AS IT HAPPENED

A Memoir

AS IT HAPPENED

A Memoir

WILLIAM S. PALEY

DOUBLEDAY. & COMPANY, INC.
GARDEN CITY, NEW YORK
1979

Library of Congress Cataloging in Publication Data

Paley, William S., 1901–
AS IT HAPPENED
A MEMOIR

ISBN 0-385-14639-6
Library of Congress Catalog Card Number 78–73191

Copyright © 1979 by WILLIAM S. PALEY
Printed in the United States of America
All Rights Reserved
BOOK DESIGN BY BENTE HAMANN

First Edition

CONTENTS

ACKNOWLEDGMENTS

I am deeply appreciative of the assistance a number of people have given in the preparation of this book.

John McDonald, an outstanding business historian, brought his notable talents to the original selection and organization of the material that forms the basis of the story. His integrity, his keen editorial insights and research guidance were of inestimable value.

Alvin Moscow, who aided in the preparation of the final manuscript, brought to that work not only his very special abilities as a biographer but also a professionalism that was both demanding and unstinting. His assistance was extremely important and appreciated.

Much of the information about CBS was researched and verified through reference to the company's fine historical files, which were compiled so efficiently under the direction of Margaret Kennedy. Her associate, Linda Savasta Mancia, was another tower of strength in the many months of work.

Geoffrey Colvin, Harriet Heck and Terry Ryan were of great help in exploring and verifying a tremendous volume of material, and Rosemary Barthold Grieco was both meticulous and expert in translating dictation into manuscript.

I have been privileged to be associated with several generations of outstanding people at CBS. To all of them, I express my appreciation for their help in the living of this story.

To the Memory of

BARBARA CUSHING PALEY

AS IT HAPPENED

A Memoir

Preface

Over the past fifteen years I have thought several times about setting down something about myself and my work at CBS. Now, here at last, I am sitting down to make a real try, tape recorder in hand, a pad of paper at my side, alone late at night in one of my favorite rooms which exudes a nice warmth. I decorated this room over the years, picking and choosing every piece of furniture, every work of art, and each of them has a special meaning and a story for me, like the painting "La Voilette" by Matisse. It is a comfortable room—a bedroom-sitting room—in which I can relax and think and reflect.

What kind of person am I? I ask myself that, as I begin this effort. The answer is not simple. My life spans the century and, as I see it, I should do two things: I must narrate the more significant events in which I was a participant, especially those which influenced our world as we now know it, and I must reveal, if I can, something of myself and my world.

I wonder if I can put enough of myself in it. Am I reflective enough or personal enough? I am not a very demonstrative person. I am not good at flattering people or even complimenting them. I have worked for years with people at CBS whose skills I have admired and who have not had from me the kind of acknowledgment they deserve or would like to get. I like to believe, however, that they understand me and know how I feel about them.

Of course, I like praise myself, even flattery, and certainly I like to read a good notice when it appears, but I feel somewhat embarrassed when it is presented to me directly in person. I tend to brush it off and try to change the subject. As for unflattering or critical comments which sometimes come my way, I have an urge to reply, to correct misrepresentation, to set matters straight—which of course means putting things more in my favor. Some of that is certain to find its place here.

I don't think I am a very easy person to know. Perhaps that is a strange thing to say at the beginning of a work like this because I hope to make myself known in this book. Yet it is my impression that although I have had a multitude of acquaintances in my life, many of whom call me friend and whom I call friend, I have had very few intimates. Apart from these few, I think I do not like the idea of depending on others. I don't feel safe. When I find myself becoming dependent on one particular person I start to worry about what would happen if he or she were no longer there, and about who could take his or her place. Of course, I am not self-sufficient and have to lean on many people. But I always keep my reserve.

In a sort of treaty with the reader, I have decided to declare here what I will tell and not tell. As a matter of taste I will not write about my intimate personal relations. That would either be unfair to others or beyond my capacity for expression. I will take up not only the successful aspects of my life and work, but also the qualified successes in some areas, the failures in others, the good memories and the regrets.

This is a new experience for me. Until this writing, the only time I have spoken up has been for the various organizations I have represented. Now I speak for myself.

I am sure that I may have unconsciously rationalized some events, especially painful ones, to make myself feel better about

2

them, or to present myself in a better light. Still, I do want to try to be objective. After all, presenting myself is what I am doing here.

I have enjoyed extraordinary success in life, as much as I or any American could dream of, and I leave it to the reader to judge how well I used my opportunities.

Chicago

I was a child of immigrants. They were not poor immigrants, as were so many who came from Eastern Europe
and Russia in the later nineteenth century; my family was among
the fortunate ones with a stake to invest in the new world. My
grandfather, Isaac Paley, was well heeled enough upon his arrival
in Chicago in 1888 to entertain the aristocratic notion of enjoying
the freedom of the United States without actually working. His
vision of life was acquired from observing the gentry of the old
world, or perhaps from reading nineteenth-century Russian
novels. Things did not turn out as he intended, but I cannot help
wondering whether something of my grandfather's feeling for
the value of leisure and luxury did not brush off on me.

Grandfather Isaac was a tall, handsome man who wore a Van-
dyke beard and carried himself like a patriarch. As I remember
him, he would sit next to a samovar, drinking tea and chat-
ting with friends all day long. They did most of the talking;
he did most of the listening. He had a presence that I think
caused many to hold him in awe.

My father, Samuel Paley, once told me the story of how the
family happened to come to the United States. My grandfather

had had a rather special position among Jews in Russia. He lived in a small town called Brovary, near Kiev, and was the Czar's representative in the town. The state functions he performed were rather modest. When anyone from the court came through the town, he had to see to it that the horses were changed and that accommodations and other services were provided for the personage and his entourage. But my grandfather's office brought with it a certain tangible privilege. He could go wherever he wanted, in contrast to most Jews, who were confined more or less to particular neighborhoods.

If there were pogroms in the town, my father did not tell me of them. And yet, somehow, I have the notion that Grandfather Isaac thought that the time had come when emigration might be a wise course for the family. With permission to travel and also the wherewithal, as the owner of a prospering lumber business, he made a voyage to America, around 1883–84, taking his nine-year-old son, my father, to visit and see if he liked it. He did like it, returned to Russia, and apparently made plans. Four years later he moved everyone to Chicago. The entourage was considerable: himself; his wife, Zelda; my father, who was then thirteen; three other sons—William, Jacob and Benjamin; and three daughters, Sophie, Sarah and Celia.

My grandfather Isaac failed the capitalistic test. He soon lost most of his money in bad investments. But he himself was above the mere material side of life. I don't remember his ever working for a living.

Grandmother Zelda was different, indeed the opposite of my grandfather in temperament. She was small and full of spark and punch, but she was a complainer. She would sometimes shout at my grandfather, but to no avail. He was serene. Yet, she had influence—the strength in the family, I think, came from her. My father and Uncle Jay took after her, and some of her spirit must have come down to me. As I heard the story in the family, when my grandfather lost his money, my grandmother and the older children saw that somebody had to go out and make a living. William, the eldest, and my father, who was next in age, left school and went to work. My father sold newspapers, then worked in a piano factory, and then in a cigar factory, where as an apprentice he came upon his destiny.

It was not long before my father got the idea of opening a cigar store with one cigar maker working in the front window, which was not uncommon in those days. The cigar maker, sitting at a table in the window, rolling cigars by hand, was not only functional but was an attraction and an advertisement. Passers-by would stop to watch and perhaps come in to buy. Between his factory job and his own store, my father learned all about tobacco and discovered that he had the gift of recognizing the various qualities of tobacco and of blending them in attractive combinations of flavor. It was his particular genius and became his lifelong vocation.

He must have been ambitious too in those days, carrying two jobs. His brand of cigars began selling so well that he decided to go out and sell them to other cigar stores. Eventually he gave up the factory job, put more cigar makers to work in the back room of the store, and found himself in the cigar business. It was a short step from there to opening a cigar factory of his own. He made a good product, built a business, and became successful at an early age. In 1896, the year he was naturalized at the age of twenty-one, he had probably become a millionaire.

Two years later, he married Goldie Drell, who was sixteen. Three years later, on September 28, 1901, I was born. Not long after that he moved the business and the family to Detroit. I had a nurse then (a sign of the family's prosperity) whom I remember for only one thing, going hand-in-hand with her many times to visit photographers who would tell me to look at "the birdie." I must have been little more than three years old.

Sometime in these years my father's best customer, a wholesaler, went bankrupt, leaving Samuel Paley with so great a loss that it virtually put him out of business. Back we went to Chicago where my father had to start over again; thereafter I had no nurse.

My father, evidently not completely broke, acquired a house

for us on Marshfield Avenue, in a residential neighborhood not far west of the Loop. I long remembered it as a large house, at least fifty feet wide. The houses on the block were attached, like the brownstones of New York, but next to our home was an empty corner lot, which my father constantly talked of buying to protect that side of our house.

My life on Marshfield Avenue, as I remember it, was a child's dream come true. The houses on the block were full of children of about my age and we played endlessly in the vacant lot and in the cellar of my house which served as a "club."

Then we moved "up the ladder" to an apartment on Logan Boulevard in a more elegant neighborhood of northwest Chicago. My memory blurs the borders of time, for still later we moved again to an apartment hotel in the suburb of Rogers Park. School and playmates changed, but our home life remained the center of my existence.

Our family was closely knit, and its strong inner bonds of love and tradition generated classic centripetal forces which had considerable influence on me. Father, mother, my sister Blanche and I dined together every night when my parents were home. My father was frequently away on business—and on each and every occasion he was welcomed home as a returning king. There was an aura of love in our home; our father and mother lived for each other and for the children, and we knew it.

My mother was a handsome, even beautiful woman. She was on the stout side as I first remember her, but then she decided to become thin and she became thin—which suggests a touch of vanity and more than a touch of resoluteness. Her cooking was fabulous, which led me to care about good food for the rest of my life. She catered to my father in every way, simply taking it for granted that her role in life was to make him happy and comfortable.

My father was a short man with a black mustache and intense eyes that looked out rather gaily and confidently and yet seemed somewhat startled. He always stood erect and wore a coat and vest and a high stiff collar which was then in fashion. He had an odd configuration of hair—it was full on the sides but he was bald through the middle, forming a ski-slope shape from front to back. When his full head of hair started thinning, he worried about it and he believed the then current notion that if you shaved off the thinning area, your hair would grow back full again. So he had his hair shaved off through the middle. When he came home that night and bent down to kiss me, I started to cry, "That's not my father." But I grew accustomed to his new hair style; and I suppose he did, for the middle of his head remained forever bare.

I will never forget the very first automobile my father bought for the family and the excitement on that Saturday when we were all supposed to see the new car and meet the demonstrator, the man who was to teach my father to drive. My mother was a bit behind schedule and so I waited for her while my father and sister went ahead. When my mother and I came out, we found my father and sister gone. Apparently they had started without us. We waited impatiently. Finally, we saw my father and sister walking toward us, alone and without the car. I'll never forget the expression on my father's face. It seems that while turning a corner, my father was told to push the brake pedal. Instead he put his foot down on the accelerator and the car ran into a brick building at considerable speed. The new car was demolished. Two weeks later, another car was delivered, an Overland. My mother drove it; even I, although under age, drove it short distances to and from the garage. My father bought other cars, a Winton, a Cadillac and others. But he never drove again.

Such incidents stand out in my memory because they were so rare. My father earned and commanded the total respect of his family. He was a very capable businessman, loved all aspects of his growing cigar business, and at dinner would tell us in great detail what had happened that day. I was fascinated. From the time I was a young child, there was no doubt in my mind—or his—that I would get an education and then go into his business and succeed him. I admired him enormously and thought of doing great things to help him.

If I learned the sense of the life of leisure and relaxation from my grandfather Isaac, I certainly learned the fascination of work from my father. He was too busy becoming a successful businessman for me to develop an intimate relationship with him when I was growing up, but the bonds of love and respect were always there unshakably. From as far back as I can remember, whenever we met, we kissed each other on the cheek, and we kept to that tradition all his life, even in public, including the occasions when we came together in meetings with the directors of CBS.

Although we lived in unquestioned consciousness of being Jews, my family was divided on the religious aspect of being Jewish. Neither my grandfather Isaac nor my father showed much interest in religious formalities. But since my mother was more religious than my father, they would go together to the Reform synagogue on the High Holy Days. Mother's father, Morris Drell, was a student of the Torah, a dedicated scholar who spent his whole day studying and interpreting it. He was a member of an Orthodox synagogue and made religion the center of his life.

Every Friday night we would go to my grandfather Morris' house where he recited the ceremonial blessing over wine and bread on the eve of the Sabbath. To me, an uncomprehending child, it was worse than boring. I had to listen to prayers in Hebrew which I didn't understand. I often thought how wonderful it would be when I was grown up and would not have to go there every Friday night.

My grandfather Morris had done all he could to keep me in the old faith, but to no avail. He walked five miles to the synagogue for my confirmation because Orthodox Jews are not permitted to drive in cars on Saturday, the Jewish Sabbath. I did have the honor of standing up alone before the congregation to recite the Ten Commandments in Hebrew, even though I had memorized the text phonetically and did not understand a single word. It was a measure, however, a true measure of the cultural distance between the two sides of my family.

9

In Chicago my family lived a modest middle-class life, occasionally going to the theater and having parties with friends at home. My mother would often stay home, preferring, she said, to use the time to prepare the after-theater supper. She would say to my father, "Why don't you take Willie with you?" Thus, to my delight, I went to plays at an early age. Then I got a job on Saturdays as a sort of "candy-butcher" in Chicago theaters. I would march up and down the aisles of the balcony with a tray, hawking candy and other treats, and I would see the play. The first performance I ever saw on this job, ironically, was called *It Pays to Advertise*. As I remember that play, an advertising man came up with a brilliant idea to save a soap company from imminent bankruptcy. He proposed that it advertise and sell a soap to be called "Number 13 Soap—Unlucky for Dirt." The soap was a huge success and the company was saved! I was surprised that no one ever used that slogan in the real world. It made a big impression on me.

New Year's Eve was always an important night for a party in our home. Family and close friends would gather to talk and drink and, I guess, get a little tipsy. My father would dance the *gezotski* (more properly the *kozak*), which he had learned as a child in Russia. He had short but strong legs. With ten or twelve plates placed in a close circle, he would dance around and between the plates and never break a one. At almost every party, anywhere, someone would say, "Sam, come up and do your dance." He was a good dancer and continued dancing to a very advanced age. I never learned the *gezotski* or any folk dance but I took to ballroom dancing and the dreamy and close body dances of the twenties when my turn came later.

My father was very neat and orderly, almost to a fault. Every moment of his life was planned in fine detail. And he was a hypochondriac, imagining all kinds of ailments for which he hurried to his doctor and took medicines of all kinds. My mother did the opposite: she never complained, threw away doctors' prescriptions and got well on her own. Some say that I tend to be a hypochondriac. I deny it. At times I have been more concerned about my health than my mother was about hers, but I have not come anywhere near the real hypochondria of my father.

My father was a very gentle man, but when he got angry he got terribly angry. One night when I was just old enough to drive, I asked him if I could have the car. "Yes, if you're home by eleven o'clock," he said. Out riding with some friends, I forgot all about the time and my promise. I got home at one o'clock and found my father waiting for me in a state of fierce temper. I had disappointed him—in more ways than one, he said. "You remember when I asked you to be home at eleven, a friend of mine was present? After you left, my friend said to me, 'You know damn well he's not going to be home by eleven.' And I said, 'My son, when he says he's going to be home by eleven, he'll be home by eleven.' I took a very strong stand, and you let me down, son, you let me down." I was crushed. But it didn't improve my character.

Not long afterward I was stopped for speeding while having one arm around a girl. The officer took my name, address and telephone number, and said that instead of giving me a ticket he was going to call my father and tell him about it. Terrified, I rushed home and appealed to the desk clerk of our apartment hotel: "Do me a big favor. When that call comes in on the switchboard, pretend you're my father, please, and take the message." The officer did call. The clerk answered and said, "Yes, this is Mr. Paley, what is it? Really? He did that? My God! What a bad boy he is. I'll see that he's properly punished for it." I escaped my father's wrath but not the guilt, and I was troubled by what I had done.

The birth of my sister, Blanche, on May 11, 1905, when I was nearly four years old, affected my life profoundly, even at the very beginning. My mother and father had asked me what I wanted for my birthday, and I gave a classic reply: a baby sister. (I wonder if or how they planted *that* idea in my mind.)

One night there was a commotion in the house. The next morning my father came in to me and said, "Well, you have your wish. You have a baby sister."

I was taken to my mother's room where she had given birth to a daughter. I saw this tiny object in a crib and thought my parents were fooling me. She looked like a doll, so, just to check, I put my finger in her eye. She screamed, of course, and already I was in trouble.

Now with a real baby sister, I came to be unhappy about my request. It seemed logical that if I hadn't asked for her, we wouldn't have had her. As the older child, I was typically jealous of her for taking my place as the favorite.

Not long after my sister was born I got the feeling that my mother did not approve of me or did not think I was as good as she wanted me to be. As we grew up, my mother gave so much attention to my sister that I thought she regarded me as less worthy. She also made comparisons between me and other boys. Then and there a strong ambition was generated in me to be a success. I wanted to prove to her or anybody else who found fault with me that "Darn it, one day I'll show you!" Along with my own conflicting self-esteem, I had both a strong love for my mother and an antagonism to her. And yet I wanted to be with her. I remember one occasion when she started to go downtown and I followed her along the street. She told me to go back to the house. And I wouldn't go back. Finally she turned around in exasperation and said, "Okay, let's go back home then." When we got home she took me to the basement and gave me a whipping—one to be remembered.

The worst of it all was my impression that she did not find me attractive. She would complain: other children were brighter than I was; they looked better, or did something better; when I got clothes, the clothes never looked right on me; everybody else looked neater. I am not sure now if she really felt that way about me or was just trying to make me try harder. But the effect on me was a feeling of inferiority. I felt sorry for myself. I believed I was born unattractive.

This complicated relationship with my mother was eased when I got into the outside world. When at the age of about twelve, I went to my first dance, given by a neighbor on Logan Boulevard, I sat like a wallflower. One girl in particular made it clear somehow that she liked me and wanted to dance with me. Another did the same. I was surprised and thought at first that they were fooling, but apparently they weren't. It occurred to me for the first time that I could be attractive and that put me in a good state of mind about how girls might feel about me. There was no question about how I felt about them.

I had an early passion for reading, especially for Horatio Alger stories. I went to the public library almost every day, and when I found a Horatio Alger book I had not read before, it was like finding a gold mine. I would read late into the night with great excitement about disadvantaged young men who worked hard, were virtuous and ended up marrying the boss's daughter or getting rich. My mother was forever telling me to turn off the light and get to sleep. But I remained intrigued by the Horatio Alger heroes.

At school I was often a good student, sometimes an indifferent one, and on occasion a poor one. It all depended, it seemed, on circumstances. At first, things went badly in the grammar school near Marshfield Avenue—a school, I must say, whose methods were devised without sensitivity to the minds of children, or as we would say today, of any understanding of child psychology.

At eight or nine years of age I got over my strong desire to stay at home to be near my mother. But I still didn't like school. I took extreme measures to avoid going to school: I would pretend to be ill, or would inflict some minor injury on myself to justify not going. I played hooky and signed my mother's name to excuse slips. On more than one occasion I crawled out of the classroom while the teacher's back was turned. And all for one reason: I felt put down by the school, and indeed I was put down, quite literally.

The school operated on a system designed to crush the morale of half its students. Each class divided the bright students, who were assigned one side of the classroom, from the presumed less-than-bright ones, assigned the other side. The farther down front you were on either side, the brighter you were; the farther back, the more stupid. I spent miserable days in the last row of the lower side, which had only one advantage: I could easily slip out to freedom.

One day the teacher announced a special fifteen-minute recess, a break in our routine, and because I was not feeling well, I sat and dozed with a book open in front of me. When all the children were back from the recess, the teacher asked me to stand up. I stood up, wondering what I had done now, and the teacher solemnly addressed the class, saying that while all of them had gone out to play, I had stayed behind to read and to prepare myself for the next lesson, whereupon she moved me from the lower to the upper half of the class.

I had not deserved to be branded stupid and I did not, of course, deserve to be commended for being a devoted student, but the combination of these artifices changed my life at school. No longer did I skip classes. Through the remaining years of grammar school, through high school, and into college, I ranked first, second, or third in my class. My career as a good student lasted until the end of my first semester at the University of Chicago, when the dean wrote to my father that I was one of the best students ever. Then something happened, and I ended that year in the lower part of my class.

Before then, and when I was old enough, I worked for my father in his factory during the summers. I swept floors, ran errands, looked around and learned. Father sent me to the banding department where they put the bands around the cigars and I learned how to do that. He sent me to the "kitchen," where they mixed tobaccos and I learned how to do that. Almost every day I walked or ran to the downtown post office to buy federal bonding stamps, one of which had to go on each box of cigars. I would get the cash and run downtown, get the stamps and run back. I would try to see how fast I could make it and I got to be very fast, always striving to be better than before.

As a child I learned that I had a good ear for music, perfect pitch, so that I was able to tell if a note was even a fraction off. My mother took me to a concert given by Mischa Elman on probably his first concert tour in America, when he was a young lad in short pants. He played the violin so beautifully that I decided then and there that I wanted to become a violinist. But the violin teacher we consulted turned me down because I could not sing notes perfectly at the right pitch. I was crushed. Instead, I studied the piano for years, taking lessons from successively more advanced teachers, and I did very well. I even gave a concert once and there was some thought of my making a career as a pianist. But I never really liked the piano all that much and my piano playing came to an end when I went away to school.

In the fall of 1917 my family sent me away to complete my high school education at the Western Military Academy in Alton, Illinois. I put on cadet uniforms, shined my buttons, stood at attention for examination every morning, drilled at times during the day, fought mock battles and twice a week went to town—Alton—for candy bars. When you wanted to show yourself to be an independent creature, you bought snuff from a dealer who came around the school. You put it on your lips and little by little took some on your tongue and swallowed it. That made you one of the boys. I tried it just once, got sick, and gave it up forever.

That year marked a turning point in my life: I was away from home for the first time and I overcame being homesick and got used to being on my own. When I had left home, I was quite short; at the Academy I sprouted. I grew so fast I needed three sets of uniforms in one year. The isolation was good for studies. In that one year I accumulated two years of high school credits and was admitted to the University of Chicago at seventeen. I also met the qualifications to enter the Army as a second lieutenant, except for my age, and my father, who refused to give his permission. This was a heavy blow to me. I wanted to be an officer and wear one of those Sam Browne belts diagonally across my chest. A Sam Browne belt signified, at least to my mind, that you were an officer who had served overseas and that you were a hero.

I started in a college dormitory and then was admitted to a fraternity, Zeta Beta Tau. The fraternity house was a new life and great fun.

At Chicago I was at or near the top of my class—until I fell in love. She was a lovely young woman, older than I, my first true love. She was the most exciting person I had met to that time. She lived far out on the north side of Chicago, but that did not stop me. Every night I would go out there by streetcar and elevated train, arriving late in the evening. I would leave her in the middle of the night and get back to college in time for only a couple of hours sleep, and with little time for study. Failing to manage both love and study, I chose love. I just squeaked through the second semester.

We separated only because of Samuel Gompers. In 1919, Gompers, himself an immigrant from England, and a cigar maker, as well as founder and lifetime president of the American Federation of Labor, sanctioned another strike against my father's cigar factory. There had been many before. My father decided to relocate, and so he and I took the train east.

Going East

The Great War had ended, New York was alive with the spirit of the new times, and the streets were thronged with streetcars, automobiles, carts and horses and people moving at a much faster pace than they did in Chicago. It was a great, tall city and I was enchanted. While my father went about his business, I investigated the reputation of New York as the most sinful city in the world. On my first outing alone, I walked down one avenue for three or four blocks, expecting to be accosted by New York women who, I had been told in Chicago, fell into the arms of any young attractive man. When I was not accosted, I felt discouraged. It never occurred to me that my information might be wrong. I tried a Broadway hotel which, according to my information, was known as a gathering place for the most glamorous people of all. There were indeed glamorous women present but no one saw fit to send me a note or even a seductive glance. At seventeen years of age, it was depressing. Youth was not to be served anything but lunch. I tasted none of the city's pleasures. Most of the time I followed my father around or waited for him while he investigated the possibilities of opening a new factory on the East Coast.

I indulged in another fantasy which was to stay with me longer than my youthful naïveté regarding women. My hard-working father had often spoken of eventually retiring to an orange grove in California. "As soon as I have $25,000, we're going to move to California," he would say, "and we're going to buy an orange grove and have a little house and we're going to have a marvelous time." I, too, dreamed about that orange grove as the ultimate goal in life. I could really visualize myself picking an orange off the tree and sitting under the tree and eating the orange. It would be a lovely, lazy life. When I wasn't eating oranges, I would be a beachcomber on a nearby beach. So, every once in a while in Chicago I would ask my father, "Dad, how much money do you have?"

"Why?" he would reply.

"Have you got the $25,000?"

"No, I haven't," he would say.

One day, however, I said, "You must have $25,000 by now."

"Yes, I have."

"How about the orange grove?" I asked.

"Well," he replied, "you know . . . it isn't convenient for me to go out and buy that orange grove now."

In New York, approaching my eighteenth birthday, I made plans for the future and my orange grove. My horizon for aging was thirty-five, which was nine years younger than my father was at that time. It came over me then as a firm conviction that I was going to be rich when I was thirty-five. And I decided that at thirty-five I would retire and spend the rest of my life as a beachcomber, with or without an orange grove. But I would have complete freedom. I thought quite a bit about it and recognized that my father and men like him got caught up in the web of business and constantly postponed retirement and the pleasures of leisure. In order not to get caught that way myself, I made an oath to myself and a solemn vow that I would retire, no matter what, at age thirty-five. Having made that vow, I imagined it a personal deal that I had made with God, or some superior being, which meant, logically, that if I did not live up to my oath, I would be punished.

My father found a site for his new cigar factory in Philadelphia rather than in New York, and no sooner had he taken the space, ordered equipment, and engaged a foreman than he received word from Chicago that my grandfather Isaac had died. He rushed back to Chicago, leaving me to supervise the Philadelphia factory for what he expected would be a few days. Business and family affairs kept him in Chicago for almost a month. While he was away, I took charge in Philadelphia. After all, I had been my father's protégé. I had absorbed his business philosophy at the dinner table, worked summers in the Chicago plant, and understood the cigar business as much if not better than any well-taught young apprentice.

My first task was to hire cigar makers for the new plant, mostly women, as was the custom in Philadelphia, but no sooner had I begun than the entire cigar industry in Philadelphia was struck over working conditions. However, I went out and argued with the union leaders and workers that it was unfair to strike our new plant over working conditions since no one had yet ever worked for us. I promised the workers higher wages and better working conditions than any other cigar factory in the area because we were producing a better-grade and more expensive cigar. I also gave bonuses to girls who would find other girls to work in the new plant, provided picnics, boat trips and free entertainment, and succeeded in hiring all the workers we needed to start. Then, the first sign of real trouble came not from the union but from the president of the local association of cigar manufacturers. He charged into Father's office, intending to demand that we stop our operation. But he stopped short when he found sitting behind the boss's desk a teen-ager. Nevertheless, when our identities were straightened out, he said in a threatening voice, "You can't run your factory while we are having a strike. You must close down. We don't want to give those girls an outlet to work anywhere else." I became as angry as he was, for I knew where my loyalties belonged. I was adamant in telling him that we would not be influenced by threats and intended to go about our business of making and selling cigars. By the time my father returned with the family, we had the Philadelphia plant running full force.

The responsibility thrust upon me by my father and my ability to stand up to that irate cigar manufacturer marked a turning point: I became conscious of the fact that my boyhood had ended and that there were things in the world I could do and do well.

I returned to college that fall, at the Wharton School of the University of Pennsylvania, where the curriculum was divided between business and liberal arts courses. (I continued working for my father during the summers.) My factory experience had propelled me into adulthood and at college this time I took my studies seriously enough to get by. But I had no drive to excel in the classroom as I had in earlier years. In another little revolution, I became half student, half playboy. I threw myself into the heady life of the Roaring Twenties and began to enjoy college life enormously.

While I was at college, my father gave me a moderate but quite adequate allowance, and yet when a good business proposition came my way one year, I grabbed it. It was a new-style shirt with an attached collar and it buttoned down. An alumnus fraternity brother who had become a wholesale shirt salesman showed the fraternity boys the new kind of shirt and I decided to go into business. I ordered a huge load of those shirts, because the more you bought the lower the unit price. I recruited football heroes, baseball players, track stars, and all kinds of people whose popularity, I thought, might make them supersalesmen on campus. I paid them a generous commission and made myself a healthy profit of about $1,000.

While my allowance was strict, my father was not stingy. He gave me an Essex automobile which helped make me become noticed on campus. In my senior year I became head of the fraternity.

In the late spring of 1922, after leaving college, I went to work full time for the Congress Cigar Company. My father gave me a salary of twenty-five dollars a week, no title, and one big assignment. He called me into his office one day and announced that the company had intended to build a combined factory and office building which he hoped would be the most up-to-date one in the industry. "You will be in charge of the whole project, the plans, construction and everything." I was not surprised at his willingness to trust me with so great a responsibility. It was his style of management. He ran the production end of the business, and as his young lieutenant I was expected to learn all the other operations of his company.

After some investigation, I decided that the key to the new plant would be central air conditioning, and we put in what I believe was the first such system in the cigar manufacturing business. Natural weather was often either too dry and made the tobacco crack and crumble or too damp, which made the tobacco soggy and too closely packed in the cigar. The conditions increased the cost of the cigars. An important amount was saved once the factory was opened and operations went at full tilt. Our new factory at Third and Spruce was a beautiful building, eight stories high, and colonial in style.

My father's investment in the new plant was a sign not only that his business was doing well but also that he expected it to expand even further. Samuel Paley was ready to ride the economic wave of the twenties: he had standardized his product years earlier, at about the time that Henry Ford standardized his, but of course the operation was on a much smaller scale. To facilitate economies in production, my father stopped making numerous varieties of cigars and concentrated on a single brand, La Palina (a play on the family name), which was a special blend of Puerto Rican and Cuban tobaccos for the filler, encased in a binder of Connecticut tobacco, with a Java wrapper. It appealed to the taste of a wide public. Designing the La Palina was a test of my father's skill in the art of blending tobacco, and the triumph of his life. It was not a Model T type of cigar (a five-center) but a high-grade cigar (high grade meant a cigar that sold for ten cents or more) offered at a moderate price. La Palinas came in about twenty shapes and sizes, selling for from ten cents to three for a dollar.

For years my father's business had been regional, with its principal markets centered in the Middle West but after moving east, we went national in marketing, advertising and all other aspects of the business. When I went to work for my father after college, he had expanded from one factory producing about 75,000 cigars a day to six factories in several eastern states producing about a half-million cigars a day. The new, modern factory was the seventh. Congress Cigar was soon producing and selling a million cigars a day, and we could advertise La Palina as "America's largest selling high-grade cigar." Sales later rose to close to 1.5 million cigars a day. Sales and profits more than doubled between 1922 and 1927.

The Paley family of course prospered accordingly. To me, my father was a genuine hero, the founder, president and prime mover of a growing, exciting business. But he was not alone in running it. There had always been, as far back as I could remember, Uncle Jay (who had changed his name from Jake), Uncle Ben and the sales manager, Willis Andruss, the only one in the top group who was not a Paley. If I learned anything about selling, it was from Andruss. I got to know Uncle Jay and Uncle Ben well only after I was admitted into the inner circle of the business.

Uncle Jay was taller and younger than my father, quite a handsome man with dark hair. He trained me in finance. Uncle Ben was different. He was the youngest, slouched a bit, had a kindly face and a wonderful smile. It was easy to want to hug him. He was not the best of businessmen. Tell Ben your hard luck story and he would empty his pockets for you. A quiet and slow-moving man, he lived a life separate from the family. He was a great man for the races. The combination of gambling and his happy-go-lucky style worried his two brothers, so they persuaded him to put a good deal of his money in trust. In the company he was a good buffer in many situations because he could reach anybody and had many friends who would do him a favor.

I lived a two-sided life, industrious and fun-loving. I seldom got to the office late and I always fulfilled my obligations, and, I think, made a positive contribution to the business. After hours, I plunged again into the joyous and hectic life of the 1920s. I took a one-room apartment in the Warwick Hotel (equipped with a little pantry and a fold-down Murphy bed) and I felt truly independent and free to dance, drink, and gamble and enjoy the night life—just as long as I got to the office on time the next morning. As a young man I drank, dated show girls and gambled in the fashion of the time. My friends and I wined, dined and danced our way through nightclubs, speakeasies and restaurants and somehow survived the bootleg booze.

I almost did not survive gambling. In Boo Boo Hoff's well-known casino I ran $10 up into a small fortune of $40,000 over a series of spectacular evenings. I was possessed. I could not lose. I got to the point where I thought I had been put on this earth to break the gambling houses of the world. Monte Carlo was next in my vision. My winning streak lasted about a month. In the following months I lost $45,000—which left me $5,000 in debt to Boo Boo Hoff.

"Never mind," he said, "just pay me as you go along, little by little and don't let it worry you too much." So shortly afterward I put together a hundred dollars and went to another gambling house in search of a new winning streak. I lost the hundred dollars. Worse, the next afternoon a couple of hoodlums came to my office and said that Boo Boo was very unhappy about my losing to other gambling houses: he was calling his debt and expected me to pay up by five o'clock the following Saturday.

Terrified, I imagined that I might be dumped to the bottom of the Delaware River. I could not go to my father; it would hurt and disappoint him terribly to learn that his son was a gambler and at such high stakes. So I went to Uncle Jay. Although very disapproving, he finally came through and gave me the five thousand dollars. I paid my debt to Boo Boo Hoff. But I wasn't cured. For some time afterward I went back to gambling houses to try to repeat that miraculous winning month. It wasn't until I went to New York to work in radio that I lost interest in going to gambling houses, and after that the urge never came back.

My favorite organization, of which I was a charter member, was a group called "The Hundred Club." We occupied a small house on Locust Street near Broad Street in the center of town, where we would lunch every day. It was a close-knit and lively men's group. We ate well and we played cards for small stakes. After lunch we hurried back to our offices and sometimes returned for dinner.

My friends and I met with the cry, "Let's have some fun." I was always ready to go. One of my favorite friends was Ben Gimbel of the famous department-store family. With all the money he ever needed, Ben never took life very seriously. He loved show business, show people and practical jokes. Some of his practical jokes were funny and others were very cruel. His cousin Nathan Hamburger once gave a dinner party at the family house while the parents were out of town and Ben put a sign up on the door, QUARANTINED: DIPHTHERIA. Poor Nathan waited long into the night for his guests to arrive. Ben and I, Larry Lowman, Henry Gerstley and a few other young men formed a group that made the rounds of many dances and parties. I worked hard but I didn't have any sense of final responsibility; when I left the office I was able to throw off all my cares.

At the Congress Cigar Company, I advanced to the status of vice-president, with duties that consisted of buying tobacco, overseeing production and dabbling in advertising. In 1927 my salary rose to $20,000 a year. Much of the work was routine, but a few episodes stand out, doubtless because they redounded to my credit in the eyes of my father and uncle.

On one occasion, one of them asked me to audit the operations of a dealer who bought tobacco for us abroad. It was a big job, and checking the complex transactions took a long time. The dealer had a fine reputation, and my father and uncle found it hard to believe what I had uncovered. They made me prove my claim that the dealer had outrageously falsified our accounts. Then my father confronted the dealer with the proofs I provided and in an emotional scene the dealer collapsed, confessed and begged to be forgiven. My father, who thought he knew the dealer as a friend, promised not to take him to court if he would resubmit the accounts. When all the new bills were in, we found that we had saved a couple of million dollars in overcharges. It was a big moment for me.

One year my father sent me to Puerto Rico by myself to buy tobacco. I think we were the largest buyers of Puerto Rican tobacco, competing in that market with numerous dealers who bought for resale to smaller manufacturers. When I arrived I found that the tobacco crop was large and there was an oversupply in the market. The farmers were vulnerable to a terrible crash in prices, and the dealers were talking of making a killing. But the other buyers could not do so without reckoning with us. The farmers would wait to see what we did.

Our office manager and I went out into the field to visit the farmers and found them in a miserable state at the prospect of extremely low prices. One could argue in the abstract that low prices for a large crop is a natural economic law, and the farmers should take it as it came. But, the more I thought about it, a quick killing seemed wrong for them and foolish for us. I reasoned as follows: if prices fell too low, the farmers would go under and would have difficulty producing the next year's crop, and we had a long-term interest in their financial health. We were not interested in a quick turn of profit but expected to come back year after year to buy tobacco in an ongoing relationship.

As the largest buyer, Congress Cigar could influence the market price, and the decision was mine to make. I spent a week in Puerto Rico deciding which lots we wanted to buy, and I concluded that, at thirty cents a pound, the farmers could get their money back with a profit. This price would fit satisfactorily into our cost structure. I gave the signal, and our buyers went out all

over the island closing deals at thirty cents a pound for the tobacco lots I had selected. That night when I got back to the
hotel, a delegation of dealers was waiting, ready to kill me. I explained my position to them, but they had sent a cablegram to
my father telling him I had gone crazy paying ten or twelve cents
a pound over that year's expected price.

When I heard from my father, I cabled him an explanation,
and back came his response: "You're absolutely right." The
farmers responded with many gifts including a hundred-year-
old bottle of brandy. When I returned to the office in Philadelphia, my father gave me a raise in salary.

While selling cigars so successfully we watched with interest
the phenomenal growth in the sales of cigarettes throughout the
country (from about 16 billion to about 82 billion a year in
twelve years) and we were tempted to break into this related tobacco business. So we introduced a cigarette called "Palina" and
advertised it as having "a dash of Java." I was put in charge of
sales and advertising. We put a tremendous effort into that new
venture and it was a bust. People smoked a Palina once but not
again. In Akron, Ohio, I tried to give a package of Palinas to a
cab driver. He looked at it and passed it back, saying, "Thanks
very much, buddy, but I've already tasted them." I felt crushed.
When we came to analyze the problem of taste, we found it was
not the tobacco but the cigarette paper. The best cigarette paper
was made in France and we just could not purchase this paper
because the entire output had been taken up by other American
manufacturers of cigarettes. We closed down the business and
took our losses, which were quite substantial. As cigar makers,
we had thought only about tobacco and overlooked the fact that
cigarette smokers smoke paper too.

The high point of both my business and social life came in
May of each year when my father took me to Europe with him to
buy tobacco in Amsterdam. My father was training me to be a tobacco buyer. I went to Amsterdam to learn that art from him, and
then to Paris to enjoy life. We went to Amsterdam for the Java

wrapper, which was so important to the flavor of La Palina cigars. In fact, we advertised "Java Wrapped—the Secret of the Blend." Since Java (along with Sumatra, another prime source of tobacco wrappers) was then a colony of the Netherlands and the tobacco from the area was brought to Amsterdam to be sold, that city became the center of international tobacco auctions.

Manufacturers, wholesalers, brokers and speculators would gather in a great opera-house-like room called Frascati's. On one side of the room was a platform occupied by the auctioneer and his attendants. The other three sides were formed of balconies in the shape of horseshoes, with each tier divided into boxes. The boxes were occupied by the important tobacco buyers. On the floor between them were congregated the professional traders or brokers. Tobacco was sold in lots, one lot at a time. The buyers sent in their bids to the auctioneer in sealed envelopes until a gong rang out, signaling the end of the bidding. The auctioneer then opened the envelopes in the presence of all assembled and would say something like, "Lot number 1234 sold to . . ." and announced the party who had bought it. Bedlam would break loose among the brokers on the floor below. Each lot was made up of tobaccos of various grades, and a winning bidder usually would want to keep only what he needed for his particular kind of tobacco business; a speculator might want to resell the whole lot in separate pieces. Thus a second round of trading would begin, not through the auctioneer, but openly among any or all present, mainly among the brokers on the floor, as in a commodity exchange.

Soon the gong would ring again, and silence would come over the crowd while the auctioneer opened the bids for the next lot. Then wild trading would resume as the lot or part of it was resold in pieces. I don't know to this day how these people understood each other. Their piecemeal trading was done with fingers and hands and signs of one kind or another. Everyone made little notes and everything always went all right. At the end of the day, everyone knew what he'd bought or what he'd sold. It was very exciting, and profits could be substantial. A speculator might make or lose a million dollars on a single lot. Even a manufacturer had to take the risk of reselling what he didn't need.

We did our important homework for days before this dramatic event. The auctions were held every Friday for six weeks. During the intervals, my father and I and our broker would prepare our sealed bids for certain of the large lots, each of which would run in the millions of dollars. We knew of course what our requirements were when we arrived in Amsterdam. We were, I believe, the largest buyers present, and it was no secret that we were interested in buying for our own account only Java tobacco for wrappers. We would be sellers of anything else that came to us in the auctioned lots. Since the lots were mixed we had to examine them in their entirety, not only for what we wanted to keep but also for what we would want to resell to the other manufacturers and the wholesalers and speculators.

Each morning we would get up about five o'clock, have breakfast and go to our broker's office. Since the lots were too large to be examined in full, samples of each grade of tobacco in a given lot would be provided to the brokers for the potential bidders. The samples always truly represented what was in the lot; there was never any question of one's being misled. When we looked at a handful, we knew that a thousand bales of that kind and grade of tobacco would average out the same.

It was in this appraisal phase that I saw my father's talents most vividly at work. We arrived at work at daylight, for natural lighting is essential in judging the appearance and color of tobacco, especially wrapper tobacco. We discussed the grades—there might be as many as fifty in a single lot—with our broker and his staff of experts who would hand us the samples. We—I say we, but I just stood there watching and listening and trying to learn—would then judge which lots we wanted to bid on and how much we should bid. The art of the sealed bid is not simple. My father, though he took advice, would settle on the bid himself. Into it would go his calculations of what the lot was worth to him—that is the value to him of the portions of the lot he intended to keep for use in his business; the potential but uncertain value of the resale of the portions he did not want to keep; and in the end what to bid competitively against the other buyers who were valuing the tobacco and making similar calculations. One wanted to bid high enough to get the lot and yet no higher than was necessary. The bidding usually ran into the millions. It was scary.

Everyone took security measures to safeguard the amount they intended to bid. We put our evaluation of tobaccos and bidding prices down in code in little black books which we kept under lock and key. Since everyone knew his principal competitors and the nature of their interests, the mutual guesswork was quite sophisticated. If you lost a bid on what you needed, you would have to buy those portions of the lot at a higher price from the winner, typically a speculator, in the second resale auction. It was a coup to make a winning bid for a lot at a reasonable price that got you what you wanted. You couldn't win them all of course and even when you did, you couldn't be sure that you had not overbid for the lot. This led to a good deal of bluffing after the auction. Everyone lunched and dined together and it hurt deeply to hear someone say his losing bid was a very low amount. It was an old trick: if you were taken in by someone's boast that he had bid far lower than your winning bid, you might be tempted to bid lower next time, and lose. You never really knew what had happened in the bidding—losing bids were not revealed by the auctioneer.

These uncertainties made our weeks in Amsterdam a lively affair. We bought huge supplies of tobacco for the business, no matter at what level of prices, in order to have enough stock on hand to meet our needs for more than a year. It was the only way to guarantee the quality of La Palina cigars. Our mission was basic to the business at home.

We worked with great intensity and concentration and for long hours over the many details involved in judging, bidding and buying tobacco in Amsterdam. The Dutch were strict in the attention they paid to every little detail that went into those tobacco auctions. And I learned from their insistence on methodology that if you get the details right, the final work product will be correct.

After the auctions my father and mother would usually go to Vichy to appease his hypochondria with health-giving waters, and I would go directly to Paris for two or three weeks of play. My companions were known as "the smart set," who followed a routine one spring season after another. There was a right place to have lunch every day, a right place to have dinner; after dinner there was another place, and then began the night life, ending up usually in Montmartre at a romantic bistro run by a black woman called Bricktop. I was an American in Paris in the twenties.

The larks of my own twenties life had no firm rationale. More often than not, the lark was inspired by whim or challenge or, on occasion, a feeling for the extravagant gesture. In the spring of 1928, when I was staying at the Ritz with my parents, a friend who was an automobile buff talked me into accompanying him to the factory of the most famous builders of auto bodies in the world, Hibbard and Darrin, just outside Paris. He wanted to buy a Hispano Suiza, a very fine car in its own right, for which Hibbard and Darrin had built a special convertible body.

The car was beautiful and unique. The top could be folded far back and the doors had an original shape, tapered in from each side, which gave them a high-style look. It was the only body design of its kind in existence. All in all, it was probably the most beautiful car I had ever seen. I was taken with it. My friend quailed at the price, $16,000, and said, "It's too damn expensive." I said, "I think you are a fool. If I had that kind of money, I'd buy it."

At that time I did have money in my own name, but it came from the family business—and to me was sacrosanct. As a matter of family ethic, I would not use those funds without my father's approval. So I did not consider myself—my free self—to be rich. However, I did own some stock in my own name, and later in the day, when I checked with my stockbroker, I found that my stock had risen to just about the price of that Hispano Suiza—some

$17,000. I was amazed. It seemed that my wish had been fulfilled. I had said that if I had the money I would buy that car, and now I had the money. It was dazzling to have the car of cars within my grasp. So, I put in a sell order and in a few minutes received word that I had the cash to my credit in the Philadelphia broker's office. I bought the car and had it delivered to the Ritz.

I was uneasy over how this extravagance would appear to my father or my mother. In the course of talk at the hotel, I casually commented, "By the way, I bought a car." My mother was indifferent, but my father's interest perked up. "Where is it?" he asked. "Downstairs," I replied. We went out on to the Place Vendôme in front of the Ritz, and my parents looked around. The Hispano Suiza was sitting nearby, the prettiest picture on the street. But again my father said, "Where is it?" I pointed and my father said, "You're crazy. I don't see any car." There was a pause, and he said, "You don't mean that big thing over there, do you?" I said, "Yes, as a matter of fact I do." His face got red, and he started to say something harsh to me, when my mother intervened and said, "Now, Sam, take it easy. Your son bought this, I guess, with money that was his to spend and that he had a right to spend, and he will probably get a lot of fun out of it. Don't spoil the fun."

My father quickly suppressed his disapproval. I engaged a chauffeur in Paris for a couple of weeks to drive me and my friends on our daily round of pleasure spots until the early hours of the morning. Later, in Philadelphia, I began to think my father might have been right in his first reaction to the car. I didn't like driving it. It was so unusual that it drew crowds of people whenever it was parked on the street. It seems that one of the paradoxes of youth, at least of mine, was that I wanted an attention-getting object without the attention. It may be that I haven't changed much in that respect in the last fifty years.

A Young Man's Fancy

The first radio I ever saw was a primitive crystal set. A friend clamped the earphones on me and I was dumbfounded. It was hard to believe that I was hearing music out of the air and I never got over the surprise and the fascination. I quickly found someone to build such a set for me, because there were no ready-made radio sets at the time. As a radio fan in Philadelphia, I often sat up all night, glued to my set, listening and marveling at the voices and music which came into my ears from distant places. A few years later I became a sponsor.

While my father and uncle were on a trip in Europe, leaving me more or less in charge, I bought an hour program to advertise La Palina cigars on the local station WCAU. Cost? The munificent sum of $50 per broadcast. But when they returned, my uncle upon going over the books immediately spotted the new expenditure. "What kind of foolishness is this?" he demanded. "Cancel it right now." Reluctantly, I followed instructions.

A few weeks later at a luncheon, my father remarked, "Hundreds of thousands of dollars we've been spending on newspapers and magazines and no one has ever said anything to me about those ads, but now people are asking me 'What happened to the

La Palina Hour?'" A feeling of vindication rose within me, for I had argued about advertising on radio with my uncle, and to my surprise, my uncle now agreed. He admitted to my father that he had ordered me to cancel the program and that he had since been asked about the program by friends. So, he said, perhaps he had been wrong.

At about the same time, my father was approached by one of his very close friends, Jerome Louchheim, a well-known and highly successful building contractor in Philadelphia, with a personal appeal that Congress Cigar advertise its La Palinas on a small radio network in which he had recently bought a controlling interest. The network, called the United Independent Broadcasters, was still in financial difficulties in New York City and Louchheim asked for my father's advertising as a token of his personal friendship. So, my father agreed to advertise and put me in charge of organizing a program. I put together a program called *The La Palina Smoker,* a half-hour show that featured an orchestra, a female vocalist whom we called "Miss La Palina," and a comedian as a master of ceremonies. It turned out to be a pretty good show.

Over the next six months I made frequent trips to the United Independent Broadcasters' offices in New York and became rather well acquainted with this little network and its activities. UIB had been formed by Arthur Judson, the celebrated concert manager, and a few associates, as a vehicle for putting the classical musicians he represented on the air. Incorporating the network on January 27, 1927, Judson had arranged with the Columbia Phonograph Company that in exchange for its financial backing, the network would be known on the air as the Columbia Phonograph Broadcasting System. He had managed over that first year to sign up sixteen stations as network affiliates, each of which would receive ten or so hours of air time a week from the network.

Arthur Judson and his associates had a lot of trouble getting on the air. But after eight months of strenuous preparations, the network made its debut on Sunday, September 18, 1927, with its own twenty-two-piece orchestra. That same evening, it put on an ambitious performance of the Deems Taylor–Edna St. Vincent Millay opera, *The King's Henchman,* featuring artists from the Metropolitan Opera Company. It was a gala première and a great achievement, but at a cost they were unable to bear. The UIB group went broke and was unable to meet its payroll. Hearing of the network's financial distress, Isaac and Leon Levy, who owned station WCAU in Philadelphia, an affiliate of UIB, brought the wealthy Jerome Louchheim to the rescue. Louchheim bought an interest in the network and was elected chairman of the board of directors on November 7, 1927, and the Levys bought a smaller portion of its stock.

Shortly afterward, the Columbia Phonograph Company withdrew its participation, accepting free advertising time in payment for its interest. UIB then dropped the word "Phonograph" but continued to use the name Columbia Broadcasting System on the air. In its first full year of operation, UIB had taken in $176,737 in net sales and had paid out $396,803, for a net loss of $220,066. Louchheim had failed in all his efforts to turn the company around.

Some ten months after taking over and having bought the controlling interest in the company, he approached my father and offered to sell the network to him, saying, "Sam, why don't you buy it from me? You at least have a cigar to advertise and you can make some use out of it. I can't use it; I have nothing even to try to sell over it." My father later repeated the gist of this conversation to me, as well as his answer: he had no interest in the matter whatsoever. Louchheim had told him he had bought "a lemon," that the network's books were a mess, and that he wanted out. But my father did not want to invest *his* money in such a venture.

I became tremendously excited at the prospect and the network's shaky condition did not deter me. It was the great promise of radio itself that impelled me to act and to act immediately. I did not know what it would cost to buy control of UIB or whether Louchheim would sell it to me. But I had the money to

buy it. I had about a million dollars of my own and I was willing to risk any or all of it in radio.

The source of that million dollars was a family affair. When I went to work for Congress Cigar in 1922, my father put a block of its stock in my name. As the company was privately owned by the Paley family (except for a modest amount of stock owned by Willis Andruss), Congress Cigar stock then had no known market value. Financially speaking, my shares did not impress me at the time. But in 1926, Congress Cigar went public with the sale of 70,000 shares, and the company was listed on the New York Stock Exchange. After the sale, 280,000 shares remained privately held. The following year my father arranged to sell 200,000 shares to the Porto Rican-American Tobacco Company, and my father and Uncle Jay entered into an employment contract to continue running the company for a number of years (they retired in 1931). Some of my stock went with these sales and so I came to have on my own account a little over a million dollars. This was the money I always regarded as sacrosanct, not to be spent or invested without my father's approval.

Nevertheless, on my own I went to see Louchheim whom I had long known as a family friend. He was much older than I, rich, and an important figure in Philadelphia, a man who did not waste words. A bit in awe of him and in view of my youth, I feared that he might think I was not serious about what I had to say. But I told him straight out: I wanted an option to buy his UIB stock, or a substantial amount of it.

Louchheim, it turned out, owned about 60 per cent of the shares in the company. I asked for just over 50 per cent, that is, just enough to secure absolute control. We settled on 50.3 per cent. He asked for $200 a share, though I had no real way to judge the value of the stock. That came to $503,000, and I must say I did not blink an eye. I was satisfied because the sum came to only about half of my personal fortune. I knew that I would have to put in more, perhaps all of what I had when I got into the network. Indeed as part of the deal with Louchheim, I agreed also to place $100,000 in acceptable securities with the

American Telephone & Telegraph Company as a bond for its wire services, in place of the similar bond which Louchheim had put up. UIB itself still did not have sufficient funds for the bond. In exchange, I got Louchheim to agree to place his remaining shares in a voting trust for five years—with the important provision that the Voting Trustee would vote for directors whom I nominated— an arrangement that further secured my control and made sure that my management policies in UIB would be stable at the directors' level.

Louchheim, for his part, drove a conventional hard bargain. The price of the option he said would be $45,000, to be applied to the purchase price when I picked up the option, to be forfeited if I did not. The option was to run ten days. I am able to be so precise about these terms because I still have in my possession a copy of that option-contract. It is dated September 19, 1928. I was still in my twenty-sixth year.

I cannot recall just when I went to my father to ask his approval. Ours was an old-fashioned relationship in which he was the authority figure, especially when it concerned money I had received from Congress Cigar stock. But in this instance there was another ticklish question. The problem was how my desire to go up to New York and run UIB might affect my position as his heir-apparent in the cigar company. The fact that as a family we no longer held the controlling stock in Congress Cigar, and that my father and Uncle Jay had a limited contract to manage the business, left me somewhat freer than I might have been otherwise. Nevertheless, it was still my intention to continue in my father's footsteps. I would promise only to take a leave of absence for a few months to put the network in shape and then to leave it to be operated by a professional management while I returned to my career in the cigar business. I knew my father expected to pass the management of the business on to me, so I had to explain my intentions to him.

On the other hand, I realized that my father would be disturbed if he thought his disapproval would embarrass me. I was troubled even by the thought of possibly disturbing him. Our relationship was then a crucial thing in my life. Family tradition, going back to my childhood, prevented either of us from knowingly giving offense to the other. It was also in our style to be polite and somewhat formal with each other. My father had always believed in giving me or letting me take responsibilities, even in fields where I had little experience. I was very conscious as a young man of my father's confidence in me. It was not an uncomplicated confidence. We had our differences in philosophic outlook. My father, a self-made man who had known adversity, was far more cautious than I and, despite his confidence in me, he thought me rather rash. He also had a strong preference for tangible things: land, factories, physical products. UIB had nothing but office furniture; no radio station of its own, no tangible properties; just prospects. So, with considerable trepidation in my heart, my plans hanging in the balance, I approached my father. I put it to him straight: did he think I should do it or not?

He asked for a day to think it over and then he surprised me. "Yes, I would do it," he declared. And he went further: he and the family would relieve me of some of the burden; they would join me in buying some of Louchheim's stock. They took approximately $100,000 worth of stock, leaving me with about $400,000 worth. Later, I asked him why he was so congenial about it and he explained: "Well, I figured that if it were a failure, you'd lose some money, but you'd have gained a lot of experience. And if it were a success, what you were going into seemed to be more interesting. It would give you a more interesting world to work in than the field I was in. So, on balance, I didn't think it was a bad risk." He also anticipated something I didn't: that if I made a go of it, I would not come back.

On September 25, I closed the deal and on the next day, September 26, 1928, was elected president of a patchwork, money-losing little company called United Independent Broadcasters.

I left Philadelphia for New York unaware that I was starting a new life. I moved into an apartment in the Elysée, a smart little hotel on Fifty-fourth Street between Madison and Park, which had one of the best French restaurants in town. The economy was booming, the stock market had begun its last wild rise before the crash, and the theatrical district, through which I passed on the way to work, was in its glory. The marquees read *Strange Interlude, Show Boat, Animal Crackers, George White's Scandals, This Thing Called Love, The Front Page* and a score of others. I attended the theater many evenings during the 1928–29 season.

My office high above the Paramount movie theater was geographically at the hub of this playland, but only geographically. In comparison with stage and screen, radio then ranked nowhere in show business. In the twenties, movie stars disdained the upstart medium. Only musicians took to it. Radio was for music, popular and classical, along with bits of news, talks, vaudeville-like skits and, on occasion, the broadcasting of big events such as political conventions. A native radio art had not yet been created. But I had the gut feeling that radio was on the threshold of a great awakening, that marvelous things were about to happen and that I had come to the medium at the right moment.

UIB had about a dozen employees in a few offices on one floor of the narrow Paramount tower. Most of the money spent in furnishing the suite had gone into the large, fancy, wood-paneled head office, which seemed to have been designed by UIB's early promoters to impress advertisers and prospective investors in the network. On the day of my arrival a new office boy, Albert Bryant, a stocky fellow with a sober face and a witty smile (he would later become a CBS executive) saw me as a callow youth like himself, without any real business to attend to. Bryant barred my way and insisted on a good deal of identification before he would let me in. It was the first hint of how I would be received. Although I wore clothes styled for older men, for the next few years I would usually be addressed as "Young man . . ." as if some pearl of wisdom or admonishment were about to follow.

The nominal head of the network when I arrived was Major J. Andrew White, a good broadcaster, who was known around town for his natty dress, which included a pince-nez with a ribbon and a white carnation in his lapel. He had style. He asked me one day for an advance of $500 and, when I gave him the money, he said, "Thanks, it's going for a secondhand Rolls-Royce." Major White understood radio at the microphone. But the business of radio or radio operations were not his talent or even within his knowledge. He took no offense about standing aside when I took over. He was happy to have someone take over the day-by-day running of the network, while he put programs together.

In those days we didn't make records or tapes. We auditioned programs live. The potential sponsor would sit in one room and listen to the program, which would be wired in live from a studio performance. Major White would introduce it, saying who was in it and what it was about. The show then would go on and the person we were trying to sell would listen and buy it or not. Major White was adept at presenting programs in this way and on the air. For a time I put him in charge of programs, and since I did not intend to stay long, I kept myself in the background while Major White continued as public spokesman for the network.

Some of the original group stayed on in CBS for many years, even to retirement. Some were not in the right job. Major White had brought in one young radio announcer as his assistant and office manager, which was typical of the confused state of affairs. He had no idea how to manage an office. He drove me crazy, giving me the wrong answers to everything. One day soon after I arrived, Major White was ill and unable to broadcast a football game. So with my fingers crossed, I sent the inept office manager to Chicago to substitute for White. He had told me he had had some experience broadcasting local sporting events. As a result I lost an impossible office manager and gained the best and most famous sportscaster in the country—Ted Husing.

I could see why Jerome Louchheim had sold me his interest in the company. There was no one there who could grasp all of the strands that had to be pulled together to make the network a success. So, once I settled in, I began to analyze our problems and priorities.

The network was too small. We needed many more station

affiliates to give us national coverage if we were to compete with the much larger National Broadcasting Company. We needed programs that would attract a larger audience and give us, in the language of the trade, "substantial circulation." We had to sell time to advertisers. We had to build an organization in a field in which there was little experience to go on. Most important, we had to get control of the finances. We were not going to break even that year, but we had to slow down our losses.

All these matters needed attention more or less at once. But there were some logical priorities and there was one lifesaver: 1928 was a presidential election year. Herbert Hoover and Al Smith were engaged in a lively campaign in which whistle-stop journeys were no longer sufficient. Radio played an important part on both sides. The Republican and Democratic parties in their local and national election campaigns would spend a couple of million dollars on radio time. NBC got the lions' share and we got the overflow business, perhaps a couple of hundred thousand dollars. Without it, the need for immediate revenues would have been the first order of business.

In sorting out the other problems, I could see that building an organization would take months of time and trial. Programming would take time and so would the development of contacts with advertisers and ad agencies. It was apparent I would have to take on that job. But most pressing was the problem of expanding the size and designing the composition of the network itself.

When I arrived on the scene, AT&T had not yet completed its radio line from coast to coast. The final link between Denver and Salt Lake City was scheduled for December, less than three months away. The only coast-to-coast broadcasting was done up to then on a temporary and irregular basis through the use of long-distance telephone lines. But the real thing—permanent radio lines—was coming by Christmas 1928. NBC had kept up with the development of radio lines, and, with the last link in place, would be prepared to announce the first regular national network. UIB had not kept up. But the opportunity was still there to catch up in several areas of the country and to race NBC for the Christmas announcement.

We had affiliations with only sixteen stations in eleven states, permanently connected by AT&T, which formed the nucleus of our network. Their call letters are still music to my ears: WNAC (Boston), WEAN (Providence), WABC (New York City—later changed to WCBS), WOR (Newark), WCAU (Philadelphia), WFBL (Syracuse), WMAK (Buffalo), WJAS (Pittsburgh), WKRC (Cincinnati), WADC (Akron), WAIU (Columbus, Ohio), WGHP (Detroit), KMOX (St. Louis), WJAZ and WMAQ (Chicago), KOIL (Council Bluffs, Iowa, near Omaha, Nebraska). I have a number of these old-fashioned microphones in my office today.

Compared with NBC, this was not much of a network. NBC had fifty-odd affiliated stations in its two major networks—the "Red" and "Blue," plus a regional "Orange" network on the West Coast. Behind it stood the resources of the great Radio Corporation of America (RCA). RCA had formed NBC in 1926 by consolidating its own small network with a larger one owned by the American Telephone & Telegraph Company. NBC (in which General Electric and Westinghouse were minority shareholders until 1930) bought the AT&T network for one million dollars (that became the Red Network) and combined it with RCA's network (the Blue). In setting up NBC as its broadcasting arm, RCA had a major motive which our fledgling network did not: as a manufacturer of equipment, RCA wanted to create a demand for its radio sets as much as to create radio programs.

Whatever its motivation, RCA was aggressively expanding NBC and our competition was not welcome. Indeed it was not even acknowledged. Not long after I came to New York, I asked somebody to arrange a meeting for me with Merlin H. Aylesworth, then president of NBC, so that we could know each other and talk about the future of radio. My friend came back two days later, ashamed, and reported he could not arrange the meeting. He said Mr. Aylesworth had thought about my request and said he didn't want to meet me, because if he did, that would mean that they were acknowledging us as competition. As a matter of policy, NBC did not recognize CBS, just as an established nation might not recognize a newly formed state. He wanted to keep it that way. Aylesworth said we were too small. It made me wonder. Later we met and became very friendly.

The first order of business, if I were to succeed in making UIB grow, was to change the basic document of networking, the contract between the network and its affiliates. The original 1927 contract had played a major role in almost breaking the company financially. It had obligated the network to buy ten hours a week from each station affiliate at $50 an hour. Under the various contracts with the affiliated stations, which differed somewhat, the network was committed to pay out some $7,000 a week, whether or not it sold sufficient time to sponsors to cover that cost.

When Jerome Louchheim had taken over the network, they tried to plug the drain on the company's cash with a new formula. Their new contract required the network as before to pay the stations for the time it used for commercial programs, but it now obliged the stations to pay UIB for the sustaining programs originated by the network. However, after operating for the better part of the year under this new contract, the company was still losing money. It just did not have enough sponsored programs to pay its total operating costs and the stations did not buy enough sustaining programs to cover our losses.

So, I decided to revise the contract once more in order not to make it less, but to make it more attractive to station affiliates. I hoped to attract additional stations to the network and at the same time I wanted the contract to protect the network from financial losses. I devised a package of compensations giving something of greater value to each side. I proposed the concept of free sustaining service: that is, to make the sustaining programs available to the affiliates at no cost. And I took the bit in my teeth: I would guarantee not ten but twenty hours of programming per week, pay the stations $50 an hour for the commercial hours used, but with a new proviso. The network would not pay the stations for the first five hours of commercial programming time; that is, we would pay the affiliates $50 an hour for all commercial time used in excess of five hours a week. The twenty contract hours were set forth at specified times, and to allow for the possibility of more business to come, the network was to receive an option on additional time.

And for the first time, we were to have exclusive rights for network broadcasting through the affiliate. That meant the local station could not use its facilities for any other broadcasting network. I added one more innovation which helped our cause: local stations would have to identify our programs with the CBS name.

This new arrangement was beneficial for both parties, for in those days local radio stations had plenty of time on the air to dispense and little cash. We offered programs of a quality that no local station could produce; and by going to twenty hours of such programming we could "sustain" a local station. On our side of the deal, the five free hours of commercial time assured us of some income that we could keep.

We put this proposition to our existing affiliates and received their agreement in November 1928. That put us in a position to offer it as an attraction to other local stations among the four or five hundred then operating in the United States, some of them hooked up to small regional networks. By telegram I invited a carefully selected number of unaffiliated stations from the South to a meeting in New York City. Twelve of their representatives came. This was a crucial meeting for me. We met in a room at the Ambassador Hotel, where I presented them with all the advantages of affiliation under my new formula for sharing commercial and sustaining time on the air. After some debate over the terms and conditions, the meeting ended with every station signing up. Suddenly, in one day, we had a southern leg to our network. Later, a few more stations came in from the Middle West and signed up. The Pacific coast remained a tantalizing plum, if we were to become nationwide.

The only possibility of our getting to the West Coast quickly was to hook into a regional network. There was one West Coast group called the American Broadcasting Company (no relation to the present network of that name) with headquarters in Seattle and five stations along the coast, plus one in Salt Lake City and one in Denver, with an AT&T-leased landline from Denver to the coast. Our relations with this network were rather unreliable. It claimed to be the third-largest network in the country, but it went into receivership the following August and vanished, leaving a new problem.

It was a hectic, busy two months—November and December—in which I was scurrying about trying to sign up affiliates and at the same time to acquire a station of our own. Operating on alternate nights on leased time from WABC (New York) and WOR (Newark), we badly needed our own station from which to originate programs. I negotiated with WABC and WOR, both of which were willing to sell. Simply because it was cheaper, we bought WABC in December 1928 for $390,000. The acquisition gave us a transmitting station and a studio on top of Steinway Hall on Fifty-seventh Street—and also some unusual assets of the WABC company, Atlantic Broadcasting. Desperate to sell local time, the station management often accepted merchandise instead of money. And so, coming to us with our purchase of a radio station were live chickens, kitchen appliances, pieces of jewelry, and whatnot. UIB's fixed assets—in furniture, equipment, and improvements to leased premises—amounted to only about $25,000. Everything else was rather airy. The net worth of WABC at book value was about $130,000; the difference between that and the purchase price we listed in our books under the old accounting euphemism "Good Will."

Where did we get the money? For that kind of expansion, we were undercapitalized. We issued 2,500 new shares of our stock at $200 a share to raise $500,000. I subscribed to about $200,000, raising my total investment to $600,000. The other shareholders took up the rest.

During this hectic autumn, one goal slid away almost unnoticed and was lost forever: my intention to return to my father's cigar company. Only in retrospect would I realize how lucky I had been to have been there, on the scene, when the technologies of mass production, national advertising and national communications in broadcasting came together. At the time, I had some intimations of the future, but I really did not dwell on the bigger picture. I simply realized that I had an affinity for this new life in broadcasting. I loved what I was doing every day. The decision to make broadcasting the core of my new life came over me naturally, and my father took my decision just as naturally.

On My Own

Three and a half months after I bought UIB, I like to
think I startled the nation and particularly NBC with
my first appearance on the air, January 8, 1929, when I announced that CBS now had the largest regular chain of
broadcasting stations in radio history. At least one newspaper
headlined the news: COLUMBIA SYSTEM TO HAVE WORLD'S LARGEST
NETWORK.

It was literally true, but only literally. We had tripled our
broadcasting coverage and now served forty-nine stations in
forty-two cities across the nation. NBC was divided into two
separate networks, neither of which had as many fully affiliated
stations as we did. So we were the largest radio network in the
world. Actually, we were still a small, informal organization,
groping our way as we went along. But we wanted to make a
splash when we announced our debut as a new national network.
We had lost the race with NBC to be the first with coast-to-coast
broadcasting—by two weeks, and that only because someone
had goofed in making certain technical wire arrangements.

Behind that announcement, however, had gone a tremendous
amount of planning and work in reorganizing the structure of the

company. When I had taken over, the network consisted of three companies: UIB, which supplied the station time; the Columbia Broadcasting System (the old phonograph company), which sold the time; and Arthur Judson's company, which supplied the programs. The Columbia Broadcasting System was the name then best known to the public because it was the broadcasting arm of UIB. To preserve that name, I abolished the broadcasting arm as a corporate entity and changed the name of UIB to the Columbia Broadcasting System, Inc. I became president of the newly christened company and named Major White as managing director.

That left me with the problem of Arthur Judson, whose company supplied the network by contract with its programs. The trouble was that Arthur Judson, a serious musician and a great impresario, was interested solely in music and cared nothing about vaudeville or comedy. His programs lacked variety and, I thought, were a drag on our future expansion. So I went to him, and said: "Arthur, we are not going to be a success with your kind of programming. Your organization does not know how to turn out all that we need. We have to make a deal with you so we can do our own programming." He was surprised and deeply disappointed—and tough-minded—and we negotiated a long while before we agreed on a plan relinquishing his services and leaving us free to do our own programming. By December 1928, I had reorganized all the corporate parts of the company into a single entity, the Columbia Broadcasting System, Inc.*

For broadcasting, we divided our new network into six groups of stations, so that an advertiser could buy time on only the group or combination of groups that best suited him. In addition to the "basic network," which covered the Northeast and the most populous areas of the Midwest, five other groups covered the South, Midwest and the Pacific coast. With our network of forty-nine stations in forty-two cities we estimated that we were within radio range of 87 per cent of the population of the coun-

* On April 18, 1974, because of extensive diversification, we changed the name from Columbia Broadcasting System, Inc., to CBS Inc. For purposes of simplicity in this book I shall usually refer just to CBS.

try, though only about 33 per cent of the homes in the United States then had a radio, and we were broadcasting only twenty-one hours a week. Nevertheless, I recognized the potential cultural significance of this new instrument—network radio broadcasting—which would pull our far-flung country together. I could see the boom coming in the manufacture and sale of radio sets.

It was an exciting, hectic period of time and I had that feeling of being on the threshold of great, wonderful happenings. Everything seemed new and innovative, and I had the energy of youthful enthusiasm to spend on solving problems that arose on a daily, if not hourly, basis. In those days we didn't even have the basic contract forms. When we made a sale, we would write a new contract each time. We hired someone who had worked for NBC and knew something about their forms—rate cards, affiliate controls, sales and purchase papers, and the like. But setting these up took a while. Meanwhile I would go out and sell, sell, sell network time.

One day, when I was laid up with a bad back, I considered the problem of how to persuade our advertisers to buy a wider area of the network coverage. In those days, advertisers were selective and usually bought only the basic network and whatever supplementary groups they wanted. Seldom did an advertiser take the whole network. It dawned on me that the difficulty of selling the whole network was our own fault: we had not recognized that different areas of the country represented by the network could be of varying value to an advertiser. But if we gave an important discount to an advertiser on condition that he would take the whole network, it might be worth it to him. It also would greatly increase the coverage of our programs, give additional programs to many of our stations, and raise our overall income as well. We introduced the plan and it worked.

Standard forms and contracts did not change the atmosphere of business, which remained informal at all levels. Even in our most important deals, negotiations were most informal. When, for example, the ABC (Seattle) network was about to fold, we took over ABC's landline lease, and it was a life-or-death matter for us to establish a connection with a strong regional Pacific network. I knew of only one network on the West Coast with suitable stations that were not tied up with NBC. It belonged to a man named Don Lee. He owned stations in Los Angeles and San Francisco and was hooked up with several affiliates.

Don Lee was a rich man who, in addition to his radio interests, had long been the franchised dealer for Cadillac cars for the entire state of California (when General Motors granted wholesale dealer territories). His company, Don Lee, Inc., had bought station KFRC (San Francisco) in 1926 and station KHJ (Los Angeles) in 1927, and was in the course of expanding its operations into a network with a half-dozen affiliates up the coast to Seattle and Spokane. Because of Don Lee's reputed business ability, I wanted not only to have his network merge with ours, but also to get him to be our West Coast representative.

I had heard that he was satisfied with his regional radio operation and was not interested in a national affiliation. But I knew the value of national network programming, or the promise of it, which no single station or regional group could equal. The best talent wanted the big audience and all that meant in fame and fortune. I also figured that the problem of the difference in time zones between the two coasts could somehow be resolved. And so in a brash flush of enthusiasm I picked up the telephone and called Don Lee in Los Angeles.

Mr. Lee himself came on the phone and I spilled out my story. Although he probably knew less about me than I did about him, he made a good guess at the sound of my voice. When I had finished, he addressed me as "Young man . . ."—the salutation I was getting used to—but then surprised me. He told me I was talking about a substantial matter that was not for the telephone; if I thought it was important I should get on a train and come to California and talk to him. It was true, I had been hasty. In those days, it took more than a week to go by train to the coast and back. To leave the office for such a time had seemed impossible to me. But I changed my mind fast. I told him I would be there.

When I got off the train at Los Angeles several days later, a unique business experience began for me. Mr. Lee's chauffeur, waiting at the station, told me that there was reserved for me a bungalow at the Ambassador Hotel—a grand place with vast grounds, cottages, and a large swimming pool. I checked in, but I did not spend much time there. Upon my arrival, I was told that Mr. Lee wanted me to pack a bag: we would be leaving that night.

I met Mr. Lee and several of his friends at his home. He was a short man with a round, half-bald head, flaring ears, and smiling eyes behind shell-rimmed glasses. He spoke crisply and to the point. "We're going off on my yacht for a few days," he said to me. "It looks to me as if you could use it."

When I first laid eyes on his yacht, the *Invader*, it took my breath away. It was absolutely the most beautiful and said to be the fastest sailing vessel on the Pacific coast. When we put out to sea, I discovered all the comforts of home aboard this graceful sailing ship, and yet my mind was on business. The next morning I sought him out and said, "Now, Mr. Lee, let's talk about this affiliation I came out here to discuss."

"Mr. Paley," he said, "there's a rule here and you might as well know about it right now, and that is, no one discusses business on this boat."

"That's fine," I answered, "but I have to get back to New York, Mr. Lee. What am I going to do about it?"

"You'll just have to wait until we get back to Los Angeles. Then I'll be glad to discuss business with you."

I was young enough to think that I was losing all kinds of precious time, but after a while I decided to relax and enjoy myself. Along with several attractive guests, I talked and read and sat in the sun, and joined in lively lunches and dinners. When we got back to Los Angeles four days later, I went straight to Lee's office. "Well, now," I said, "let's get down to business."

"I'll discuss business only if you'll agree to come back on the boat for another three or four days," he said. "You still look tired."

I didn't care how "tired" I looked, I was not going to waste another four days. Now knowing Mr. Lee better and on a first-name basis, I decided to refuse. "I just can't do that, Don," I said. "I must get back to New York. I have a business that needs me, and I've already been away too long."

"Well, that's too bad," he replied. "Unless you can arrange to come back on the boat, we have nothing to discuss."

"In other words," I said, pressing the logic, "if I do agree to go back on the boat, we *do* have something to discuss."

He agreed, and I asked for a few minutes to think about it. I called my office in New York, caught up with some of the things on my desk, and told them I'd be away for another week. Then I returned to his office and said, "Okay, I'll go back to the boat." We went back on his yacht for another four days, without mentioning a word of business.

Finally back in his office again, he said, "Now we will talk business." He pressed a button for his secretary, who came in. "Mr. Paley," he said, "is now going to dictate the terms and conditions of the contract that will exist between us, on the basis of our stations becoming affiliated with CBS."

"What terms and conditions?" I said.

"The terms and conditions that you dictate."

"What does that mean?"

"Whatever you dictate and whatever you think is fair, I'm prepared to sign," he said.

I told him that I thought that was a dirty trick, putting the whole burden on me. But it was the only way that he would do it. So I leaned over backward to be fair, and I am sure that I came away giving him much more than I would have if we had done some arguing and negotiating.

I still have a copy of that contract. It is dated July 16, 1929, and was to take effect the following January. He knew what he was doing. He had understood the values of national network affiliation. I made him our West Coast representative. The deal was a good one for both of us. All he had wanted to do during the yachting distraction, it seems, was to get to know me; in fact we became good friends.

We remained close, and the business relationship between CBS and the Don Lee stations remained stable until he died five years later at fifty-three years of age. The affiliation with Don Lee entrenched CBS on the West Coast and gave us a secure coast-to-coast network.

From the first half of 1929, advertisers began to come our way. Our net sales were running at an annual rate of about $4 million and CBS began to look promising enough to attract the attention of the movie moguls. I first became aware of such outside interest in the early spring of 1929 when William Fox—later of Twentieth Century–Fox—came looking. I was not eager to sell part of CBS, but I was interested in what Fox might have to say. With all our accomplishments, I knew that in spite of our own big talk we were still a small company with modest resources and still unproven in competition with the giant RCA with its two NBC networks. After such a large, rapid expansion of our operations, I wanted breathing space and I was tempted by the idea of the security which an association with a strong, established company in a related field would provide. The movie people had tremendous financial resources and I thought there might be some connection between their knowledge of show business and what we needed in broadcasting. I was anxious also to ease up on the structural and financial problems of the business and to concentrate on programming, which I felt would be the most important element in building a network.

Flattered of course that a movie mogul of such stature should ask to see me, I was conscious of my youth and inexperience and, in short, I was in awe of William Fox. I listened to his overtures at dinner and again at his office. He was "interested" in broadcasting and wanted to have his company buy into CBS. No doubt there was a good deal more on his mind, as there was also on mine. Radio was exciting enough intrinsically and for its potential growth. But there was even more in the air. The movies were caught up in the revolution of the "talkies." Al Jolson had been heard in *The Jazz Singer*, the first feature movie to combine both music and dialogue with motion pictures, only a little more than a year earlier; and it was only about eight or nine months since the first all-talking feature picture, *The Lights of New York*, had opened on Broadway. So there was the possibility that if sound could come to film, film could come to sound. The union of radio and motion pictures, in a word, television, was already in its experimental stage and was expected to emerge in public in a few years. As entertainers, the movie moguls had reason to cast an eye at radio. It seems likely too that movie people had an eye on RCA, which not only owned NBC but was also affiliated with one of the big movie companies, RKO. There was reason for talk on both sides.

Mr. Fox looked mean and he acted like a powerhouse—both impressions gained from the way he dealt with me. "If we join you, you know, with our financial backing and our know-how in show business," he said, "we'll make you into something." He wanted to know if he could send his people to CBS to look at our books as a prelude to any sort of deal to be made. I said yes, he could have anything he wanted. His people spent several weeks at CBS and then he called me to his office and declared, "Well, I've got good news for you."

"What's that, Mr. Fox?" I asked.

"I've decided to buy a half interest in your company."

"Well, that's fine," I said. "On what terms?"

"I've been giving a lot of thought to that and I want to be fair. I'll buy a half interest at the same rate you paid for your interest in CBS."

I had my hat on his desk. I picked it up with one hand and shook hands with him with the other, and said, "Mr. Fox, it was nice to have known you," and walked out of the room. I was furious.

He kept calling me at my office and I did not return his calls. He had insulted my intelligence. I would not have anything more to do with him. Instinctively I knew there was no use talking further to him.

But the rumor that William Fox was out to buy CBS reached Adolph Zukor, head of Paramount and kingpin of them all. Anything that Mr. Fox was doing was of interest to Mr. Zukor. Before long, a representative of Mr. Zukor came to see me.

Zukor was the biggest name in the business. Twenty-some years earlier he had been one of the pioneers of the motion picture business. He had come from Hungary in the 1880s and from penny arcades and nickelodeons he had gone on to produce short films and features—some say he introduced the feature film in the United States and the star system as well. He "discovered" Mary Pickford, Douglas Fairbanks, Rudolph Valentino, and Clara Bow. When I met him, he was fifty-six years old, rich, and famous. He had gathered into Paramount all the functions of movie production, distribution and exhibition through the Paramount chain of theaters. When his representative came upstairs from his office to mine in the Paramount building, it was like receiving a messenger from a legend. But I was better prepared after my run-in with Fox.

Zukor's man came right out with it: Zukor wanted to know whether CBS was for sale, in whole or part. I met him head-on: "Look. We are small and we could use a well-financed partner. Paramount is acceptable because it is in a related business. But I don't want to waste any time negotiating. The information about our business is available. I've got a price and if Paramount wants to meet it, fine. If not, don't bother talking about it."

"What's the price?" he asked.

"For a half interest, $5 million," I declared, without a gulp.

"You don't mean that, do you?"

"Yes, sir, I do," said I.

The next day he came back and, like Mr. Fox, said, "I've got good news for you. Mr. Zukor is so enamored of CBS and what you've done with it so far that he has authorized me to close a deal with you for $4 million."

That was of course a conventional bargainer's response to an asking price. But I had decided on a firm price. So I told him, "You didn't understand me. I said to you not to bother me unless Paramount was willing to pay $5 million."

He said, "Well, you're kidding. We're negotiating. Don't tell me you won't take $4 million?"

"I'm telling you now and I'm not going to tell it to you any more," I insisted, "the price is $5 million, and not one penny less. If you want to waste time negotiating, let's call the whole thing off."

He came back again the following day. "Now I've got something you can't refuse. I am authorized to give you $4.5 million." I said, "The answer is no, and I am not going to discuss it with you further."

Meanwhile Uncle Jay heard about it and came up from Philadelphia. "Is it true?" he demanded. "Paramount has offered you $4.5 million for a half interest in CBS and you turned it down?" I said yes. "Young man, success has gone to your head," he cried. "You're out of your mind. You know that, don't you? Look how much money you would have made in such a short space of time." I insisted that I would not sell a half interest in CBS for less than $5 million. He said, "Well, I'm here representing myself and your father to tell you that's the most arrogant thing we ever heard of. Now, you pick up that telephone, you get hold of this man and you just hope to God that $4.5 million offer is still good."

"I'll do nothing of the kind," I said. "I told this man $5 million. I meant it and I still mean it and I'm not going to budge."

It was only a few hours later that I got a call from my father: "Young man!" Lord, that salutation didn't help my father's case. He started to give me the same argument. "Your uncle tells me," he said, "that you're being very stubborn, very arrogant." I listened patiently and I said, "Well, okay, you can think I'm stubborn and arrogant if you want to, but I have figured out what I want to do. I have the right to say yes or no to Paramount, and my answer is no."

The next day Paramount's negotiator telephoned and said, "Mr. Zukor would like to meet you."

I said, "Fine," and I joined him for lunch. There were Mr.

Zukor and about twelve other people of his executive staff sitting there. I was alone. It was the first time I had ever seen him and he did not look like my ideal of a tycoon. He was a short man, no more than five feet high, who walked with his feet turned in, and even when he smiled he had steely eyes.

When we got around to talking about the business of CBS, he remarked, "You know, one of the reasons I want to buy your company—it's not just because of broadcasting—is that I've heard a lot about you and I want you to be a part of the Paramount family."

I replied to his compliment, "Well, that's fine, Mr. Zukor. I appreciate that and I am flattered. But all I've got to sell is my company, and I will go with it."

"Well," he continued, "we think very highly of you as a person and it's a tribute to you. As for me, I've negotiated all my life rather successfully and I've never been in a business deal where a man started out with a price and stood by it to the very end. There must be some give and take. If you ask $5 million, it doesn't mean you have to stick by it. Four and a half million dollars as a counteroffer seems fair to me."

I repeated what I had said before. "Mr. Zukor, it may seem unfair to you, but my price is $5 million."

"Why?"

"I'll tell you why," I said. "I'm selling the future, not the present. Things are going very well, and in two years CBS will be making enough money to make the purchase attractive to anybody. Don't call it stubborn," I said. "Call it conviction."

There was no deal and I went back to my office. But the day was not over. About five in the afternoon, the middleman came to see me. "You're the damnedest kid I ever came across," he declared. "They've accepted your proposition. They will pay you $5 million for half the stock of CBS." We made the deal and it was completed and signed by all parties concerned on June 13, 1929. Five days after I made the deal I received the nicest note from Uncle Jay, saying he was both surprised and pleased.

Zukor then took to telephoning me from time to time to ask if I would agree to run companies he was thinking of buying. They were usually in the business of leisuretime activity—radio-manufacturing companies, pool-table companies, bowling-equipment companies. Later, he wanted me to be his right-hand man in the Paramount complex. I always said no—all I wanted to do was to run CBS. He argued that I could run CBS with my left hand and manage his expanding entertainment empire with my other. But I knew my limits, and I knew that my ambitions were in broadcasting alone. I said I was afraid I just couldn't do it. One day in his office he said to me, "Well, don't you even want to know how much I intend to pay you?"

"I don't think it makes much difference," I replied, "but anyway, what do you have in mind?"

To my astonishment, he offered me $450,000 a year. When I gasped, he added, "But this isn't all. There's a bonus system here and on the basis of earnings last year, you would get an additional $150,000."

"You mean $600,000 a year?"

"Yes," he said.

"Mr. Zukor," I said, "I don't think anyone in the world is worth that much money."

And that's when, without a smile, he said, "Bill, you're wrong. I'm worth much more." His income I would guess was about $900,000 a year, maybe a million.

After visiting his estate at New City, not far up the Hudson River from Manhattan, I found my estimate of his income easy to believe. The estate included the large house in which he lived, a smaller building that housed a movie theater, and several guest cottages, all looked after by a large staff of well-trained servants. Although Zukor never played the game very well, he had an eighteen-hole golf course with a private pro. It was, in sum, far above any standard of living I had ever seen at that time, and yet he took it all in stride, not the least bit self-conscious about the extraordinary luxuries with which he surrounded himself. He acted as though he had been born to the manner. Still, when he offered me the astonishing salary that might someday approach his, I held my ground in refusing. Finally he said, "Well, don't give me a definite answer now. Think about it and come see me tomorrow." I didn't have to think. My mind was made up. I went to him the next day and said that I had given the matter consideration but that I was sorry, I would stand by my first reaction. Thanking me politely, he said he thought I was making a mistake. I'm sure he thought I was silly to throw away the opportunity to make all that money and then probably to be his successor.

The CBS-Paramount agreement called upon the stockholders of CBS as a group to sell half their stock to the Paramount company. For the CBS stockholders it was a sensational deal, not only for the proceeds to be received, but also because, by the measure of the deal, the company would now be valued at $10 million. Only nine months earlier I had bought half the company's shares from Louchheim for a half-million dollars, which put a value on the company of one million dollars. Thus, allowing for the stockholders' subsequent subscription of an additional half million, CBS had increased in value about sevenfold in less than one year. The real increase in value, of course, was in CBS's new substance: affiliates, our own station, rising revenues and even brighter prospects.

With a single shareholder, Paramount, owning 50 per cent of the stock, and fifteen other shareholders dividing the other 50 per cent, one might suppose that Paramount would have working control of CBS or that by purchasing one additional share from any shareholder, Paramount could gain absolute control of CBS. But such was not the case.

The mechanics of our agreement provided that we would increase the total number of shares in CBS to 100,000, half of which were designated "Class A" and went to Paramount. The other half, 50,000 shares, were designated "Class B" and were divided among the individual stockholders. The division of stock into two classes, with each electing its own directors, meant that neither side had absolute formal voting control. A majority of stockholder votes on each side would elect that side's directors. To gain absolute control, one side would have to cross over and obtain more than half of the stock on the other side. It was not possible for anyone to gain such control over our side because altogether the Paley family including myself controlled a majority of the Class B stock.

Such structures should never be overlooked in corporate life, but in this instance, it was the intention of all parties, that neither side should have full control. Informally, however, as president and operating head of CBS, I exercised control. Mr. Zukor for Paramount wanted it that way just as much as I did.

There was one other aspect in negotiating the sale which would have considerable consequences in the future of CBS and my life. We got into an argument over whether Paramount would pay for the CBS stock in cash or with Paramount stock. Speaking for myself and the other CBS stockholders, I insisted upon payment in cash. I was dealing with Paramount's treasurer, Ralph Kohn, when this subject of cash or stock came up and when we reached an impasse, he said Mr. Zukor wanted to see me about it. In his office, the head of Paramount asked: "I understand you are insisting on cash?"

"That's right, Mr. Zukor."

"Why won't you take stock?"

"Well, I'd just rather have cash."

"Don't be a fool," said Zukor. "Paramount's stock is worth about $65 a share now and will be worth $150 in a year or so. You just take the stock and you'll be more than twice as rich."

I got an idea then for a compromise: it would relieve him of the need to put up cash and it would satisfy me. "I'll tell you what I'll do," I said. "I'll make you a proposal. I expect CBS to earn $2 million in the next couple of years. That was why I held out for $5 million. Now I propose to you that we will take Paramount stock instead of cash and you will agree that we can sell the Paramount stock back to you, not at $150 but at $85 a share, two years from now, if CBS earns $2 million in that time. That is, you give us the right to put the Paramount stock back to you at a price only $20 above its present selling price."

"You're asking the simplest thing in the world," Zukor replied. "If that's all you want, we have a deal. It's all set."

"That's all I want," I said.

So I sold half of CBS less than a year after taking it over. I didn't have any emotional feelings about the transaction. I was willing to sell at a price that seemed rather preposterous at the time, but which took full account of the company's prospects and brought in some immediate profits for me and my fellow stockholders. I expected Paramount would be a good source of capital for us as we grew, and of course I was glad to prove to my father and uncle that I knew what I was doing. To me it was just a good deal. I didn't worry about transferring half my risk in CBS to Paramount. That risk was covered by a "first-refusal" feature of the contract, which gave us the right to buy back the CBS stock held by Paramount at a price which matched the bona fide bid for the stock by any other party.

The sale did not change my enthusiasm over CBS or the amount of energy I expected to put into it. The day we signed the papers was just another day for me. If the deal hadn't gone through, I wouldn't have cared. CBS was my life. I felt I was going to make a success of it, and I thought I could do it with or without Paramount.

The outcome of this deal two years later, after the great crash of 1929, was quite a surprise, at least to Zukor and his associates.

At my stand-up desk in the new CBS Headquarters Building.

My mother at her home in Palm Beach.

My father among the tobacco leaves in Cuba.

Fishing with my father.

Signing the contract for Columbia Concerts Corporation.

Miss Radio of 1929, Olive Shea, cutting the ribbon to open our headquarters
at 485 Madison Avenue.

One of our early stars, Bing Crosby.

The CBS Adult Education Board.

Kate Smith.

Major Edward Bowes.

Will Rogers.

A 1935 CBS meeting in my office with (l. to r.) Larry Lowman, Paul Kesten, Fred Willis, Ed Klauber, and Hugh Boice.

H. V. Kaltenborn.

Edward Klauber.

Major J. Andrew White.

Babe's favorite pond at Kiluna.

The family at the wedding reception for Minnie and James Fosburgh at Kiluna.

A Different Kind
of Business

B roadcasting was an absolutely new, unique, fascinating, complicated and much misunderstood business in those early days. (Today, it is no longer new; all other adjectives apply.) At the start very few people could visualize it as a profitable business. We bought our home station WABC from a maker of radio sets who thought that the manufacturing side of the business would be much more profitable than broadcasting itself. RCA, the giant in the industry, had launched NBC principally as a vehicle to stimulate the sale of RCA radio sets. Almost every move anyone made in this fantastic beginning business amounted to crossing a new frontier. There really were no precedents and no limits to what you could do or try to do. It was a business of ideas.

During those early days at CBS, I wore many hats. I was the chief executive officer of the company. Also, the chief accountant, the program director and the talent scout. I worked twelve, sometimes sixteen, eighteen hours a day. The business received my total concentration until I left the office; then I would go back to my bachelor apartment, change into evening clothes, and go out for a night on the town. I had a lot of energy, a lot of ambition, and I drove myself hard in business and in pursuit of pleasure. I developed a high sense of responsibility for the success of CBS that I had seldom been called upon to have when working for my father. Now I was out on my own and no longer had my father or Uncle Jay looking over my shoulder. My life was changing as rapidly and as dramatically as the life of the infant CBS. We were both maturing day by day.

Quite early in the game, I had evaluated the essential elements of broadcasting and came to believe that the crux of this business was programming—i.e., what went on the air. It seemed logical to me that those who put on the most appealing shows won the widest audiences, which in turn attracted the most advertisers and that led to the greatest revenues, profits, and success. We started to grow and we originated more and more network programs from our key home station WABC. But half a year later, it became plain to me that CBS had an urgent need for more and larger studios from which we could originate better shows for our own local station and for the network. So even before I made that $5 million deal with Paramount, I signed a ten-year, $1.5 million lease for six floors of space in a new building going up on Madison Avenue at Fifty-second Street. It was seen at the time as a very high risk for such a fledgling company, but I considered it an absolute need if CBS were to succeed in competing with NBC. What amazed me was that the builder agreed to make substantial structural changes in the building at a considerable cost to himself to accommodate our need for two air-conditioned, windowless, double floors for our studios, without ever checking our credit rating. I wondered about his business acumen, but I was told he regarded me as a good risk. He must have been, as I was, supremely confident about the future of CBS.

After the Paramount deal, I was committed to the goal of CBS earning $2 million by September 1931. So, in July 1929, we moved from four rooms in the old Paramount Tower to four floors (two of them double floors) in this modern building on Madison Avenue at Fifty-second Street. The three upper floors housed six large studios, programming offices and the broadcasting equipment rooms; the executive, sales, accounting offices all were crowded on the one lower floor. I moved my original paneled office over intact to the new building, but now I had my own private secretary, Frank Kizis, who dressed in a dark suit, black tie, and stiff collar, sitting in an outer office. For the formal opening ceremonies of the CBS headquarters, President Hoover spoke over the CBS network from a hookup in the White House. Olive Shea, Miss Radio of 1929, cut the ribbon, and I beamed my youthful smile in black tie and dinner jacket.

The new building was a great stride forward. Now CBS had its own ample studios from which it could originate its own programs. As time went on we expanded our facilities constantly, eventually taking over most of the building, which we would occupy for thirty-five prosperous years. Still, we were a tiny organization, initiating, innovating and building on ideas extemporaneously, with the vitality of youth and a lot of excitement and creativity. What CBS now needed was more men of executive ability in its youthful ranks; what I needed was help of all kinds. So, in 1930, I hired two men, who devoted almost the rest of their lives with me to CBS.

Edward Klauber came aboard to help relieve me of paperwork and nagging administrative detail. I almost passed him by. When he first came to the office I saw a short, heavy-set, taciturn man who walked with his hands behind his back, Napoleonic style, and who at forty-three seemed to me an old man. But an intermediary persisted and, because I really needed someone badly, I saw him again and reconsidered. His background was superb. Born in Louisville, Kentucky, he had studied medicine briefly, abandoned that for a newspaper career, had risen from reporter to night city editor of the New York *Times*, and then had gone into public relations. He joined CBS as "assistant to the president" and little by little created his own job, relieving me of more and more problems. He was an indefatigable day-and-night worker, always keeping in touch with me, providing me with written reports and eventually becoming my adviser on all sorts of things, rising to vice-president and later executive vice-president of CBS. In time, Klauber developed a strong sense of possessiveness toward me, which in later years caused management problems. Nevertheless, he became one of the considerable assets to CBS in its growing years.

The second important figure to join CBS in 1930 was Paul Kesten who, at thirty-one, was closer to my age, a slim, dynamic man with blond hair and piercing eyes, a meticulous dresser and a good conversationalist well versed in many subjects, who had worked in advertising since he was twenty years of age. Hired as our director of sales promotion, he just bubbled from the start with ideas and strategies for promoting the network. For instance, because we were so small and still chasing the great NBC, he suggested that CBS should always talk publicly about radio as a medium rather than about CBS directly: this lofty view would make us seem bigger than we really were. Kesten was a master of this approach. He sent out non-partisan surveys and reports on the ownership and use of radio sets, the coverage of stations and programs, the income levels and habits of listeners, the use of automobile radios. He created a flow of bread-and-butter information and statistics for everybody in the new industry. And underneath it all, he was very competitive and eager to portray CBS as the equal of NBC.

Kesten and I were so compatible that we understood each other in a kind of mental shorthand. We could cover a lot of ground in a few minutes of conversation. We saw eye to eye from the start on the importance of design and good taste. In those early days it was necessary to persuade some advertisers about what was tasteful and effective in the spoken advertisement on radio. Kesten had a feeling for elegance and taste along with a touch of majesty, with which he presented the image of CBS to certain advertisers. We proved to be able to work together as a unique and effective team.

All this helped clear the way for me to concentrate my own efforts on the top priorities of the new network: thinking up new programs, finding the talent to perform in these programs and finding the advertisers who would pay for it all. All were equally important and they had to mesh at the same time and the same place. There were more ways than one, I learned, to put a show together and to get it on the air.

The best way, of course, was to have sponsors come to CBS with plenty of money and willingness to accept every proposal I put to them. We even had a few like that. Foremost among them was the Grigsby-Grunow Company, the largest manufacturer of radio sets in America. With about a quarter of the whole market, they sold about one million Majestic radio sets in 1929 and they loved CBS because they hated RCA. The Radio Corporation of America was their chief competitor, with whom they were continually battling in the courts over patent rights. They first sponsored *Majestic's Two Black Crows,* a very popular blackface comedy much like *Amos 'n' Andy* of later years and they sponsored the *Majestic Theater of the Air,* a fine program which introduced to radio listeners such outstanding personalities as Ruth Etting, Fanny Brice, Edgar Guest, Dolores Del Rio, Helen Morgan and several contemporary American composers, including one named George Gershwin at the piano. And the Majestic people were enthusiastic enough to sponsor the *American School of the Air,* a half-hour educational program that went out on the air twice a week and later five times a week. It was designed to be used in classrooms across the country as an educational vehicle and an aid to teachers. Majestic Radio was our first big sponsor, buying just about everything I proposed, with three or four shows running at the same time. They were very important to CBS in the beginning, a lifesaver, and there were other radio manufacturers who came to CBS because they were in competition with RCA.

But most of our advertisers—the vast majority—had to be wooed to CBS, and the method I used was to entice them with good ideas. In our offices, my associates and I would dream up radio shows of all types. I would take our best ideas to an advertiser and say, "If I could get you so-and-so, would you agree to give serious consideration to that program?" If there seemed to be some real interest, I would then approach the entertainer and say, "What if I could get you so much money for a weekly show, would you . . . ?" I would then bring the sponsor and the artist together in a studio for a live audition. If it clicked, a new CBS program was born. This involved a lot of running back and forth between the parties, pleading, persuading, selling and negotiating. Each situation was different; no formulas applied.

In preparing the 1929 winter schedule, it occurred to me that if CBS was the number-one network, as we were advertising ourselves, then we ought to have the number-one popular orchestra in the United States. Clearly, that was Paul Whiteman, a giant among jazzmen and big bands. It was a formidable idea. Would Paul Whiteman come with us? Would any sponsor pay his formidable price?

I took the idea to Lennen & Mitchell, the advertising agency for P. Lorillard Company, the makers of Old Gold cigarettes. After talking to his client, the account executive said, "Get Paul Whiteman and you have a deal." I found Whiteman performing at the Drake Hotel in Chicago and during a break, I introduced myself. A portly man with great presence, Whiteman looked at me and laughed. "Young man, you don't think I'm going to do a regular program on *radio*, do you?" He had made spot appearances before, but I tried to persuade him of the advantages of a regular weekly program. He thought it would debase his reputation. We talked a bit and he went back to lead his band. Then he returned and we talked some more.

We talked until well after midnight. How I persuaded him I no longer remember. His fame was already great, but usually he played for only a couple of hundred people at a time. I just stayed with him, talking of the magic of radio and of vastly greater audiences than nightclubs or Flo Ziegfeld had to offer. And we talked of money. It was late that night or near dawn of the next day when he said, "By God, you've sold me. I'll try it."

I rushed back to New York to give the good news to my associates and then made my way to Lennen & Mitchell. They were equally delighted and the contract was signed soon afterward. I forget what they paid him, but *Variety* reported it was $30,000 a week for the band and $5,000 a week for himself. The sponsor controlled the program and most often named the radio show for the product that was being advertised. Thus, we had the *Majestic Theater of the Air*, the *Emerson Effervescent Hour* and the *Listerine Program*. NBC had the *A & P Gypsies* and the *Cliquot Club Eskimos*. And so, at 9 P.M., Tuesday, February 5, 1929, Paul Whiteman opened on CBS in a weekly *Old Gold Program* with that wonderful blues singer Mildred Bailey as his regular singer and a young comedian, Eddie Cantor, as his guest star. His theme song that night, as ever more, was Gershwin's *Rhapsody in Blue*, the masterpiece of symphonic jazz of the twenties. Paul Whiteman's presence on the air added immensely to the stature of CBS. He was, purely and simply, the best of his kind.

Will Rogers was the most popular comedian of his time, better known to the public than the President of the United States. He was beloved as the cowboy performer who twirled his lasso and "razzed" bigwigs, politicians, businessmen, and every conceivable contemporary theme, including new inventions like radio. He was an actor, lecturer, author, newspaper columnist, Broadway star and Wild West showman. Will Rogers was one performer to whom radio could not offer fame or riches. Nevertheless, I had an idea in mind for a program and I suggested it to E. R. Squibb & Sons because I had already tried to sell that pharmaceutical company air time with four or five different proposals. The man I saw at Squibb was Theodore Weicker (the grandfather of Senator Lowell Weicker of Connecticut) who was then first vice-president and later president of the company. Theodore Weicker personified the Squibb company as he wanted it to be—the model of integrity, meticulous in detail, bound by the highest ethical standards and exacting ways. I presented him with my idea for a solid and humorous program and threw out my own lasso: "Suppose you had someone like Will Rogers to star in a Squibb program?" Mr. Weicker looked up at me and said, "Ah, you're starting to interest me. Let me think about it."

We left the matter there while I went on a tour of CBS

affiliates, going through Chicago to the West Coast in early March 1930. I met Don Lee on business in San Francisco and later we drove down for a holiday at a resort in Agua Caliente, Mexico. No sooner had I reached my room in the hotel than a call came in from someone in our New York office. "You've hit the jackpot," he shouted. "We got a call from Squibb today and they said, 'You get Will Rogers and we'll go.'"

Having sold Weicker on Rogers, now I had to deliver Rogers, and of course, I did not have him to deliver. In fact I had never met the man. But I knew that he, like many other stars of the stage, was very wary of attempting humor on radio to an unseen audience. In one of his syndicated columns, he explained it better than I can:

> If you are in a Theater, you know about the type and class of people that you will face, and kinder frame up your act accordingly. But on the Radio, you got every known specie in the world, and here is the hard part that very few have figured. On the the stage when you tell anything and it gets a laugh why naturally you kinder wait till the laugh is over, and then go on.
>
> Well, that little microphone that you are talking into, it's not going to laugh . . . So that is what I would say is the principal hardship on the comedy fellow doing his stuff over the air.

I understood that Rogers was in Los Angeles, but I had no taste for driving back that evening, and so before dinner I wandered around a Mexican gambling casino. The roulette tables were crowded. One in particular was surrounded by spectators four or five deep. At the edge of the crowd, I stood on my toes to look over them, expecting to see some spectacular betting—and who did I see? Will Rogers, of course, playing roulette. The coincidence was stunning; I thought, a lucky day for Paley.

When Rogers and his wife were leaving the casino, I intercepted them near the door, and introduced myself, asked for a few minutes of his time, and told him my idea about a weekly humor program on CBS.

"Oh, young man, it's very nice of you to think of me," he said with a twang, "but I couldn't possibly under any circumstances go on radio, except to visit."

"Well, let me tell you a few things about radio," I replied. "You might change your mind."

"No, no," he said, "I know a lot about it."

His wife, a tall and gracious woman, then interrupted and said, "Now Will, this young man wants to talk to you. Listen to him." He could withstand me but he couldn't resist her.

I gave my by-now standard talk about the enormous size of the audience, how he would give enjoyment to people who would never have an opportunity to see or hear him, how—but I got nowhere. It was soon time for them to go and so I said, "Could we meet again?"

He began to reply, "Young man, I think . . . ," when his wife again intervened. "Will, this young man wants to meet you again. The least you can do is to meet with him." He gave in and agreed.

When we met the next morning I argued with him all over again. He brought up what he regarded as "the principal hardship" of a cold microphone: lack of audience reaction. I covered that immediately with a promise: I'd provide him with a studio audience.

He seemed to be taken with the concession, and he wavered. He turned to his wife with a quizzical look and she said, "Will, it just might be fun. You might enjoy having your own program. Why don't you give it a try?" That was it. Rogers turned back to me and said, "Okay, go ahead and make the arrangements."

So Betty Rogers was responsible for bringing Will Rogers to millions of radio listeners. Only recently did I learn that he passed all of his big decisions on to her.

The philosophical comedian came to the studio of our affiliate, KHJ of Los Angeles, on Sunday night, April 6, 1930, to begin a thirteen-week series called the *Will Rogers Program*. He was scheduled to talk for about ten minutes of a half-hour variety program with music. For the first promised studio audience, we rounded up about forty people from the office and the studio. Will Rogers' monologue and their laughter went out over the air together.

It was not money that brought Will Rogers to CBS, but some other interest. We—or rather Squibb—paid him $72,000 for this series, and I understand he gave it all to charity. It was the challenge of radio and an unseen audience—and his wife.

I doubt if there was a single comedian coming from the stage who did not have some problem adapting to the microphone. They all thought about it and studied it. One man drew millions of people to their radio sets for years on end with his dry, urbane wit, delivered in the flattest imaginable voice. Yet, though he was an experienced vaudeville performer, radio comedy did not at first come easily to Fred Allen. He came to CBS through an ad agency in October 1932, and in his memoirs, *Treadmill to Oblivion*, he describes how he made the transition from the stage and brought a new style of humor to radio:

> Analyzing the comedian's problem in this new business, it seemed to me that the bizarre-garbed, joke-telling funster was ogling extinction. The montony of his weekly recital of un-related jokes would soon drive listeners to other diversions. Since the radio comedian really had to depend on the ears of the home audience for his purpose, I thought that a complete story told each week or a series of episodes and comedy situations might be a welcome change. It would enable the listener to flex his imagination, and perhaps make him want to follow the experiences of the characters involved. This, if it worked, would insure the radio comedian a longer life.

Man-and-wife teams turned out to be the great and enduring comedy shows of radio. Fred Allen had his Portland Hoffa, and that same year, 1932, CBS brought to radio George Burns with Gracie Allen, Goodman Ace with Jane, and the inimitable Jack Benny with Mary Livingstone. In each instance, as all old radio fans know, the comedy was based on a frustrated man trying to cope with a dizzy dame. Everyone laughed at Jack Benny's stinginess and scratchy violin, at Gracie Allen's lost brother, and at

Fred Allen's sardonic view of almost everything, including network vice-presidents.

Although we introduced many of these comedians and saw them on their way to stardom, we could not hold them all forever. There was a drifting back and forth between the networks, depending largely upon what particular night or time slot the advertiser wanted or where he thought his advertising message would be most effective. The situation was always very competitive and for a long time we were the underdog.

There were major disappointments in those early days, particularly over the ones who got away. In 1929, I sold Standard Brands on the idea of sponsoring Rudy Vallee when he was an obscure nightclub singer. His shows had been broadcast locally on our station WABC in New York. But I did not have a contract with him and when I tried to sign him up, I learned that Standard Brands had taken my idea to NBC because, I suppose, NBC had the prestige. I felt cheated, angry, but there was nothing I could do about it. Rudy Vallee went on to become the first entertainer to be made a star solely by radio and he should have been on CBS.

Nor can I ever forget or really forgive what happened with my protracted and determined efforts in 1931 to get the Metropolitan Opera on a weekly CBS broadcast. I fought my way through Edward Ziegler, the Met's assistant general manager, who was not enthusiastic, and on to the renowned Otto Kahn, lofty patron of the arts and president and chairman of the Met. In his investment banking office of Kuhn, Loeb & Company, Mr. Kahn was dumbfounded that I would even think the august Met would ever allow its operas to be broadcast. He thought radio would distort the beautiful music and cheapen the Metropolitan Opera. But I persuaded him to visit my office and to hear the Met's performance as it would be received by a radio listening audience.

We put our microphones into the opera house and piped the performance by closed circuit to my office, where Kahn, Ziegler, and Giulio Gatti-Casazza, the Met's general manager, sat without expression and listened. I was a bundle of nerves. We heard the overture and several minutes of singing into the first act and still no one reacted. Then Kahn leaped to his feet and exclaimed: "I can't believe it. It's simply marvelous . . . and just imagine, hearing that wonderful music and those marvelous voices and we don't have to look at those ugly faces!"

With Otto Kahn's zealous go-ahead, I proceeded without any trouble over the next few weeks to arranging broadcasting details with Edward Ziegler. Then one day he came to my office, shaken and white, and announced with some shame that Kahn, while visiting Paris, had met the head of the law firm that handled RCA legal matters, who had convinced him that the Met should broadcast from NBC rather than CBS. It was a callous, dirty trick and I felt terrible about it for weeks.

It was frustrating and doubly galling to come up with new ideas for a show or to persuade an entertainer or an advertiser to try this marvelous new medium of radio and then to find that, once persuaded about radio in general, some would choose NBC over CBS. True, in those early days NBC was the more prestigious network and it had the larger, better-equipped studios, fancier offices, more people working for it and greater financial resources behind it. But I thought CBS made up for all of that with our youthful zest and drive and our better ideas for new and popular programs. And yet it caused me considerable anguish until one day my whole attitude of being the perpetual underdog changed.

I was walking down Broadway and on one side of the Great White Way was the Capitol Theater, the largest and most beautiful movie house of its day, showing a rather mediocre movie, and on the other side was a very ordinary, rather run-down theater showing a movie that I had heard was very good. And there were far more people lined up to see the good movie in the ordinary theater than there were in front of the resplendent Capitol. The analogy struck me so forcibly that I never forgot it. "You know," I said to myself, "for radio, it's what goes into a person's house that counts. The radio listener doesn't know what kind of office I have, what kind of studios I have, he only knows what he hears. And I can forget about all these advantages my competition has

. . . I just have to put things on the air that the people like more. And that's my job. I've got to find things that will be popular. . . ."

I began to tell advertisers that story about the Capitol Theater versus the good movie in the smaller movie house, asking them which they would choose. Invariably they would choose the good film over the more spectacular house and that little story became a very strong point in my being able to persuade advertisers to sponsor programs on CBS.

That insight affected me too, for I became extra careful about spending money on anything in the company that did not affect the product, the program itself. When it came to talent, I would give them anything—or almost anything—they wanted in order to get them on CBS. And I began to pay attention to finding worthwhile and cultural programs to balance the music and variety shows in order to help improve the reputation of CBS for good taste and social responsibility.

When it came to finding new talent, I seemed to have a good ear. I "discovered" Morton Downey, the melodious Irish tenor, and Bing Crosby, the easygoing baritone, and Kate Smith with her voice of pure gold, and the Mills Brothers, a jazz ensemble who could sing like an orchestra, and others, all around 1930 and 1931, and I signed them to CBS contracts on a sustaining or noncommercial basis. I first heard Downey at a supper club on Park Avenue. Kate Smith came to CBS when she was fed up with fat-girl parts in Broadway shows. The Mills Brothers wandered into CBS after hitchhiking from Cincinnati. The head of our artists bureau, Ralph Wonders, telephoned and asked me to tune in to our audition room in order to hear a new quartet. "Sorry," I said, "I'm already late for lunch." But he persuaded me to listen to one song. An hour later I was still listening and calling for more. This was the most remarkable quartet I had ever heard. We signed them up immediately, put them on the air a few days later, and they became the musical sensation of the nation. I never did make lunch that day. But the Mills Brothers and I earned a lot of lunches over the years.

The incomparable Boswell sisters, who sang in a Chicago theater, were brought to my attention by our Chicago station manager, Leslie Atlass, and after hearing them I signed them to a CBS contract for a regular sustaining program which went on the air three times a week, starting in June 1932. They not only swept the country with their popularity, they set a new style for singing trios for years to come.

I first heard Bing Crosby's pleasant baritone voice while taking one of my marathon walks (in those days before jogging) circling the deck on the S.S. *Europa*, on my way to Europe for business in June 1931. Each time I circled the deck I would pass a teen-age boy on a deckchair, listening to a phonograph recording of the same song, "I Surrender, Dear." One voice on that record stood out, pure, dreamy, melodious with a unique phrasing of the lyrics. When I stopped to look at that record, there was the name in tiny print: "Chorus by Bing Crosby." Although he had sung with bands and singing groups before, I had never heard of him. But I cabled the CBS office: SIGN UP SINGER NAMED BING CROSBY.

When I returned, Ed Klauber told me that he and our programming people had decided to drop the project because they had learned that Crosby was unreliable, failing to show up for scheduled performances, in trouble with his union, and so on. I was furious. I explained to them rather forcibly that I was not trying to buy reliability but a unique and wonderful voice.

Within a week, Crosby came in from the West Coast, but accompanied by a very able lawyer, who had seen to it that NBC learned of my personal interest in his client. His price for Crosby was $1,500 a week on sustaining time and $3,000 a week if and when a sponsor was found. It was an astounding price at the time, in fact an outrage, but I did not want to lose him. I negotiated as hard as I could, but we finally settled for his asking price. Crosby got off to a rather rocky start at CBS, missing his own opening show, but there never was any question about the quality of his voice, and he went on to the pinnacle of success in the world of entertainment—radio, stage, screen, television, recordings, comedy, and, of course, golf. And there was nothing wrong with his reliability, either.

What made Bing Crosby's first contract with CBS so extravagant was that he came to our network as new or developing talent, just as had Morton Downey, Kate Smith, the Mills Brothers, and others, to be put on the air on a sustaining basis; that is, without advertiser support. Under this new contract policy, we usually paid such talent a little over $100 a week, or at most $500 a week, until we could find a sponsor. Then their salaries could go much higher. We put most of them in the toughest tryout spot, opposite the most popular program on radio, NBC's *Amos 'n' Andy* from 7:00 to 7:15 P.M. It was an expensive innovation for CBS but well worth the risk. To our utter delight, just about everyone we "sustained" in that tryout slot found sponsors and went on to become a star in the world of entertainment.

My good ear served me well some years later, when in August 1942, I first caught a glimpse of and heard a skinny, young man sing a couple of songs with the Tommy Dorsey orchestra in a bit part of the MGM movie *Ship Ahoy*. He received no billing and the theater manager, when I asked him, had no idea who the singer might be. The next day I found someone at Columbia Records who knew of him and I suggested that he be signed up as quickly as possible. So, CBS signed up Frank Sinatra for Thursday nights 8:00–8:30 P.M., starting in October, and later we moved him to five nights a week, 11:15–11:30 P.M., in a program we called *Songs by Sinatra*. Two months later, Sinatra sang at the Paramount Theater on Broadway and brought the house down, becoming the singing sensation of the country. We immediately moved him to our top musical program *Your Hit Parade* as the featured singer and his ensuing fabulous career is entertainment history.

More and more programs came to the networks from advertising agencies which had developed their own program departments to serve their corporate clients by creating new shows and talent and by controlling them.

A good part of my work was involved in persuading these advertising agencies or corporate sponsors to put their own shows on CBS or to sponsor one of our own concepts. Everyone in those days, it seemed, had ideas about what the listening public would like to hear on radio. A certain degree of delicacy was required in such negotiations. One of the big advertisers of that period was the Liggett & Myers Tobacco Company, makers of Chesterfield cigarettes, whose vice-president in charge of advertising, W. D. Carmichael, was an old-fashioned, courtly southern gentleman. Carmichael came in on one occasion for a studio audition of a new show. At the end of the program, he turned to me and in a soft, well-mannered voice asked, "Mr. Paley, what do you think?"

I looked at the expression on his face, thought awhile, and replied, "I think it is a pretty good show, but I don't think it is for you."

With a "Thank you very much, Mr. Paley," he left CBS. My associates were upset, for they thought he was ready to sign up. But I wanted a longtime relationship with this advertiser, based upon honest advice and not just a sales pitch. Later, when I went to him with a program I could more heartily recommend, he bought it without hesitation, and from then on he sought my advice on all programs he sponsored on CBS as well as those he placed on NBC.

Among the early radio advertisers, the most pre-eminent sponsor of them all was George Washington Hill, the eccentric genius who headed the American Tobacco Company, makers of Lucky Strike cigarettes. Very early on, Hill had recognized the advertising potential of radio and he spent a fortune advertising American Tobacco products, all of his radio budget going to NBC. I made an appointment to see him one day in late 1930 or early 1931. The night before that meeting, I was unable to sleep.

A prospect like George Washington Hill was extremely important to CBS, and his exalted position in business absolutely frightened me. I went to that unforgettable first meeting in Hill's office at 111 Fifth Avenue wearing a new, ultraconservative business suit with a high, stiff collar. When I first laid eyes on the famous personage, I saw a medium-sized man with black bushy eyebrows, wearing a dark suit with suede patches over the elbows, a black bow tie on a white shirt, and a cowboy hat.

He sat at his desk in deep concentration, without looking up, an enigma to me. I stood there feeling like an ill-clothed scarecrow next to him.

Without a hope for his Lucky Strike advertising, I announced that I would like to get his account for his Cremo cigars, which were made by the American Cigar Company, a subsidiary of American Tobacco. Without a word, he handed me a pad and a pencil.

"What's this for, Mr. Hill?" I asked, perplexed.

"Well," he said, "I like to buy ideas. That's the most important thing. If you want some of my business, you bring me an idea for a program, and if I like it, I'll give you the business. It's as simple as that." So I accepted his challenge and left with his pad and pencil.

I went back to my program associates, and together we developed a presentation of four good ideas. When I took these to Hill, he had his office filled with his own people and I had four or five of my staff with me. We put up idea number one. He listened to it patiently and then turned to me and said, "Mr. Paley, that's a very good idea. I compliment you. I can see now that you people are very creative, and you're the kind of people I'd like to do business with and get to know better. But there are just one or two things to consider about the idea." He then proceeded to explain why he couldn't use it.

We then put up idea number two, and he said, "That's even better," and he was more convinced than ever that we were creative. Again, however, it was "except for one or two things," and he proceeded to give me reasons why it wasn't good enough, as far as he was concerned.

The same thing happened to idea three and idea four. Then he made a long speech about how excited he was about our creativity and how much he admired our abilities. He asked us please not to be discouraged because he was sure that we would get together . . . we were a ray of sunshine come into his life. So, although we had not accomplished anything, we left feeling encouraged.

The next day I told my associates, "I think we made a mistake.

We shouldn't have gone there with four ideas, we should have presented just one idea, something we really believed in. Let's come up with one thing like that."

In about a week we had something. I called him and he never hesitated: "Come right down any time you want to." We went to his office and put on a big act about this one—and it was a good idea, a very good idea. I was crazy about it. He listened to it attentively and, when it was all over, he said, "Well, everything I've said before I say again, except more so. But there's one little thing about the show. Let me tell you why I can't use it." He gave a long discourse about that, and we thanked him very much, and bowed out.

When I got back to our office, I was dismayed. I thought about it for three or four days, and finally had a hunch. It occurred to me that perhaps Mr. Hill subconsciously preferred ideas he himself originated over those thrust upon him by people who had something themselves to gain. I called him and said I wanted to come and see him about a matter that didn't have to do with broadcasting—and I made up something about a cause I was interested in. I discussed it with him, and when I was finished, he asked, "What about the idea department? Anything new?" And I said, "No, Mr. Hill."

"Aw, don't tell me that, Mr. Paley. You were just so close," he said.

"I know it," I said. "It's not your fault, but I think we've given you the best we have, and it isn't good enough. And, you know, we can do just so much, and then we have to, I guess, become realistic about certain things. I don't think you can look to us to give you anything that you think is down your alley."

Then I added, ever so casually, "Just to give you an example, someone on the staff came in yesterday with an idea, and he was very excited about it, and I just knew it wasn't right for you." He pounced on that. "What was it?"

"Someone had an idea that men like military music, martial music," I went on. "And instead of going on the air one day a week, get a strip six days a week, with Arthur Pryor's band, very popular. The idea is that men would like that. It would make them feel like puffing up their chests." And then I threw it away, saying, "Oh, it's one of those things, you know. That's how discouraged I am. Forget it."

"Paley, wait a minute, wait a minute!" He started pressing buttons. A small, frail-looking man, Vincent Riggio, rushed in with some other people. "Men, I want you to hear something: we go on the air six days a week and we have Arthur Pryor's band doing military music." He got up from his chair and marched up and down, singing, "Zoop-de-doop, zoop-de-doop, zoop-de-doop!"

"Can you imagine what that'd do?" he shouted. "Men will throw out their chests and feel manly and proud. I think this is it. What do you think, Riggio?"

Riggio said, "Not quite sure I like it."

Such bizarre conferences were not unusual in Hill's office, I was to learn. I was interested in Riggio's reaction, for I knew he had a special relationship with George Washington Hill. From a salesman, Riggio had become the number-two man in American Tobacco and ultimately would succeed Hill as president after Hill died in 1946. Hill always consulted with Riggio on big decisions, explaining to me, "If he likes something, it's okay. If he doesn't take to it, then America won't like it. He is the average American listener personified!"

So, there I was alone with Hill and Riggio and a few other American Tobacco men. Hill put the idea of martial music to Riggio, and Riggio didn't like it. So, Hill went over it again. "Imagine, men all over the country. Zoop-de-doop, zoop-de-doop, boom! Do you get it? Do you get it? Can't you feel your lungs stretching out? Can't you imagine the excitement?"

"George, you know me," said Riggio. "Don't quite like it, don't quite like it. Not overcome by it."

Hill then became more vehement. "Okay, let me just make it crystal clear what this is all about." Again he went over the same thing, except in a louder voice. Finally the third time around, Riggio exclaimed, "Ah, I got it! I got it! You're right, you're right. I like it, I like it." Hill remarked calmly, "I thought you'd see it.

Mr. Paley, you get in touch with the band. I'll call up the ad agency. How soon can we start?"

We got the contract for six days a week with Arthur Pryor and his band, starting March 16, 1931.

Every week Hill came over to CBS to hear the songs scheduled for the following week's programs. He had a list and, as Pryor's band played the marches, he would cross off those he didn't like. Then substitutes would be played, from which Hill would choose the replacements. They were rather tedious sessions that I nonetheless had to attend. Still, I was much luckier than Merlin Aylesworth, president of NBC, which later carried Hill's Lucky Strike program, *Your Hit Parade*. Hill visited NBC every week to hear the songs for the program, which he insisted should be good, straightforward dance music, because that's what the public wanted. To test the songs, he would make Merlin Aylesworth get up and dance to each one with his secretary. Merlin, not a very good dancer, told me he hated every second of it. But what could he do? Whenever I saw him I'd ask how his dancing was coming along. Furious, Merlin would yell back at me, "You don't know how damn lucky you were. He could have had you marching up and down to that military music." We had a lot of fun kidding each other about our respective roles in helping George Washington Hill decide what music was best for the American public.

Eight months later, Hill switched from the Pryor band to Bing Crosby for the Cremo cigar account. Although I worked hard to get along with that eccentric genius of advertising, for I had a healthy respect for his knowledge and his intuition, still at times he could be a very difficult man. When the zany CBS comedy team of Stoopnagle and Budd poked some fun at Lucky Strikes, Hill flew into one of his famous furies. In their fifteen-minute, twice-weekly show, Stoopnagle and Budd had become famous for their take-offs on advertised brands and most advertisers were delighted with the free plugs for their products. It was silly stuff, such as calling Palmolive soap "Palm Grape Soap," or something like that. They did it every week. But when they got to Lucky Strike cigarettes and called them "Lucky Strokes," I was summoned to Hill's office the next morning. And he was in a rage:

"Mr. Paley, I have spent—I don't know—millions and millions of dollars advertising this brand, Lucky Strike cigarettes. And you, without my permission, had the nerve and the bad taste to take the good name of Lucky Strike and make fun of it and cheapen it. It's the worst thing that's ever happened to a sponsor on radio, and you're going to pay for it."

"Mr. Hill, it wasn't meant, I'm sure, for that program to do anything that would be disadvantageous to your brand of cigarettes. Advertisers stand in line waiting to have their brand names used by Stoopnagle and Budd."

"I want no lecture from you, Mr. Paley, as to the importance of a brand or a trademark and what can happen to an image if the wrong things are said about it. I think it was awful. And I want compensation for the damage done."

"How much do you think you ought to have?" I asked.

He said, "Well, we're friends. It isn't so much the money, but I want to get over the principle. I want $50,000."

"That is a lot of money, Mr. Hill, and I want a little time to think," I told him. "Let me go back and talk to a few of my associates. It's a lot of money for me to pass on without consultation."

"All right, Mr. Paley," he said, "I hope you come to the right decision."

Back in my office, I wrote him a note saying I had thought about it, and if he felt so strongly that his brand had been damaged and if he thought that the damage could be symbolized by money and if he thought $50,000 was the right amount, then in light of our very friendly and mutually advantageous relationship, I was acceding to his request—"and enclosed you will find a check for $50,000." I sent it by messenger.

Within an hour I got a hand-delivered reply in which he said that he admired the way I had responded to his feelings, that he was very pleased, and in the circumstances, it would not be necessary for him to take the $50,000, so he was returning it, enclosed.

Once that was settled, I thought everything was going along happily, when one day out of the blue, Hill called me to his office and declared, "Mr. Paley, we're canceling our contract. I can't tell you why, but I've got to cancel it. Don't ask me any more questions."

I didn't like losing the business and I did not know if and when Hill might come back to CBS, but from time to time he asked me to lunch at the Metropolitan Club. He was a hardheaded businessman who, I thought, would buy something from me when he was ready.

His cancellation of *Cremo Presents Bing Crosby* perplexed me and it was not until two years later that Hill gave me an explanation. It involved the fact that the Cremo cigar was advertised and sold as a machine-made cigar, which supposedly had a big advantage over the hand-made variety because no worker's saliva would touch the cigar wrapper in making the cigar. Cremo was known, if you please, as the "no-spit cigar." But the cigars sold so well that his production manager, without informing Hill, had to augment the machine-made production with hand-made cigars and, of course, "spit" was involved. So, George Washington Hill's advertisng slogan had become a lie. Fearing exposure and a setback for his company for deceiving the public and preferring not to trust me with the secret, he had just canceled the program and left CBS without an explanation.

All I could think was that relations with an advertiser could get quite rocky.

While I spent most of my time buying talent and selling advertisers, in the office Paul Kesten perfected the formula of combining research with promotion. He began turning out a small avalanche of surveys which reported accurately the known facts and trends concerning radio broadcasting. His survey reports, bound in attractive little booklets, covered the growing range of the CBS network, the increasing number of radio sets in the United States, a breakdown on radio sets owned according to incomes, the impact upon the sales of brands advertised on radio and which shows gained what level of popularity.

One survey, conducted by an independent statistical analyst revealed in 1934 that the radio dramatic sketch had taken over the number-one spot in popularity from the jazz bands, which came as a surprise to most of the nation. In 1931, CBS had introduced *Myrt and Marge;* in 1932 came *Easy Aces, Skippy, Just Plain Bill, Bobby Benson* and *Buck Rogers;* and in 1933 came *Jack Armstrong.* The big bands fell to third place but still were very popular and bandleaders' names became household words: Paul Whiteman, Ben Bernie, Wayne King, Glen Gray, Ted Weems, Abe Lyman, Guy Lombardo, Fred Waring, the Dorsey brothers. Second in popularity and growing steadily were the new "variety" shows which combined music and sketches. There was *The American Review,* which featured stage and screen celebrities such as the Marx brothers and Ethel Waters, and *The Camel Caravan, Ward's Family Theater* and others.

By 1935, Paul Kesten was so overburdened with work that he turned to a young man who had just earned his doctorate in psychology at Ohio State University and had written an intriguing statistical paper showing that man's ears were more effective than his eyes in absorbing information and intelligence. Kesten thought that young man had a future in radio. He invited the young psychologist to join CBS, eventually to take over the research department, so he himself would be free to concentrate on promotion. Kesten had someone telegraph him the following persuasive appeal on August 29, 1935, a copy of which is still in our files:

MONDAY OK HOPE YOU DECIDE TO COME TO CBS STOP SINCE OUR TALK SEVERAL NEW RESEARCH PROBLEMS HAVE ARISEN WHICH I THINK WOULD INTRIGUE YOU STOP I DON'T KNOW OF ANY OTHER ORGANIZATION WHERE YOUR BACKGROUND AND EXPERIENCE WOULD COUNT SO HEAVILY IN YOUR FAVOR OR WHERE YOUR TALENTS WOULD FIND SO ENTHUSIASTIC A RECEPTION.

The young man left Ohio for CBS, became director of research and later would become president of CBS. That was Frank Stanton.

Despite the general economic depression and hard times which swept the country in the thirties, those were big years for the growth of radio broadcasting and for CBS. Entertainment on radio was free. Advertisers came to recognize the true value of advertising over the airwaves. CBS's net sales increased from $4,172,000 in 1929 to $12,984,000 in 1934. Our net profits more than quadrupled from $474,000 in 1929 to $2,274,000. That was a clear indication of our growth and of our future direction. But the most important figure to me came at the end of 1931. Our net profit that year reached $2,203,000. We certainly had made more than the $2 million I had promised Adolph Zukor at Paramount.

After Hours

O ne of the highest, enduring dividends of my association
with CBS was that it brought me to that magical city
of New York. I had fallen in love with New York from afar (as
far as Philadelphia, that is), living vicariously through the pages
of *Vogue*, *Harper's Bazaar* and *The New Yorker* the glamorous
life of the New York set during the Roaring Twenties. Buying
United Independent Broadcasters in 1928 gave me the opportunity not only to visit New York more often, but actually to live
there!

Many nights, after leaving my office and most of my cares
at CBS, I would go to the Central Park Casino, near the park's
Sixty-fifth Street transverse road. The Casino, hailed as "the
swankiest restaurant in New York," was the unofficial nighttime headquarters of Mayor Jimmy Walker, where the so-called
"swells" of the city came to meet and socialize in black tie
or white tie and tails, along with their beautiful wives and
lady friends dressed in long gowns, sparkling jewelry and the
latest coiffures. Its dining pavilion in silver and maroon decor
offered one of the finest cuisines in the city; its ballroom with
walls of black glass and golden murals featured the best of

the society orchestras and provided a leap to fame for Eddie Duchin on the piano. It was a fabulous night spot until Robert Moses, then the Parks Commissioner, ordered it leveled to the ground to make way for a children's playground. He insisted that the City of New York should not provide public land for expensive nightclubs.

Then there was the Mayfair Club Dance every Saturday night in the Crystal Room of the old Ritz Carlton, one of the most beautiful rooms in all of New York. There the literary and theatrical people of the city met with the socialites for the sumptuous high point of their week. While the Casino in the Park was a public nightclub for anyone who could afford its prices, the Mayfair Club was for members only. Thorstein Veblen might have called it conspicuous consumption, but to those who partook of the festivities it was clean, carefree fun for its own sake. Frankly, I had no trouble and no qualms embracing the beautiful night life of New York.

My decision to separate my business life at CBS during the day from my social life at night came rather naturally. I could see the dangers of socializing with my office associates, or with the advertising agency men, or corporate officers who were so important to me in the development of CBS. I just did not want to mix the two. I feared the one-dimensional kind of existence it might lead to and the risk of encumbering my business affairs with my social ones. This separation was more or less understood and accepted at CBS and became a long-standing way of life for me.

As a young, energetic and curious bachelor, I soon found new friends and adapted readily to a social life, revolving around the theater, nightclubs, weekends on Long Island's north shore, parties until dawn, and the flickering and flaming romances of the time.

In keeping with the spirit of this new mode of life, I treated myself to a rather luxurious triplex apartment on the top three floors of a newly completed building on Park Avenue at Fifty-eighth Street, and I hired the most marvelous English butler-valet, named Watts, to preside over it all. I had the apartment decorated to suit my purposes. The top floor was designed for parties with built-in seats and lounges surrounding a semicircular bar against one wall. On the opposite side of the room, an upright piano was built into the wall, with only the keyboard showing. French doors led to a terrace and a roof garden, where couples could escape the din and noise of music and conversation. It was a good party room and came to be used well for that purpose.

The first floor, which contained my bedroom, a guest room, and a large dressing room, fit the fancies of a New York bachelor. The dressing room was lined with closets and had a desk, a couch, a massage table which folded into a door. But I could not get to like my modern bedroom, and after the first couple of nights, I moved into the guest room, where I had my old furniture. For the next three years, I slept in the guest room and left the master bedroom in its modernity, clean and empty. The living room and dining room on the second floor were done conventionally in oak paneling by another decorator.

Every morning a man came in to get me out of bed, which always was a terrible struggle because of my late hours. His instructions were to pull me out of bed no matter what I said or did. Every morning I fired him. But he would pull me and haul me and get me up and into some morning calisthenics. Then I'd take a shower and he'd give me a quick massage and he'd say, "Fired, am I?" and I'd say, "Oh, no, no, no, just kidding. Come back tomorrow." This went on every morning. By the time he left the house, I would be feeling fine and ready for another full day of work.

Most of my parties were private affairs for personal friends, but some were in the service of CBS. In 1930 we had brought together the seven leading concert bureaus in America and formed the Columbia Concerts Corporation. A subsidiary of CBS under the leadership of Arthur Judson, it represented more than one hundred of the best-known classical artists in the world. Upon Judson's suggestion, I entertained some of these artists in a series of parties. I remember best the one I gave for Arturo Toscanini, whom we represented, and who conducted the New York Philharmonic Symphony Orchestra on a CBS broadcast every Sunday afternoon.

My butler-valet, who knew his job well, gave me extraordinary service. He could arrange a large dinner with only a few hours' notice. But on this occasion I gave him special instructions well ahead of time. I had heard that Enrico Caruso had loved good food and that his chef was the best Italian chef in the world, and was still living in New York. I sent my man out to find him. He found him in retirement but willing to come out and cook a dinner for the great Toscanini. Three days before the party, Caruso's chef arrived to begin preparations for the great project. We bought special foods and special utensils according to his orders. I invited friends of Toscanini, a few concert managers, some CBS people, and other friends of mine—about twenty, in all.

On the day of the party, a friend came by and casually remarked that Toscanini had sworn off Italian food for as long as Mussolini was in power. I didn't believe him. I thought he was pulling my leg, but I wasn't sure. That night, when the guests were at the table, I waited nervously for dinner to unfold. The first dish was served. Toscanini looked at it and said, "No, thank you." The waiter brought the second course and Toscanini looked at it and said, "No, thank you." I signaled the butler to bring the broiled chicken I had ordered held in reserve. The maestro ate plain chicken, while the rest of us feasted on the best Italian meal I have ever tasted.

The party came off very well. Toscanini drank martinis and champagne. After dinner in the upstairs room, I risked having a CBS jazz group sing for him, and I was delighted to see the great Toscanini tapping his finger in evident pleasure as he listened.

At a party in the home of Mr. and Mrs. Harrison Williams (she was one of the extraordinary beauties and leading hostesses of the time), I was fascinated by one Fats Waller who played piano. I invited him to come in for an audition. We signed him up, and he became one of the favorites on the CBS schedule. Talentscouting did not always work out that well, however. At a fashionably dark and romantic nightclub, I came upon one singer who had a special and haunting voice that sounded better and better to me as the night wore on. We arranged an audition for the next day. My associates and I sat in my office and listened to his voice over the speaker from the audition room. I couldn't believe what I heard. The voice was cracked, off key, and just terrible. It seemed that he could sing well only in dark clubs around midnight, and that we could not provide. I endured a great deal of kidding from friends at CBS over that audition.

My association with Paramount and Adolph Zukor introduced me to the mythical never-never land of Hollywood in the thirties where, as a young bachelor, I met and got to know the gods and goddesses of the silver screen. I made my debut on that scene soon after Paramount had bought 50 per cent of CBS, and Jesse Lasky, who was in charge of all Paramount production, gave an ultra-lavish party in my honor at his sumptuous beach house at Santa Monica, California. Just about every glamorous movie star I had ever heard of came to that party. The champagne flowed all night, and I felt as though I were in unbelievable paradise. Invitations to other parties followed, and as time went on, I found myself at various dinner tables talking with Marlene Dietrich, Joan Crawford, Norma Shearer, Jean Harlow, Madeleine Carroll, Ginger Rogers, Loretta Young, Paulette Goddard, Norma Talmadge. I met the moguls of motion pictures too—people like Sam Goldwyn, Louis B. Mayer, Harry Cohn, the Warner brothers, and, of course, David Selznick, who became one of my best friends. Even after I bought back our CBS stock from Paramount I continued to visit Hollywood every year, and my relationships with the movie greats continued.

New York for me was even more magical. I could never fully anticipate the surprises the city would hold. Not long after I moved here, Harry Hurt, a stockbroker and friend, dropped by the apartment and invited me to join him on a dutiful visit to his sister who lived nearby. When I walked into his sister's apartment, my knees almost buckled. There before me, my friend's

sister, was the woman of my dreams. For years, back in Philadelphia, while a teen-ager, I had come across her photograph in
Vanity Fair, Vogue, or *Harper's Bazaar,* and I had become enamored with one of the most attractive women I had ever seen, a
myth personified in a photograph. I was introduced to her and to
her husband, a well-known man-about-town. So startled was I
at coming face-to-face with this girl of my dreams that I scarcely
said a word, nor did I detect any particular sign of kismet upon
her beautiful face.

A few weeks later, my friend telephoned: a terrible thing had
happened. His brother-in-law had died in a fall from his apartment. After a while, we met again and she invited me for a
weekend to her summer home in Manhasset, Long Island. I
arrived just in time to be told that we and her other guest were
invited to a neighbor's home for tea. We drove only a few
hundred yards down the road and turned into the spacious
grounds of a lovely country place. The main house was white
clapboard, quite old, very simple, with an elegance and beauty
which struck me as being just right. It belonged to Ralph
Pulitzer, the son of the publisher of the *World* and the St. Louis
Post-Dispatch, who had let it out that summer. As I wandered
about the house and grounds, I could not help but think that this
house on these grounds represented the kind of home I myself
would like to own and to live in someday.

The woman of my Philadelphia dreams and I became good
friends. At the beginning, we became quite fond of each other.
We remained rather close but finally we went our separate ways.
As I turned thirty, I was convinced that I would never get married, and in fact was sure that I would never want to get married.
Bachelor freedom suited me just fine. My social circle grew wider
and wider each year, like the ripples in a pond.

One summer I rented a house at Sands Point on the north shore
of Long Island and came to know Herbert Bayard Swope, retired
editor of the *World,* better than I had before. I spent many
happy, playful hours at Swope's home. He did not give parties as
such; events just went on and on in his home. His house was the
only one I have ever known which was organized on a twenty-

four-hour-a-day basis. Servants worked in shifts around the clock. Meals were available at any hour one wanted to eat. One guest might have breakfast at 5 A.M., while another at the same table might be eating a steak before going to bed for the night. Some guests never found the time to go to sleep, for fear of missing out on some game being played, or some event or some liaison. Swope particularly liked what he called his "stormy dawn sessions" of backgammon. As befitted an important newspaper editor, he had a guest list varied beyond imagination, and one never knew whom one might run into. I remember Howard Hughes sitting in a corner by himself in nondescript ragged clothes, looking like a statue of himself, speaking to no one, oblivious to everything going on about him. That occasion, as I remember it, was the day or the day after he returned from his record-breaking flight around the world. Writers, editors, playwrights, poets and publishers were in and out of the Swope home, many of them members of the well-known Algonquin Round Table, named for the hotel on Forty-fourth Street in Manhattan where they met for lunch and sparkling conversation. Their chief outdoor sport—and the extent of their physical exercise—was croquet, which they played with passion and vehemence. This became the croquet era of my life, although it did not in the long run replace my own enthusiasm for golf.

One memorable weekend I joined a luncheon group on Long Island and met Dorothy Hearst, wife of Jack Hearst, who was the son of Mr. and Mrs. William Randolph Hearst of the famous newspaper chain. My convictions and faith in bachelorhood soon slithered away. Dorothy was beautiful and she had a quality that enveloped me. She was very bright and had strong opinions on a good many subjects. I was taken by her good looks and her grace, and as it happened, she was attracted to me too. All of this led to a new life for both of us. Eventually, she divorced Jack Hearst, and on May 11, 1932, we were married in Kingman, Arizona, a long way from reporters, where my Los Angeles lawyer knew the justice of the peace. We went to Honolulu for several weeks on our honeymoon.

Marriage brought a more settled social life for us among new as well as old friends. Our circle, combining her friends and mine, widened. Of course, I had to give up my bachelor apartment. My butler-valet, who was no longer the boss of the house, left me. We rented a house at 35 Beekman Place, and, because we liked the little street so much, we bought a five-story house at number 29. We planned to modernize it, but the contractor—the same one who helped build Radio City—told me it wouldn't cost much more to tear the house down and build a new one that would be fireproof. So we had it torn down and built another, six stories high. Meticulous about architectural details, I put my heart and soul into this first house and most of the people who visited us thought it was one of the most beautiful in New York. I didn't. After we moved in, I didn't like it. It had no charm or warmth for me. It was antiseptic. We left it (and later sold it) and moved to a lovely old house on East Seventy-fourth Street. We adopted a son, Jeffrey, and then a daughter, Hilary, bringing a new dimension into our lives.

Though we were not members of the Algonquin Round Table, we came to see more of this group than I had as a bachelor. Among those we came to know quite well were Alexander Woollcott, Bob Sherwood, Heywood Broun, George Kaufman, Neysa McMein (the artist), and Harold Ross, editor of *The New Yorker*. Woollcott was a sort of leader of the group, a great story-teller in private as well as public, and I brought him to CBS to spin his stories to the wide radio audience on a program called *The Town Crier*. There were many conflicts within the group. They would quarrel and not talk to each other for days or weeks. Then there would be a lot of letter writing, apologies, and tears.

We also met some of the group at the Kaufmans' and at Moss Hart's. The Kaufmans gave wonderful parties where everyone had to perform. One would write a playlet, for example, and the others would play the parts. I qualified by playing one of the minor figures in a one-act play. Not being a professional writer, I did not have as much in common with them as they had with each other; I was just happy to be in their company. I remember Harold Ross as always being rather rough and scowling. Raoul

Fleischmann, the owner of *The New Yorker*, confirmed the stories I had heard about Ross and his staff. They dominated him. Raoul said he wasn't allowed to go into the editorial department; if he so much as opened the door, they would yell, "One more step and we're going to leave." Years later he wanted to sell *The New Yorker* and I offered to buy it from him. I was interested in the publishing business and had great admiration for the magazine. But after a couple of weeks, he came back and said the editorial staff just wouldn't allow him to sell the magazine, especially to a corporation.

During the summers of the middle thirties, Dorothy and I rented country houses on Long Island, and in 1938, we rented the Ralph Pulitzer estate, Kiluna Farm, the same beautiful place I had seen years before on my very first visit to Manhasset. While renting, we looked around, planning to buy a house on the Island, but nothing so grand as Kiluna Farm's eighty-five acres, with its guest cottages, barns, indoor tennis court, swimming pool, greenhouses, and gardens. One day my real estate broker suggested, "Why don't you buy Mr. Pulitzer's place?" I told him that I did not want to insult Ralph Pulitzer with the maximum I had set for a country home. Without my making a bona fide offer, the agent on his own approached Pulitzer with the information that I was in the market for a house at a certain price. He returned reporting that Pulitzer had quickly agreed to sell Kiluna Farm at that price, saying, "I'd like to have Bill Paley living in my house." So, in December 1938, I bought Kiluna Farm, and another of my dreams had come true.

Over the next forty years I made few changes in the house I loved from the first moment I had seen it. We put a terrace in the back of the main house and extended the gardens somewhat, but the old house stands, largely as it always has, on one of the few hills on Long Island, overlooking Long Island Sound in the distance. The indoor tennis court, with its glass roof for daylight play, and its indoor lights for night play, is unchanged. A new swimming pool has been put in, but the old swimming pool deep in the woods remained for those who preferred privacy. I once asked Ralph Pulitzer why he had put the pool in such a faraway and secluded location, and he told me, "When I built the pool, men liked to go in swimming without the tops of their swimming suits." How life has changed. The main house retains its quiet simplicity and the patina of age.

Through my business dealings with the investment banking firm of Brown Brothers, Harriman in the early thirties, I became acquainted with Averell Harriman, whose extraordinary combination of human qualities I admired. He was to have an influence upon my life and my own sense of values. Averell was a natural patrician with a real sense of public service. And he transmitted to me certain pleasures of life about which he knew a good deal, particularly the love of art which became the primary avocation of my life ever afterward. Averell's wife, Marie, owned an art gallery on Fifty-seventh Street, dealing mainly in French Impressionist and Postimpressionist paintings and some contemporary American art.

Averell and Marie had a way about them of combining a sense of style with a feeling for fun in life. In the family home, called Arden, up the Hudson River near West Point, they lived in a veritable castle, built by Averell's father, who had made a vast fortune developing the Union Pacific Railroad, and children rode their bicycles through the great halls. There, I was introduced to people from all walks of life, and after my marriage the Harrimans lured Dorothy and me on several jaunts which remain memorable.

On one of our trips in the mid-thirties, to the Salzburg Music Festival in central Austria, Averell insisted that I join him in a "shoot" to which he had been invited in Hungary. "No, no," I said, "I've never shot a gun in my life." But Averell waved off such an answer. "Don't worry," he said, "I'll show you everything you have to know about shooting and you'll have a good time." One could never be certain if he were joking or being serious. I knew he was a health buff, was careful of what he ate and swore by the help rendered by osteopaths. So I was not too surprised when once he advised me that if I wanted to live a long life, I

94

should upon waking up every morning put on my socks so that my feet did not get cold. Or that he once gave me a walking stick for Christmas and explained that the top could be unscrewed, revealing a secret button, and that by pressing the button, I could take oxygen from the cane. "One should always have a cane with oxygen," he remarked, and to this day I still do not know if he was kidding.

So, for my first "shoot" I reluctantly accompanied him to Vienna, where I was outfitted with the proper clothing and shot-guns, and while our wives went on to Budapest, by train, Averell and I drove across the border to a grand old castle, somewhere in Hungary, arriving about two in the morning. Averell loaded a shotgun with blank cartridges, placed a candle on top of a ward-robe, and taught me how to aim and shoot at a flickering flame. He instructed me on the rules of gun safety and the gentlemanly conduct expected in shooting birds. We practiced through the night. "By the way," he commented ever so casually, "don't let on that you've never shot before." When I protested, he insisted, "People get nervous when they shoot with someone who has never shot before; there are some dangers in shooting, of course. But don't you worry, I have instructed you and there'll be no real danger. . . ." He was so sure of himself. But the danger I feared was not bodily harm but rather the prospect of the humil-iation of a pretender.

The next morning, dressed properly as a hunter, I met the others, some ten men. We spread out in a line on a field, at ready. The first bird out came past me. I closed my eyes and pulled the trigger. The butt of the damn gun hit me hard in the shoulder, nothing like shooting blank cartridges, and Averell had not told me about that. Of course, I missed the bird. My lack of expertise went unnoticed, for the others seemed to be missing too. Then, when I had begun to worry—I was still missing and they were hit-ting their birds—I only half closed my eyes and tried for a bird that came by very high, a shot I should not have attempted at all, and, lo and behold, the bird fell. Pure luck. But through the af-ternoon, I began to get the hang of it. I passed, I think, not as a

rank beginner but just as a bad shot. And so it went until our final
night when at a farewell party, Averell raised his glass in a toast
and recounted our "secret." That changed my status in that group
of strangers from one who had been barely accepted to that of a
bon vivant who had risked humiliation to be among genuine
hunters. It all meant next to nothing, really, except that at the
time I had caught the fever of a new hobby. I had learned something completely different and I plunged into a new world of sensation. It is hard to describe. In any event, on our way home, I
went to Purdey's, the famous gunmakers in London, and ordered
a pair of custom-made Purdey shotguns, fitted exactly to my own
proportions. I went hunting in this country on occasion using
those shotguns with much pleasure.

On the way home from that same trip, Averell coaxed me into
accompanying him on a tour of art dealers and their private collections in Paris. He described it as an art hunt. Aside from some
sporting prints I had collected, I knew little about painting and
had little interest in art. Over the next two or three days, I saw
several private collections of paintings that intrigued my sensibilities: oil paintings signed by artists then not as well known as they
are today: Cézanne, Derain, Renoir, Gauguin, Monet, Picasso . . .
I was hooked, and I did not know why. Back in New York, I
began to read about these artists and their works and I searched
them out in the galleries of New York. And I grew to love these
Impressionist paintings. In the presence of these works of art
which touched me, I felt a sensuous, aesthetic delight. I cannot plumb the depths of these feelings with words, but they
would in time result in my wanting to surround myself with this
kind of painting.

Although inspired, I recognized that these unique works of art
were bought and sold for rather large amounts of money and that
a collector inevitably had to think about market values. My urge
was to buy, but I had to think about what I could afford to pay
for the paintings which so appealed to me. One can view great
art at an orderly and leisurely pace in museums where collections
are more or less permanent. But for the private collector, only
a few works of art ever become available and only at certain

times and places. So, the opportunities to buy and to collect take place in rather disjointed episodes, and because few men can spare the enormous amount of time involved in searching out paintings that they want to own and that are for sale, collectors must rely to a great extent on art dealers and agents to do the legwork.

I bought my first major Impressionist painting through the well-known dealer Valentine Dudensing in New York, who had urged me with his usual passion to start small, to buy a rather insignificant painting, to live with it awhile, and then gradually build up a collection with finer and finer pieces. But I did not want to buy mediocre paintings. "I'd rather have one good thing than five or six mediocre ones," I told him, knowing intuitively that I must be very careful about the first picture I purchased. I knew it was to be the beginning of something important in my life. I rejected this and that and waited until he finally came to me with a painting I liked. In September 1935, I bought it and I have it still and I love it as I did at first: a Cézanne landscape called "L'Estaque," the name of a village in southern France.

Averell used an art agent in Paris who later became Europe's most famous publisher of popular art books, Albert Skira, who became my agent, too. With his vast knowledge of art, the dealers, and the collectors, Skira was an inspired agent who would direct me to the best paintings available of the period I preferred. "I've found something that I think is awfully good. Come and look at it," he would say, and I would rush off whenever possible to see what he had found. Then, if I liked it, either he or I would negotiate with the owner or dealer on terms. Through Skira, I began to acquire a number of French Impressionist and Postimpressionist paintings.

There was a sport in collecting, too. One memorable art dealer in my early collecting days was a snappy fellow who lived extravagantly on the Champs-Elysées. He had two loves: art and the horses. When the horses were good to him, he would be insulted by any price offered for one of his paintings. But when he lost at the races, he was casual, almost flippant, about selling. "What do you want and what do you want to pay for it and take it away," he would say, all in one breath. He lived with flair. On one occasion, he sold me the rug on the floor of his office. Another time, when I had bought several small pieces, he came across a folded and crumpled water color in the back of his desk drawer. When I admired the painting, he exclaimed, "Take it, take it, a gift. . . ." At the Knoedler Gallery in New York some time later, I had it pressed out and discovered he had given me a Cézanne.

He also introduced me to the son of the famous Ambroise Vollard, one of the great art dealers of all time, who discovered and admired the French Postimpressionists long before most people appreciated their work. Vollard had left most of his collection to this boy's mother, who then passed it on to her son. The son's apartment in Paris contained virtually nothing but paintings, great bins full of them, unframed canvases arranged in large portfolios. He would flip them over: twenty-five Cézannes, thirty Degas . . . I never saw such a collection in my life. I even managed to buy some from him.

I enjoyed the European art galleries, but private collections were usually far more interesting. Once I went to the apartment of Cézanne's son, Paul, who as a matter of courtesy allowed me to see his personal collection. I was taken with a self-portrait of his father. "If this painting ever comes on the market," I told Skira, "I would very much like to have it." Somehow, Skira came to an agreement with the artist's son that if he ever decided to sell it, I would get first refusal. Two years later, a cablegram from Skira arrived, saying Paul Cézanne had decided to sell his father's self-portrait. I cabled back immediately, yes, and it is now in my living room in New York. This head of Cézanne, with a beard, wearing a yellow sombrero, is, I believe, one of the best of his self-portraits.

The men dealing in the art world were (and still are for the most part) highly individualistic personalities, a pleasure and a challenge to know and to deal with. But if these men had their personal idiosyncrasies, the artists and painters themselves lived in a fantasy world of their own. My greatest pleasures came from knowing and buying paintings from the artists themselves. In the mid-thirties, I would often visit the studio of André Derain, who had been one of the avant-garde leaders of French art, although by the time I met him his influence had been adversely affected by the critics. Nevertheless, I liked his work, especially his earlier paintings. A man with great force of character, he went on painting austere landscapes and portraits in his own style, which was avant-garde no longer. Nor was he among the most organized of men. Once in his studio I came across a half-finished painting of two Italian actors rehearsing, which I particularly liked. "Why don't you finish it?" I asked.

"Oh, I'll get around to it someday," said Derain.

"No, I want to buy it and I want you to finish it now," I insisted. So, he put that painting up on his easel and while I waited, he completed the work. Of course, you cannot tell now, but if ever the painting is examined scientifically, some art historian will be perplexed to find that the upper part of the two men was painted during Derain's prime, before 1925, and the lower legs were done some years later. To me, it's a very interesting painting, and beautiful, too.

On another occasion, I came across a small painting in a dark corner of Derain's studio, which was so covered with grime that I could hardly make out its true colors. I had to use all my powers of persuasion to get him to clean away the dirt. Then I announced, "I'll buy it."

"Oh, you don't want to buy that," he said. "Yes, I do," said I. "I'll give it to you," he said. "I don't want to take it," said I. But he insisted, "Yes, you've got to. As a friend, you've got to take it." I remember that scene as if it were yesterday, it was so representative of his personality. That small painting, "Head of a Boy," hangs in my office at CBS now. It is one of my favorites, done during Derain's best period.

This same period, I came to know Matisse, who agreed to do a painting of my wife Dorothy. Every day I accompanied her to his studio for the sketches—he must have done fifty sketches of her—but when he was about to start to paint, he fell ill, and said, "I can't finish it this year, but next year we'll do it." He never did do the painting. Later he sent one of the sketches to Dorothy for

Christmas. In his apartment, I came upon a painting of a woman with a veil, which I absolutely loved, and asked about it.

"Everybody in the world has been trying to buy this painting for years," Matisse said.

"Well," said I, "there must come a time when you will want to sell and here I am and I want to buy it."

He looked at me and murmured, "Let me think about it." Finally, some days later, he said: "All right, if you really want it, you can have it." So I bought it. Today, in my bedroom, is that now famous painting "La Voilette."

In contrast to most painters, Matisse had a passion for order. His brushes not in use were always clean, there was never a speck of paint on the floor or on his clothes, and yet he was the most imaginative of painters. His genius lay in using colors side by side that had never gone together before, and achieving an aesthetic balance in his paintings which eluded the best of others. So, I took an inordinate sense of pleasure when he complimented me on what he called "instinctive sense of balance." I had shown Matisse several series of photographs I had taken while in Paris and he advised me avuncularly at one point: "Please, whatever you are doing (as a career), drop it, and take up photography seriously." I admired him enormously as an artist, but I declined to take his advice.

Matisse's son, Pierre, had opened a gallery in New York and the first time I walked into his gallery he was struggling with a wooden crate. I introduced myself and asked "What's in there?" Matisse explained that he had asked his father to send him "something exciting" so that he could achieve a bit of status for his new gallery. "This case contains the painting my father sent me. I haven't even seen it." We opened it, and, oh, my God! I almost died, it was so beautiful. It was called "Odalisque." I thought it was the best painting Matisse had ever done and so I said, "I like that. I'd like to buy it. What's the price?" He quoted me one. I said, "I'm going to buy it and I'm going to take it right home with me now." The next day he called me up and said, "All hell has broken loose. I didn't realize people all over the world have been trying to buy it. It just got out that my father sent it to me. I've had telephone calls and cablegrams from all over the world about it." He was a gentle, honorable man. "If you'd like to make some money," he said, "I'd like to buy it back from you. I'd pay you a good price and still I could make some money on it." I declined his offer as gently as possible.

It must be remembered that these French painters were hardly as famous then as they are now. But collectors like myself bought their paintings because they held a very special appeal for us, not because we envisioned the future fame that would be accorded to these artists and their paintings or the high monetary values that would be put on them.

There was a famous collection in Berlin—the Schmidt Collection, about which Skira approached Averell and me, saying that this whole collection was for sale for $400,000. It was a fantastic opportunity: approximately fifty important paintings. Averell and I agreed to buy the collection together. Then each of us was to select what he wanted from the collection and pay the amount that was represented in the value of each picture—the value to be determined by a third party. Those we did not want would be sold for us by the Marie Harriman Gallery. At the last minute Averell got cold feet, saying he had changed his mind because it was too much money. I pleaded with him, begged him. He was adamant. So we had to tell Skira we were backing out. Skira nearly cried. "You can't do this. You must buy it," he protested. He then appealed to me, but I said, "I can't. I can take half but I can't go all the way." We allowed our option to lapse, and the collection was bought by the Wildenstein Gallery, which made millions on the deal. I bought a Cézanne still life from the collection and at a high price. So there was a great opportunity lost, however you measure it.

On another occasion, I was plain lucky—I was in St. Moritz when Skira telephoned from Geneva. "I've got a great painting here. You must come right down and see it."

"Albert," I said, "I just got here and I'm dead tired. I've been leading a very energetic life in Paris for the last couple of weeks." When he insisted, I finally said, "Listen. If it's so good, why don't you bring it up here?"

"I can't," he responded. "It's too large. I can't get it in my car."

"Well, get a truck," I said jokingly.

"I can't do that."

"Well, I'm sorry. I'm not going to Geneva," I told him.

The next day, a truck pulled up in front of the Palace Hotel in St. Moritz and the painting—a Picasso—was taken out and put in the lobby. I liked it. I asked Skira the price, which was quite modest. I said, "That's fine, I'll buy it." Then I asked, "Whom does it belong to?"

He replied, "That's the one thing I can't tell you. I'm sworn to secrecy. There's no question about its authenticity." There certainly wasn't and I took it. It is the painting called "Boy Leading a Horse," now one of the best known of all of Picasso's paintings. It's priceless, and I have promised it to the Museum of Modern Art in New York.

I was always curious about who had sold it to me. Years later, at the museum, the mystery was cleared up. A famous Berlin dealer named Thannhauser came up to me and said, "Mr. Paley, I'll bet you've often wondered who owned that 'Boy Leading a Horse.'"

"I sure have."

"Well, let me tell you a story. When you were in the lobby of the hotel looking at that painting, I was on the outside looking through the glass. And I was shivering. I needed that money so badly that I had smuggled the painting out of Germany. I had to have the funds and I didn't want anyone to know who owned the painting because it would be traced and I would have gotten into trouble. I was the owner of that painting." He had somehow got many of his paintings out of Nazi Germany and eventually came to New York with them. He sold some, lived very comfortably for the rest of his life, and left the balance of his collection to the Guggenheim Museum, where it now remains.

Although I pursued no conscious pattern in buying paintings, but only followed my taste in selecting them, I have been told by artists and other collectors that they can see a pattern and a kind of taste that is a sign that one person put the collection together. That is the sort of comment about style which pleases a collector.

Trial and Error

When the net earnings of my fledgling network passed the golden mark of $2 million by September 1931, I heaved a sigh of relief and pleasure. I notified Paramount that CBS wanted it to fulfill its contractual obligation to buy back at $85 a share the Paramount shares it had given CBS shareholders in lieu of cash for its 50 per cent ownership of CBS. The network had fulfilled its contractual obligation to reach cumulative earnings of $2 million during two years and now wanted to be paid in cash, as promised. The catch was that Paramount was in no condition, financial or otherwise, to buy back its stock at $85 a share. Paramount stock, never having recovered from the 1929 crash, was selling on the open market at below $10.

Adolph Zukor and I had been two supremely confident men when the Paramount-CBS stock deal had been made in 1929. He had been certain that in two years, Paramount would be selling at $150 a share, and I had been equally sure CBS was worth the $5 million paid because it would have earned $2 million. My confidence had never been shaken, except possibly once in mid-

1930 when the first of the Crossley ratings* was published. Based upon telephone interviews with a small sample of the population, Crossley reported that just about everyone was listening to NBC programs. NBC's *Amos 'n' Andy* had a Crossley rating of 53.4, *Rudy Vallee Varieties* got 36.5, the *Lucky Strike Dance Orchestra* got 27.8 and so on. As for CBS, with the exception of only two shows, the more popular of which had a 12.0 rating, no CBS program did better than 3.3. That first Crossley rating hit us like a blow to the solar plexus. There were cries of anguish in the CBS offices, but most of us were angry with disbelief. It just could not be so. We were certain that at least some of our programs were more popular than those of NBC. I was furious. The danger of losing advertisers was real, for no matter how talented our performers might be, who would want to sponsor a CBS program that only a few would listen to?

Paul Kesten came up with the solution and like all good solutions, it was simple. We hired the prestigious accounting firm of Price, Waterhouse and Company, whose integrity could not be questioned, to conduct an unbiased study of radio network popularity. Price, Waterhouse devised a simple survey which *Fortune* magazine later described this way: "So basic were their facts, so simple their presentation . . . the entire advertising fraternity was impressed."

What Price, Waterhouse did was send out several hundred thousand postcards to random homes in cities and towns where CBS had affiliates, asking listeners simply to name their favorite radio station, tear off that portion of the card and drop it in the mail. The results were reassuring. In the ten largest American cities, the survey showed CBS stations were favored seven to three over one of the NBC networks and five to four over the other. In all sixty-seven cities covered by the CBS network, we rated 34 to 31 over the first NBC network and 32 to 31 over the

* Organized by Archibald Crossley, the Crossley rating (officially called the Cooperative Analysis of Broadcasting) was the first national rating and represented the percentage of the entire radio-owning population listening to a program.

other. Thus, the ratings war began between CBS and NBC; but at least we did not lose our advertisers.

Nor did we lose our momentum. Economic indicators for the whole radio industry pointed upward: radios in use, number of listeners and time sales to sponsors. The radio industry was growing despite the onset of the Depression. Radio gave people free entertainment, free education, and free information. Network radio gave manufacturers a lively coast-to-coast marketplace for their brand-name goods.

Ironically, when serious negotiations with Paramount got under way, I found myself face to face with John D. Hertz, a businessman of considerable substance, whom I had declined to hire at CBS. Hertz had built up one of the largest taxi fleets in Chicago, founded the concept of rental cars, and retired a rich man, only to be bored by retirement. Zukor had recommended that I hire him as my right-hand man at CBS. Although I had liked the man, I told Zukor that he might, because of the importance of the job, have a negative influence upon the ambitions of the young management team at CBS. So, I suggested that Zukor hire him instead. Now, with Paramount in trouble, Zukor was moved off to one side and Hertz, as chairman of the finance committee, had become the key man at Paramount. But in our negotiations, he tried to handle me the wrong way. I was barely thirty years old and he tried to overpower me into agreement, threatening again and again, to get a better price elsewhere on Wall Street than I was offering him. What I proposed was to buy back the CBS stock for the same amount that Paramount owed us on it, namely $4 million. Paramount wanted more.

I knew that Paramount could not raise $4 million on its own and I thought that no one else would make such an offer as long as CBS stockholders had the first-refusal right to match any offer. I challenged Hertz to find another buyer, if he could, and I stuck to my price.

As we came up to the deadline for those negotiations, Paramount brought in Otto Kahn, the famous investment banker, and he tried the reasonable approach. "Mr. Paley, the people at Paramount are having trouble with you," he declared. "They want to sell their CBS stock to you, but you are offering them only $4 million for it, and they think it's worth much more than that. After all, you just made your $2 million."

I was just as reasonable. "Mr. Kahn," I said, "they have a right to ask what they please and they have a right to go out and get a higher offer. All you have to do is go out and get that offer, and then as you know from the provisions of the contract, if you get that offer, you have to give me the right to meet it. It would then be up to me to meet it or not."

"You know damn well that it's very hard to get another bid under these circumstances," he said.

"I don't really know about that," I retorted.

"Well, I'm telling you it is. I think you ought to pay them more."

"No," I insisted, "I won't do it."

"In other words, you've made up your mind, you're not going to offer any more."

"That's right."

"Young man, you're too much for me," said Otto Kahn, "I am authorized to act for Paramount and I accept your offer."

So, the CBS stock returned to its original shareholders in an approximate exchange for the Paramount stock held by us. We paid $4 million for the CBS stock and Paramount used that $4 million to buy back its shares at $85 a share, as agreed upon. Various amounts of shares had been sold on both sides since the original purchase, so that only those stockholders who still held their shares participated in the buy-back.

On behalf of the thirteen early CBS stockholders and myself as the major stockholder, I decided to convert about half of the returning CBS stock into cash. In these negotiations, I brought in three investment banking firms—Brown Brothers, Harriman; Lehman Brothers; and Field, Glore. They bought back half of the stock held by Paramount at $82.21 a share, part of which they sold to their clients at a later date.

So, when all the negotiations ended and the legal papers were signed and the exchange made, I walked away from that final meeting with a check from the investment bankers for $2,000,004.88 and CBS stock worth slightly more than that for me and the other CBS stockholders. My share amounted to a substantial amount of that cash and 10,577 additional shares of Class A CBS stock. Aside from all this, of course, the other half of CBS was represented by 63,250 shares of Class B stock, of which I individually owned 39.7 per cent and was the voting trustee of another 27.7 per cent.

I was on my way to becoming a truly rich man and yet it did not seem to touch me emotionally. There were no celebrations. I walked out of that meeting alone shortly before midnight, stopped at an all-night restaurant, had a cup of coffee, and went home to bed. The Paramount-named directors duly resigned from the CBS board and I named four new directors of my own choosing, three of them from the Wall Street investment banking firms. We planned, when the time was right, to list CBS on the New York Stock Exchange. CBS was on its own merry way. And I began planning my own retirement from the network.

The year before I had told a reporter for the London *Daily Mirror* that I intended to retire at age thirty-five, and over the next three or four years I told others, all in an attempt to reinforce for myself the vow I had taken at eighteen to get rich and retire. And when that fateful day of my thirty-fifth birthday approached in September 1936, I truly faced one of the most dreadful dilemmas of my life. Because of the success of CBS, I had all the money I had ever hoped for, more than enough to quit work and live a life of leisure. And yet I did not really want to retire. But how sacred is a solemn vow and promise one has made to oneself? Even at the age of eighteen? Would I be punished if I broke the vow? Would my luck run out? Would something really terrible happen to me? Those were serious thoughts in those days. I carefully analyzed the alternatives and concluded that I really did not want to become a beachcomber or pick oranges off trees. Life was not meant to be devoted to the acquisition of money, followed by a lazy life of leisure. At eighteen, I had been too young, too immature, too unknowing to set an unalterable path for myself. Now, at thirty-five, I knew that life was meant to be lived to the fullest, day by day to the very last one. Money was not the issue. My life with CBS was fascinating, adventurous, and even of some social significance. Radio was reaching into the homes of millions and millions of Americans across the country; the average listening family had its radio turned on for more than five hours a day, and CBS was a major source of entertainment, information, and news for so many Americans. How could I quit? I loved my work. I was thoroughly involved in selling and organizing and programming and constantly looking for new station affiliates. I also spent a good deal of time in Washington, testifying before congressional committees of one kind or another, talking with various congressmen about the rights of broadcasters, and I traveled to the West Coast at least once or twice a year to try to develop new programs. It seemed that I had to be everywhere. There was hardly ever any let-up and I enjoyed the pace and the excitement. So, my thirty-fifth birthday came and went and I never looked back. Besides, we were making some exhilarating strides in our competition with NBC. In the 1934–35 season, radio's top five programs all were on NBC; in the 1936–37 season, four of the top five were on CBS!

The reason behind this turnabout was simply that I had managed in the season in-between, 1935–36, to lure away three of the most popular entertainers from NBC—Major Bowes, Al Jolson, and Eddie Cantor. Major Bowes's original *Amateur Hour* was the most popular radio program of its time: listeners loved to empathize with the amateur performers and to try to second-guess who would win the competition for the most applause and who would get the gong that cut short the performance. When Major (Edward) Bowes switched sponsors and signed up with the Chrysler Corporation, I cultivated our relationship, even going to watch his broadcasts and attending the parties which followed in his luxurious apartment on top of the Capitol Theater building, of which he was part-owner. When I thought he would agree that it made no difference to him which network he went

Aboard the *Queen Elizabeth*.

After signing a Latin American network contract in Brazil.

Paul Whiteman.

Franklin D. Roosevelt.

Anschluss, the Nazis on the march.

The *World News Roundup,*
with Robert Trout.

Orson Welles at a news conference after *The War of the Worlds.*

Good-bye, Mr. Chips brought James Hilton, Laurence Olivier, and Cecil B. DeMille to Lux Radio Theater.

With Paul Kesten.

With souvenirs of early CBS affiliates.   Elmer Davis.

At a wartime dinner for Ed Murrow, with Archibald MacLeish (l.).

In World War II, I served as Deputy Chief of the Psychological Warfare Division of SHAEF under General Eisenhower.

At SHAEF with General Eisenhower (front right), R.A.F. Marshal Tedder (front left), and a few others.

CBS war correspondents (l. to r.) Edward R. Murrow, Paul Manning, John Daly, and Robert Trout.

Winston Churchill.

Charles Collingwood in
working clothes.

Presenting an eighteenth-century Chinese bowl
to Lowell Thomas on his twentieth anniversary
on the air.

Frank Sinatra starting out on CBS.

on, I made my sales pitch to Walter Chrysler. By then I had a set sales talk as to CBS's youth, energy, good affiliate stations, competitive coverage with NBC, and our better promotion plans. Walter Chrysler was a business man. He asked a good many pointed questions and I answered them as best I could. I tried to impress on him how progressive and how fast-growing CBS was and how much we could do for Chrysler. But the decision was entirely his and he did have a big investment involved in sponsoring Major Bowes. Why should he switch? Major Bowes had been a proven winner on NBC. I'll never forget my fear or my bad case of nerves when I came to him for his final answer.

Chrysler faced me grimly from behind an enormous desk. "Sit down, Bill, I've got some bad news for you," he said.

I sat down and thought, Oh, Lord.

"I don't know how you're going to take this. I like you, but I've been thinking about it and thinking about it, and I might as well blurt it out. I've decided . . ." He paused for a terrifying second. "I've decided to put Major Bowes on CBS."

I jumped out of my seat, ran around his desk, threw my arms around him and hugged him. He grinned. My emotions sent tremors up and down my spine. This was the coup of coups. Major Bowes on CBS!

We also took the *Lux Radio Theater* away from NBC. Created in 1934 to do adaptations of Broadway plays, the *Lux Radio Theater* was moved by us to Hollywood for the 1936–37 season to do adaptations of motion pictures. With Cecil B. DeMille, the movie director, as host, the *Lux Radio Theater* enjoyed tremendous popularity for many years—many of them, in the top ten.

Taking *Lux* to Hollywood was a sign of a major change in broadcasting, linking the entertainment worlds of radio and motion pictures. In late 1936, in anticipation of technological improvements in transmitting, we took steps to establish a permanent CBS base in Hollywood. We bought our own radio station in Los Angeles, KNX, and its studios. We also bought the 1,500-seat Vine Street Playhouse, and then, needing still more studio space, we leased the Music Box Theater on Hollywood Boulevard. The idea was for CBS to have the capability of originating radio shows from the West Coast, serving that area and time zone more effectively and, more important, having ready access to motion-picture stars. Our biggest venture, however, was a plan to build a new radio center of studios, offices, and theaters on Sunset Boulevard between Gower and El Centro streets, renaming the site "Columbia Square." When the new complex, designed by William Lescaze and built at a cost of $1,750,000, was opened on April 30, 1938, *Radio Daily* described it as "technically and physically . . . perhaps the most advanced radio home in the world today."

The need for studio space and facilities nearly doubled in the latter half of the thirties, not because of additional programs but rather to accommodate the need for more rehearsals and technical equipment. Radio broadcasting was becoming more sophisticated. The rather slapdash broadcasts of the early days began to give way to better sound and better programs.

Radio drama ran the gamut of aesthetic tastes from thrillers, to melodramatic daytime serials, to adaptations of classical theater, to news and experimental forms of serious drama. All types of radio drama developed, becoming more sophisticated in form and technique. The thrillers, suspense stories, and daytime serials were commercially successful. They suited the fancy of most listeners, attracted sponsors, and helped pay for the more serious and experimental programs which appealed to the minority of listeners with the so-called "highbrow tastes." In the early days, listeners made it a point to listen to *The Shadow* every week just to hear that cynical laugh and the voice which said, "The Shadow knows . . ." And then there was *Gangbusters*, with its special sound effects, a long-running success and a forerunner of the cops-and-robbers shows on television. In time, dramas written especially for radio developed into an art form, which received high critical acclaim.

But it was the daily daytime serials which attracted the most loyal audience on radio, as they would later on television. They became part of the fabric of life for housewives across the country; they generally sold brand-name products in proportion to their popularity; and for the radio stations then, as for television stations now, the degree of success of their daytime programs could well determine the profit-and-loss statement at the end of each year. In the radio days, that success depended largely upon two people, Frank and Anne Hummert, who were without question the most prolific producers of daytime serials.

For most of the thirties, this husband-and-wife team created just about half of all the serials on the air. Hummert, who had been one of the top writers in the advertising business, perfected the genre of soap opera, the to-be-continued melodramatic depicting of the troubles and woes of so-called ordinary people. Virtually every program Frank Hummert created was eagerly bought by one or another advertiser, and Hummert had much influence on which network got his newest brainchild. He had married his young assistant, Anne, a most attractive and capable woman who ran their large staff of writers and production people. Frank himself was rather eccentric and crotchety, instilling fear in most people, because he controlled so much of his segment of the business. But I liked and admired him as a person and a real professional. I made it my business to join them for lunch two or three times a month at the Park Lane Hotel, where Frank always ate raw vegetables and complained of a stomach ailment and of people he did not like. We talked mostly about daytime serial plots, truly his favorite subject, never about business, and I believe this relationship helped bring to CBS some of our most popular, long-running serials, such as *Just Plain Bill*, *The Romance of Helen Trent*, *Our Gal Sunday*, *Ma Perkins*, and others. Daytime serials, often referred to as soap operas, became an American phenomenon.

Then as now, the sponsors of programs usually sought the widest possible audience for the advertising of their products. Defining and mapping these sales markets by age, income, region, and other categories became a specialization of the advertising agencies, and of course a matter of bread-and-butter interest to us.

From the beginning I saw that the business side of broadcasting required us to reflect in our programming the taste of the majority. But at the same time I also realized that we should balance popular entertainment with programs which would attract the minority tastes. So while I chased the top entertainers, talent, and sponsors, my associates and I worked equally hard to bring serious drama, classical music, and educational broadcasts to CBS. I wanted CBS to represent the finest quality in broadcasting and in programming, and through these years we sought and embraced the opportunities for bringing something new and important to the public via radio. The *Cavalcade of America*, a series of historical dramas, was one of the few such programs to attract a sponsor, the Du Pont Company, despite its small audience.

Most of these more serious programs never won sponsors or did so for only a short time. They were too "highbrow" for most listeners, and so CBS would pay to put them on the air, always hoping to find a sponsor and seldom succeeding. Orson Welles was a case in point. I was astonished by his extraordinary ability when he appeared at a charity fund-raising party and at the last minute, without rehearsal, put on a stunning dramatization. We brought Welles to CBS to form a dramatic group called the *Mercury Theater of the Air*, which competed at 8 P.M. Sunday with NBC's popular Edgar Bergen and Charlie McCarthy on *The Chase and Sanborn Hour*. Then Orson Welles made radio history on October 30, 1938, with his broadcast of *The War of the Worlds*, in which he simulated news bulletins reporting the landing on earth of men from Mars. So real was his dramatization that millions of Americans panicked. CBS was sued by people who claimed they had suffered from shock and in some cases, heart attacks, because of the program. The *Mercury Theater* became famous. And Orson Welles soon found a sponsor, Campbell Soup, and was launched on a career of numerous triumphs on the air, in the theater, and in the movies.

The *Columbia Workshop* was our own experimental theater of the air, a proving ground for new radio techniques. In order to keep it as flexible as possible, we decided never to offer it for sponsorship. Under the direction of Irving Reis, who had been a studio engineer, the *Workshop* was chartered to put on experimental radio dramas which would innovate special sound and electronic effects, music, direction—all "with no restriction save the essential and reasonable one of good taste." And it did just that. Its new sound effects, which influenced the entire industry, simulated such things as a trapped fly buzzing against a window, a torpedo being fired from a submerged submarine, five hundred bombing planes in action. New voice effects were created with electronic filters for radio portrayals of ghosts, leprechauns, and all sorts of characters. Its performance of Archibald MacLeish's *The Fall of the City*, a poetic drama featuring Orson Welles, was an all-time pinnacle of radio drama, an outstanding event in my own broadcasting experience and a sensation in 1937. By the time it left the air in 1942, the *Workshop* had made a remarkable record in the new genre of radio drama. Outstanding writers of the day, including W. H. Auden, Dorothy Parker, William Saroyan, Irwin Shaw, and Stephen Vincent Benét, had written half-hour dramas especially for the *Workshop*. Another genius of serious radio drama was Norman Corwin, who had a special following of listeners for his sensitive radio arrangements of the works of American poets, verse plays of his own, and a variety of documentaries uniquely contrived for radio. He was a genius of the medium and his radio dramas are among CBS's classics.

Of all the arts, the one easiest to put on radio was music. One had only to play a record. Popular music flooded the airwaves at the beginning of broadcasting and then slowly gave way to comedy, drama, and variety. Classical music filled more than 25 per cent of all CBS broadcast time in the beginning, largely because of Arthur Judson's influence as a concertmaster. But classical music throughout the thirties leveled out to about 10 per cent of our air time. I had lost out in bringing the Metropolitan Opera to CBS, but I already had signed the New York Philharmonic Symphony for CBS Sunday afternoon broadcasts. A succession of great conductors was presented to the American public via those Philharmonic broadcasts: Arturo Toscanini, John Barbirolli, Artur Rodzinski, Bruno Walter, Dimitri Mitropoulos, and Leonard Bernstein. CBS had its own Columbia Symphony Orchestra, directed by Howard Barlow. Deems Taylor served as our musical consultant. In the mid-thirties we commissioned twelve American composers—some well known, some obscure—to compose works specifically for radio performances. When we broadcast five of these original works on a single program, Aaron Copland, one of the composers, hailed it as "a red letter day for American music," and commented: "It shows . . . that the Columbia Broadcasting System really believes in the native composer's product and in the capacity of the radio audience to understand and enjoy it."

At the start, it was not all that easy. I tried to persuade Jascha Heifetz, the great violinist, to perform on radio, but he turned me down, saying, like many others, "My music is for the elite, for those people who really understand it, and that means that it belongs in the concert hall." In time, he and others like him came to see that radio concerts could attract and convert millions to the magical beauty of the world's greatest music. The local affiliated stations also had to be persuaded to give hours of free air time to classical music, for such programs invariably received low ratings. In time, they came to understand the audiences' appreciation for stations that would bring symphony orchestras, chamber music groups, famous conductors, and brilliant soloists into their homes. Thousands upon thousands of programs of classical music were presented on CBS radio through the thirties and afterwards, which considerably influenced the musical tastes of America.

In line with our obligation for social responsibility, we broadcast the *Church of the Air*, in which CBS provided free air time on Sundays for clergymen representing the Protestant, Catholic, and Jewish faiths, in proportion to their published membership. However, we did prohibit them from being sponsored or from making appeals for contributions or discussing secular subjects. This policy grew out of an earlier mistake we had made in dealing with Father (Charles E.) Coughlin. I had scheduled him in a program coming from his Shrine of the Little Flower, in Royal Oak, Michigan. Before that he had broadcast locally over our affiliated radio station in Detroit for some years and had organized the Radio League of the Little Flower for which he collected contributions. He was indeed a powerful, popular orator from the pulpit. But after a while he strayed far beyond his theological talks to messages of hate and extreme political views. We soon insisted upon seeing his scripts in advance. We then refused him air time for one especially inflammatory advance script and strongly suggested he confine himself to a religious theme. That Sunday he appealed to his radio audience to write me personally in protest against the restrictions imposed upon him. Almost 400,000 letters poured into CBS, almost all of them in protest against our action. Nevertheless, we canceled Father Coughlin forthwith. We could not allow anyone to violate our policy of forbidding the abuse of air time. Father Coughlin arranged to continue his particular radio sermons by buying time over a number of independent stations throughout the country and buying lines from AT&T connecting these stations for simultaneous broadcasts. He became rather a *cause célèbre*, but that is another story.

From the very beginning of the network, we had prohibited sponsors from mentioning the price of their products on the air. The theory was that this would somehow cheapen the image of radio. But in 1932, in the depths of the Depression, one advertiser in particular appealed to me directly with the argument that listeners had every right to know the price of an advertised product as an important factor in their decision to buy or not buy.

That made sense to me. So, that same year, CBS lifted the self-imposed taboo, and sponsors from then on could advertise their prices as well as their products on the air.

We also inaugurated various types of informational and educational programs. We brought experts and authorities to the microphone to talk on books, business, history, astronomy, chemistry, music appreciation, and current subjects of interest. CBS formed an Adult Education Board of distinguished educators to advise us, and I met with them for a full day twice a year to hear and to discuss their recommendations. Our *American School of the Air*, an outgrowth of the early program sponsored by Majestic Radio, became a CBS non-commercial educating tool five days a week as a supplement to regular classroom instruction, and we distributed a teacher's manual to go with it. Surprisingly, the program seemed to attract many adult listeners outside of the classroom, judging from the fan mail received. We also had an advisory board to help us set policy and choose programs suitable for children. But one year when we adopted the advisory board's recommendations by canceling our so-called "blood and thunder" shows for children, our sponsors deserted us on the replacements. The children deserted us too, turning to the same type shows on other networks.

Out of necessity and based upon our past experience, we began to establish certain broadcasting policies covering the use of the CBS network for advertising and for the fair dissemination of information. In 1935, we set a fixed limit, specified in minutes and seconds, on the amount of advertising on any program. We barred the advertising of any products which we believed were socially taboo. And we set specified standards for broadcasts designed for children. On news and all public information broadcasts, we enunciated a formal policy based upon fairness and balance. We declared CBS to be "completely non-partisan on all public controversial questions, including politics." We said we would sell time on the air only for the advertising of goods and services and would refuse to sell time for propaganda. We made one necessary exception: we would sell air time to a political party during a campaign for the election of candidates. For all other discussions of public issues, we would allot time at our own expense so that we could maintain a policy of fairness and balance. The fundamental, basic concept behind these policies—then as now—was that the broadcasters—not government regulators—should exercise editorial judgment and take editorial responsibility for what went out over the networks. These policies, first established in 1935, worked and worked well through the years. The mistakes we made, we wanted to correct ourselves. I enunciated that concept then and I believe in it even more strongly now.

Those years were truly the heyday of radio broadcasting. In the decade of the 1930s, radio grew from infancy to maturity. New ideas, improved ideas, experimental ideas could be implemented without fuss or immense expense within hours or days. Mistakes and poor judgments could be corrected as easily. The pace was fast and glorious. We learned as we went along, by trial and error, and in the end we established broad policies and sound traditions that govern radio and television today.

Press-Radio War

R adio news grew and developed alongside the entertainment and cultural segments of broadcasting all through the thirties. Yet, from the very beginning, it always remained a separate, distinct entity and special part of broadcasting. At CBS, my associates and I recognized radio news as a unique service we could provide to the public, and we realized early that the prestige of our network would depend to a considerable extent upon how well we could provide such service. It seemed to me that if radio could broadcast the news of the day and special events, it would be a highly desirable service to the more serious listeners. In return, those listeners would appreciate radio—and particularly CBS—for giving them more thoughtful fare than just entertainment. It must be remembered that when I came to CBS in 1928, radio was looked upon by most people as a gadget, a toy, an amusing instrument of light entertainment.

Up until then, news on the networks had been scarce and episodic. At CBS, we had only a single teletype machine bringing us the news from the United Press, and we announced any big breaking stories from time to time.

In 1928, CBS covered the Republican and Democratic political conventions, the campaign speeches, and the election returns as they came in on election night. Radio brought Al Smith and Herbert Hoover right into your home. But the true magnitude of what a national network could do in covering a live news event dawned upon us and upon the nation with the all-day and into-the-night broadcast reports of the inauguration of President Hoover that first Monday in March 1929. The President-elect's reception at the White House, the auto trip to the Capitol, the swearing-in, the ceremonial parade, the speeches, the inaugural ball—all were described as they occurred by CBS and NBC. The broadcasts broke all records for number of microphones used, announcers, technicians, miles of cable, and, finally, the size of the audience, estimated at 63 million. The significance of radio coverage of that event was inescapable.

The public interest in radio news encouraged us to expand our news and public affairs services. So, in the first few months of 1929, soon after CBS's debut as a coast-to-coast network, we inaugurated our first regular daily news summary, our first regular program of political analysis and our first regular public affairs show. The first daily news summary over CBS was a five-minute segment which we introduced in a half-hour morning program called *Something for Everyone*. Then we hired two well-known newspapermen, who had experience on radio, to broadcast weekly fifteen-minute news commentaries for CBS: H. V. Kaltenborn from New York and Frederic William Wile from Washington.

CBS made giant strides in its news service in 1930 principally because of two other men who joined the network that year. When Ed Klauber came aboard as my assistant to help relieve me of administrative matters, he spent a good deal of his time, because of his long experience on the New York *Times*, as my adviser, guide, and mentor on how CBS should handle news. Paul White was hired away from the United Press and the United Features Syndicate to run our infant newsroom.

Klauber and I tackled a variety of problems which arose at the network. Our method was to discuss any given problem until we had exhausted the possibilities and alternatives involved. Once we made a decision we would get it down on paper and that would become a guiding policy for the network. Thus we agreed there would be no editorializing during news broadcasts, commentaries would be kept completely separate from the news itself, CBS news would be accurate and objective.

That was easy enough. But beyond that, we both wanted our radio news and commentaries to achieve a fairness and a balance. If we gave one side of a controversy, we would give equal time to the other side; if we presented a speaker with one viewpoint, we would try to counterbalance it with a viewpoint from the other side. It all seems rather simple now, but in those early days, it was absolutely new territory to explore.

We also decided that in hiring men for the CBS newsroom, we would favor the good newsman over the pleasant speaking voice. I became convinced that journalistic judgment was far more important in a radio newsman than any other quality. All of our future hiring at CBS News would reflect that very early decision.

These were long-range policies, but the most tactical decision we made was to give the man in charge of the newsroom the authority to interrupt regular programs with news bulletins. In the long run, this decision was instrumental in making CBS News one of the most important departments of the whole network. In effect, we were putting news on an equal—or perhaps superior—basis vis-à-vis the entertainment and commercial segments of the network. Thus, the ground rules and guidelines for radio news coverage and broadcasting, the professional ethics involved, all were laid down very early in the history of CBS. Paul White, himself an old news service hand, was instrumental in implementing these policies in our newsroom. He is also to be credited with setting the tone, vigor, and spirit of broadcast journalism, especially at CBS.

Our expansion of news and special events began when I sent Frederic Wile to the London Naval Disarmament Conference in January 1930. There he recruited Cesar Saerchinger, a forty-year-old reporter for the New York *Evening Post* and the Philadelphia *Public Ledger* to complete that assignment for him. We then decided we wanted someone to stay in London to cover Great Britain and the Continent for us and Saerchinger became that man. Some would call him CBS's first "foreign correspondent," but actually he was more of a "public affairs" man than a broadcaster. His job was not to cover news but to arrange for eminent persons to speak or to be interviewed on CBS about current events in Europe.

In the fall of 1930, Lowell Thomas, then well known for his personal adventure books and for his colorful travel lectures, came to see me about becoming a broadcaster. I was immediately impressed with him. Here was a man who had had remarkable experiences around the world. He was suave and well-spoken, a kind of hero to the American public. My enthusiasm for him got him on the air. I gathered the key editors of the *Literary Digest* and directors of Funk & Wagnalls, who were looking for a new personality for commentaries on current events, in the CBS board room. Then I signaled Lowell Thomas at a microphone in one of our audition rooms. He spoke without preparation and without a script. His voice was piped into the board room and one of the most fabulous careers in radio was launched. Because of prior commitments, the *Literary Digest* split the account: NBC would broadcast Lowell Thomas in the East and CBS would broadcast him simultaneously in the West. We introduced him over CBS as "a new radio voice, informing and entertaining you with the latest news of the day." He was a natural radio personality and was well received. I would have liked to keep Thomas for CBS, but the next year NBC signed him exclusively. Sixteen years later, in 1947, he came back to CBS and stayed with us until his closing night, May 14, 1976: forty-six years on the air—one of the longest runs in broadcasting history.

During that one year, 1930, we put on more than six hundred domestic public affairs broadcasts, and, following the Naval Disarmament Conference more than eighty international broadcasts. At the time we limited ourselves to some extent to broadcasting fully anticipated news events. However, sometimes we were lucky to be on the spot at the right time. One of our affiliates had a microphone at an Ohio prison for a concert given by the prisoners, when a fire broke out. An inmate seized the microphone and began broadcasting the horrors of the conflagration. In the background the listener could hear the crackling and roar of the flames, the shouts of the firemen, and the screams of the dying. We tied the prisoners' broadcast into the network and millions of Americans experienced this awesome event in which 320 inmates perished. As a broadcast, it was a harbinger of the news world to come: one day, even raging battlefields would be brought into the home.

In April 1931, CBS laid claim to being the number-one news network. At the top of all our press releases, we wrote: "Columbia—the 'News' Network." We based our claim on the number of times we interrupted our regular commercial programs with bulletins of spot news, which were much more frequent than those of NBC. With a United Press teletype machine in our newsroom, it was a matter of policy to have our announcers interrupt programs with important bulletins. In fact, we urged the United Press to give us more news bulletins, more stories of national rather than local interest and more service from 8 A.M. to 12:30 A.M.

It was perfectly obvious to us that radio was particularly well suited for the communication of news to the nation. More than the printed word, the spoken voice could travel over the airwaves to remote areas of the country and the world, crossing the barrier of literacy, and reaching the widest and most diverse of audiences ever known. It was faster, more intimate, and more revealing. We were so vigorous in our pursuit of news for radio and so delighted with beating NBC in this area and so pleased with how well we were doing that we completely overlooked the rumblings and reactions of the newspaper establishment.

From the very beginning newspaper publishers were of two or more minds about radio. Some bought radio stations, or made connections with them, and so became part of the broadcasting industry. Others worried about competition for the advertising dollar. Still others believed as we did that news bulletins on the air encouraged readers to buy newspapers. On the whole, however, most newspaper publishers worried increasingly about the competition of radio news, seeing it more as a threat than complement to the press.

Nevertheless, we were taken by surprise when the American Newspaper Publishers Association at their 1931 annual meeting passed a resolution favoring newspaper control of radio news broadcasting. For two days at their convention, the publishers castigated the competition of radio in news and in advertising and many suggestions were made on how to curb radio from broadcasting the news received from the wire services before the newspapers themselves hit the streets. In the end, the publishers convention appointed a committee to confer with the press associations—the Associated Press, (AP), United Press, (UP), and the International News Service (INS)—with the aim of "bringing about proper regulations of such news broadcasting." The publishers also resolved that radio program logs "if published, should be handled as paid advertising."

This twofold threat was alarming. With the slump in newspaper advertising and the steady rise in the popularity of radio, newspaper publishers felt that radio was stealing advertising away from them. They were determined to fight back. Personally, I felt it was the slump in the economy during the Depression. Nevertheless, the tension between the press and radio increased throughout that year and the next.

In matters of this kind, it seems there is always one incident or another that triggers the explosion. Some say it was our coverage of the Lindbergh kidnaping. CBS was tipped off by telephone from a Newark newspaper. NBC got the news too, but withheld it until the newspapers came out. CBS put it on the air immediately, and followed it with intensive live coverage. We brought Boake Carter, a radio commentator from WCAU in Philadelphia, into our team on location in New Jersey, near the scene of the crime. Of all the crimes up to that time, none captured the attention of the nation so grippingly as the kidnaping of the Lindbergh baby. Our rapid-fire bulletins on that story irked the newspaper press. But we had our own sources of information and the publishers could only frown. Radio's live coverage of the 1932 conventions, particularly the Democratic Convention, with its emotional contest between Alfred Smith and Franklin Delano Roosevelt, captured the imagination of the radio public. All this brought about the competitive resentment of a good many newspaper publishers. They applied pressure upon the wire news services. The newspapers, as the major paying clients of the wire services as well as a source of news stories, apparently reasoned: Why should they allow this news to be given to the radio networks, which were competing with them for the public's attention and the advertising dollar?

Whatever the causes behind it, the United Press in the middle of the 1932 presidential campaign suddenly cut off its regular service to CBS and NBC. We struggled along without the wire services until election night. Strangely enough, the UP had signed a separate contract to supply us with election returns from across the country. Then a few days before election night, it canceled that contract. But through a comedy of errors, we survived. The AP, not knowing of UP's cancellation, also agreed to supply us with returns. Then, on election night itself, the UP must have discovered that its competitor was giving us the returns, for suddenly its teletype machine in our newsroom began chattering in the election returns. And to complete the circuit, the INS hastily installed a teletype in our newsroom. So, for the first time, CBS had all three news services at its disposal and we devoted the whole night to the election and capped it all off by putting the new President-elect, Franklin Delano Roosevelt, on the air from Hyde Park, New York. Radio, through its two major networks, beat all the newspapers in the country with the election results.

Newspaper publishers were chagrined and angry over the success of radio in covering the election; some were still furious at radio's growth in listeners and revenues at a time in the depths of the Depression when newspaper advertising revenues were falling off. At CBS we received rumors and then reports which confirmed the newspaper publishers' intention to band together to deny the news wire services to radio stations or the networks. What came to be called "the press-radio war" broke out. It was serious business. Not only did the newspapers intend to cut off their news stories but they threatened to stop printing our schedules of daily programs (except as printed advertising) in their papers. Thus radio listeners would not be able to know or to plan what they wanted to hear on radio.

With my blessing, Ed Klauber wrote to Karl Bickel, president of the United Press, insisting that no one in radio had any desire to injure the press and no one had done anything in that direction. However, his letter stated firmly, "there must be news broadcasting and we have no intention whatever to recede from this field." Pleading for peace and cooperation, we then made our own threat: if the newspaper publishers cut off our source of news, within forty-eight hours we would set up a news-gathering agency of our own. Bickel replied that he too was for peace and cooperation but that he would have to be guided by the wishes of the newspaper publishers.

Our reconciliation efforts came to nil. The following month, April 1933, the Associated Press, at its annual meeting of subscribing newspaper publishers, voted "that the Board of Directors shall not allow any news distributed by the Associated Press, regardless of source, to be given to any radio chain or chains. . . ." The UP and INS soon followed with a similar ban.

Then the American Newspaper Publishers Association at its 1933 annual meeting voted to stop listing radio programs in their newspapers except as advertising matter. Actually, it was a threat that was never widely implemented. *Broadcasting* magazine headlined the conflict succinctly: "A.P. and A.N.P.A. Declare War on Radio." All our efforts to make peace with the newspapers failed. NBC struggled along without the news service, telephoning around the country for its information, but since we proclaimed CBS as the number-one news network, I finally made the decision to set up a news-gathering service of our own. The Columbia News Service was an unprecedented effort in broadcasting and Paul White, a great, hard-working newsman, spear-headed the remarkable job of putting together a world-wide news-gathering organization in a very brief time. He set up news bureaus in New York, Washington, Chicago, and Los Angeles and had their managers line up stringers (local newsmen engaged to work part-time) in almost every city in the country with a population of more than 20,000 and in some other less populous locations. NBC did not engage in any news-gathering operation. We were alone in confronting the publishers and wire services. For three months the war continued. CBS went on to purchase the Dow Jones ticker service, which brought us news from Washington as well as from the financial centers. In England we bought the services of the Exchange Telegraph, and the Central News Agency for coverage of Europe, Asia, Africa, and parts of South America.

Dispatches flowed into our newsroom. Paul White and his staff prepared three news programs each day, two five-minute newscasts and one fifteen-minute summary. White did so well that on occasion we had news stories that the newspapers missed. We even received inquiries from some newspapers about the cost of buying our news service. We had become competitive.

The newspaper publishers became even more angered. They must have begun also to worry about a new competing news service. On one occasion, Kent Cooper, general manager of the Associated Press and one of the most eminent newsmen in America, came to see me and tried to frighten me into making peace with the publishers. From his august perch atop the news media, he predicted dire consequences for CBS if we did not agree to limit the amount of news we would broadcast in competition with the newspapers and wire services. I recognized the greater facilities and the greater access to news of the three wire services and all the 1,800 newspapers in the United States, but I did not like to be threatened. And told him so. Frank B. Noyes, president of the Associated Press and president of the Washington *Evening Star*, was one of the publishers who carried out the threat of dropping the listings of CBS programs from his newspaper, while carrying the listings of NBC. The publishers then threatened through their National Radio Committee to carry on their fight against radio incursions into the news field in Congress, which was then beginning to consider the provisions of a federal communications act.

During the year, I had conferred several times with David Sarnoff, president of RCA and with M. H. Aylesworth, president of NBC, and we decided in November 1933 to meet with representatives of the press to discuss ways in which we in radio could live in peace with the newspaper publishers. In December, I met with Roy Howard, chairman of the Scripps-Howard chain, who agreed to act as an intermediary. Two days later, Aylesworth and I met with Associated Press's Kent Cooper and United Press's Karl Bickel, and we laid the groundwork for a press-radio peace meeting, which was held at the Hotel Biltmore in New York on December 11, 1933. There representatives of CBS, NBC, and the National Association of Broadcasters (representing local stations) met with the chieftains of the three wire news services and such newspapers as the Des Moines *Register* and *Tribune,* the Nashville *Banner,* the New York *Sun,* and the Hearst and Scripps-Howard chains.

We negotiated long and hard. The publishers wanted to get CBS out of the news-gathering field and they wanted to limit radio to announcing brief news items supplied by the newspapers through the wire services. Furthermore, they insisted that the news supplied to radio should not be used in competition with the newspapers. That is, they wanted radio news summaries to be broadcast only after the publication of the morning and afternoon papers.

I insisted with equal vehemence that radio was not invented as a service to hold things back: radio's function was to bring news and public events to the public faster than any other medium because it was able to do just that. Speaking for NBC as well as CBS, I argued that we had an obligation to broadcast news as fast as we got it.

The result of all this was a compromise, which came to be

called "the Biltmore Agreement." We agreed on behalf of radio to drop our own news-gathering facilities, including the Columbia News Service, and in exchange, the publishers agreed to set up a special radio news bureau that would cull the news from the three wire services and send radio networks and stations two five-minute news summaries each day. We agreed to air the two news programs only at 9:30 in the morning and 9:00 in the evening. In return, they agreed to send us flash bulletins of news of "transcendent importance" for immediate broadcast. We agreed not to sell advertising for the two news-summary programs, but they agreed that we could find sponsors for our news commentaries.

The agreement was a trade-off and it accomplished its one immediate purpose of bringing peace in the family of newspapers and radio news coverage. The broadcasting of live news was not mentioned at all. That was our own exclusive field and not negotiable. It was also tacitly understood that the newspapers would continue to carry the listings of radio program schedules.

What the Press-Radio Bureau agreed upon did not come into being until the following year, on March 1, 1934, and by that year, no one was paying much attention to any of the provisions of the so-called agreement. The number of flash bulletins had increased dramatically. Almost all spot news was being supplied to the radio stations as news of "transcendent importance." Radio commentators again began to use spot news in their analyses and commentaries. Then other competing radio news agencies arose to sell their services to disgruntled radio stations, so that in 1935, the UP and the INS joined in the competition to sell news to radio stations. For all intents and purposes, the Biltmore Agreement was dead. The time schedules for radio news summaries fell by the wayside and even the stations which subscribed to the Press-Radio Bureau were able to broadcast news summaries as early as 8 A.M. and 6 P.M. In short, none of the restrictions imposed upon radio worked for very long. In the end, radio could not be held back from performing its vital role in bringing the news to listeners faster than any other medium.

I wondered afterward about the wisdom of my decision to abandon the Columbia News Service. But one cannot know the road untraveled. CBS might have had an earlier lead in developing its own news-gathering prowess. But at the time, we really did not have a need for such a large organization to put together the short news summaries customary at that time. When the need arose in later years, CBS moved on its own without hesitation to gather and to broadcast news from around the world.

The ultimate, long-range effect of that press-radio war of the thirties was the demonstration and proof that fledgling radio could stand up to the newspaper barons of the day. The two major networks, CBS and NBC, came head-to-head against the dominant newspaper and wire services and, despite some lingering bitterness, radio (and later television) won recognition as full-fledged members of the Fourth Estate, co-equal with newspapers in the dissemination of the news. Radio would never be controlled or dominated by the print media.

Live News

On the day the German Nazi Army marched unresisted into Austria, March 11, 1938—the prelude to World War II—I was home in New York with a cold and a fever. Ed Klauber telephoned to tell me that Vienna had refused us the use of its facilities to broadcast from that city. I thought of the director general of the Austrian broadcasting service, whom I had met several times in Vienna, and remembered that we had had a rather pleasant working relationship. Not quite realizing just how bad things might be, I reacted as I often do when a problem arises. I picked up the telephone.

The overseas operator put me through without difficulty to Vienna to my friend, the broadcasting director general. I told him how distressing it was that his organization was not allowing us the use of the facilities we needed to broadcast from there. In a tearful voice he broke in to say, "I am sorry, Mr. Paley, I am no longer in charge here. I cannot do anything . . . I would if I could." There was a sob and then a click. The connection was broken and he was gone.

I thought about it for a while and realized that every capital in Europe must be seething in reaction to Hitler's takeover of Austria. Whether or not we could hear from captured Vienna, it would be interesting if we could switch from one capital to the other and give reports from all. But was it technically feasible? I called Klauber and asked him to put it up to the engineers. Their first reaction was gloomy—it couldn't be done. I insisted that there must be some way. Within an hour, Klauber called back to say that it would be a very tricky operation, but it probably could worked out. I urged him to proceed with haste.

At the time, CBS had a staff in Europe consisting of two men: Edward R. Murrow and William L. Shirer. Neither of them at the time was really a broadcast newsman. Murrow had been hired by CBS in September 1935 as "Director of Talks" and his job was to arrange for personalities to give informative talks over the network. When I first met him, I was so impressed with him— he was such a sober, earnest young man at twenty-seven with that elongated, somber face—that I wrote a memo to Ed Klauber, who had hired him: "Mr. Murrow might be the best one in this organization to be responsible for all of our international broadcasting." We needed such a man, for our broadcasts from Europe were on the rise. A year and a half later, in 1937, we assigned him to London as our European director. I had great faith in him. But when he came into my office for a talk on the day before he left for Europe, I had no idea that this assignment would set in motion the career of the greatest broadcasting journalist of his generation.

He was the head of our foreign staff, a staff of one. When we wanted to expand it in the summer of 1937, Murrow showed his gift for recognizing the talents of others by engaging William L. Shirer, an experienced foreign correspondent for newspapers, who had broadcast occasionally for CBS. Shirer's regular assignment, from a base in Vienna, like Murrow's from his base in London, was to arrange broadcasts and do interviews. On March 10, 1938, both happened to be away—Murrow in Poland and Shirer in Yugoslavia—arranging musical broadcasts for segments of the *American School of the Air*.

Fortunately, Shirer, who years later was to write *The Rise and*

Fall of the Third Reich, the definitive book on the subject, got back to Vienna the next day, to witness Germany's invasion and takeover of Austria. The only broadcaster on the scene, Shirer tried to get on the air to New York, but Nazi soldiers escorted him out of the broadcast studios with bayonets.

He reached Murrow in Warsaw and explained that broadcasting in Austria was shut down. Murrow, having been in touch with Paul White in New York, suggested that Shirer fly to London and go on the air from there with an eyewitness account of what had happened. Murrow would head for Vienna.

The day after the takeover, Shirer went on the air for CBS from the BBC studios in London and reported in personal, telling detail:

> Austria's resistance to Nazi Socialism actually collapsed at 6:15 P.M. yesterday when it was announced on the radio that the plebiscite had been indefinitely postponed. . . . When the radio announcement came over the loudspeaker, the Fatherland Front people and the workers melted away and stole home as best they could. On the other hand, it was the signal for the Nazis to come out and capture the streets of the capital. And yet, as late as 6:00 P.M., the picture had been quite different. I was walking across a large square just a block from the Opera, at six, just as two lone policemen were driving a crowd of 500 Nazis off the square without the slightest difficulty. A half hour later you would not have recognized Vienna as being the same city.
>
> With the announcement that the plebiscite was off, the Nazis suddenly poured by tens of thousands into the old inner city. . . . I saw a strange sight: twenty men, bent down, formed a human pyramid, and a little man—I suppose he was picked for his weight—scampered over a lot of shoulders and, clutching a huge swastika flag, climbed to the balcony of the Chancellory.

By the next day, in line with my instructions for a European news roundup, Murrow and Shirer had recruited American newspaper correspondents in Paris, Rome, and Berlin. Murrow had

Babe and I starting our honeymoon trip to Europe.

It was always funny with Burns and Allen and the Jack Bennys.

With Amos 'n' Andy (Freeman Gosden, left, and Charles Correll, right).

Edgar Bergen and Charlie McCarthy.

Hubbell Robinson headed
TV programming.

Lucy and Desi.

Frank White and Ed Wallerstein found long-playing records stacked up well against the same music on old-fashioned discs.

The Materials Policy Commission submits its report to President Truman.

Secretary of War Robert Patterson giving me the Medal for Merit.

Stokowski conducts.

Election Night 1956 with Walter Cronkite.

Alistair Cooke, when *Omnibus* was on the air.

Edward R. Murrow's inaugural *See It Now* broadcast in 1951 gave the audience a simultaneous look at both the Pacific and Atlantic coasts, marking a new era in television.

With our early color camera.

Faye Emerson and Arthur Godfrey.

When Television City opened, Frank Stanton and I surveyed the scene.

persuaded German authorities to open a line for him from Vienna, and our CBS engineers had managed the technicalities involved. So, at 8 P.M. on March 13, 1938, two days after the event, CBS broadcast its first round robin of European news and commentary on the Nazi invasion of Austria. We called it the *CBS European Roundup*. Pierre Huss of the International News Service reported from Berlin; Edgar Ansel Mowrer of the Chicago *Daily News* from Paris; Shirer, and Ellen Wilkinson, a member of Parliament, from London; Murrow from Vienna. Shirer also read a report from Frank Gervasi of INS in Rome. From Washington, D.C., Senator Lewis B. Schwellenbach of Washington commented from the American point of view.

In the CBS studio in New York, Robert Trout played a role which has since become familiar but was then unknown. Trout was a remarkable extemporaneous broadcaster. He belonged to that small group who could talk in front of a microphone without notes for twenty, thirty, sixty minutes, two hours, without stopping. H. V. Kaltenborn could do the same and then comment on and analyze what he had said. In that *European Roundup*, Trout may have been the first anchorman in the profession.

Ed Murrow's broadcast that night from Vienna, his first solo performance as a newsman, gave a hint of the unique sensibilities he would put to use throughout the coming war:

> This is Edward Murrow speaking from Vienna. It's now nearly 2:30 in the morning and Herr Hitler has not yet arrived. . . . From the air, Vienna didn't look much different than it has before, but, nevertheless, it's changed. The crowds are courteous as they've always been, but many people are in holiday mood; they lift the right arm a little higher here than in Berlin and the 'Heil Hitler' is said a little more loudly. There isn't a great deal of hilarity, but at the same time there doesn't seem to be much feeling of tension. Young storm troopers are riding about the streets, riding about in trucks and vehicles of all sorts, singing and tossing oranges out to the crowd. Nearly every principal building has its armed guard, including the one from which I am speaking. There

are still huge crowds along the Ringstrasse and people still stand outside the principal hotels, just waiting and watching for some famous man to come in or out. As I said, everything is quiet in Vienna tonight. There's a certain air of expectancy about the city, everyone waiting and wondering where and at what time Herr Hitler will arrive.

For the time, it was an extraordinary feat of logistics and planning. Each correspondent reported live, some thousands of miles away from each other and each of their reports had to be scheduled precisely to the second. It would not be long before we would be able to have such widely scattered correspondents talk to one another on the air. In 1938 this new technique was immediately recognized as an unusual event in news. We put it on again the very next night with a somewhat different cast of correspondents. By bringing together in one program an anchorman at studio headquarters and correspondents on location, we were doing something that would become the important format of modern news broadcasting. The *European Roundup* became the *World News Roundup*, which is still on the air at 8 A.M. Eastern Standard Time, Monday through Friday.

It was six months from the Austrian invasion to the Munich crisis. In that period, Murrow and Shirer, who now formed the nucleus of a growing CBS foreign news-gathering organization, cabled dispatches to our newsroom in New York, drew upon the services of newspaper correspondents, gave their own broadcasts, and arranged broadcasts by participants in events. Hitler's demands on Czechoslovakia and the threat of imminent war that September gripped the attention of the American public as had no other foreign event. For the next eighteen days—to the signing of the Munich Pact by Hitler and Britain's Prime Minister Chamberlain on September 30—CBS was immersed in the crisis day and night. I was either at the studio or constantly listening from wherever I might be.

Live news and on-the-spot broadcasting made their mark. I was so excited that I sent Murrow and Shirer this cable: "Columbia's coverage of the European crisis is superior to its competitors and is probably the best job of its kind ever done in radio broadcasting."

CBS presented more than a hundred special broadcasts on the Munich crisis from Europe, particularly from London, Prague, Paris, and Berlin, but also from Rome, Geneva, Godesberg, Munich, Nuremberg, Trieste, Stratford-upon-Avon, Warsaw, and Budapest. The use of numbers to describe something can be boring but they convey briefly the ferment at CBS. About sixty members of a small home-office staff threw themselves into work on the news. Despite the technical and programming intricacies, we put on fourteen *European Roundups* during the eighteen days of the Munich crisis. Kaltenborn himself broadcast about a hundred analyses of the situation, a tour de force that made him famous. He seemed to live at our Studio 9 in our Madison Avenue headquarters. Altogether, with the numerous spot bulletins, the news summaries, the commentaries, and the analyses, CBS put on a total of nearly five hundred broadcasts on Munich in less than three weeks.

Still, at this time, CBS had a foreign news staff of only three men, Murrow, Shirer, and Thomas Grandin, whom we had engaged in 1938 and stationed in Paris. On a temporary basis we hired a number of stringers—correspondents of European and American newspapers and wire services—in foreign capitals, who were on call to broadcast for CBS on special occasions. It was just good enough for emergencies of the moment but in the event of war we were understaffed and weakly organized. By mid-1939, Czechoslovakia had fallen, Albania had been invaded, and both Germany and Italy were flaunting their further aggressive intentions. An all-European war was a distinct possibility. Yet, to many Americans, peace still seemed more likely. Quite apart from personal considerations, from a management point of view it was important for us to have an opinion: Would there be war? Or would there be peace? Should CBS enlarge its permanent news organization in Europe? In July 1939, we sent Paul White to London to assess the situation.

White reported back uncertainty about the imminence of war, but he recommended in a letter the addition of one more foreign staff member "to be taken into this office as soon as possible, and trained not only for substitute work here (in London) in the event of a crisis, but also for a European post with us in the event that no crisis arises or the war becomes postponed indefinitely."

On July 26, Ed Murrow wrote to Ed Klauber from London: "I think that such plans as can be made have been made for covering the next crisis, which I remain convinced will not result in war." The upshot of this uncertainty about the war was that in August we added one new correspondent to our foreign staff. Ed Murrow persuaded a twenty-six-year-old, hard-working newsman, Eric Sevareid, to join CBS. Sevareid at the time was holding down two jobs: city editor of the Paris edition of the *Herald Tribune* and night editor of the United Press in Paris.

Back in New York, we added two distinguished journalists to our staff of news analysts. One was Major George Fielding Eliot, who had served in both the Australian infantry and the American Army and had gone on to write books and lecture on military topics. The other was Elmer Davis, a Rhodes scholar and free-lance writer who had met Ed Klauber when both had worked for the New York *Times*. Klauber and Paul White lured Davis to CBS to pinch-hit for Kaltenborn who was off on a three-week trip to Europe and to take on a special, new five-minute nightly news broadcast from 8:55 to 9:00 P.M. Davis came aboard and stayed with CBS for three years, until June 1942, when he was chosen by the government to head the newly created Office of War Information.* Thus before the war started, we had in White,

---

* Elmer Davis' inimitable style as a writer and a man can be discerned from this very nice, handwritten note he sent:
"Dear Bill—
In the hustle of departure I failed to express adequately my real regret at leaving Columbia. Not only did you give me the nation-wide audience that made this transition possible (I will tell you a year from now whether that was a favor or not) but I always found Columbia a good place to work. It has always been my good fortune to work for civilized employers but Columbia was the most pleasant of the lot. With considerable apprehension I leave a job I know I could do for one which I may not be able to do at all, looking backward at what will presently seem a lost Paradise."

Murrow, Shirer, Sevareid, Kaltenborn, Eliot, Davis, and Grandin, the foundation of one of the most distinguished news organizations ever assembled by any branch of the media.

We also established a short-wave listening station on Long Island to pick up broadcasts from Europe. That facility enabled CBS to put overseas news on the air quickly. Oftentimes, we broadcast news which was picked up by the American newspapers and wire services who had so disdained us in earlier years. These arrangements to enlarge our news staff were made none too soon.

The Stalin-Hitler Pact was announced on August 21 and by the end of the month, war was at hand. Germany invaded Poland on the night of August 31. Britain and France mobilized. There was a pause of two days. We reported the mobilization in detail, and, along with the whole world, waited for the response of Britain and France. On September 3, 1939, from London, Murrow reported the start of World War II:

> Forty-five minutes ago the Prime Minister stated that a state of war existed between Britain and Germany. Air raid instructions were immediately broadcast, and almost directly following that broadcast air raid warning sirens screamed through the quiet calm of this Sabbath morning. There were planes in the sky. Whose, we couldn't be sure. Now we're sitting quite comfortably underground. We're told that the "all clear" signal has been sounded in the streets, but it's not yet been heard in this building.
>
> In a few minutes we shall hope to go up into the sunlight and see what has happened. It may have been only a rehearsal. London may not have been the objective—and may have been.
>
> I have just been informed that upstairs in the sunlight everything is normal, that cars are traveling though the streets. There are people walking in the streets and taxis are cruising about as usual.

The crowd outside Downing Street received the first news of war with a rousing cheer, and they heard that news through a radio in a car parked near Downing Street.

The responsibilities of reporting a war were enormous. As the intermittent alarms came in faster and faster, the spot bulletins and special events of broadcasting became general news. We emerged transformed. In late 1939 and through 1940 and 1941, while the war abroad hung like a shadow over the United States, our newsroom and the studio next to it became the most intensely active and growing places in our broadcasting organization. We continued to expand staff and facilities. Our newsmen worked with a passion almost around the clock. Copy flowed like a deluge into our newsroom from three main sources: our own correspondents at home and abroad, the newspaper wire services, and our short-wave listening post, which received broadcasts from a mélange of foreign sources. Our home-office staff distilled and prepared newscasts, which we broadcast day and night in regular summaries, bulletins, analyses, and in roundups.

Both abroad and at home our news staff grew rapidly. From the *ad hoc* organization of stringers and the permanent staff of four foreign correspondents on September 1, 1939, we jumped to fourteen regular foreign correspondents by the end of the year, to thirty-nine in 1940, and to more than sixty in 1941. In a short time, CBS News became one of the three or four outstanding foreign news organizations in the United States, in both numbers and quality. The new strength of our domestic news organization also became evident when, in 1940, we sent thirty-four staffers to the political conventions. Among the personalities in CBS News not already mentioned, some forgotten now, some still famous, but all distinguished, were—I like to mention their names—Mary Marvin Breckinridge, Cecil Brown, Winston Burdett, Charles Collingwood, William J. Dunn, Erland Echlin, Harry W. Flannery, Farnsworth Fowle, Bill Henry, Russell Hill, Larry LeSueur, Howard K. Smith, Betty Wason, Leigh White, and William L. White.

Much has been written about the journalistic accomplishments of the members of CBS News in the war, and the routes they traveled and the hazards they faced to get the news home. We sent Bill Shirer to Germany and, to his extreme distaste, upon the fall of France, he entered his beloved Paris with the German Army. Ed Murrow, chief of our foreign correspondents, held the United States in thrall with his broadcasts of the Battle of Britain. His very personal manner of speaking, punctuated by the everyday sounds from the streets and the explosion of bombs, became in the United States the best-known and most respected broadcast voice of the war.

There was no substantial public issue about the rapid buildup of American forces for national defense, but throughout the country there was a conflict of opinion about American involvement in the war. For me, as chief executive of CBS, the dilemma was how the network should handle the great debate. We had long-standing policies in both news and public affairs: unbiased news and the presentation of opposing opinions of representative public figures. Radio, like television, is a particularly sensitive medium. Like the press, we use our editorial judgment in the selection and presentation of news. But unlike the press, radio, being a medium of sound, can carry emotion and the bewitchment of live personality.

These were delicate matters at the outset of the war in Europe. Two days after Britain declared war on Germany, I had Klauber issue a memorandum to the CBS organization reiterating our standing editorial policies—a position adopted afterward by the other networks and by the National Association of Broadcasters. I insisted that as an organization CBS had to be thoroughly objective in reporting the war: we would be fair and factual; we would maintain a calm manner at the microphone; the sound of a newscaster's voice would not betray any subconscious emotions or prejudices. There was no great difficulty in carrying out these directives in straight news or in public affairs, despite the subjective element in the selection, writing, and presentation of news, common to all journalism. I merely emphasized the need to try consciously to avoid bias.

When President Roosevelt proposed revision of the Neutrality Act, we broadcast his address and then provided a free forum for one of the most extended debates ever heard on a radio network. We presented thirty-four speakers with different points of view in the five weeks before Congress voted on the Neutrality Act.

We took no position on the issue, not because as citizens we had no opinions, but because we believed the overwhelming need of the public was to be given the basic information on which to make its own choices. Certainly, with the issues of war and peace to be decided, the personal opinions of broadcasting journalists had no place on the air. Their work was to provide objective information for others. The professional reporter would be checked by the questions of a professional editor, except when his broadcast was live and checking was impossible.

For each distinguished correspondent whose name the public has learned, there have been unknown editors and producers who have asked hard questions of the reporter himself. Our journalistic strength comes not only from our correspondents, but also from the producers and managers who constantly oversee this whole editorial process.

In the field of news analysis, however, it was more difficult to enforce such policies. It was not easy at times to know where to draw the line between analysis and personal opinion. None of our wartime analysts—H. V. Kaltenborn, Elmer Davis, George Fielding Eliot—disagreed with me on policy. Indeed, Elmer Davis, in an article in *Harper's* in November 1939, and later before a congressional committee, brilliantly explained and defended our policy. Each did, however, step over the line of objectivity on occasion, and at one time or another I had to take a stand.

In the early summer of 1940 I was called by James Forrestal, one of Roosevelt's aides (and an old golfing friend), and asked if I would take a new government post, Coordinator of Inter-American Affairs. I told him that I wasn't right for the job but that I knew someone who was. I recommended Nelson Rockefeller, whom I had come to know through our work at the Museum of Modern Art. I was aware that Nelson had business interests in South America and spoke Spanish, and had some feeling for the people there. Forrestal called Rockefeller, who accepted the post, an event of no small importance, for it was the beginning of his career in politics.

A few months later, I received another request from the government. This one came from the President himself, and so I could hardly refuse. While I was having lunch in Washington with Jesse Jones, the Secretary of Commerce, an aide handed him a note. He turned to me and said, "Bill, are you supposed to be having lunch with the President today?" I said no, and he told his aide, "Some mistake. Just call back and say no. A few moments later the aide reappeared and announced, "Mr. Secretary, the President is in his office waiting for Mr. Paley to join him for lunch." Jones firmly declared to me, "You must be mistaken. You have a date with the President." I knew I hadn't, but obviously I had been commanded. I was whisked by limousine into the White House grounds, nudged through a couple of doors and found myself standing before Franklin Roosevelt.

"Bill, sit down. I've been waiting for you," he said. A metal box on wheels was rolled into his office and placed beside him at his desk. From it, he took out our lunch, handing my plate to me and placing his on the desk in front of him. He said he had heard I was in Washington and wanted to see me.

The President was gracious, charming and serious, all at the same time. He remarked that he had learned that I was contemplating a trip to South America in order to extend the CBS network to that area. I explained that I was planning such a trip but that plans for short-wave broadcasting to Latin America were still in the formative stage. The President talked of his concern over Nazi propaganda and its influence over radio stations in Latin America. Our country ought to do something to counteract that Nazi influence, he said, adding that he would appreciate it if I would take on that assignment.

Such a request from a President, particularly in times of emergency, is a moving thing. I promised I would do what I could and would report to him.

After a quick exchange of letters with the President, I left for a seven-week swing on November 8, 1940, through the major nations of South and Central America, accompanied by Mrs. Paley, Paul White, and Edmund Chester, our Spanish-speaking director of short-wave broadcasting activities. We returned to the United States with contracts with the most important stations in just about every country we visited—sixty-four stations in all, a Latin American network! The contracts provided that CBS would beam to Latin America our entertainment, cultural, and news programs in Spanish and Portuguese. Sustaining programs would be provided free and sponsored programs, if any, would provide a share of the advertising money to the stations broadcasting the programs. All in all, it was quite an exciting and adventuresome trip in which I met heads of states as well as the owners and directors of radio stations.

I gave President Roosevelt a detailed report and analysis on what my staff and I had learned about the influence of Nazi Germany in each of the countries I visited.† I surmised (and accepted the probability early on) that if we entered the war, the U. S. Government would take over our new Latin American network as part of the war effort. And, of course, that is what happened. Because of wartime delays in the delivery of material for our two new short-wave transmitters on Long Island, our broadcasting to Latin America did not start until May 1942. Six months later, the government requisitioned the network and began sending its own broadcasts south of the border. The man in charge of the operation was Nelson Rockefeller, the Coordinator of Inter-American Affairs.

On December 7, 1941, I was up at Kiluna Farm for the weekend, talking with one of our weekend guests, Ben Hecht, the writer, when someone rushed into the room, shouting that Pearl Harbor had been attacked by the Japanese. I turned on the radio for the news and then (taking Hecht into town, too) drove to the

† I gave an abbreviated similar report to the American people in an article I wrote for the April 1941 issue of *Fortune* magazine.

CBS headquarters. There was nothing much I could do that night except, like Americans throughout the country, listen to the radio.

The next day, Ed Murrow, on leave from London, came into the office and told me he had met with the President at the White House the night before, hours after the news of the attack on Pearl Harbor! Murrow had had an appointment with Roosevelt for that evening, but after the news of Pearl Harbor had been broadcast, he had telephoned the White House on the assumption that his appointment would be canceled. But no, he was told, the President still wished to see him, if he would be willing to wait until the President finished his work. Murrow waited hours in the residential quarters of the White House. It was after midnight when he was called in to see the President. He described President Roosevelt on that night of Pearl Harbor as being very well composed, serious and eager to learn what Murrow could tell him of the events, personalities, and atmosphere of the European theater of war. Murrow was amazed that on that day of days, the President of the United States would take the time to keep an appointment with him. But to me it reflected the high esteem in which Ed Murrow was held in the White House and throughout the nation. The previous week I had given a dinner to honor Murrow for his wartime broadcasts from bombarded London and it seemed that almost every eminent American pressed us for an invitation. The guest list grew to one thousand. Edward R. Murrow had become a national hero, our most famous war correspondent, for he had been America's eyewitness to Britain's "finest hour." After Pearl Harbor, he was most anxious to get back to London.

When our country declared war on the Axis powers, CBS, like every other institution in the United States, converted itself in its own way to a total war effort. We adopted war themes on many of our programs. In dramatic shows, characters met wartime problems; the *American School of the Air* brought war news, information, and instruction to children; *Country Journal* gave farmers help in solving wartime agricultural problems; *The Garden Gate* promoted Victory gardens; *Church of the Air* broadcast talks by chaplains. There were new series exclusively about the war: *They Live Forever, The Man Behind the Gun, Our Secret Weapon.* Kate Smith conducted War Bond drives. Some of our company-owned stations went on a twenty-four-hour-a-day schedule, serving as part of an air raid defense system and also providing entertainment for defense workers on the overnight "swing shift."

Some of our most difficult problems lay in the presentation of the news. From day to day and hour to hour, the news took on immediate and personal meaning for almost every American. Consequently, while the journalists' responsibilities for accuracy and completeness had not changed, the weight of these responsibilities had increased enormously. We accepted government restrictions on news that would affect the military—troop movements, new inventions, movements of merchant vessels, and the like—to avoid giving vital information to the enemy. It was more difficult to draw the line on controversial subjects which the public had a right to know.

News reports would affect American public opinion and could have an important influence on the war effort. There were legitimate differences of opinion, for instance, about the division of the war effort between the Far East and Europe, about the British, about the "Second Front" to relieve the Russians, and so on. We had to strike a balance between serving the cause of our war effort and maintaining objectivity in our news reports. About this time, I decided that as head of CBS I had better make a wartime visit to London and get a closer perspective on the war.

In late August 1942, I flew to London by Pan American Clipper, a journey then of many hours, in the pleasant company of my Kiluna Farm neighbor and future brother-in-law, John Hay Whitney. Jock was in the Army Air Force and was being transferred to London. From all reports, especially those of Ed Murrow, I knew that I would meet people who, though ravaged by raids from the air, had come through with a quality of perseverance seldom matched in human history. I had also heard but not yet realized how normally and casually, at least on the surface, they went about their business, even pleasure, while under fire.

I was met by a friend, Randolph Churchill, son of Britain's Prime Minister. He had come into my life in the early thirties on one of my trips to England, and we met thereafter in England or in New York from time to time. I was delighted to see him and his wife, Pam (now Mrs. Averell Harriman). On my first night in London, they took me out to dinner and to a nightclub afterward—a reception characteristic of these English even in a war-torn capital. Late that first night, I met Jock again and we walked home together along dark streets to Claridge's, traditionally the "American hotel" in London. General George C. Marshall, United States Chief of Staff, and Harry Hopkins, representing President Roosevelt, had stayed there shortly before we did, and one had the feeling of walking through history.

The next morning I received an invitation to lunch with Dwight D. Eisenhower, who had just been appointed Commander-in-Chief of the Allied Expeditionary Force, in anticipation of the invasion. The appointment was still a secret at the time. It was simply a get-acquainted meeting at his flat at the Dorchester Hotel. We had a mutual associate in Harry Butcher, who had been a CBS vice-president before the war, in charge of our Washington office, and who spent most of the war as Eisenhower's Naval Aide and confidant, sitting in on everything that concerned the General, guiding his relations with the press and broadcasting. He, in fact, kept a diary of events for Eisenhower.

The first meeting with Eisenhower was pleasant, casual, and, I think, a time-out period of relaxation for a man who carried such heavy responsibilities upon his shoulders. Nothing was said, for instance, about General Marshall's recent visit to London which resulted, I found out later, in a major change in war plans. (They had decided to attack the "underbelly" of Europe through North Africa first, rather than conduct a direct invasion across the Channel.) Instead, General Eisenhower and General Carl (Tooey) Spaatz, commander of the U. S. Eighth Air Force, who made a fourth at the lunch aside from Harry Butcher, inducted me into the realm of "short snorters," a special "society" of air travelers who had crossed the Atlantic. You became a short snorter by having another person sign and date one of your dollar bills, and you did the same to his bill, after which you were obliged to carry that bill with you always. If you were challenged and failed to produce your signed dollar bill, you were fined a dollar. So, they signed my bill and I signed theirs, and became a short snorter.

The two generals impressed me. Behind their genial horseplay, they showed strong character and seriousness of purpose in the deadly business of war. I soon thought of Eisenhower as one of the most engaging men I had ever known. Later I was to learn that he was far more effective in small groups than in addressing large audiences. At any rate, at the time I certainly appreciated the General's hospitality. It was the start of a long friendship.

The British themselves extended to me hospitality such as I had never received before. With their nation's survival at stake, they felt a friendliness for their American allies which was extraordinary. British friends and acquaintances of mine fostered this atmosphere by giving small, intimate dinner parties where people got to know one another personally. What with lunch and dinner engagements every day, the giving and receiving of interviews, and work at the office, I was kept busy. For me there was also a long-standing personal attraction to London. I had friends there, like Alfred Duff Cooper (Viscount Norwich), the writer and diplomat, who had been Minister of Information in the first years of the war. Duff was a short, solid, strong man, highly educated and cultured, with a temper that was truly terrifying when out of control. His wife, Diana, was a great beauty. Their son had lived with us at Kiluna Farm since the war had started. They expressed their appreciation by giving a small dinner party for me in a private dining room at the Dorchester. The guests included Prime Minister Churchill and his wife, Clementine; Brendan Bracken, who was then Minister of Information in Churchill's Cabinet; Ronald Tree, an M.P. and cabinet adviser on American affairs, and his then wife, Nancy; and a few others —about ten in all.

I came to the party with a memory of having met Churchill once before in the mid-thirties, at which time he was looked upon as a rebel and was in disfavor with the Establishment. Randolph had invited my wife, Dorothy, and me to a weekend of golf at Chartwell, his father's country place, and I had sat silently then as a young man through a long lunch listening to Churchill complain about the lack of military preparedness in England. So, when I came to the Duff Coopers' party that night in 1942, I was eager to see Churchill again, now at the height of his political and personal powers.

He truly was a great human being. The public and the private man were one and the same; vision and reality came together in a single truth. Churchill had about him that rare quality of personal grandeur, not only upon the world stage but at the dinner table. The legend of his fabulous capacity for drinking, I think, has been exaggerated. At political and military meetings, I have been told, he drank hardly at all and only chewed the end of a long cigar. But when he relaxed in the evening, he relaxed according to legend: cocktails, wine through dinner, champagne after, then brandy. But he scarcely showed it. His was a tongue that hardly needed loosening.

He was at his best that night, even a bit euphoric, and with good reason. Recently returned from Cairo and the front at El Alamein, he talked about the war at the eastern end of North Africa. He described how the British had been in retreat but had stopped Rommel at the El Alamein line. Only later did I realize that while he talked about East Africa he said nothing about "Torch"—the code name for the forthcoming Allied invasion of North Africa which was at that time top secret. Although he had just been to Moscow to tell Stalin the Second Front was off and "Torch" was on, he said nothing about it.

The guests took turns expressing their views. I listened, saying little, content to learn and observe. It did not occur to me that I would be expected to perform. It was about half-past eleven and for some time I had had a need to visit the men's room. But no one else had left the table and so I sat there, very uncomfortable. Then the Prime Minister turned to me and said, "Mr. Paley, you have just come from New York. We would like very much to have you tell us what the attitude in America is toward the war in Europe and toward us in particular. Anything you could tell us would be greatly appreciated."

That was certainly a key question in every Briton's mind. However, the first priority on my mind was how to find the men's room. And so I answered him, saying, "Mr. Prime Minister, if you'll excuse me for a minute, I'd be glad to answer your question." I got up, left the table, and went to the room I needed so badly. Upon coming back, I was jittery. One did not address the Prime Minister of Great Britain—at least I didn't—without a certain degree of nervousness. I hoped that the party had gone on to some other subject and that I'd been forgotten. Not at all. Not a word was being said at the table. When I sat down Churchill looked at me and said, "Well, go ahead, Mr. Paley."

I gave my interpretation of the current attitudes of Americans toward England. Churchill may have been worried about some anti-British feeling in the United States, and perhaps about whether the pre-war isolationist sentiment in America still lingered toward Europe. To the best of my ability, I summed up the opinions of various American groups, even of the "America Firsters" who had been so prominent on the isolationist side. I explained that there were still some people who felt that the United States should not have gotten involved in the European war. But, I said, the vast majority of Americans, including some ardent isolationists, were now very much in favor of our war efforts to help destroy Hitler.

During that evening, I had another head-on encounter with the redoubtable Churchill, which will ever remain in my memory. Being a new and eager "short snorter," I had inducted Duff Cooper and, much to my surprise, he immediately turned around and challenged Churchill. The Prime Minister truly snorted that of course he was a short snorter. He implied he had invented it. But he failed to produce his bill. He also refused to pay the fine. He insisted he could not be challenged on the ground, only in the air. My host appealed to me and I felt honor-bound to disagree with the Prime Minister.

"Well, sir, I hate to contradict you, but I was inducted recently into the society and I understand that you could challenge another member at any place, on land, sea, or in the air."

"Not true," said Churchill. "Who inducted you?"

"General Eisenhower and General Spaatz," I said.

"Oh, they said that, did they?" said he. "Well, they're wrong, they're wrong."

"Okay, they may be wrong, but here's *my* bill," said I, challenging him. "Just sign it, would you?"

"One isn't suppose to sign it on land," he persisted.

"Well, sign it anyway, won't you, please?"

So, he signed it, "Winston Churchill" and then with a baleful look at me, added "(*with reservations*)."

The morning after the Duff Coopers' party I heard that the story of my exit from the dinner table to the bathroom was being bruited about London. In the English tradition of supreme personal discipline, many of those who heard the story thought I should have remained at the table, no matter what. My host, Duff Cooper was of that opinion, much to my surprise.

When I saw Eisenhower again before leaving London, he asked if there was anything he could do for me. I told him the short-snorter story and suggested, I thought whimsically, that he lodge a plea with the Prime Minister concerning the dollar he owed me. A couple of weeks after I got back to New York I received a note from Averell Harriman, who was then stationed in London as the chief overseas administrator of Lend-Lease. Enclosed was a dollar bill, which Churchill had asked him to pass on to me. He explained that Churchill had been told by Eisenhower that he was wrong about the rules and that Churchill had said he was "paying up." I still have that short-snorter bill framed in my office.

British hospitality is a special genre, unduplicated anywhere else in the world. Although I had visited England many times before, it was on this wartime trip that I became more conscious than ever before of the understated qualities of the British national character, traditions, and sophistication. In some of the most formal, stately country homes and castles, owned by the same families for generations, if not hundreds of years, I came upon the most splendid furniture, furnishings and paintings, much of it of museum quality. In the best of these houses, everything was arranged in a sort of casual manner, rich but not ostentatious. The overall impression was one I would keep with me the rest of my life.

Ditchley, the country home of Ronnie and Nancy Tree, was for me at the time the most beautiful home I had seen in England. Ronnie, born in England of American parents, and Nancy, who came from Virginia, were fabulous hosts to me over many memorable weekends I spent at Ditchley during this trip and upon my returns to England later in the war. Apparently Winston Churchill agreed, for he spent almost every weekend during the war at Ditchley, rather than Chequers, the country estate which the government provided for the Prime Minister. One reason went beyond the magnificent hospitality: Ditchley was safer, for the Germans must have known the location of Chequers.

In the round of social engagements, I met Lord Louis Mountbatten, shortly before he was appointed Supreme Commander of Allied Forces in Southeast Asia; I conferred with U. S. Ambassador John G. Winant and with Averell Harriman; spent weekends at Lady Baillie's residence, called Leeds Castle; and one evening at Lord Beaverbrook's country house, Cherkley, in Surrey, less than an hour's drive from London. The evening was, like England itself, memorable.

Ed Murrow drove me to Beaverbrook's, warning me beforehand that the British press lord took particular pleasure in extracting indiscreet information from his guests by getting them as drunk as possible. At the dinner table, where among the guests were Lady Mountbatten and the author H. G. Wells, Lord Beaverbrook apparently decided to focus on me. When I declined his offer of wine, he asked, "Will you have some whiskey?" To that I agreed, and a bottle of scotch was brought to the table. He poured lavishly.

"I hope you will drink with me, sir," I said.

"Oh, I like scotch, too," he replied with a laugh.

So, we drank through dinner and then through most of the night. I was very careful to see that he drank at least as much as I did. And we traded stories. But I was not privy to any war secrets and could expound only on what I had read in the newspapers or heard on the radio. Beaverbrook, who had recently resigned as wartime Minister of Supply, and had just returned from a special mission, as a personal envoy of Churchill, fascinated the party with many tales of wartime diplomacy and the battle-front—quite indiscreetly. Very early the next morning, around six o'clock, his lordship, now completely sober, telephoned and solicitously asked if I had enjoyed the evening before.

"Oh, yes," I replied, "I couldn't have had a better time."

"Of course, we spoke very freely."

"Yes, we did," I admitted.

"Of course, everything we said was completely off the record, wasn't it?"

"Oh, completely," I assured him. "I wouldn't *think* of repeating it to anybody."

"That's fine," said he. "I appreciate that."

In London, I saw Ed Murrow every day and the more I was with him the more he impressed me. By nature, he was prone to see the worst side of things, a true pessimist, and yet, at the same time, he was inspired by some higher mission that overrode his inherent gloom. On the air and off, he was the soul of integrity. He was fearless, strong-willed, and honor-bound by his convictions. It all came across in his wartime broadcasts. He radiated truth and concern. And America recognized and reacted to it.

In Britain, Murrow was Mr. U.S.A. He knew everyone of consequence in Britain's war effort and in government as well as numerous plain Londoners. Everybody who knew him trusted him. As a self-appointed guide to wartime London, he introduced me to all or almost all the British cabinet ministers, and afterward we would discuss our impression of what we learned. From him I learned of Eisenhower's concern over public opinion in England, including the manifold problems of introducing American troops into the compact British society. These discussions often took place at the Murrows' flat, not far from the CBS office on Hallam Street, with his wife, Janet, joining us.

As my admiration grew, I also worried about him. I tried to convince him that he was a damn fool to go out on so many night bombing missions over Germany. "You've done it and you know what the feel of it is. You can talk about it authoritatively. What do you have to gain to do it the second, third, fourth, or fifth time?"

He would always say, "Oh, I agree with you. I think it's silly and I won't do it any more." Then, a couple of nights later, I would find out that he'd gone on another bombing expedition over Berlin.

When I complained, he would say, "Oh, I'm sorry. But this was one I just couldn't resist."

He gave me the feeling that he had a death wish. Ed seemed unable to refrain from putting himself in danger. He did not want to report on danger without having experienced it himself. When describing the air raids over London, he would stand on top of a building and broadcast live. Bombs fell around him. Some dangers are a necessity for war correspondents; but nobody required Murrow to fly night bombing missions, one of the most dangerous activities in the war—except Ed Murrow himself. Such acts were part of his nature. He drove automobiles too fast. When he drove us to the country, he scared me to death. Not many people would drive with him. Close as we became, I never learned what it was that made him live so dangerously.

As a journalist Murrow was an astute observer and man of judgment. He guided me in a number of wartime broadcasting matters. Ed and Robert Foot, director general of the BBC, persuaded me to give a talk over BBC radio the day before I left London in September 1942.

We knew the British had a vital interest (reflected in Churchill's question to me at the Duff Coopers' dinner party) in understanding the American attitude toward their country. In my radio talk I reported that there was in fact "evidence of widespread and perhaps increasing anti-British sentiment" in the United States, a feeling, I surmised, that was partly ingrained, dating back to the Revolutionary War. I also reported that there might well be some anti-American feelings in Britain, although I had encountered none myself. The important thing, I declared, was that these differences be admitted and "talked about frankly as between friends," who were pursuing a common purpose.

As for rumors that relations were bad between American and British troops, I warned that such untrue stories were being spread by the Axis, and it was the duty of transatlantic broadcasters "to defeat and dispel these rumors" by reporting "fearlessly and accurately within the limits imposed by military security" the day-to-day happenings of the war, the broader issues and policies, and also the disagreements that would inevitably arise between the Allies. Better to air any real disagreements when they occurred, I said, than to suppress them and foster distrust and disunity.

On my return to New York, I faced a number of special concerns, such as the reorganization of the news department because of the hundreds of CBS employees who were leaving to join the military service. And Ed Klauber was lost to CBS as number-two executive. After suffering a heart attack, he retired in 1943. Upon his recovery he went to work for the Office of War Information. We had the good fortune to have Paul Kesten take his place. And of course there were many detailed problems in running CBS, both on the entertainment and news sides, on a wartime basis. It occurred to me, however, that in only a few years the war had transformed our once small and inexperienced news department into a large and mature organization, one with a heavy burden of responsibility. As the war expanded, CBS correspondents went east and they went west to the ends of the earth.

Overseas

From the air, Algiers was a lovely city of French-colonial-style buildings and gleaming white houses, shaped like a large amphitheater rising up around a busy harbor. Such was my first view of the city from the sky as we arrived there in November 1943, aboard an army transport plane. On the ground it was something else: dirty, dilapidated, bustling and bristling with Allied soldiers and French Moroccan troops. Eisenhower had had his headquarters in Algiers since his successful campaign in North Africa; Italy had been invaded through "the boot" and had surrendered two months earlier. The strike against Nazi Germany through its not very "soft underbelly" was under way. I was with the Army as a civilian consultant to the Office of War Information (and later to the Psychological Warfare Division) and wore the uniform of an honorary colonel.

As the war had moved ahead since my visit to England fourteen months earlier, I had become restless and anxious to get involved more directly in the war effort. That was where the action was. The world was at war, our cause was just, and I could not help but feel that I was outside of it all, on the sidelines, at CBS. Like everyone else—or almost everyone—on the sidelines, I felt a sense of duty to take part in this crusade against Naziism. I wanted a piece of the action; to contribute whatever talents I had which could be of use. After all, I was only forty-two and felt much younger. Luckily, a request for my services came from the Office of War Information through an old friend, playwright Robert Sherwood. In a few weeks, I cleaned out my desk at CBS and with a few words of general advice left the network in the capable hands of Paul Kesten.

My assignment was to supervise the establishment of Allied radio broadcasting activities in North Africa and Italy, a six-month assignment which I optimistically thought we could complete in three or four months. I went overseas as part of a psychological warfare unit, flying from New York to Miami to Brazil to Dakar on the west coast of Africa on to Marrakesh and then, finally to Algiers. There, our whole unit was put up in a sort of fleabag hotel, and we waited and waited. After a few days I began asking around for an apartment to rent and came upon a lieutenant who offered to share his with me. I saw it that afternoon, attractive, clean, just right—and I said it was a deal.

I had been sent to Algeria on the assumption that the Allies would soon occupy all of Italy, including Rome. My job then would be to reconstitute the Italian broadcasting system. Although Italy had surrendered in September, the Nazis had taken Rome and German resistance proved stronger than anticipated. (It would take another nine months before we could occupy Rome.) I inspected radio stations in North Africa, Sicily, and in parts of southern Italy where we had gained military control. I tried to improve the radio service in these areas by adding new programs, livening up old ones, and, in general, attracting larger audiences for the information and entertainment broadcasts that went on the air.

Nevertheless, Algiers was far removed from combat since the Germans had been driven out of North Africa. My major task was to have been in Italy, but there was no way I could venture much farther north than Naples until German resistance was broken. Then I learned that Eisenhower was moving his headquarters back to London to prepare for "Overlord," the cross-Channel invasion of France and the final strike against Germany. I was asked if I would head the entire psychological warfare unit in Algeria after Eisenhower left. I much preferred to be nearer the center. So I suggested to my superiors that I would be more useful in the new psychological warfare organization that was being formed to help in the Overlord project. By this time, I certainly did not want to return home; I was far too involved in the work. But the army brass did not know that. I waited for their decision and was delighted when new orders arrived. I flew to London in January 1944.

My new title became Chief of Radio Broadcasting within the Psychological Warfare Division of SHAEF—Supreme Headquarters, Allied Expeditionary Forces. Eisenhower was the Supreme Commander. SHAEF had been newly created in London for one purpose: the invasion of France. My immediate boss, as Chief of Operations, was an old colleague, C. D. Jackson, on leave from Time, Inc. Jackson's immediate superior was Brigadier General Robert A. McClure, Chief of the Psychological Warfare Division, who reported directly to Eisenhower.

London at the time was an international metropolis beyond one's ordinary imagination. The streets were alive day and night with men in uniforms of all the Allied nations. A spirit of camaraderie pervaded the very air we breathed. The tide had been turned. We all knew the armed forces were being gathered in England for the major assault upon the Continent. We did not know where or when. But we knew we were living through the planning stage. English pubs kept regular hours; people gathered around pub pianos and sang songs which would become international favorites.

One became acutely aware of the preciousness of life when the first of the German V-1 rockets were launched against England. I was having lunch with C. D. Jackson, when one of the first such pilotless rockets struck London. First there was the buzz, then an eerie silence, and then the explosion. It sounded as if it had hit next door. Actually, the rocket had struck a row of stores about three blocks away. C.D. and I made our way to the bombed area and saw a great many people dead, some lying in the street, some still sitting on chairs inside stores where they had been shopping.

The V-1 raids went on night and day. The rockets came to be called buzz bombs because of their sound in flight. When the buzz would suddenly shut off, it meant the rocket was falling; the explosion would follow in seconds. It was terrifying. Experience taught you to estimate where the rocket would hit from the sound of the buzzing and the sudden silence. Then two months later, the Germans introduced the V-2 rocket. Its impact was worse: the V-2 was completely silent; the warning buzz was gone. For me, the terror was gone too; one's safety had been taken out of one's own control.

As Chief of Radio Broadcasting, my first two major assignments were: managing the American broadcasting over BBC facilities to enemy and enemy-occupied territory, and preparing for the world-wide announcement of D-Day, the cross-Channel invasion to the occupied countries of Europe as well as those that were free. Our broadcasting to the enemy was generally of two types, black and white. "White" propaganda was that which truthfully identified its own source, and stuck to the persuasive truth; "black" propaganda identified itself falsely and lied outrageously when necessary. One of the best of our black operations was a German radio station—that is, a "German" station broadcasting supposedly in Germany when in fact the entire operation was run by Sefton Delmer, a bearded British news correspondent, from a small village outside of London. Delmer worked in a closed compound. From the moment one entered the gate, only German could be spoken there. Everything was aimed at creating the illusion that this was a part of Germany.

The Allied intelligence operations were so good that after D-Day we could supply valuable information to this radio station and to others, which would be broadcast to German troops even before their own legitimate stations could put it on. Our black station's primary mission was to gain the confidence of the

German troops and their commanders so that in time of battle, when their communications were interrupted, the Germans would turn to our station for basic information. Then *and only then* would we give out wrong information to misdirect them. Ultimately, it proved quite effective and promoted chaos in the enemy operations.

On the "white" side of my work, I succeeded by some rather fancy infighting in persuading the British Information Ministry to increase the amount of air time over BBC apportioned to our OWI operation reaching the European countries. Competition among the allies in London for air time was fierce and it was considered quite a coup for OWI when their time on the air was increased from one to two hours a day to four to five. OWI had set up its own American radio studios in London for French, Dutch, Belgian and Norwegian news broadcasts to the Continent. I was the OWI hero of the hour.

One of my tasks at the Psychological Warfare Division was to produce the broadcasts that would inform the world of the long-awaited invasion. We needed recorded messages from leaders of all the occupied countries—France, Norway, Belgium, the Netherlands, and Luxembourg—to be broadcast to those countries, as well as translations to be broadcast elsewhere. The first and most important communication would be from General Eisenhower. His message had been recorded well in advance, and it had been approved by the military, the State Department, the White House, and many other organizations. One day, not long before D-Day, Bob Sherwood was in my office and I gave him the top-secret transcript of Eisenhower's message to read. Suddenly he exclaimed, "My God, he can't say that."

I said, "Say what?"

Sherwood read me the line: "To patriots who are not members of organized resistance groups, I say, 'Continue your passive resistance, but do not needlessly endanger your lives before I give you the signal to rise and strike the enemy.'" In other words, Eisenhower could be interpreted as telling these people that he would give them an order to endanger their lives needlessly. It was a subtle point and no one had caught it. Since it was crucial that Eisenhower's statement be flawless, I decided we had to change that phrase.

I telephoned one of his aides who spoke to the General, then called me back. "Eisenhower is too damn busy for a re-recording." Then he quoted Eisenhower: "'You tell Bill Paley to fix it up somehow. Any way he wants to fix it up is all right with me.'"

The only way I could change it was to erase the part we wanted cut and insert a new, clearer phrase with a much needed pause at one spot, spoken by someone else. The phrase now read: "'. . . but do not needlessly endanger your lives; wait until I give you the signal to rise and strike the enemy.'" The pause in the middle of the sentence was all-important. We tested many voices and decided that the one that came closest to Eisenhower's was General McClure's. We erased the phrase as spoken by Eisenhower and inserted a new one spoken by McClure. Then we played it back. It was terrible. Anyone could tell that it was someone else's voice.

Once more I called Eisenhower's aide, asserting that we had no choice: we simply had to make a new recording. A big argument ensued, but eventually I convinced him to put it to the General in the strongest possible language. Eisenhower finally agreed. "But you have to be out here at six tomorrow morning," said the aide. "That's the only time he can do it." The next morning we drove our camouflaged truck, filled with sophisticated recording equipment, to his headquarters, strung a microphone inside, and Eisenhower, grumbling and sore as hell, made the new recording. The first message was now ready.

We recorded Haakon VII, King of Norway, at his house on the outskirts of London. An old man overcome with emotion over the coming invasion, he wanted only one person in the room with him as he spoke. So I stood there watching and soon after he started reading, he broke down and cried. "Never mind, just take your time," I said. "We'll do it over again. We have plenty of time." He started again, got a little further this time, then again broke down and wept. As gently as possible, I reassured him—

surely he would get through it the third time, I told him. But he didn't. In the end we had him read as far as he could before being overcome, then stop and collect himself, then continue until he broke down again. We edited out the weeping and spliced together a complete continuous statement.

Charles de Gaulle posed yet another problem. He had been flown in from North Africa in Churchill's plane just the day before D-Day and was told that we needed a statement from him immediately as the French leader-in-exile, to be broadcast to France and other countries at the time of the invasion. He said that he wanted to read Eisenhower's statement first. I arranged this and was later informed that after he had read it, de Gaulle took offense that Eisenhower hadn't mentioned him by name. He sent word that he had nothing to say to his people in France.

I replied by messenger that this was vital and that he had to say something. He replied that he was very sorry. Desperate, I sent word to Anthony Eden, Foreign Secretary, explaining what had happened and asked him to intercede. He did so and failed. Eden then called Churchill and Churchill called de Gaulle. Their conversation, as reported to me, was along these lines:

Churchill: "Look here now. We've asked you to give a message to the people of France for use on D-Day. I understand you refused to do it. If you persist in this posture, the plane that took you from North Africa to London is being warmed up now and would be very happy to take you back."

De Gaulle: "I don't know what you're talking about."

Churchill: "That message our people wanted you to record for broadcast to the people of France."

De Gaulle: "Oh, I didn't understand. Of course I'd be very happy to do that kind of message."

We recorded his statement at about 5 A.M. on D-Day. When it was translated we found that it was rather vague and did not mention Eisenhower by name; it even seemed a little unfriendly. We sent it to Anthony Eden and asked his advice. He said he didn't like it either but it was better than nothing, so we decided to use it.

160

Four days before D-Day, I had taken a group of translators to a safe place outside the city and told them: "For security reasons, you people aren't going to leave here until a very important event happens. You'll know pretty soon by the work I'll ask you to do that it's right around the corner. If you have any messages for your families, give them to me and I'll see that they get them. In any case, they'll be told not to worry about you. You're in good hands. You're doing a very important job." They then went to work translating all the recorded D-Day messages into other languages. These translations were also recorded. Even after the job was done, the translators could not be dispersed. On D-Day morning, they were brought to my D-Day station in a small room deep below ground in a BBC building filled with broadcasting and recording equipment. This was a reward for the outstanding job they had done, for now the translators could see, close up, their translations in use in broadcasts to Europe and beyond. BBC transmitters were aimed at different parts of the globe. Each recorded message in each of the different languages had to be placed on a separate transmitter in order to reach the intended audience. Stations in the United States also rebroadcast the messages by shortwave to other parts of the world.

Obviously we could not broadcast the recorded messages until we received a signal from military headquarters in Normandy that a strong foothold had been secured and the invasion was on its way to being successful. To give us the news as quickly as possible, one man going ashore at Normandy carried a radiotelephone linking him directly to me. He was to push a button, I would pick up my phone, and if the invasion had succeeded he would say the code word "Topflight." I would then start the broadcasts.

The de Gaulle problem had been resolved, the translation had been completed, and I was trembling with raw nerves. Suddenly the special phone rang. I picked it up and said, "Yes?" The voice on the other end said, "Testing." I put the phone down. About five minutes later it rang again and again I was startled. The voice said, "Testing," so again I put down the phone, not only jittery but irritated. A few minutes later it rang a third time and again the voice said, "Testing." This time I said, "You son of a bitch. I don't know who you are but if you do this to me once more I'm going to find out who you are and I'm going to knock your head off. Now don't call again until it's real. Understand?" He apologized. Some time later the phone rang again. I picked it up and a voice said, "Topflight." I gave the signal, and instantly, without a hitch, the world was informed of D-Day.

Several weeks after the invasion, I went to Normandy to inspect our division's units at the front, particularly the mobile loudspeaker units which were used there to beam our appeals for German troops to surrender. These loudspeakers were usually set up during the night and used the following morning to call upon surrounded pockets of German units to give up their fight. This proved to be very effective. Our problem was that we did not have enough of these speaker systems. Upon my return to London, General McClure arranged for me to return to the States for three weeks in order to report to the War Department and conduct some other business for SHAEF. This allowed me to visit my home in New York for a short while to accomplish some personal business which had weighed heavily on my mind.

As with many men, the war was an opportunity to reflect on the course of my life from a distance. One of my conclusions was that my marriage was no longer a success. I thought it would be best for both Dorothy and me to divorce and to go our own ways. Believing that she felt the same way, I anticipated an amiable agreement to part. To my surprise, when I reached home I found that she did not share the same feelings. Her answer was she was not ready to call an end to our marriage. It was impossible to work things out in the time I had. The impasse would have to wait until after the war to be resolved.

Before I had left London, my chief, General McClure, had asked me to see what I could do about getting more equipment for our loudspeaker systems. When I reached Washington I mentioned this to someone in the military command, and he said, "Well, the thing to do is to see General Marshall." General

George C. Marshall was Chief of Staff, the highest-ranking man in the Army, the grand strategist of the war. I protested that my loudspeaker systems were not important enough to take up with General Marshall, but the man insisted that to get anything done quickly I must go to the top. An appointment was made for the next day.

For the first time I met Marshall, a tall, handsome man with a long, dignified face that gave the impression of strength. Everything about him inspired confidence. He welcomed me warmly and said, "Before we talk about your purpose in coming here, let me give you a briefing on where we stand today." He led me to a large war map, covered with flags and other symbols showing the locations of every important unit in the war. He showed me Europe first—this was just days before Operation Anvil, the Allied invasion of southern France. Then we talked about the war in the Pacific. He spoke straight and to the point. His statements did not signify optimism or pessimism; they were simply factual. They gave me a strong feeling that everything was in good hands.

Rather sheepishly, I explained our need for equipment. The general pressed a button, a high-ranking officer came in and, after a few words from the general about what I needed, thanked him and left. When I returned to headquarters in Europe the equipment was there. This, in the Army, was the equivalent of a miracle. General McClure didn't know what to think: he was happy to have the equipment, but he was furious at me for having gone to Marshall on so trivial a matter. I tried to explain that I had simply taken advantage of an opportunity, but I don't think any explanation quite satisfied him. General McClure, a graduate of Kentucky Military Institute rather than West Point, was a soft-spoken, hard-working, determined military man of great integrity. He had none of the bluster, pomp, or faked toughness of so many army men of high rank. As an American military attaché in London early in the war, he had developed a deep understanding of the British and a great sympathy for Anglo-American friendship. I had the greatest respect and admiration for the man.

I rejoined the headquarters of the Psychological Warfare Division in London. As the Allied armies advanced, we moved our headquarters to Paris, where my job then was to prepare for the takeover of all means of communication in Germany upon the expected Allied victory. But moving the Psychological Warfare Division of SHAEF into Paris was not a simple transfer. The main headquarters for SHAEF was at Versailles and there was a standing order that because of limited living quarters, no additional U.S. military staff were to be billeted in Paris. General McClure and I thought it absolutely necessary for us to be at the communications hub of France and the war effort at the time. So, McClure sent me on ahead of the division to persuade one Major General Roy Lord that we had to be billeted to Paris rather than Versailles. General Lord was chief of staff to Lieutenant General John C. H. Lee, who headed the American Communications Zone (called Com Zone) in Paris, which was responsible for the flow of all American supplies into France. General Lord lived in an impressive apartment, the penthouse of the George V Hotel. Despite his reputation to the contrary, when I saw him he was warm and congenial. He asked me to sit down, have a drink, and talk. I explained that our vital concern was communications. There was no place that could match Paris as a communications center and it was imperative that we take advantage of the city's facilities. He smiled and said he'd think about it. The next day, General McClure arrived in town, spoke with General Lord, and found that he had assented—we could make our headquarters in Paris. But there was one condition: I would have to take a new job on Lord's staff, producing special information for the top officers of Com Zone, while continuing with my job for the Psychological Warfare Division. I didn't like it—I wasn't sleeping much as it was—but General McClure had given his word. I took the post but soon found a deputy who was fluent in French and he did most of the work.

One consequence was that I got to know General Lord well. He had risen through the ranks with astonishing speed through a combination of brightness and brashness. He had come to his present job simply by marching into General Lee's office and announcing that he thought that he could be of great help. Lee was impressed and tried him out as his assistant and then recognizing his brightness, made him his chief of staff.

General Lord startled me one day, in my civilian naïveté, while talking on the phone with General Patton, who was complaining bitterly that his army was running out of ammunition. Lord said that there must be some mistake—ammunition was on the way. When he put the phone down he said, "I had to say that. As a matter of fact I'm not sending him ammunition, I'm just sending him gasoline." Shocked, I asked why. He said, "Well, as long as he keeps chasing the Germans, they'll run. If he ever stops, they'll turn on him. Therefore, I think it's more important for him to keep on chasing than for him to have ammunition." I thought, "My God, what a chance this man is taking." As it turned out, Lord did get enough ammunition to Patton in time to protect him if the Germans had turned. But for a critical period of time, Patton had pushed the Germans back many miles in one of the great chases of the war without the ammunition needed to protect himself.

I was housed in a small apartment at the George V Hotel. At the same time, I had at my disposal a penthouse on the Rue Barbet de Jouy on the Left Bank, owned by an American friend of mine who had asked me, as a favor, to look after it as a prized possession he could use after the war. Thus I could live in splendor whenever I wanted to. When Duff Cooper came to town as the British ambassador to France, I gave a dinner party for him and his wife at the Barbet de Jouy penthouse. Of course all Americans were heroes, at least for a little while, in the newly liberated Paris of 1944. I think we have never been more popular in any time or place.

My own unit did not have much time to join in the joys of French liberation. We worked almost every waking hour—sixteen to eighteen hours a day. I continued as Chief of Radio until one day General McClure called me in and asked me to succeed C. D. Jackson, his deputy. I said that I couldn't do that to my friend, but McClure put in a call to Jackson, who was in Washington, and C.D. told me that for serious reasons he could not continue in the job and that he would feel better if he knew I would take it. I accepted.

McClure thought that as his deputy I ought to be a commissioned officer. I told him that I would rather be regarded as a civilian expert in my field than as a military man. Saying he was sorry I felt that way, he accepted my refusal. The next day, an old friend from OWI came through and when I told him the story, he said, "You're a damn fool. Don't give up the chance to have full authority over the military members of your organization. This will become more and more important as you go into Germany." He convinced me. While my own staff knew and respected me, it would prove a great advantage in dealing with the Germans to have some clear sign of my authority. I told McClure that I had changed my mind. He called General Bedell Smith and within forty-eight hours the authorization came from Washington: I became a colonel in the U. S. Army.

As General McClure's deputy, my most immediate task was to put in final form the writing of the *Manual for the Control of German Information Services*. In the complete reconstruction of German life that the Allies planned to undertake as soon as the country was conquered, our division would have charge of the entire press, all magazines, radio, film, theater, and the concert halls. This manual would be the operational guide.

We stated our goal at the outset—"To eliminate Naziism and German militarism from any influence on German information media"—and described the three phases by which we would pursue that goal. First, all German information services would be shut down; second, Allied services would be substituted for the defunct German ones; and third, there would be a gradual transition back to German control of information services under a system of licensing by the Allies.

The manual sought to explain how all this would be done. For example, there was a section on how to requisition and confiscate equipment; how to choose licensees; how to choose German employees (including "Guidance on How to Recognize a Nazi"). There were separate sections for the press, radio, film, music, etc. For radio we described a network system much like the one in the United States. While under Allied control, network programs would originate at Radio Luxembourg and be rebroadcast by stations throughout Germany; during certain periods the local stations could cut away, according to a system of cues, and broadcast local programs.

For each of the different media we compiled large glossaries of technical terms in English and German (for example, "voltage doubler circuit" became *Spannungsverdoppelungsschaltung* [*die*]). There were also highly detailed sections on the history of German information control during the war, administration, finance, and more. It was a large piece of work. Producing it became my chief occupation in the months before Germany was conquered; applying it would be my job afterward.

After the first draft of that manual had been approved, with the exception of one small section, I took deathly ill and was rushed to the American Hospital in Paris and put in the intensive-care unit, where under drugs I slept for forty-eight hours. I was tested again and again for a suspected heart attack but in the end the diagnosis was that I had suffered complete exhaustion. I remained bedridden for the next week, deprived of cigarettes and stimulants, and was slowly nursed back to health.

I celebrated V-E Day, May 8, 1945, in a small hotel room in Heidelberg with Richard Crossman, a British intellectual and colleague in the Psychological Warfare Division, who spoke German fluently and possessed one of the cleverest minds I've ever known. After the war as an M.P., he rose to cabinet rank and later became editor of the *New Statesman*. Somehow that day, when we heard the news of Germany's surrender, we found a bottle of wine, and put it under running cold water from the faucet and although it was still lukewarm, enjoyed it far more than its temperature or vintage would have merited. We tuned a little radio in to London and heard the city going completely wild. With London, we celebrated. The unbounded exhilaration of that moment was the greatest imaginable contrast to the events of the next day.

Dachau is only about two hundred miles from Heidelberg, and Richard Crossman and I were in one of the first parties to reach that concentration camp, just hours after the Nazis had fled and the Americans had arrived. I can add nothing to the many existing descriptions of Dachau; I can only confirm them and mention the feeling of dread that comes over me when I remember our visit, even now. The hundreds of bodies stacked outside the crematorium and the thousands of starving, emaciated people still in the barracks can never be erased from the memories of eyewitnesses. I saw some of these people fall dead in front of me, while on their way to get food in a barracks. In that day we saw more than it was possible to comprehend. I will never understand it and its effect on me will never diminish.

That night, when we reached Munich, the head technician of the German Broadcasting Service came to call on me. With tears in his eyes, he told me how happy he was that the Americans had arrived and that Munich was liberated. He described how all during the war he had prayed for Allied bombers to aim at the radio transmitters clustered there to serve most of Germany. He said he used to get on the roof of one of the transmitter buildings as the planes were flying overhead, hoping to see one come right toward him. He was very impressive. Of course, now he wanted to be helpful, if he could, to the Americans. After he left, I had him checked and within a couple of hours received a report that he had been head of the entire SS organization in the Munich district. I had him arrested.

The next day, Crossman and I drove some sixty miles to a medium-sized town called Regensburg to fulfill a promise Dick had made to a young German who worked for the BBC, that once he reached Germany, he would visit the young German's mother. It was an eerie trip for we were two Americans driving unarmed along a road which was lined with thousands of German soldiers, most of them still holding their rifles, waiting to surrender. Forty-eight hours earlier, they would have shot us.

When we reached our destination, the boy's mother greeted us calmly and politely. "Thank you for coming," she said. "I've been expecting you." Seated in her living room, Dick gave her in fluent German all the news he had about her son. I could not understand all he was saying, but I was amazed at how relaxed and unfeeling her face seemed to be. She just stared at Dick and hardly said a word. I thought, my goodness, how can a mother who hasn't seen her son for so many years get news about him for the first time and be so unmoved by what she's hearing? Then I looked down at her hands. They were both bleeding. She had dug her nails into her hands, so intense were her feelings.

With Germany conquered, the Psychological Warfare Division moved in and occupied a part of a small town near Frankfurt called Bad Homburg. We took over a compound that had been a training school for railroad employees—about twenty-five houses, a big auditorium, a dining hall, and a kitchen. It could not have been better suited to our needs.

The work in Bad Homburg was strenuous but smooth; everything had been well systematized. Our job, as noted, was to carry out what we had described in the manual. Newspapers, magazines, radio stations, theaters, concert halls—all were reorganized and put back into operation. Radio was non-commercial, but all the other enterprises started to generate profits that soon became substantial. We put the accruing money into a special account; I don't know what became of it. It was a great business, and while I knew that each concern would one day become independent and go its own way, I soon had the feeling that I was sitting on a vast, if fictional, empire.

Shortly before V-E Day, General Lucius Clay had come to Germany as Eisenhower's deputy in charge of the military government. He was a tough, able, awesome man. He held staff meetings once a week, and one week General McClure asked me to go as his representative. There were perhaps forty officers sitting around the table with Clay in the center on one side. Every man in that room, except me, had from one star up to four; I was the lowly colonel. Clay made some announcements and then asked for reports. When he came to me he said, "Colonel Paley, I find in my house a lot of Nazi literature. I suppose this is the condition in most houses throughout Germany. What do you intend to do about this literature?"

"General Clay, we're going to announce plans in a few days by which all this literature will be turned over to special committees of German citizens in each city and town," I reported. "It will then be repulped and turned into new paper on which will be printed democratic literature."

"Colonel Paley, I don't think that's enough," he said. "I think it's dangerous for that material to be here and I want it destroyed immediately."

"General Clay, don't forget how the whole world condemned Germany for having destroyed what they called democratic decadent literature," I said. "Now you don't want to put us in the position of having emulated that."

"I don't agree, Colonel Paley, and since you seem to be in opposition I'll ask my chief of staff to prepare orders immediately that call for the destruction of all Nazi literature throughout Germany."

I stood up to object again, but he said, "That will be all, Colonel." There was utter quiet. I don't think anyone else there would have dared to talk to him like that, but I had no stake in a military career.

The next day Clay's chief of staff asked me to help him write the order. Instead, I went over and gave him a rip-snorting sales talk about the importance of getting General Clay to countermand his order. I finally got him so worked up that he marched into Clay's office to argue the point, emerging fifteen minutes later with a smile. Clay had agreed, the order was rescinded.

In mid-July, 1945, Eisenhower disbanded SHAEF, leaving Berlin and Germany under the control of the Allied countries individually, each with its own sector. My job became correspondingly smaller, since I was working only for the American forces, not the Allies. By this time I had the feeling that there wasn't much more I could do and so ought to leave. My papers had just been drawn up when General Clay, who had taken Eisenhower's place in Germany, astonished me by offering me a job on his staff. His representative told me that the post carried with it the rank of general with one star. The job sounded interesting, but I declined; if the Army had offered four stars I still wouldn't have stayed. It was time for me to go and that was it. On August 24, nine days after Hirohito informed his people of their defeat, I flew to London and from there to New York.

I came home with a disconcerting conflict of feelings experienced by many other returning men. The indelible impressions of the horrors of war commingled in my mind with a feeling that life had never been so exciting and immediate and never would be again.

Transition

The war formed an interlude of great meaning in my life. It widened my horizons, deepened my maturity, brought new and lasting friendships, and gave me, above all, the space and time away from New York to reflect seriously and to gain a new perspective on my own life and upon CBS and broadcasting.

I returned to the United States in early September, 1945, and was demobilized that fall. But before returning to work at CBS, I went off alone to Colorado Springs, where I spent a week re-thinking some of the ideas and decisions that had been on my mind. I wanted to be as objective, as logical, and as certain as possible before launching into a new civilian life. Now forty-four and no longer that "young man" of so many years ago, I knew without a doubt that I wanted to make a new life for myself. Although there was no other woman on the horizon, I realized that Dorothy and I were not the happiest of couples and we both deserved better. I decided again to ask for a divorce upon my return to New York.

The future of CBS presented a multiplicity of problems and opportunities in the dawn of a post-war world. I had been doing a lot of thinking while overseas about the future of CBS. Paul Kesten, who was running the company in my absence, had kept me informed with long, detailed, personal letters that he wrote on weekends away from the office. Basically, CBS was in good financial shape, but we were still a poor second in audience ratings. NBC with its greater financial resources and far superior broadcasting facilities along with good "know-how" could attract and buy entertainers and creative talent easier than could CBS.

In one fifteen-page, single-spaced letter after V-E day and before my return, Paul Kesten had outlined his strategy for the future of CBS. In essence, he proposed turning CBS from a mass medium into an elite network, beamed at ten or perhaps 15 million homes rather than 30 million. He wanted CBS to become "the one network that never offends with over-commercialism, in content, in quantity, or in tone . . . that presents superb and sparkling entertainment . . . (and) an important forum for great public figures and great public issues, for education, for thoughtful and challenging presentation of the news and the issues growing out of it. . . . To be the network that is *never* corny, blatant, common, coarse or careless, that is *always* bright, stimulating. . . ." He envisioned network programming which would constitute a national magazine of the air. His plan would entail changing the entire structure of affiliate stations. He wanted to find new affiliates which would agree to give CBS a solid block of ten hours of network broadcasting a day and then to find advertisers who would sponsor these nationwide programs. "Perhaps it will strike you, Bill, that I've merely expressed briefly the things we've told ourselves we've been—or wanted to be—these many years," he wrote with his usual enthusiasm.

What his plan really amounted to was giving up the fight against NBC and giving up a national, cross-section radio network for a narrower, specialized network of dubious potential. His was not the answer I sought. We had discussed all this many times before the war. I always saw network radio as primarily a mass medium. To survive, CBS had to give the majority of people the kind of programs it wanted to hear in popular entertainment.

173

We could and did endeavor to do this and at the same time to introduce new, more sophisticated shows and themes and talent, which we at CBS thought listeners would learn to like.

I thought I had figured out the real root of CBS's competitive problems in attracting and holding our entertainment talent, in appealing to affiliate stations and to the public. It lay in the lack of control over the programs we put on the air. Most of our entertainment shows were produced and controlled by advertising agencies and by producers on the outside. CBS just sold the time, and put the shows on the air. Of course, we had the right to accept or reject programs submitted to us and we did sometimes suggest programs to the outside producers. But we were at the mercy of the sponsors and the ad agencies. They could always take a successful show away from us and put it on NBC for whatever reason they saw fit.

It seemed to me that the answer for CBS was to originate, produce, and put on some of its own shows and to sell them to some of the advertisers or to the sponsors directly! That would involve a major change in the industry. Instead of being merely a pipeline, we would have some control over the programs we broadcast. This had the advantage of permitting us to schedule our programs in the time slots most advantageous to our overall programming design rather than leaving the scheduling to the whim of an advertiser.

I fully understood and anticipated that this strategy would be risky and expensive. We would have to build up our own production department, facilities and staff to produce our own shows. Agencies and sponsors would resist giving up control over their programs. Yet, there would be certain advantages for them in my new scheme. They could buy finished products from us for which we would be fully responsible. It would all depend, I decided, on how well we could create programs that belonged to us. But the change held out the best hope for the objective I had in mind: I was determined that CBS would overtake NBC as the number-one radio network. I was not satisfied with second place. I would grant NBC its greater reputation, prestige, finances, and facilities. But CBS had and would continue to have the edge in creative programming. *That,* I thought, would be the key to success in post-war broadcasting. Creative programming would attract the top entertainment talent to CBS and would also create new talent along the way. And this time, with CBS in command over its own programming, we would keep the talent and the programs we attracted.

Looming on the horizon, as I was well aware, was the coming of a whole new system of broadcasting: television. With the war now over, the final technology involved in bringing television into the home would be rushed to completion. CBS had operated two experimental television stations off and on since 1931; but with the advent of the war, all laboratory work had been suspended. However, Paul Kesten had kept me informed of the research and development of a system of color television which he promised would put CBS in the forefront of the new industry. Color television had been "Kesten's baby" since 1936 when he had brought into the company a young, brilliant Hungarian physicist named Peter Goldmark, who had been hired as an expert in the technology behind color television. I realized that once the technology was established, television would need an enormous staff and facilities to produce the various kinds of programs shown over the picture tube.

In preparation for this future in radio and television, my most immediate concern was for reorganizing the company. No longer could I do everything myself, as in the early days of radio. Someone was needed to share the workload. And I had just the man in Paul Kesten, who had worked in harmony with me since 1930 and who had run CBS in the years I had been away during the war. So I worked out in my mind a division of responsibilities at CBS. I would promote Paul from executive vice-president to president in charge of all day-to-day activities of the company. I would move up to chairman and chief executive officer and devote my time to the broader, more strategic concerns of radio and television development, including particularly my new ideas on programming, which I considered the essence of broadcasting. In short, the way I planned it, Kesten and I would run CBS and face the future together.

With all that settled in my mind, from Colorado I went off to the hills of Hollywood to visit and enjoy my friend David O. Selznick, who had won the fame and fortune he deserved in producing *Gone With the Wind*. David and I were kindred spirits, good friends who seldom if ever talked business, but enjoyed each other's company and the fun of those huge, lavish parties for which he was renowned. I spent a week with him and others in the movie colony, shedding the tensions of the past war and the future business plans, and then returned to New York.

I moved into the St. Regis Hotel, which put my domicile only four short city blocks from the CBS offices on Madison Avenue. Dorothy and I agreed upon a separation and put the divorce proceedings into the hands of our attorneys. The negotiations between the lawyers on a property settlement, however, were long and drawn out, consuming almost two years, and our divorce did not become final until July 23, 1947. A small party of my associates welcomed me back warmly at 485 Madison. My office was there, waiting for me as I had left it almost two years before. Paul explained that he had decided to leave the office unoccupied rather than use it himself. It was good to see him and get down to business once again. We reviewed the years I had been away, what had happened at the office and in the industry, and a host of new critical problems facing us. I could hardly wait to spring my reorganization plans upon him. And then, and I shall never forget it, I was stunned to hear him say he could not become president of CBS.

He explained that he had been sick, that he had a terrible arthritic condition, and that it would not respond to any treatment. He was in constant pain. In order to get to the office at nine, he had to get up at six in the morning (and his bachelor quarters were in a hotel only four blocks away). His arthritis had become progressively worse through the war years and it would not get better. He had been holding on by the skin of his teeth. He believed he was dying.

I sat there in shock, listening to those words. Looking at Paul, you could not tell that he was at all ill. He seemed as young, vigorous, and brilliant as he always had been. He was only forty-seven. I could hardly believe him. He wanted me to know, he said, that after thinking long and hard about my homecoming, he was sorry to say he wanted to retire.

He implored me not to worry about my plans for the top management of the company because he had a young man who had worked his way up in the organization and was every bit as good as he was; this man was Frank Stanton.

I had known Stanton before going overseas, but not very well. Kesten had brought him into our research and sales promotion department in 1935, promoted him to director of that department, and then, while I was away, called upon Stanton to help run the company. In 1942 Stanton had been elected a vice-president of CBS, and in 1945, while I was still in Europe, he had been made general manager of the company and elected to the board of directors. I remembered Kesten writing for my approval of that last promotion. Now in the office, Kesten sang the praises of his thirty-seven-year-old protégé, who had earned a doctorate in psychology based on his studies of radio audience preferences and tastes. He told me how well Stanton had learned the overall operation of the entire organization and how well he got along with our affiliated stations. He described Stanton in glowing terms: capable, conscientious, hard-working, energetic; a man of integrity and good taste. Paul and I agreed that he seemed to have all the qualifications the job of president required. His age was not an obstacle; CBS was a zestful organization for young men. I agreed with Kesten's choice, for I had that kind of faith in his judgment. But I persuaded him against resigning and he agreed to take the position of vice-chairman. I also advised him to seek whatever medical help could be found and then to return so that the three of us—Paley, Kesten, and Stanton—could run CBS.

Shortly afterward, I invited Stanton and his wife to lunch at Kiluna Farm and then took him aside to explain my plans for a new management team at CBS. I told him of Kesten's health problem; how Kesten had recommended him for the post of president; and what I had in mind about the job. We discussed the possibility of his becoming president. Stanton was very restrained in the discussion, but said he would be very happy to assume the responsibilities I had in mind.

During the following three hectic months, I plunged headlong into the many problems facing our organization. Starting to work closely with Stanton, I concluded he did indeed possess the qualifications that the job of president required. Gradually, we established between us a different kind of rapport than Kesten and I had shared. Where Kesten was warm, outspoken, and easy to work with, Stanton was more reserved, reticent, and rigid. Yet, Stanton proved himself to be very bright and articulate, willing and imaginative. He was every bit as effective as Kesten in dealing with the people and problems in our daily operations. A few days before our January board of directors meeting, I called Stanton into my office and told him that I was now prepared to propose him to the Board as president of CBS. He expressed his pleasure and appreciation. In all that time, I never considered anyone else for the job. And so it was done. On January 9, 1946, the Board elected me chairman, Kesten vice-chairman, and Stanton president.

At that same meeting we promoted Ed Murrow from war correspondent to vice-president and director of public affairs, which included our news department. Ed and I had talked about his future before I left England and had discussed in great detail how best to convert our wartime news organization into a strong and permanent news department covering world-wide events on a regular basis. Ed had the experience, the news judgment, the scope and depth of mind to head the department, and I told him so. He had some misgivings about walking the executive corridors of CBS. But he was the man in whom I had complete confidence. When he returned to New York in late 1945, we worked together on policy matters concerning the news department and he decided to take the job, which placed him on the executive ladder above Paul White, who became director of news broadcasts in the public affairs department.

Ed turned out to be a very good operating executive, particularly in dealing with people in the news department and in helping shape the philosophical policy decisions taken by CBS in the post-war period. I think Ed rather liked the idea of being a news executive, at least at the start, although his nature was to be rather taciturn about it all.

After a while, I began to sense that he might be unhappy about not being on the air. It was nothing that he ever said, but he had been the most famous radio news personality to come out of the war, and I thought that he missed the action and excitement of live broadcasting. From time to time I would speak to him about it. But he could be stubborn.

"Ed, would you like to go back on the air?" I would ask.

"Oh no," he would say, "I'm happy. Everything is fine."

But his mournful face would belie his words. We went over that dialogue several times in several forms, until finally one day I spoke bluntly:

"Ed, I have a strong feeling that you really want to go back on the air. I can tell you're sort of miserable."

"I'll only go back if you order me to," he said.

"Okay, Ed, I order you to."

He broke out in a great big smile. "Okay, I'll go back."

He resigned as vice-president in July 1947 and that fall returned to broadcasting with a daily news program which led to his famous series *Hear It Now*. And that led to *See It Now* on television and on and on. Edward R. Murrow returned to his proper niche: broadcasting. He set standards of broadcast journalism and ethical integrity in presenting the news, which are still admired and emulated by journalists throughout the free world. It would be nice to say that Ed was always happy in his role as a newscaster, but one could never be sure of his true mood from that somber and sad visage of his. He reported on the world but he also carried the weight of the world upon his shoulders.

Even after he left his executive post, Ed always had a rather

special position at CBS because of the exceptionally close relationship we had developed during the war. He was perhaps
the one man for whom I breached my personal desire for sep-
arating friends from business associates at CBS. Ed and I would
get together quite often, and he seldom if ever made an important career decision or personal move without consulting me as a
friend. In CBS affairs, Ed jumped the chain of command and
dealt directly with me. In fact, as a broadcaster, he had a rather
unusual employment contract with the company—unique as far
as I know: it allowed him to cancel if ever I ceased to be chief
executive officer of CBS.

Some years later, Ed Murrow failed to take my advice and I
have wondered about it ever since. He was asked by some of the
leading Democratic politicians of New York to run for the Party's
nomination for U.S. senator.

"Do it, I think you'll win," I told him when he asked. "And if
you do," I added, "I don't think you'd be very far from the
highest post in the land."

"Well, I feel uncomfortable about it," he replied. "I wasn't
born here in New York and I don't feel I know this state well
enough to represent it."

"Ed, that's a lot of nonsense," I said. "You've lived here for
years and you know what the problems are. You're a smart guy
and of course you could represent the people of this state."

But I could not persuade him. Because he had been born in
North Carolina and did not know New York State *perfectly,* his
inner integrity prevented him from stepping into the political
waters.

One unfortunate consequence of my friendship with Ed Murrow, I think, was the development of a rather strained relationship between him and Frank Stanton. I think Stanton did not
approve of the idea of Murrow's going over everyone's head in
his dealings with me—which is understandable—and perhaps
Murrow did not like the idea that I was so close to Stanton. I
never could quite figure it out, nor could I do much about it.

The one and only man I met during the war whom I brought

In my office at the new CBS Headquarters Building.

At the University of Pennsylvania, May 1968, for an honorary doctor of laws degree and a commencement address.

Columbia University's Board of Trustees with University President Dwight D. Eisenhower.

I enjoyed Arthur Godfrey.

The Honeymooners, Art Carney, Jackie Gleason, and Audrey Meadows.

Shooting with Ed Murrow.

Recording *My Fair Lady* with Robert Coote, Julie Andrews, and Rex Harrison.

Studio One: George Orwell's *1984.*

Larry Kert and Carol Lawrence record *West Side Story.*

(l. to r.) Danny Thomas, Merle Jones, and Phil Silvers.

With Frank Stanton in a television studio during the 1960 Presidential Election campaign.

Ed Murrow's *Person to Person* visits Salvador Dali.

With Red Skelton.

Danny Kaye's television debut,
touring for UNICEF.

Mildred Dunnock and Lee J. Cobb in *Death of a Salesman.*

Cliff Robertson and Piper Laurie in *Days of Wine and Roses.*

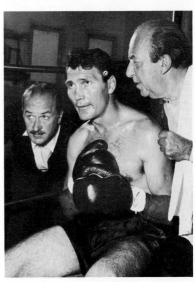

Keenan Wynn, Jack Palance, and Ed Wynn in *Requiem for a Heavyweight.*

With Eric Sevareid.

Captain Kangaroo (Bob Keeshan).

Carol Burnett.

back into my business life was John Minary, an attorney with a distinguished law firm in Chicago, who had been an aide to General McClure, under whom I also had served. One day, near the end of the war, when we were talking about the future, John revealed that he was particularly interested in managing private estates. One thing led to another and I asked him if he would come and work for me. We shook hands on it and soon after he was demobilized, he joined me in New York, took charge of my personal office, and has been handling with aplomb and efficiency all of my business affairs outside CBS ever since. With firm hand, John holds the legal reins on some of my more unbridled ideas; while he is equally capable of steering me unscathed through a bramble of legalities toward an objective well worth winning. He plays an important role in my life.

At CBS, the biggest policy decision facing me and top management was how to proceed into the new age of commercial television. The future of the medium was still unsettled. There were only six television (transmitting) stations and only a few thousand TV receivers in the United States. Television networks did not yet exist; production and programming were still in the planning stage. The television system to be adopted for the whole country was still an open and all-important question. And CBS and RCA were in direct conflict over that question.

Both networks had been experimenting with television broadcasting for a long time. CBS went on the air experimentally in July 1931, and I had told the New York *Times:* "Personally, I believe television will be in operation on a commercial basis by the end of 1932." Of course, I was wrong. In 1940 we proposed to an industry committee which was considering technical standards for television that standards for color television also be adopted. In 1941 the FCC, acting on the recommendation of the committee, approved limited commercial broadcasting of black and white without approving any single standard, and at the same time authorized experimental field tests of our color system.

World War II had created a hiatus in all television development and so there we stood at the end of 1945 poised for action, with the RCA black-and-white system virtually assured of FCC approval and the CBS color system not yet approved but, in our estimation, far superior to the black-and-white system.

Soon after my return to CBS, Kesten, Stanton, and Dr. Goldmark made a major presentation to me of the CBS color system, including a demonstration of one of Dr. Goldmark's models. They all were absolutely enthusiastic about the system and our chances of winning FCC approval, which would make the CBS color television system the standard for the whole industry. In color technology, we were far ahead of RCA which had focused its research on black-and-white transmissions. At the time, CBS was operating two television stations, one broadcasting four hours a week in black-and-white and the other broadcasting experimentally in color. The dilemma, of course, was that the two systems were incompatible. If the public bought black-and-white sets, it could not receive CBS color programs; if it bought CBS color, it could not receive black-and-white. But, argued Kesten and Stanton, everyone agreed that color television was vastly superior, technically and aesthetically, to black-and-white. It was just a matter of the public waiting perhaps one year more for the fully developed color system to be approved by the FCC rather than buying black-and-white sets immediately. In fact, Kesten had indicated publicly eighteen months before, in April 1944, that CBS would soon be putting color television on the market and that the public should not be sold inferior black-and-white TV sets which would soon become obsolete. That had thrown the television industry, particularly the manufacturers of sets, into utter turmoil. How could they gear up for manufacturing television sets when RCA and CBS might be telecasting on two completely different systems?

While I listened to the enthusiastic predictions of my colleagues at CBS, I also heard the rumblings from set manufacturers who were almost unanimously opposed to the introduction of color in competition with black and white. At their behest, I met with a large group of manufacturer representatives and listened to hours of their complaints and pleadings. If CBS proceeded with its intention to introduce color broadcasts, which were incompatible with black-and-white telecasts, it would bring chaos to the industry, the manufacturers complained. They implored me to wait, to put off the CBS color system for a number of years: let them make and sell black-and-white sets to the public and then follow that with the introduction of color sets some years hence, when our color system would be more fully perfected. It would be good business for all of us, they argued. I listened most of that day. But in my own mind I could not see my way clear to countermanding Kesten and Stanton. It would be in effect a vote of no confidence in them and in all their work during the years of my being away in the war. As an article of faith, I had to go along with them.

Dr. Goldmark's laboratories and his staff of more than one hundred forged ahead with the final work involved in perfecting his color system. The system relied upon a rotating wheel which gave brilliant and stable colors, and we demonstrated it to the industry time and again. In the summer of 1946, RCA put its black-and-white sets on the market and in September of that year, we made our big move: we petitioned the FCC to authorize commercial color broadcasting using the CBS color system in the UHF band.

Our arguments were solid: CBS polls showed that viewers would wait more than a year to buy a color set instead of a black-and-white one if only they knew it was coming; they would pay as much as 48 per cent more for it when it arrived; our color broadcasts between New York and Washington via coaxial cable had shown the feasibility of networking; the ultra high frequency (UHF) band offered space for more stations than would very high frequency (VHF), and the commission itself had admitted that UHF television was inevitable. With the advantages of firm standards and color's greater inherent beauty, broadcasters could build audiences rapidly and television would be off to a fast and sure-footed start.

The essence of this battle was speed. Goldmark and his team

threw themselves into the battle. He never lost his enthusiasm and confidence in his ability to produce a color system that would win the approval of the FCC. We applied for our license in September 1946 because the number of television sets in existence at the time was estimated at only about 6,000. Thus, the incompatibility of the two systems was not all that important. The public could easily switch over to color sets, if (and a big if) the FCC approved our system.

However, if the FCC rejected our color system, then the demand for black-and-white sets would become so great, so many would be sold, that it would no longer be economically feasible to introduce color (at least, for a long time to come). And we so warned the FCC. If our color system were not licensed, we said, we would not continue our color development.

And so the die was cast, the gauntlet thrown. The future of television broadcasting, as we saw it, was involved; millions of dollars, even tens of millions, hung in the balance.

But even before the hearings began, a corollary issue caused much consternation in our offices. For the first time after the war, the FCC was accepting applications for new television stations broadcasting on VHF in black and white. CBS at the time had one such television station in New York, WCBW (later WCBS-TV) and was eligible under FCC regulations to own four more in four different cities. We could apply and presumably receive FCC approval to build four more VHF stations. But, if we did, it could be very well seen as undercutting and showing a lack of faith in our own color system. Kesten, Stanton, and our own legal department advised that we abstain from seeking licenses to build black-and-white stations. I went along with them, realizing we were taking a double gamble in sticking solely with our unproven color system. In effect, we were all relying upon the assurances of our technical staff, headed by Dr. Goldmark.

CBS, therefore, deliberately did not apply for FCC licenses to open four more television stations. Furthermore, we advised our affiliates not to bother to apply for black-and-white channels. We said CBS would come up with a better television system in color and for anyone to invest in black and white would be a waste of effort and money.

In the meantime, Paul Kesten came to the final decision that he had to retire from CBS because of his debilitating arthritis. He had sought medical help across the country and into Mexico—all to no avail. When I could no longer in good conscience try to persuade him, I cabled him in Mexico: "I can't say I was wholly unprepared for it, but your decision caused a thud within me." In August 1946 I presented his resignation to the board of directors, and Frank Stanton stepped into the second spot at CBS. We worked out a reorganization of the company and divided the workload between us. While I would serve as chief executive officer concentrating upon broad policy and strategy, Stanton would assume responsibility for implementing CBS policies, would handle the day-to-day activities, including our very important relations with affiliate stations and also our significant dealings with Congress and the FCC. The latter, which we called "the Washington beat," could be very time-consuming, for, as I explained to him, our policy was to develop and maintain good, helpful relations with representatives of government on a continuing basis. I had given a great deal of time to this "Washington beat" during the 1920s and 1930s, when the radio industry had been fighting government censorship and FCC regulations over what could and what could not be put on the air. Now, I wanted Frank to take over and speak for CBS.

As president and chief operating officer, Stanton took over very well. He knew everyone in the CBS organization and worked well with his peers and subordinates. He was equally effective with our affiliate stations and rapidly came to be an outstanding spokesman for CBS, and by extension, for the whole industry in his appearances before the public and the government in Washington.

I intended to focus my energies upon the so-called "creative" side of the business, programming for post-war radio, preparing CBS for the coming age of television, and thinking ahead about guidelines for our future.

Triumph

O ne night, at a small dinner party in New York, about a year after my separation from Dorothy, I became aware for the first time of a slender, beautiful woman introduced to me as Barbara Cushing Mortimer—"Babe" to all her friends. If our paths had crossed before, I was unaware of it at the time, which was strange, because her sister Betsey was married to Jock Whitney, an old friend and neighbor at Kiluna Farm. But that night at that dinner party, we talked for some time and, struck by her extraordinary beauty, character and personality, I invited her out to dinner the following week.

Ah, how can I describe now this marvelous woman whom I loved and to whom I was married for thirty years and more? It was obvious that Babe was one of the loveliest women in the world. Men, and women, too, stopped and stared when passing her on a walk on the avenues of New York. Whoever knew her well came to realize also what an unusual person she was, as beautiful in her inner being as in her outer appearance: tall and thin, sculptured by the Maker with a sort of Roman nose; poised, shy and yet very direct in her dealings with people. She had deep brown, often flashing eyes that saw right into you.

186

We began by seeing each other on and off and then more and more as time went on. She had been recently divorced from her first husband, Stanley G. Mortimer, Jr., an investment banker, and was living with her mother, Mrs. Harvey Cushing, on Eighty-sixth Street in New York. Then suddenly she fell ill with phlebitis and was rushed to a hospital, where she was confined to bed for a month.

Each night during that month, I went to one or another of my favorite restaurants in the city and had the chef prepare a special dinner for two. The menu would be discussed in great detail—something I was rather good at and practice to this day—and each time something new and unusual would be tried. I would then take our dinner, packed in a warming container, to her room in the hospital. We both enjoyed her delightful wonder and wild guesses at what the dinner surprise would be. Although she was ill, she admitted to no pain. Babe took illness always with great fortitude, spirit and undiminished wit.

Those evenings together in the hospital gave us a unique opportunity to come to know one another extremely well. We talked privately, night after night, with no one interrupting or distracting us, and we came to feel even more strongly than before that we belonged and wanted to be together. The decision came easily: we would get married as soon as my divorce came through.

On July 28, 1947, in Mrs. Cushing's summer home on Long Island, Babe and I were married in a small family wedding. Among those present were Babe's two children from her previous marriage, Stanley III and Amanda; her mother and her two sisters and brothers-in-law; her brother Henry and his wife; my mother, father and sister; and a few close friends. It was a happy event and the start of a glorious new life for me and, I think, for her too.

Babe gave up her job at *Vogue* magazine, where she had been an editorial assistant, and after our honeymoon in the South of France, Italy, and Switzerland, we settled down to life in and around New York, commuting between Kiluna Farm and an apartment at the St. Regis Hotel. But the centerpiece of our lives was Kiluna. I delighted in the grounds, the vista as one drives up to the house, the house itself. It has a look, a feel, an atmosphere that I cherished but cannot describe except in terms of opposites. The house was rather large, but not immense, rather grand, but not grandiose. Inside it was cozy and warm. Babe and I gave many gay and memorable parties there and often had friends come to stay over weekends. A perfectionist in everything she touched, Babe ran Kiluna beautifully.

Gardening became a passion and an art for her. She would have her plans and drawings of the gardens laid out in detail during the winter and then in the spring, summer, and fall, both vegetables and flowers would bloom into a delightful treat to the senses. Little by little over the years, Babe transformed the grounds of Kiluna into a place of simple but rare beauty. Not far from the house, she created an extraordinary dell of wild flowers around an oval pond containing floating water lilies. Trees and bushes grew higher up on the hills encompassing this dell, with paths upon which one could stroll and look down upon the serenity of what nature and Babe Paley had created. She filled our house not only with flowers from the gardens, but with beautiful antique objects we had discovered during our travels. They were a joy to live with day by day. Kiluna and Babe expressed one spirit to me: happiness.

Babe, a perfectionist, paid attention to everyone and everything in detail. She possessed impeccable taste and spared herself no effort in getting everything she did just right. Her meticulous attention to the clothes she chose to wear made her one of the country's acknowledged leaders in fashion. She headed the list of the world's best-dressed women for so many years that in 1959 she asked that her name be dropped in order to spare our children the joshing of their schoolmates. Instead she was named to fashion's Hall of Fame, a perpetual honor. Babe never really enjoyed her reputation as a great beauty or a best-dressed woman; she much preferred praise for what she was and did, especially for her accomplishments.

Her taste, sensitivity, and perfectionism extended far beyond the clothes she wore. This could be seen in each of our houses, in every one of our rooms, and even at our dinner table, right down to the varied colors of the vegetables on the dinner plate. She catered to my own special interest in food. I had developed a healthy appetite at my mother's table. As a boy, if I did not eat all that was put on my plate, my mother, in her simplicity, declared me sick and either called a doctor or fed me castor oil. As an adult, my principal hobby was discovering new restaurants, talented chefs, and unusual preparations of food. Babe joined me in trying all kinds of eating places around the world and she gathered one of the best collections of recipes of anyone I know. Food at the Paleys' was prepared, served, and eaten with care and affection.

She and I shared many interests throughout our married life. We shared life together. I do not think we were apart more than five nights throughout the thirty-one years of our marriage. She joined in my frequent business travels, although not in my business concerns. We roamed the world together in search of art, antiques, and new adventures. I joined her in some of her favorite civic projects, particularly in the development of the North Shore University Hospital in Manhasset, to which we, together with Betsey and Jock Whitney and many others in our community, devoted years of effort. We took special pride as that hospital developed into an outstanding teaching institution allied with the New York Hospital–Cornell Medical Center. In recognition of her efforts over a period of more than twenty years, Babe was elected in 1974 an honorary life trustee of the hospital.

Babe also was blessed with a natural creative talent in drawing, painting, and sculpture, and often used people around her, especially the children and grandchildren, as models. I told her that if it were not for the attention she paid to her family and social duties, she could become a professional artist. She denied it. Throughout her life, Babe developed many close and loving friends. She was very generous and giving of her time, her sympathy and her counsel. Friends in trouble sought her out for companionship, for aid in an illness, for financial help or whatever was needed.

Babe's strong feelings for family unity, I always believed, were derived from her mother. Never was there a woman who was more loved than Mrs. Cushing. In her old age, quite stout and restricted in her activities, she remained serene and happy, taking life in stride in an uncomplicated and straightforward manner. I simply adored her. Never did she make demands on her children. It was not necessary. Her children and their spouses vied to be with Mrs. Cushing as much as possible. She was beloved to the day in May 1949 when she succumbed to a heart attack at the age of seventy-eight. Her three daughters, Babe, Betsey, and Minnie, and her son, Henry, shared a twenty-four-hour-a-day vigil at the hospital for three weeks during her final illness.

The following Christmas, her presents arrived in each of our households. Mrs. Cushing always started her Christmas shopping in January, and even in her final year on earth she did not fail us. I still think of her with loving affection.

Like her mother, Babe loved children. After we were married, her children, Stanley (Tony) and Amanda, lived with us. Dorothy's and my children, Jeffrey and Hilary, lived with Dorothy, but visited us often for long and short stays. Later, Babe and I had two children, William and Kate. So, of our six children, four grew up with us at Kiluna. All six brought the wonderful joy of childhood and youth to our home and to our lives.

At my office, I worked with fierce concentration and, blessed with a high energy level, I always had very good staying power. But when I returned home at the end of a day, my work and business problems were left behind at the office. Sometimes, of course, that was not possible. Paperwork to do or telephone calls, programs to watch or hear at times kept me working at home late into the night. I did not discuss business problems at the dinner table, as my father had; I preferred to relax and to discharge the tensions built up during the working day.

Especially in the first few years after the war, the crisscrossing variety of problems, pressures, and activities which confronted me made the pre-war radio days of my career seem to be a period of pure pleasure. In oversimplified terms, the advent of television doubled the workload demanded by post-war radio.

At the war's end, radio had won the overwhelming approval of the American public and became an important social force in the country. According to the current surveys of the period, nine out of ten American families owned radio sets, more than owned automobiles, telephones, or bathtubs. More than 56 million radio sets were in use; Americans were spending more time listening to radio than they spent doing anything else, except working and sleeping.

The fifteen most popular radio programs and personalities of the 1945–46 season (according to the Hooperatings) were *Fibber McGee and Molly*, Bob Hope, *Lux Radio Theater*, Edgar Bergen and Charlie McCarthy, Red Skelton, Jack Benny, the *Screen Guild Players*, Fred Allen, *Mr. District Attorney*, Walter Winchell, *Great Gildersleeve*, Eddie Cantor, Abbott and Costello, Jack Haley and Eve Arden, and Burns and Allen. They were all wonderful, popular entertainment. The only trouble was that twelve of the fifteen top shows where on NBC; ABC had only Walter Winchell, the news commentator; and we had only two of the top fifteen, *Lux Radio Theater* and *Screen Guild Players*. We were sadly lacking, it was obvious, in star talent. We did put on some "specials" which won high critical acclaim for CBS: Ibsen's *Peer Gynt* and Shakespeare's *Richard III* on the *Columbia Workshop*, and *Operation Crossroads*, which examined the new phenomenon of atomic power. In 1947, we produced an acclaimed thirteen-week series called *One World Flight* in which Norman Corwin commemorated Wendell Willkie's famous round-the-world trip by recording interviews with leaders and ordinary citizens in seventeen countries. Nevertheless, CBS was woefully behind in audience ratings and I was determined to do something about it.

Our new Documentary Unit, the precursor of later television documentaries, was an offshoot of the entertainment programming department I had established at CBS soon after my return from the war. In a small and quiet way, with no public announcement, we began by producing only three half-hour weekly radio programs of our own, put them on the air, and then said, in effect, these particular time periods were available only to sponsors who would buy *our* programs in those time slots. At first, we met great resistance, but I had expected that. Offers for other shows in those time periods were made; but I refused them and was very stubborn about it. Finally someone came along and bought one of the shows and all my arguments to the advertisers and their agencies turned out to be true. The point was that if CBS produced its own programs, at its own expense, ad agencies would not have to maintain their own big, costly production departments. If an agency or sponsor liked what CBS produced, it could buy that show in that time slot, which was a known quantity at a clearly marked price, still collect its usual 15 per cent commission, and rely on CBS to maintain top quality. If the program got into trouble, CBS would spend as much as necessary to save the show because it had as much at stake in audience ratings as the sponsor.

We made little progress in the beginning. Shows were kept on the air that went unsold. But gradually over the next two or three years, the advertisers and the ad agencies came to appreciate the beauty of what we offered them. Everyone benefited. By the end of 1947, we had packaged thirty-six radio programs and found sponsors for only fifteen of them. And then in 1948, we had twenty-nine sponsors for our packaged programs and two of them made it to the top ten! Those two were the first of the most successful, long-running packaged CBS hits: *My Friend Irma,* a situation comedy with Marie Wilson playing the role of the dizzy dame; and *Arthur Godfrey's Talent Scouts,* an amateur performer contest which owed its popularity to the offhand commentaries of the inimitable Godfrey.

Over the years, our new policy on package programs changed the way of doing business in the entire broadcasting industry. In time, the networks superseded the advertising agencies in governing and scheduling programs on radio and later on television. But even with the success of our new policy, CBS still trailed NBC in its audience ratings, simply because the major entertainment talent of radio still preferred the more prestigious, larger network. It worried me and I thought about it a great deal. Then in 1948 some clever tax attorneys discovered a method whereby these top stars, who were paying a whopping 77 per cent of all their earnings above $70,000 in federal income taxes, could accumulate appreciable savings if they sold their programs as "properties" and paid only 25 per cent in taxes on capital gains. In the summer that year, Lew Wasserman, president of the Music Corporation of America, the largest talent agency in the country, and Taft Schreiber, executive vice-president there, came to me with a proposal that CBS buy the *Amos 'n' Andy* show, which was one of NBC's longest running, most popular programs.

I was absolutely delighted with the idea, although I balked at the first asking price. I had known the producers and stars of *Amos 'n' Andy,* Freeman Gosden (Amos) and Charles Correll (Andy) for many years. In fact I had tried, but failed, to get them on CBS at the time they started on NBC in 1929. Wasserman and I entered into long and intensive negotiations. We realized that there were tremendous advantages for both sides if we could make a deal. Gosden and Correll would build up an immediate estate for their families, MCA would collect its agent's commission, and CBS would score a positive coup in the broadcasting industry. *Amos 'n' Andy* had been an NBC stalwart for the past nineteen years. But I also had in mind how well owning *Amos 'n' Andy* would fit in the new program policy we had adopted. It also occurred to me that the more star talent I could attract to CBS at this time, the greater the head start in talent we would have for the years of television looming ahead. In September 1948, we announced to the public that CBS had bought *Amos 'n' Andy* for its Sunday night prime time. It created quite a splash.

Later that month, Lew Wasserman offered me the *Jack Benny Program* under the same capital-gains arrangements. CBS would buy the comedian's corporation, Amusement Enterprises, Inc., which included the Benny show on NBC and a number of other productions. Benny was absolutely tops in my estimation and I had no doubt that I wanted his prize show, which had been on NBC for sixteen years. With a Sunday night schedule of Jack Benny at 7 P.M., followed by *Amos 'n' Andy* at 7:30, CBS would get the kind of lift, thrust, and public image I thought it needed. Lew Wasserman and I negotiated with the ease of experience and fairly rapidly we reached a tentative understanding on the price of the Benny corporation—$2,260,000—and the compensation to be paid the most important performers, mainly Jack Benny. I thought we were close to making a final deal. And then Wasserman called the whole thing off. He made a special trip from Los Angeles to New York to tell me this personally, a kind and gracious act; still I was deeply disappointed and angry. I had learned through the grapevine that Benny's sponsor, the American Tobacco Company, had been notified of our pending deal, and they in turn had informed NBC. As a result, NBC had begun negotiating with MCA for the Jack Benny property also. There are certain forms and traditions in all such negotiations, well known to both sides, and what Lew Wasserman had done, it seemed to me, was a breach of good faith. We were in the midst of our negotiations and it was simply bad form for him to walk out on me and offer my deal to my competitor.

I brooded over this for about two weeks and late one night it occurred to me that in trying to put this deal together, I had talked with everyone concerned, except the star himself. So I picked up the phone and put in a call to Jack Benny; he was not home, but having dinner at someone else's house, I was told. I found that number and called him there. We had met casually on a number of occasions but I did not know him well.

"This is Bill Paley, Mr. Benny," I told him. "I've been negotiating with your agents and I thought we were getting along well. I thought we were going to make a deal and suddenly the rug was pulled out from under me. I think it's unfair. And I just wonder how much you know about it. I'd like to come out and talk to you about it."

He replied that he was in the middle of a dinner party and

could not talk freely at the time, but would call me in the morning. The next morning he asked me to come to California. I grabbed one of our lawyers and we flew to Los Angeles and rushed to the offices of MCA. We missed Benny, who had gone to a rehearsal, but Lew Wasserman was ready for us with another turn of events.

"Well, Bill, a very strange thing happened here only a few hours ago," he said. "While you were on your way here, Niles Trammell (the president of NBC) was here to sign the Benny contract. There was something in the contract that bothered RCA at the last minute." I learned that David Sarnoff himself had interrupted the meeting with a phone call, ordering Trammell back to New York to discuss a legal question in the contract which troubled him. I gathered that both Benny and Wasserman were annoyed. Then Wasserman handed me the contract in question. "Here's the contract we were prepared to sign with NBC," he said. "We worked on it for three days and three nights. And since they didn't sign it, Mr. Benny has authorized me to say to you: if you want this contract the way it is, he's prepared to sign it."

My lawyer and I read it over carefully. Wasserman was fair. He pointed out "the sticky paragraph" which had worried Sarnoff. It was a technicality having something to do with a possible uncertainty in Benny's corporate tax position. After studying the text, my lawyer said, "I see nothing about it that is troublesome." I conferred with him for a few minutes to make certain that I was right in thinking that this deal was completely open and above board and legally sound, and then I told the MCA president: "I'm prepared to sign the contract."

"Okay," said Wasserman. "All we have to do is change the name National Broadcasting Company to Columbia Broadcasting System."

It was as simple, as complicated, and as close as all that: changing a name in a contract, being prepared to take a giant calculated risk and to act on the spot, and being in the right place at the right time. If it had not been for my personal telephone call to Benny that night, I would not have been in Wasserman's office when Trammell of NBC had walked out.

Absolutely delighted with our luck, I returned to New York. Jack Benny was an institution on radio. His coming over to CBS had all kinds of marvelous ramifications for us. It signaled to the whole entertainment industry that CBS was the up-and-coming network, competitive with NBC, and eager to sign up stars of his caliber, and determined to put on more and more successful programs in order to attract listeners to CBS.

The Benny deal, however, was far more complicated and potentially risky than the purchase of the *Amos 'n' Andy* show. For legal and tax reasons, Jack Benny and MCA were selling me the physical property of Benny's corporation. During the negotiations, I learned that his services were under contract to his sponsor, the American Tobacco Company, for several more years and that American Tobacco had the right to choose the network on which Benny would perform. I considered this factor and concluded that CBS needed to have Jack Benny on its schedule. I would just have to convince American Tobacco to switch networks. It would benefit all of us. If American Tobacco insisted upon keeping Benny on NBC, it would create an impasse for the remainder of their contract.

The morning after I signed the contract, I went to Benny's home and we shook hands on the deal, then I flew back to New York to tackle American Tobacco. But all my powers of persuasion directed at various representatives of American Tobacco and their advertising agency BBD&O (Batten, Barton, Durstine & Osborn) in countless meetings got me nowhere. No one was willing to give me a definite answer and some of them let me know they preferred to keep Benny on NBC where he was a known quantity with an established audience for Lucky Strike cigarettes.

Depressed by this frustrating turn of events, I decided on a showdown before the situation deteriorated into a lawsuit. It was about six o'clock and I was still in my office, so I telephoned Vincent Riggio, now president of American Tobacco, whom I had known since our George Washington Hill days. Reaching him at his home on Park Avenue, I said "Mr. Riggio, something important is developing and I'd like to see you as quickly as possible."

"Come on over right away."

At his apartment I came right to the point. "By all that's right and holy, you know, you ought to be moving to CBS. We own the Jack Benny corporation. You will get just as good service on CBS as you will on NBC. These roadblocks are being put in my way and I just can't deal with them because I think these people are prejudiced in the other direction."

"What do you think I ought to do about it?" he asked.

"I think we ought to have a meeting where everybody is together at the same time so I won't have to talk to you and then talk to the agency and then talk to the lawyer and have this uncertainty go on and on. I get a different story from everyone. So, let's all meet."

"When do you want to do it?"

"Tomorrow morning."

"Okay," he said, and then went to the phone.

The next morning in Riggio's office, I took them all on—Ben Duffy, head of BBD&O, the agency's attorney, and several others from the ad agency and from American Tobacco. The arguments went round and round. Riggio sat at his desk, saying nothing. He had hardly changed at all from when I had first met him. I think I handled every argument put to me by those who wanted Benny to remain on NBC. Their primary concern was that their program would lose part of its audience by leaving NBC. I insisted that with all the publicity and excitement of Jack Benny shifting networks, his ratings and American Tobacco's audience would *increase* on CBS. But the lawyer for BBD&O backed me into a corner. Suppose I was wrong? Could I guarantee that Benny would not lose any of his audience? Would I agree to CBS paying a penalty to American Tobacco, if Benny's ratings went down? I do not believe he expected me to agree. No one could guarantee any comedian's audience ratings. No network ever had. And yet I felt confident that CBS, with the proper handling, publicity, and advertising, could increase Benny's ratings. But I could not be sure. And yet I wanted to close this deal then and there, when I had them all together. All this flashed through my mind within a second or so. Then I committed myself.

On behalf of CBS I offered to pay American Tobacco so much per point lost, if any, for each and every week that Benny was on CBS for the remainder of their contract with him. It was an exceptional offer. There was nothing left for them to argue about. Utter silence filled the room and then Riggio declared, "Okay, now you've all had an opportunity to raise objections. What about it?"

Anger, frustration, or whatever flashed on the faces of my opponents, but they had nothing more to say. It was a moment I savored. Then Riggio declared, "The matter's settled. We're moving to CBS." We signed the papers and soon afterward made the announcement that shook the industry: Jack Benny was moving to CBS. It was the start of something big, something that would have lasting effects upon both networks.

One of the major ramifications of the Jack Benny switch, I have always believed, was that it helped cause General Sarnoff and his associates at RCA to reject my offer that both our companies change over to the long-playing record we developed in 1948. Earlier that year, I had invited General Sarnoff to lunch at CBS and demonstrated for him the revolutionary unbreakable record, the 33⅓ rpm turntable, and the remarkable fidelity of sound. He came back two days later with about twenty-five of his people and we demonstrated the LP record for all of them in the CBS board room. A week later, he was back for another meeting and I remember his saying, "It's quite something for the great Victor company to take a thing like this from the little Columbia company." He then invited me and some of my associates to see RCA's own latest innovation: a 45 rpm record with a remarkably fast record-changing player. Still, he would not make up his mind about our long-playing record. Then in September, when my negotiations with Benny and Wasserman were under way, he let me know RCA would "wait and see" because he did not believe the economics of long-playing records could be worked out. Whatever the reason for Sarnoff's reluctance, RCA came out with its own 45 rpm record in January 1949, which caused incalculable confusion in the record market. They did not adopt the long-playing record until a year or so later.

While we were in the process of winning the record competition with RCA, we were in the process of losing our color television battle to them. In 1947, the FCC denied our petition to introduce the CBS color system commercially, on the grounds that it had not been adequately field tested.

While we curtailed our research into color television, we did not give up the fight. Dr. Goldmark promised and assured us that he could modify and improve his color system so that it could be received on black-and-white sets. We still believed the CBS color system was far superior to any other color system then being developed by RCA or anyone else.

After winning Jack Benny, I went after Bing Crosby, whom I had wanted to get back on CBS for fourteen years. He had left CBS for NBC and then switched to ABC in 1946 when ABC was the only network which would allow him to pre-record his radio programs. He had been the first singing star to insist on recording his songs so that only his best renditions would go out over the air. NBC and CBS had a policy that everything the listener heard on radio was live. But late in 1948, with Crosby available, I changed my mind about our pre-recording policy. It seemed to me the public did not care that much about the issue. So I sang the praises of a new and dynamic CBS to Bing and offered to find him a sponsor who would sign a three-year, non-cancellable contract. Then I went to Liggett & Myers, makers of Chesterfield cigarettes, and announced that I was coming to them first but that I was in the position to sell Crosby, the top crooner in movies and on radio, to the first advertiser who would sign him to a three-year, non-cancellable contract at $20,000 a week for the whole program. They agreed without a squabble, but attached some conditions. When I telephoned Crosby with the good news, I was excited about getting him a sponsor so quickly. I spelled out the details and then told him his new sponsor's two conditions.

"They insist that you stop knocking cigarettes, Bing," I said.

"That's easy enough to do," said the imperturbable crooner.

"And you have to make it clear that you are associated with Chesterfields. They want you to carry a pack of Chesterfields with you when you go out in public."

"But," said Bing, after a long pause, "that'll make a bulge in my pocket, won't it?"

"Yeah," I told him, "and so will the $20,000 a week."

We announced the Crosby deal in mid-January 1949, which broke the dam. That month, Red Skelton joined CBS; in February, Edgar Bergen; in March, Burns and Allen. And then the flow became a steady stream: Ed Wynn, Fred Waring, Al Jolson, Groucho Marx; and Frank Sinatra, who had left us, came back.

The migration of superstars to CBS was a landmark event in the history of broadcasting, which came to be known as the "Paley Raids." *The Jack Benny Program* at 7 P.M. on Sunday night increased the audience for every succeeding program, and CBS soon dominated Sunday night. Groucho Marx, Bing Crosby, and Burns and Allen gave us Wednesday nights. There is a story extant that David Sarnoff telephoned me after all this happened and said, "Why did you do this to me, Bill? I thought we had an understanding that we would not steal each other's talent," and that I replied sheepishly, "Because I had to." It is a cute little story but it just never happened. We certainly had no agreement whatsoever about competing or not competing with one another.

The general and I had a long, continuing, avuncular relationship down through the years. From the earliest days of radio, when he was the "grand old man" and I was "that bright young kid," we were friends, confidants, and fierce competitors all at the same time, and we understood each other and our relative positions. I always had the greatest respect and admiration for him. He had a sharp mind and a keen sense of competition. I always thought his strengths lay in the more technical and physical aspects of radio and television, while mine lay in understanding talent, programming, and what went on the air. I never could learn what made the insides of radio and television work. Nevertheless, I knowingly took the risks involved in bringing the top talent in performers to CBS because I always believed that programs were the essential products of radio and would be the same for television. And in 1949, CBS had twelve out of Hooper's "First Fifteen" programs, sixteen of Nielsen's "Top Twenty," and our average-audience rating was 12 per cent larger than that of any other network. In short, that year, 1949, CBS became number one in radio.

Interlude

The United States went to war again in June 1950—this time in a "police action" on behalf of the United Nations—in Korea, and once again I was asked to serve the government. I was the most reluctant draftee imaginable at the beginning and then found my job fascinating and absorbing. It took most of my time, with very little left over for CBS.

Stuart Symington, who was later to become U.S. senator from Missouri, was a neighbor of mine in Manhasset and a frequent golfing companion. I thought nothing of it when he remarked that there was great concern in Washington over actual and potential deficiencies in the material resources of the country. Since the United States had recently entered the war in Korea, there were fears that some natural resources—minerals, metals, oil—might be or become in critical short supply. Symington, at the time, was serving as chairman of the National Security Resources Board. He told me President Truman was thinking of setting up a presidential commission to study the entire problem of the future resources of the United States. But he surprised me when he asked if I would be interested in heading such a commission.

I laughed at the idea. "My goodness," I told him, "I wouldn't do that for anything in the world." That was his first approach. Then one night in Washington a short while later, he and I dropped in at Lyndon Johnson's house to see the senator, who at the time was a close friend of Symington's. I thought it was a casual visit until I thought about it later. Again Symington brought up the subject, this time with Johnson. "I'm trying to get Bill here to do this materials job," he said. Johnson backed him up, giving me one of his Texas pep talks and concluding, "You must take this job . . . it's a wonderful job." Then he turned and put the question to his Texas cohort, Sam Rayburn, the Speaker and most influential member of the House of Representatives. Rayburn, who had been sitting there quietly watching a wrestling match on television, looked up at me and said simply, "I agree."

To each of them I kept repeating, "Don't be ridiculous. I don't know anything about minerals and metals. There's nothing for me to do in that field." That was his second approach and I never could be sure he had not set up that meeting with Johnson and Rayburn to pressure me. The subject came up a number of times again over a two- or three-month period, but I was then so heavily involved in the critical transition from radio to television at CBS that I really did not seriously consider Symington's proposal.

But he was persistent. On one of my social visits to Washington, he ever so casually said, "Oh, by the way, we have an appointment. Just follow me." The next thing I knew, I was in the Oval Office, standing in front of Harry Truman. The President was very intent, very serious. In that even-toned, flat voice, he told me that a full survey of our mineral and energy resources was essential for the nation. The government needed to look ahead and see what the future demands on our natural resources were going to be, what shortages could be expected, and finally, what the government should do about it. It was an important job and he wanted me to take it.

"Well, Mr. President," I replied, somewhat flustered, "I am highly flattered, but I think you are making a very serious mistake. I've never been near a mine. I don't know one metal from another. I'm not an economist. In fact, I'm the last person in the world with the capabilities to do the kind of job you are now describing."

The President did not bat an eye. If he had any doubts before, he said, they had now been wiped out. He wanted somebody who had no preconceived ideas, one who would come in from scratch, one who could understand what was going on and make his own judgments based on just good sense and good evaluations. I was the man for the job, he declared.

I had no intention of saying "Yes" to anyone about taking on this job when I walked in, but how does one say "No" to the President of the United States when the country is at war and he is putting the pressure on with a direct request? I hardly knew where to begin, so I tried to find out what he had in mind.

"How large a commission do you want?" I asked.

"That's up to you," he replied quickly.

"Whom would you like to have serve?"

"It's up to you."

"How long do you think it will take?"

"Well, I don't know," he said. "I imagine you could do it in six months."

"How much will it cost?"

"That's up to you."

"What kind of cooperation will I get?"

"I'll give you a letter to the cabinet officer of every department in the government, telling them to give you anything you want. We'll give you all the cooperation you want. You can have all the money you need. So, get started!"

The next thing I knew I was standing outside the White House in a daze, gripped by a feeling of fear that bordered on hysteria. That presidential interview had taken about twenty minutes. Now I was on my own, having promised to set up and conduct a presidential commission on a subject I knew nothing about, without guidelines or instructions, without help, without any experience whatsoever. I returned to New York to tell my wife and Frank Stanton and some others at CBS what I had done. I estimated six months for the task, but could not foretell how I would divide my time between Washington with the commission and New York with CBS.

Lyndon Johnson telephoned to congratulate me. He recommended one man, a Texan, for the commission: George Rufus Brown, of Brown & Root, said to be one of the largest contracting firms in the world. I drew up a list of possible commissioners from among the many people I had met or heard of during my own career and narrowed the list down to three other men with different fields of expertise. I had already decided on a small commission of no more than five. Then I telephoned around, checking on the experience and reputation of these men and, satisfied with what I learned, called them personally. Not only did I catch each one by telephone on the first call, each one of them accepted. I had my President's Materials Policy Commission. It had taken no more than one hour.

For a commissioner knowledgeable about mining and materials, I had George Rufus Brown; for a mining and minerals expert, I had Arthur H. Bunker, president of Climax Molybdenum Company, a former investment banker at Lehman Brothers and former director of CBS; as an outstanding, highly respected economist, I had Edward S. Mason, dean of the Graduate School of Public Administration at Harvard University. I also wanted a good writer on the commission and was delighted at the acceptance of Eric Hodgins, a former managing editor of *Fortune* and of the *Technology Review* at the Massachusetts Institute of Technology. What particularly attracted me to him was his background in the subject, his graceful style, and at times his great sense of humor, which he demonstrated in his best-selling novel *Mr. Blandings Builds His Dream House.*

Staffing a governmental-study commission was and always is much more difficult than finding the actual commissioners. It is also equally, if not more, important. The research and legwork necessary for sound recommendations depend more upon the staff than the men who head the commission. I was most fortunate in filling the key staff position of executive director with Philip Coombs, a former professor of economics at Amherst College. I had met him not long before, while he was economic adviser to Chester Bowles, then governor of Connecticut. Coombs and I went to Washington together for our first view of our new quarters in the Executive Office Building, a marvelous old structure with high ceilings and large, old-fashioned rooms. On that first day there, Coombs and I mulled over our primary and perhaps most important organizational problem: How could we attract a high caliber of civil servants to staff the Materials Policy Commission when the commission had such a short (six months) life span and there was no evident crisis involved to attract the best brains to us in Washington?

After a good deal of discussion, we decided to begin by using the President's letter ordering full cooperation of all departments. This we believed would bring a number of people who would be available to us. But, I told Coombs, we would reject as many of them as necessary, particularly among the first to arrive, until we had settled on three or four of the very top people. Word would get about Washington that we were accepting only a first-class team, that there must be something very special about this commission, and the top people we did accept would attract others. And that is just the way it worked out. When we had hired our first five or six staffers, all outstanding men and women, there was a deluge of applicants for the jobs available. At the height of our work, the commission employed around a hundred and forty full-time men and women on the staff, aided by several hundred consultants working on special projects.

We had an enormous subject to cover, mountains of material to read, hundreds of experts to take testimony from, and it was all fascinating to me. The task before us was to make a comprehensive survey of the essential natural resources of the United States—minerals, metals, oil, gas, energy, timber, and water—to estimate the rate of their use in 1950 and then project the needs of the country in natural resources twenty-five years ahead to 1975, and finally, to project for the President what shortages could be expected and what policies should be instituted to deal with expected problems. At the start the full commission met every three or four weeks, but as chairman I worked with the staff four or five days a week. Babe and I moved to Washington, renting a house in Georgetown, and returned to New York only on weekends or sometimes on a Friday which I then spent at CBS.

At the end of about four months, I realized the commission could not possibly produce a meaningful report in six or even nine months. I wrote to President Truman, saying we could put together a respectable but rather superficial report in six months but that if he wanted a really good report, we would need an additional year beyond the six months and that it would cost many hundreds of thousands of dollars. What were his wishes?

The very next morning I received his reply in a letter which, in effect, said: I want the best report you can put together. I don't care how long it takes. Money is no object. Very truly yours, Harry Truman.

So, fully enticed and involved in the subject of natural resources, I plunged back into work. Eric Hodgins, whom I had persuaded to spend full time with the commission, became in effect a member of the staff and its chief writer. Because we did not have the time to listen to everyone in our formal hearings, we sent out questionnaires far and wide; we farmed out special studies to research companies; we consulted specialists throughout the country. We became a veritable "think tank."

The extension of the life of the commission meant that I would have to devote all of 1951 and well into 1952 to the project, but I thought the scope, breadth, and significance of our work was well worth the time and effort. Besides, I was receiving a broad education in economics, world trade, and the fundamentals of our country's national power, which resided in our access to natural resources.

I kept in constant touch with events at CBS through daily phone calls to Frank Stanton and the key men in the various divisions, particularly programming. I was on the telephone every night to New York and the West Coast. On some Saturdays and more Fridays, I put in a full day in meetings and conferences at

CBS. During the week, I worked daily at the commission and read material late into the night, sometimes to three o'clock in the morning. That year and a half I believe I worked harder than I ever had before. I was leading two lives.

The battle with RCA over color television continued unabated throughout that year. Late the previous year, the FCC had approved our system as the standard for color broadcasting, but RCA then began a seven-month court battle to have the order rescinded. Victory came on May 28, 1951, when the Supreme Court of the United States unanimously upheld the FCC ruling and, in effect, CBS color television. The next month, on June 25, 1951, CBS broadcast the first commercial color network program in history. It was a gala one-hour show called *Premiere*, with Arthur Godfrey, Ed Sullivan, Faye Emerson, and other stars, and a brief appearance by Stanton, Chairman Wayne Coy of the FCC, and myself. I do not believe, however, many people saw that show. There were some ten million television sets in existence at the time but only about twenty-five of them were capable of receiving CBS color. Nevertheless, true to our commitment to our own color system, we announced plans to broadcast twenty hours of color programs each week by October 15. We also made plans for marketing color television sets using the CBS system. But then we were suddenly stopped again. Charles Wilson, Director of Defense Mobilization, that October requested that the manufacture of color sets be suspended in order to conserve certain critical materials for the duration of the Korean War. The next month the National Production Authority issued an order prohibiting the manufacture of color sets. That put a halt to our color telecasts as well as to color TV sets.

However, the biggest decision and policy commitment we made at CBS that year was to go into the business of manufacturing television sets. It had been a long time in coming. When I returned from the war, I had had some vague plans in mind to diversify the business interests of CBS so that the well-being of the corporation would not be so dependent upon the government-regulated broadcasting business. In late 1947, we went so far as to make inquiries about television set-manufacturing companies which might be for sale and worth buying. The rapidly expanding consumer market for television sets was clearly apparent. Nothing came of those early explorations, but my associates and I continued to think of the possibility of going into the manufacturing end of the business. It seemed like a natural. CBS was one of the best-known trade names in the country and, encouraged by our success with Columbia Records, we thought "Columbia" television sets, backed up by our resources and reputation, would be a likely financial success in the market place.

Late in 1950, we again began looking at set-manufacturing companies as candidates for acquisition. We did not consider it practical to start from scratch in a business in which we had no direct experience. We wanted to buy a company with a management highly skilled in the technology, research, and development of television receivers. Goldmark gave high marks to the Hytron Radio and Electronics Corporation of Salem, Massachusetts, one of the oldest manufacturers in the country of radio and television tubes of all kinds and the fourth largest in sales. This was most important to us in making our decision. On June 15, 1951, we bought it through an exchange of approximately $18 million of CBS stock. The purchases included Hytron's subsidiary, Air King Products Company, of Brooklyn, New York, which made the other parts of radio and television receivers. The two principal owners of Hytron, Bruce A. Coffin and Lloyd H. Coffin (who were brothers), were elected to the CBS board of directors. For the first time in CBS history, we were in the business of manufacturing "hardware."

A month after the merger with Hytron, we once again reorganized the internal structure of CBS. Only a year before we had worked hard to integrate the functions of our television and radio departments. Now, in July 1951, we realized that could not work out well in the long run. Television was growing too fast. We separated radio and television into autonomous divisions, each with its own departments for programs, sales, promotion, station services, operations, and the like.

It was at this point that William Golden, creative director of CBS, designed a new logo to symbolize the distinct new identity of CBS Television. He came up with the superb "CBS eye," a design so simple, strong and effective that we have never changed it. Bill Golden, hired by Paul Kesten back in 1937, became one of the most acknowledged art directors in the country, a winner of an extraordinary number of awards. He insisted upon excellence in visual quality for everything associated with CBS and he not only built our reputation in graphics and advertising but also attracted the best people in the field to do work for CBS, including such fine artists as Ben Shahn and René Bouché. He died in 1959 at the age of forty-eight and was succeeded by Lou Dorfsman, who has been carrying on to this day Golden's tradition of good design with "a classic quality" at CBS.

With the separation of the management of television and radio in 1951, CBS was restructured into six separate and distinct operating units, each with its own president: CBS Radio, CBS Television, CBS Laboratories, Columbia Records, Hytron Radio and Electronics, and CBS-Columbia.

Frank Stanton, one of the most highly organized, structured, and meticulous men I have ever met, imposed, or at least tried to impose, his personality and way of doing things upon the day-to-day operations of CBS. He systematized various company procedures, chains of command, even office decor and the way CBS secretaries typed business letters. Some of the "creative" minds at CBS resented what they took to be a loss of some of their freedom and liberties, but most of what Frank instituted was necessary and gave a special quality to a growing company. About once a week, Frank would come to Washington so that we could confer on company affairs.

The President's Materials Policy Commission report took a full sixteen months to complete. The basic information on the nation's

existing natural and material resources and the projections of
what our resources and our needs would be twenty-five years
hence were all collected and collated for the first time in five
thick volumes of text, charts, graphs, and footnotes. We made
more than eighty specific recommendations for government and
private industry to act upon in order to alleviate the shortages in
energy and raw materials we envisioned.

Our basic thrust was to warn that the United States even then
was not self-sufficient in raw materials and that it would face
both shortages and especially mounting costs of raw materials in
the next twenty-five years. We warned that there was no such
thing as a purely domestic policy toward materials that all the
world needed; there were only world policies that have domestic
aspects. We were thinking of oil supplies as well as more esoteric
materials such as bauxite, magnesium, and fluorspar (which was
used for refrigerants and plastics). We stressed the interde-
pendence of nations in raw materials and we recommended
stockpiling of critical materials, an interchange of information on
supplies and demands, various methods to help eliminate waste-
ful practices, a study of international pooling arrangements, and
generally an open world-trade policy.

Having survived the following quarter of a century, I had the
opportunity in 1975 of reviewing our report and checking our
projections and predictions. The most striking impression upon
looking back was just how prescient we really were. With remarkable accuracy we predicted the trends and the directions of
those twenty-five years. We did underestimate the growth of the
country in population and the amount of the rise in consumer demands for automobiles, telephones, television sets, air condition-
ers, and the like. We were absolutely on target in predicting "the
energy problem" of the 1970s and in advocating the development
of alternate sources of energy.

The report was well received by American industry, foreign
governments, and the press; indeed, in these quarters it was a
fantastic success. People in industry would tell me they looked
upon it as "the bible." Strangers upon hearing my name would

ask me wide-eyed if I was the Paley of "The Paley Report." When I visited Europe, people there wanted to talk to me about The Report. Industry here and abroad acted on it. A *Life* magazine editorial hailed it as comparable in potential influence to Alexander Hamilton's great Report on Manufactures in 1791. It became a prime source of information for writers of articles and books. CBS made a very good documentary out of it, narrated by Ed Murrow, which brought knowledge of it to a wide audience.

In 1974, on the eve of the twenty-fifth anniversary of the base year of the report (1950), a new wave of articles about it appeared in the press. Senator Mike Mansfield entered into the *Congressional Record* this observation: "The Paley Report is just as good today as it was 22 years ago. In my opinion it is must reading for the administration and the Congress. If we will do today what Mr. Paley recommended in 1952 we will still be able to understand and to solve our problems in this new economic age."

At the time, however, there was some ideological criticism of the report from those who worried that government action to insure the nation's needs in material resources would lead to excessive planning and controls.

Some of our recommendations were acted upon, notably the development and opening of the St. Lawrence Seaway as an all-year route to the sea. This was put into effect in 1959, serving fifty-six inland ports. But in the perversity of politics, the report was largely ignored by future administrations.

After the election of 1952, I went to see Arthur F. Burns, the head of President Eisenhower's Council of Economic Advisers and asked whether I should see Eisenhower about the report or leave it with him. He said to leave it with him. As far as I can make out, not much happened.

After the materials report was issued, I formed an organization —just an office, really—called Resources for the Future to answer questions from the public about the report. Later the Ford Foundation decided to create an organization to continue the study of the nation's raw materials. I turned over to the foundation the organization and the name "Resources for the Future," which I had set up, and the foundation then expanded the organization and became its prime mover. Later I served for some years as its chairman.

Perhaps if I had gone into government, I might have been better able to push the report. Eisenhower asked me to serve as Secretary to his Cabinet, a sort of cabinet co-ordinator, but I was so deeply involved in other projects, I had to decline.

In the final months of preparing the commission report, I came awfully close to giving up CBS in order to devote myself to other things. While the report was being written, and the commission began to prepare to wind up its affairs, I myself began dividing my time more or less evenly between New York and Washington. I came to a remarkable discovery. At CBS I was so bored and sleepy that I could hardly keep my eyes open. In fact, at one board meeting, I had to prop open my eyelids with my fingers, lest I fall asleep in front of the directors of the company. But in Washington I was never sleepy or bored. I was alert, interested, and involved in the work. We entertained at our Georgetown house, were frequently invited out to restaurants and to other homes, I worked late into the night, and I thrived on it.

At first I was puzzled and then worried. I explained the whole situation to my doctor. My daily routine was the same in both Washington and New York. Each morning upon rising I would take the B-12 vitamin he recommended, have breakfast, read the newspapers, and then be driven to work. In Washington, I would be fine; in New York when we got to my office building I would feel so tired that I could hardly get out of the car. Sometimes I would tell my driver to drive around Central Park for a half hour so that I could continue my nap. Could I dread my work at CBS that much? My doctor gave me a thorough examination and concluded that there was nothing physically wrong with me. It must be my mental attitude toward CBS, I thought; nothing else was different between my life in New York and in Washington.

I came to a profound and melancholy conclusion and told Babe, "You know, I think this tiredness I feel must be because of my business. I think broadcasting is getting me down or I'm bored with it. I don't know what the hell to do."

It was an awful thought with deep implications for my life. For a long month I thought about changing my career.

One Friday evening at Kiluna, when we had a house full of weekend guests, I thought I might have trouble sleeping that night. Wanting to be alert and in good shape the next morning, I placed a bottle of sleeping pills next to my bed, just in case I needed one. The next morning the butler brought in my breakfast and went to the bathroom in search of something. Evidently it was not there because he came to my night table and picked up the bottle of sleeping pills. He took out one pill and put it on a small glass plate and put the plate on my breakfast tray.

"What are you doing?" I asked.

"I'm giving you your morning pill, sir," he said.

"I'm supposed to be taking a vitamin. That's not a vitamin; that's a sleeping pill."

"Oh no, sir. It's vitamin B-12. I give it to you every morning."

"Oh, my God, I don't believe it!"

He was a new man and the two kinds of pills did look very much alike. Unknowingly I had been taking a grain and a half of Seconal with breakfast every morning. My doctor was highly amused. My melancholy decision to change my life disappeared and I went back to my office that summer full time and fully aware. Never had broadcasting seemed more interesting and exciting.

Creative Chaos

Some people said it was radio with pictures. Others called it a form of vaudeville. Still others saw it as a way to bring live Broadway plays into the home. Hollywood insisted it would be nothing more than cheap movies. Everyone working in the medium at the beginning was trying to figure it out: what was it? what would it become, this thing we called television?

Early television was all of these things—radio with pictures, live vaudeville, Broadway and book dramatizations, cheap movies—until it developed into a unique new art form, unparalleled in its ability to communicate to millions of people at one time. But at the beginning, though we could see television, we could not see that far into the future. We were taken up with the immediacy of the intertwining problems of this new medium, the engineering, the technology involved, the economics behind it all, the building of a network, the setting of new entertainment policies, the finding of creative men and women to produce the product to be shown in the homes of America.

The financial problems alone were enormous, as were the sums involved. CBS could not sell air time or programs to sponsors until there were enough people watching television who would see the commercials designed to sell a sponsor's products. But people were not going to buy television sets unless there were programs to see. That meant we had to invest immense amounts of money to underwrite new programs which in turn would induce people to buy TV sets, which in turn would attract advertisers according to the size of the viewing audience. The principle was the same as in radio, except that experimenting on television was vastly more expensive. At the start, we had to make a firm decision to expect losses for a number of years; to hope that by developing the proper ingredients, we would break even; and then become profitable—before we lost our shirts.

And television did take off. In 1946, CBS Television consisted of one station broadcasting six to ten hours *a week*. There were so few sets in use that we gave the air time away free and charged only for the use of our studios, sets, props and costumes. Then there were just 6,000 TV sets in the whole country and CBS could only reach a fraction of them. In 1947, the number of television sets out there increased to about 250,000; New York, Washington and Philadelphia were interconnected by coaxial cable, and television advertisers increased from 31 to 181. We had begun to build a network. By 1948, the coaxial cable extended north to Boston and south to Richmond and a separate microwave link connected to Indiana, Kentucky and Ohio. In one week in April, we signed up nine new affiliates (none of them yet on the air) which gave us a total of twelve affiliated stations. This made CBS (briefly) the largest network in the nation. By August we had eighty stations, most of them unbuilt at the time, ready to join the CBS Television Network over the next three years. But then, in September 1948, the FCC announced a "freeze" to stop the proliferation of new television stations. That decision limited the country to 108 television stations then in existence for the next three and a half years. So, at CBS we were hampered in our growth, but we managed to increase our affiliates from twenty-eight in 1948 to sixty-two by the end of 1951.

Our total programming went from ten hours a week in 1946 to

twenty hours at the end of 1947 and thirty-eight hours a week by the end of 1948. One kind of program dominated the airwaves for all three of those years: live sports coverage. Baseball games, boxing matches, horse races—any sporting event, especially one with a given time schedule, was easy and inexpensive to telecast. All we needed was one or two cameras and a hookup. The presidential campaign of 1948 was a boon for the rising star of television—and presidential politics itself would never be the same thereafter. The camera brought the public right into the convention halls, face to face with the candidates. The 1948 campaign did for television acceptance what the 1928 presidential campaign had done for radio.

The key memory for me of those early days was that television, above all else, was something new and primitive and almost everything was broadcast live! That year, 1948, was the true beginning of television as we know it today. We began actually to produce our own programs from our own makeshift studios and we sent them out to the stations in our network via cable or on film through the mail. We had our first comedy, variety and dramatic programs, including a television adaptation of *Arthur Godfrey's Talent Scouts; Studio One*, which won fame as one of the most literate, adult, well-done dramatic series on television; and *Toast of the Town*, which later became *The Ed Sullivan Show* and ran for twenty-three years as the best variety program in the business. By the end of the following year, 1949, we were well on our way with programs of nearly every type, including variety shows, sports, pop music and blues, situation comedies, comedy-variety shows, mysteries, dramas, children's shows, quizzes, news and public affairs.

It was a period of creative chaos: everything was so new. Because we could not afford the more established professionals who worked in Hollywood making motion pictures, we had to find new writers, new producers, new cameramen, new directors. Out of sheer necessity, we would develop a long string of men and women whose careers were launched in early television, and who went on to fame and fortune in the world of entertainment. Stars were born, but in those early days everyone worked with fantastic speed and dedication. This medium gobbled up material at an astonishing rate. Comics who had been making successful livings in nightclubs with routines that lasted for months if not years saw their material disappear after two or three performances on television. The writers and producers of Broadway plays sold their work to Hollywood rather than have them used up in just one performance on television. *Studio One* televised wonderful classics of literature—the plays of Shakespeare, and *The Dybbuk*, and *The Scarlet Letter*. It had to develop a stable of young writers for its own programs. The early creative talents of television like Worthington C. Miner, who produced *Studio One*, raced the clock every single week to put on a one-hour dramatization of a play, a book, a short story or an original play. Productions were staged in makeshift studios at the start and every actor had to memorize his or her lines. Plays were televised live, usually by three cameras recording the scenes continuously. If someone missed or stumbled on a line, or tripped over a cable, it went on the air that way. In 1949, we finally completed our first large television studio in the Grand Central Building in New York, but even there our productions were primitive. Every live telecast was an adventure.

My friends in Hollywood would laugh and chortle over our early efforts. "You don't know how to light, you don't know how to apply make-up properly, the writing is wrong and the direction is wrong," they would say. And I would always reply: "Well, give us time. We're just starting. We can't hire you fellows; you want too much money; so we've got to teach ourselves. Naturally we're going to make mistakes, but in time we'll be okay. Don't worry about it." And, in time, we did just that. We improved and we got writers and directors who improved with time and experience and we got better actors and little by little we developed a schedule of television programs that eventually would put a severe crimp in the movie business itself.

I had complete confidence in the potential success of our television programming operation. I could see it growing before my eyes in size, scope and sophistication. It was not unlike my experiences in the early days of radio. But this time I was bolstered by the knowledge that we were now producing, packaging and selling so many of our own programs; once they succeeded, as I felt they would, we would control and keep them as long as they remained popular.

It was not until 1953 that our television network became profitable for the first time. We had finally succeeded in producing the programs that brought in the audience that attracted the sponsors. But to do that we had "invested"—or, to put it in a better way, had lost—approximately sixty million dollars.

That $60 million cost in launching television was financed out of the profits of our radio network. Radio helped give birth to television and, ironically, it was the growth of television that radically changed radio, killing off its popularity. Radio advertising sales for all networks combined reached their all-time high in 1948 and then began to decline. But at CBS, our radio advertising continued to grow for another two years. We were number one in the ratings and we had the pre-eminent stars in the entertainment field. The CBS Radio Network reached its peak year in sales in 1950—a level of prosperity for network radio that would not be seen again to this day. It was simply a turnabout. As people bought television sets, they listened to radio less. By 1951, all four radio networks were in decline, losing both listeners and advertising. So, after all those years, I found myself presiding over the decline of comedy, variety shows and dramas on radio.

In April 1951, CBS announced cuts in our afternoon and evening radio rates—a move that surprised the industry. But we found it was inevitable in the face of the clear economic facts. Within weeks NBC, ABC and Mutual made similar announcements. It was only the beginning. The networks continued to cut rates as the decline of traditional radio continued.

We all offered various new selling plans involving split sponsorship and partial sponsorship so that advertisers could spread their messages across the schedule. We also wanted to attract new, smaller advertisers and to make network radio as flexible and convenient as possible for the larger ones. In programming, ABC tried to give each night a theme—popular music, lectures, romantic stories. NBC introduced an important innovation, a weekend-magazine format called *Monitor,* in which a series of short segments—interviews, music, news and sports reports, humor, personalities, features and remote broadcasts from around the country—were all brought together under one title. The magazine format fitted the new cut-rate selling plans because individual segments could be sold separately.

At CBS we changed our programming very little during the early fifties, for the simple reason that in the *competitive* sense we were still very successful. Between 1951 and 1955 we had more than twenty of Nielsen's top twenty-nine radio shows. The other networks, with all their programming maneuvers, never came close to catching up.

However, our basic schedule—Godfrey in the morning, serials during the day, big names in prime time, dance orchestras late at night—could not stop the general shrinkage of network radio audiences. In 1951, for the first time since 1928, the CBS Radio Network lost money. Then, for the next several years it recovered its profitability.

We struggled to recapture our radio audience at CBS and studied many ingenious plans for new programming. In March 1955, for instance, I wrote to the president of our Radio Division, Adrian Murphy: ". . . about trying to find something unique which we could introduce into our CBS Radio schedule (particularly nighttime), it has occurred to me that we might use our news service, which enjoys an outstanding reputation, as a more integral part of our programming structure. What I have in mind is that in addition to the regular news spots, we would have a [new] service . . . of breaking into programs, particularly during portions where only music was being played, with news items which we consider to have national interest." That year we produced 101 news broadcasts per week—the largest number in any peacetime period up to that point.

Still, nothing could stem the tide. The turning point came in 1956, when the CBS Radio Network went into the red. It stayed there for the next seven lean years and then regained its profitability.

As I watched the tide go out on our radio network, we also lost our beachhead in the war over color television. By the time the government's order banning the manufacture of color TV sets was rescinded in March 1953, the number of black-and-white sets in use was up to about 23 million. It was an insuperable block to our incompatible color system. Peter Goldmark came up with a converter device for attachment to existing sets; but RCA in the interim also had developed a color system, which could transmit to existing black-and-white sets, without a converter. Finally, an *ad hoc* group of two hundred engineers from ninety-one manufacturing companies produced a refined color system based on the RCA system that was adopted by the FCC in December of that year.

CBS Labs continued its development of a Chromacoder camera which could be used in the new color system, but in March 1955, I summoned our top people involved in the project for a comparison test of both the CBS and the RCA color cameras. There were twelve of us there to make the evaluation in a small theater in New York. We observed a CBS live audition on two television receivers set upon the stage. Peter Goldmark, who headed the project, attended as an observer. Beads of perspiration dribbled down his face as he stood there. Frank Stanton sat next to me and the others were nearby, all of us in the first two rows of the theater. We watched in tense silence for fifteen minutes. When the program ended, there was a deadly pause before anyone would venture an opinion. I knew exactly what I thought. I stood up and said, "Gentlemen, I'll be glad to speak first. I think the RCA camera has us beat. It has better quality." I looked around and saw a general nodding of the heads. No one spoke. So I walked out and that was the end of that CBS project.

I was disappointed and chagrined. Paul Kesten's devotion to

this color system was the only thing he ever did in his long and distinguished career that turned out to be disastrous. And Stanton had carried that blind devotion for years beyond Kesten's retirement. We had had many discussions on the subject over the years and we had had many entreaties from the manufacturers to give up this fight. But Kesten and Stanton fought off such doubts as I would have, insisting the battle was there to win and the rewards would be stupendous. Dr. Goldmark, in addition to his inventive ingenuity, was a very persuasive man. In any event, I had gone along.

The consequences for CBS were considerable, not just in the loss of our color system and its out-of-pocket research costs of millions of dollars. The ramifications of that color system war got us into a terrible bind. With hindsight, I could see that we had not thought it through as carefully as we might have. Today we would have made a most thorough examination of the project and its consequences before starting. The fault lay not in our efforts to develop a color television system and failing. In fact, our efforts pushed RCA into developing their system in a crash program, which brought color television to the consumer long before it otherwise would have been on the market. The fault lay in our poor judgment in not having a fall-back position in the event our color system failed and in not having applied for licenses to acquire four more CBS-owned television stations back in 1946 or 1947. Those stations would have been ours for the asking at the time. Kesten and then Stanton had argued that the risk was worth taking, that if necessary we could apply for our stations at some later date. But no one could foresee that the FCC would freeze the number of stations allowed in 1948 and that later, when we came to buy the four more television stations CBS was entitled to own under FCC regulations, the value and the price of those stations would have increased tremendously. Nor was it only the price we would have to pay. The time, the effort, the tensions involved were incalculable. When we wanted to buy, television station owners did not want to sell. Those early stations were very profitable and it was a sellers' market.

It took us all of eight years to find suitable television stations in the right cities to complete the CBS complement of network-owned stations. In 1950, we found a station in Los Angeles still in the early stage of development and bought television equipment assets for $334,000. That became KNXT. It took us eight long years to find and to negotiate the purchase of the next three stations we wanted to buy, and they were considerably more expensive. We acquired station WBBM (formerly WBKB) in Chicago for $6 million in 1953 and KMOX-TV (formerly KWK) in St. Louis for $4 million in 1958. Our final acquisition was WCAU in Philadelphia in 1958, when we bought the television and radio station together for a total cost of $20 million. But that gave us finally our full quota of five network-owned television stations in major cities across the country.

The original aim, however, had clearly been to enter the general market and sell television sets, regardless of our color system, in a period of great demand. I even called Goldmark on that years later: "Well, Peter, I think you misled us, you know, about their [Hytron] engineers and the quality of them because after we bought the company, it seemed to me that they had a second-rate engineering department." And what was his answer?

"Well, Mr. Paley," he said, "I was interested in color and I wanted to do everything I possibly could to keep us in the race." The answer was incredible to me, but not as incredible as it had been trying to operate that company.

The trouble from the start and throughout was our inability to manufacture a top-quality television receiver for the retail market. One of my memos on the situation to Frank Stanton, whose area of responsibility included Hytron, tells the story as it happened. It said in part:

> This really leaves me up in the air. I thought everybody concerned, right from the beginning, had agreed with the principle that CBS-Columbia television receivers were to be designed to match the best in the field. I remember specifically mentioning that our sets had to be as good in every respect as those made by RCA and Philco—and better, if

there was any chance of doing so without getting ourselves too far out of line price-wise. Now Cogan [David Cogan, president of CBS-Columbia] says, in effect, that we are only able to be as good as the second-rung TV sets from the standpoint of quality. This is so inconsistent with what he said at our very last meeting when, in response to my questions, he took the position that our sets were as good as any on the market.

What we have to do is settle on a philosophy which will pertain to our TV set manufacturing activities. As I have stated so many times in our meetings, I'm very strongly on the side of producing top quality, even though we have to increase the price of our sets and narrow the margin of our profits. If over a period of time we get a stronger and stronger reputation for quality, it would be the best insurance I can think of toward giving us a chance to increase the volume of our business and to give us better sales stability when the market forces get weaker. . . .

I think it is important for us not to underestimate the value of the CBS-Columbia trademark. It is my view that even though we do not have a large advertising appropriation, this trademark, if supported by top quality, would allow us to sell in a price range comparable to RCA and Philco. As a matter of fact, if we sell *below* those two trademarks we automatically, I think, put ourselves in a lower grade of quality in the eyes of the trade and the public. Naturally, however, I do not recommend boosting prices without an equivalent increase in the quality of the product—so if we match the RCA and Philco prices, we also match their quality.

These are not easy questions to be sure—but we are not going to come to sound decisions in developing our long-term aims and objectives unless, when we discuss these questions, we all have the same facts in mind and remain consistent in our decisions, at least among ourselves, until they are changed among ourselves. This, I'm afraid, has not been happening.

It never did happen. Eight months later, in May 1952, I again wrote to Stanton, this time on complaints received from our distributors: "The letters from distributors add up to an intolerable situation. . . . We simply must bring about (at CBS-Columbia) the recognition of the importance of quality in the line." I warned him that "CBS will be getting the backlash of these unfortunate reactions to the detriment of our general operation."

Hytron became a persistent headache. We called in outside industrial engineers and tried to follow their recommendations. We got the resignations of the Coffin brothers, who were running the picture-tube end of the business, and also of David Cogan of CBS-Columbia, the division which manufactured the set. We hired three or four different managers to run CBS-Columbia. None of them made a success of it. Nothing seemed to work. Then, five years after we got into it, I decided to discontinue the manufacturing and sale of radio and television sets. We went out of that part of the business.

We continued on for another five years in the electronics end of the business: manufacturing tubes, semi-conductors and the like. And we continued to lose money. It was an agonizing, impossible situation because someone could always recommend just one more effort to save the situation. Finally, in 1961, I called in our financial vice-president and asked him, "How much do you think it will cost just to close down the whole thing and sell off what can be sold?" He came back within a week and said, "It'll cost about $12 million." I thought about that and about the cost of continuing and gave the order to shut it down. We liquidated it, sold off the plants, paid off our contractual obligations, and the cost came to within 2 per cent of the estimate, not counting the original cost and some operating losses along the way. We took our lumps and were out of the whole affair.

In retrospect, with today's knowledge and management methods, it is easy to see that before getting into Hytron, we should have made a thorough and professional evaluation of the whole industry, the company, its management, its product, the marketing projections. If we had done that, we would not have bought Hytron. Then sheer inertia and false optimism kept us in it for ten nagging years. It was much harder to decide to quit and admit failure than it had been to buy the company in the first place. I agonized over that decision to stop. Looking back it is not difficult to see that when we bought Hytron, we understood little or nothing about manufacturing television sets. Nor did we have the right touch for it. It just did not excite us as broadcasting did. Closing down Hytron made me a happy man again. I had got rid of an expensive headache. One might think men occupying such lofty positions as do William S. Paley and Frank Stanton always learn from such mistakes. We would never do such a thing again, would we?

But a few years later, CBS Laboratories developed a marvelous little invention called Electronic Video Recording, or EVR. It consisted of a small, round plastic cassette and a cassette player which, attached to any ordinary television set, would play a twenty-five-minute color film or a fifty-minute black-and-white program on the screen. When we announced EVR in 1967, the New York *Times* ran the story on page one and called it "a revolutionary electronic device." The possibilities for its use indeed seemed unlimited in education, in industry, in government, in the professions and in the home. There were predictions of a new billion-dollar business in the making and CBS was in the lead with the first such system on the market.

Both Goldmark and Stanton were enthusiastic about the video recorder and their projections on potential sales. But this time I was worried about getting into manufacturing again and I extracted a promise from Stanton that he would keep tight controls over expenditures on the project. I told him I did not want another Hytron situation. Later, I called him and Goldmark in again and insisted that EVR be offered to General Electric or a company like GE so that we could form a partnership with a company really knowledgeable in the field. I did not want CBS to go it alone on EVR; I simply felt uncomfortable and inexperienced in the technology business.

Much to my surprise a few months later I learned that we had not formed a partnership with GE or an American company but with Imperial Chemical Industries, Ltd. of England and CIBA United Kingdom, Ltd. They would develop EVR in Europe and we would license Motorola, Inc. to make the video players in this country, while CBS's EVR Division would manufacture the cassettes in a factory in New Jersey.

I was promised and assured that the EVR operation would not escape our strict managerial and financial control, as had Hytron. But over the next four years we encountered great problems in manufacturing here and abroad. When I called in outside consultants, I discovered our original marketing projections were absolutely unrealistic and overstated by a huge amount. It seemed to me we were once again in a hopeless situation, pouring millions of dollars into an invention for which there was only a questionable existing market. Our costs relative to projected sales were far, far out of line. Then several people associated with the EVR project began to admit to me that they were wavering on their earlier estimates for the success of the video recorder.

Except for a few specialized applications, we never did get to the market with EVR. The manufacturing problems seemed to overwhelm hopes and dreams. Finally, in 1971, after consultations with some of my associates, I had to say, "Enough, we've had enough." We sold off our overseas interests and began to phase out our domestic operations, and eventually wrote the whole venture off. I began to look upon Peter Goldmark, whose fame as an inventor for CBS had spread far and wide, as a thorn in my side. That year, he turned sixty-five and retired from the company.

On the other hand, we did manage to find a way to reverse the decline of network radio. By the mid-fifties, it was clear that to survive in competition with television, we would have to find a new role for network radio. Although our daytime schedule was more than 90 per cent sponsored, our prime-time evening shows were more than 80 per cent sustaining. Even our greatest stars could not stop the rush to television. Jack Benny left radio in 1958; Bing Crosby left nighttime radio in 1957 and quit his daytime program in 1962. It was sad to see them and other old-timers go. *Amos 'n' Andy*, which had been on radio since 1926 and on a network since 1929, left the air in 1960, and I wrote to

Gosden and Correll how I felt about it: "I just wanted you to know what a depressing feeling it gives me to face up to this fact."

As the fifties ran out, CBS shortened its network schedule, turning over more time to the affiliates. They did not need a network to send them recorded music to compete with the increasingly popular independent local radio stations which were featuring popular singers, rock and roll and charismatic disc jockeys. At CBS we considered rock and roll and decided we did not want to compete in that type of music and disc-jockey banter.

Financially, network radio on all three networks hit bottom in 1960. Sales were off about 75 per cent from their high in 1948. Any other industry would have been wiped out with that precipitous drop in sales. But network radio had a place in American life. If it was no longer in the living room, then it was in the kitchen, the bedroom, the automobile, almost everywhere else. And by the end of 1960, we at CBS had come up with a drastically new programming pattern, featuring more and more news and information programs. All serials were canceled, all weeknight entertainment was canceled, and two of the four weekend dramas were canceled. CBS News began producing, for the first time, more than half of the entire radio network schedule.

We had made new arrangements with our affiliates for carrying our network programs and before long our news and information programs took hold. We began to move ahead rapidly. Our radio network sales jumped 50 per cent in 1963 and for the first time in seven years, we showed a profit. In the sixteen years since then, CBS Radio has shown a profit every year, except two, largely because of the financial successes of CBS's seven wholly owned local radio stations. Of all the networks, only CBS owned the full complement of seven AM and seven FM radio stations allowed by the FCC: WCBS, New York; WEEI, Boston; WCAU, Philadelphia; WBBM, Chicago; KMOX, St. Louis; KNX, Los Angeles; and KCBS, San Francisco, each with an FM counterpart.

Our own seven stations followed the news and information format, augmented by talk shows in which listeners phoned in; but

Off the shore of Normandy for *D-Day Plus 20 Years* with Fred Friendly, President Eisenhower, and Walter Cronkite.

The first Kennedy-Nixon debate, at WBBM-TV, our Chicago station.

With Senator Kennedy.

The senator with Bob Sarnoff, Frank Stanton, and me.

Vice-President Nixon with Frank Stanton and me.

Lyndon Johnson at the last party in the Johnson White House.

In the Congo with Robert Murphy (left, standing) as
Patrice Lumumba sits with clasped hands.

With Winston Burdett in Africa.

Leonard Bernstein.

John Hammond.

Goddard Lieberson.

Simon and Garfunkel.

Bob Dylan.

Barbra Streisand.

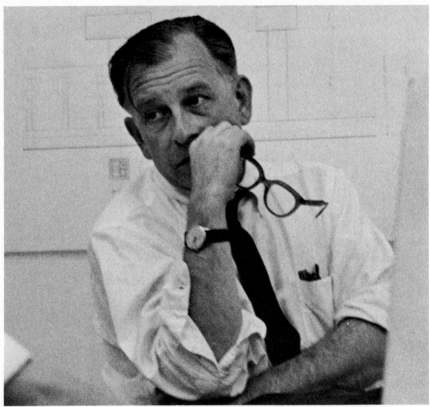

Eero Saarinen, original architect of CBS's new Headquarters Building.

Feeling the unique texture of the granite on the building.

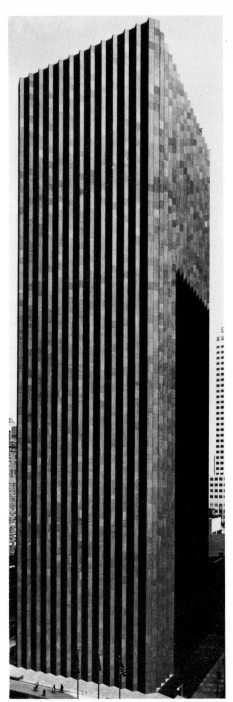

As the building began.

The Headquarters Building—a
matter of great pride.

Work in progress.

Picasso's "Boy Leading a Horse," in my city apartment.

only KMOX in St. Louis, which originated the call-in talk format, was successful with it. The other stations, while offering an alternative to popular music and disc jockeys, suffered competitively. In 1966, most of our own stations ranked fifth or below in their respective cities; WCBS, our home station, ranked ninth in New York City.

Turning my own attention to WCBS, to which I myself listened, it seemed to me that we needed to find a special, new format. It had to be something wanted by the public as an alternative to rock and roll music; it had to be something we in particular could do exceptionally well; and, finally, I wanted something which, if it did succeed, could not be easily duplicated or taken away from us by any other local station. I wanted to use the basic skills and strengths of CBS to help our own local station.

The answer was news. We would go to an all-news format. WINS, the Westinghouse station in New York, had already tried it with some success. But we had far more resources in the news department than WINS. I thought that if WCBS provided a solid news service around the clock, it would attract a kind of premium economic audience which would entitle WCBS to charge more for its advertising than most other stations in New York, just as the New York *Times* charges more than other newspapers for its advertising.

Would you believe that I was fought on this idea every inch of the way by the executives in charge of WCBS, and also by the head of our Radio Division? An elaborate presentation was drawn up to prove or to try to prove to me that if WCBS were changed to an all-news station, it would lose more than $5 million a year. Such formal presentations are taken very seriously in the company, and yet I felt sure in my bones that a news format could be a success. I asked for further studies on the subject. Again, I was presented with facts and figures projecting at least a $5 million-a-year loss. I retorted that with the news format, our New York radio station would be in time *earning* more than $5 million a year. The arguments went back and forth until I came to the conclusion that there ought to be a change in the radio management. Eventually, when John A. Schneider came in as the head of our new Broadcast Group, to whom our radio stations reported, he was asked to reorganize the Radio Division. By the end of 1967, two years after I first proposed the idea, WCBS adopted an all-news format throughout its air time.

The format consisted of national and world news from the network, local news reported by the station's own correspondents, live coverage of breaking stories, traffic reports, weather reports and the like. Slowly, the audience increased. After taking losses in the first two years of transition, WCBS became more and more profitable. Today, it ranks third among all the New York City radio stations, and it is well on its way to the profit goal I set for it so arbitrarily.

As for the CBS Radio Network, it is devoted today to news, sports reports, features, public affairs programs and live sports coverage. In this, it has changed little since the mid-sixties.

The radio network will never regain the popularity or financial importance in CBS that it enjoyed before the advent of television. In the early fifties, it was offering affiliates up to about eighty hours a week of regularly scheduled programs; today it feeds only thirty-five hours a week of regularly scheduled programs. And yet, there is real life in radio once again. The network in the course of a week now reaches more than 25 million listeners, about half of them tuned in to one of our wholly owned AM or FM stations. Advertising revenues have also increased through the years; in 1978, for instance, our Radio Division's sales were the best in the history of the company.

It does my heart good to see radio on its way up again, not so much for the profits but because I have a particularly warm feeling for radio. After all, it was my first love in this business.

From Radio to Television

For the performers—the talented men and women who put their careers, their reputations and their egos on the line every single time they reach out to an audience—the switch from radio to television was, in a word, terrifying. "Only one thing seems consistently apparent to me, and that is you just have to be twice as good on television as on any other medium." The man who wrote me that in a letter in 1949 was perhaps the best-known, most beloved star of radio and the motion pictures at the time: Bing Crosby. He had signed up to return to CBS Radio and I had written to him in California proposing that he consider a television variety series. His reply made the point: "Anytime you let down (on TV) for an instant you've lost your audience's interest, and it's a struggle to recapture it again." He turned down my offer, but said that he might "take a fling at it" in another year or so. He was sure he could do a good show, he said, but it would take a lot of work.

What bothered Crosby and many other stars was that in those days most television was live. Unlike the movies, one couldn't cover mistakes by retakes or choose between good, better, and best performances on successive takes. Bing had always preferred to use recordings for his radio performances. From any performer's point of view, live telecasts were akin to walking on a high wire without a net. And videotape would not be introduced until the mid-fifties.

Crosby was right to hedge at the start. A series is a weekly grind with a high risk of failure. Failure would diminish his drawing power in both movies and personal appearances. Nevertheless, I pursued him on the subject and Bing took his "fling," making his television debut on CBS in February 1951. But it was only a one-shot appearance. Not until 1964 did he consent to a weekly series, and that was as an actor in a domestic situation comedy on ABC, which lasted only one season. Thereafter, he confined his television performances to guest appearances and hosting "specials" which were videotaped.

For many stars, the switch to television was even more difficult because their shows had been fashioned for radio. No one knew this better than Freeman Gosden and Charlie Correll of *Amos 'n' Andy*. The two of them alone had played a whole cast of characters simply by changing their voices. On radio it hadn't mattered that the performers were white. When *Amos 'n' Andy* came to television, Gosden and Correll stayed behind the scenes and helped in a nationwide search for black actors to play Amos, Andy, the Kingfish and all the rest. The show went on CBS Television in 1951 and was an immediate hit. But in fact it had not made the transition successfully. Five days after the first broadcast, the National Association for the Advancement of Colored People (NAACP) denounced the show as insulting to blacks.

Here was a difference between radio and television we had not foreseen. Gosden and Correll had created a warm and funny fantasy world in the listener's imagination on radio. When that world became visual, it also became concrete and literal. *Amos 'n' Andy* remained on radio in some form until 1960. But the television show, under attack by black leaders for its entire life, left the network after two seasons.

We soon learned that creating television programs was a dynamic art with a life of its own. Producers had to find new forms or new variations on old forms. What worked on radio or on the stage or even in the movies did not necessarily work on the small screen. Above all, the latent, unexpressed interests and tastes of an audience change from year to year. What succeeded last year or five years ago may not work this year or next—especially on television. These were the concerns of all of us: network management, department heads, outside producers, directors and, above all, the performers.

Some performers made the transition to television easily, despite all their fears, and some did not. But the fears were there, spoken or not. Everyone in the entertainment world knew what had happened when sound came to the silent movies: many of the top dramatic stars of the silent screen were laughed and ridiculed into retirement when audiences heard their squeaky, untrained voices in the "talkies." John Gilbert, the masculine idol of the day, turned out to have a high, thin voice, and his fate was sealed with his first talking role in a movie.

One would think that a ventriloquist would fare better on television than on radio and yet that did not happen to the acknowledged master of the art. Edgar Bergen and his impish wooden sidekick, Charlie McCarthy, were loved by millions of radio listeners, but he appeared on CBS Television only twice during the 1950–51 season. He was terribly bothered by the fact that on radio he had grown careless about not moving his mouth while throwing his voice to Charlie McCarthy. On television, he could be seen moving his lips when they should have been tightly shut. I don't really believe this bothered the audience as much as it troubled him.

Red Skelton, on the other hand, whose pantomiming had to be imagined by the radio audience, made an even greater hit when he was seen on television. He was a natural vaudevillian with an intuitive feel for what makes people laugh. Yet before every television show, he was always awfully nervous, sweating, suffering terribly. But when the time was called, Skelton would walk out on stage and perform his own wonderful, special skits, at which

233

he was unique and a master. His show was frequently top-rated through the fifties and sixties on both CBS and NBC.

Burns and Allen were another matter. George Burns was enthusiastic about the possibilities of television, but he was at a loss for a format. He just did not know how to go about it. On stage, he always played the straight man with Gracie Allen, yet in real life George was one of the funniest men alive. No one appreciated this more than Jack Benny and myself. Jack was not in actuality a very funny fellow, but he loved to laugh at other comedians' jokes. He made a wonderful audience of one. And George Burns was obviously his favorite comedian. Jack would laugh so hard that he would slap his thigh uncontrollably at good jokes. People around him enjoyed rating jokes by the number of times Jack slapped his thigh. I think the record was an eight-slap rating for one of George Burns's punch lines. George had only to start one of his stories and Jack was ready to slap his leg.

In those years, I made a practice of visiting the West Coast at least twice a year, sometimes more often. Aside from the time spent on CBS business with radio and television people in Hollywood, a good deal of my social life in California was spent with many people in the film world, especially my old friends from the pre-war radio days. But these social relationships were important. We frequently discussed entertainment ideas and projects as close friends will, and in many instances my well-informed friends were helpful when CBS was looking for special talents for acting or production assignments. There were great parties, dinners and get-togethers in Hollywood where fun, good talk and business were all one. On occasions when George Burns was present, I always knew we were in for a night of big laughs.

George would tell stories, presumably true, of Jack and himself in the old vaudeville days. He would have us in stitches, Jack roaring with laughter and slapping his thigh, me rolling off my chair to the floor at parties. George would keep a straight face. He would hit a punch line, we'd laugh. Then he'd stop and when we thought he was through, he would add a topper. Then he'd wait and say, "But that's not all," and he'd add another topper, and on and on. Perhaps the anecdotes and jokes were not all that great, but it was the way George Burns could tell a story that was so humorous. You liked his stories because you like him so much as a person. That was his appeal to vast audiences, I think, but George himself did not seem to know it. He was confident only in private gatherings and I had to point out to him that he had unusual qualities which would work on television.

One day at lunch I confronted him and said, "You can do it." But he insisted, "I haven't got a format. I don't know how to do it. I'm a straight man. Gracie does the jokes. What part do I play?"

"Why don't you start the program in front of the curtain and do a monologue with your cigar and tell some jokes," I suggested. "Then when the curtain comes up, the two of you go into your usual kind of routine. Perhaps halfway through the program you could come out and do another monologue leading into another routine."

"That sounds interesting," he said. "Maybe I can work something out on that basis."

"Well, try it anyway," I said. "Make up a character, a story line, not just a string of jokes, and come show me what you've got."

He tried it and it worked. I think he worried that there would not be enough for him to do if he and Gracie just continued their radio act on television. But with George doing a monologue—the monologue of a straight man who was also funny—followed by the dialogue with Gracie, the show gained just enough structure to keep people interested and to hold their attention. Burns and Allen played on CBS Television from 1950 until Gracie decided to retire in 1958. After that George confined himself to specials and guest appearances and became the television presence the whole country knows today, a reflection of how funny he can really be in private.

Jack Benny worked hard to prepare himself for the transition to television. It took about a year and a half after my first talk with him before he was ready to make his première appearance on network television. And then he would agree to going on only once every eight weeks. His humor was highly calculated and was prepared with enormous effort. Some of the best writers in the business were on his staff. But he himself possessed a wonderful instinct for what was good and what worked for him on the air. He kept most of the cast of his radio program and retained that old familiar comedy format on television. Some new visual trademarks were added—the long stare, the hand to the cheek, the mincing walk—but he was the same stingy, vain, harassed character the audience knew on radio. On his first network television appearance, October 28, 1950, Jack brought the house down with his very first line, pitting his reputation for stinginess against his reputation for vanity. "I'd give a million dollars to know what I look like," he said. America understood Jack Benny and loved him.

Jack understood that comedy was more than just being funny. The audience has to like or at least take an interest in the comedian as a person or as a character in a situation. Jack would often explain to me and to others: "People tune in to me every week, not because I have a great show every week. I can't and nobody can. But they get in the habit of wanting to know what I am up to."

The number of his shows was gradually increased each year until the full complement of weekly broadcasts was reached. *The Jack Benny Program* on CBS usually ranked in the top ten until 1957, after which it was only moderately successful. When his contract with us expired in 1964, Jack Benny went to NBC but lasted there for only one season. He then devoted himself to only occasional (but excellent) specials. I think Jack was hurt when CBS did not renew his contract in 1964, but he never said anything about it to me. One of the very sad things about all entertainment stars is that like athletes every one of them knows his or her career must end someday; but when that day arrives, it is very hard to accept the inevitable. After Jack left CBS, we did not see each other for some time but then our friendship was renewed on very cordial terms. A few days after Jack died in December 1974, CBS did a special tribute to him and I made one of my rare appearances on television to express some of my feelings about a great entertainer and a good man and, in part, I said:

". . . I can never see another Jack Benny coming along. He left, however, with those who are professionals, a conviction, I think, after they knew how he prepared himself, that to produce a successful show or program of any kind—and maybe particularly a comedy program—a great deal of work and sweat has to go into it. . . .

"Jack had a great respect for his audience. . . . He regarded them as adults who appreciated good humor, who were sophisticated and who couldn't be talked down to. He never talked down to his audience."

Then there was an effervescent redhead named "Lucy" who would become an American institution on television—and she did not want to make the switch either. I really seemed to have done a lot of arguing and persuading with radio stars back in the late forties and early fifties. Lucille Ball, that extraordinarily talented comedienne, one of the true greats in the entertainment world, was the star of our radio show *My Favorite Husband* and I wanted to move her and the show to television in 1950.

"Not without Desi," she said firmly.

I told her that was impossible. Desi Arnaz, her husband, was a Cuban bandleader who spoke with a thick Spanish accent. He had acted only in some low-budget B-films and had appeared on an unsponsored, unmemorable radio program. But Lucy wanted him to play her husband in the television version of *My Favorite Husband*.

"Lucy," I tried to explain as gently as possible, "he's a bandleader, he can't act. What'll we do with him?"

"Bill, I'm sorry," said Lucy, explaining that Desi traveled all the time on one-night stands with his band and that she wanted a more normal married life; she wanted to have a child, and she put him and their life together above her career. "I'm not going to go on the air unless it's with him. If I can't do a television show with him, I'm going to travel with him."

Her mind was made up. I could see that. So after arguing for a bit more, I agreed. The writers were put to work and they came up with an idea for a female star married to a Cuban orchestra leader. And they found the simplest, most obvious situation comedy—a no-talent girl married to a struggling band leader whom she is always trying to help with her ideas and sketches. It turned out to be a marvelous vehicle for both of them. Desi Arnaz proved to be highly talented as an actor, much to my surprise and everyone else's. Then he also demonstrated that he was a very good business manager and producer of other situation comedies for television; in fact, one of the best in the business.

Their show was renamed *I Love Lucy* and it became one of the most important programs in television history. It was the top-rated program on television for four years, and second and third in two other years. In 1952–53, the season Lucy had a baby—both in real life and as Lucy Ricardo on television—the series had an average audience rating for the season of an incredible 67, which meant that an average of 67 per cent of all the people who owned television sets in the United States were watching *Lucy* every week of that season. Today, if a program wins a rating of 20 to 25 of the potential audience, it is deemed a success. A mere 18 per cent is enough to keep it on the air. That historic high for a series has been approached only once since then. And that was when *Lucy* received a 59 the following 1953–54 season.

When you count the reruns, *Lucy* still has a claim today to being the most popular series in the history of television. No series has been rebroadcast as many times as *I Love Lucy*. It was in fact one of the very first filmed series in the age of live television. Because the show only had two or three sets, it could be put on film without stretching the budget too far.

Ed Sullivan was hired as temporary master of ceremonies for a variety program I wanted in 1948 because the CBS programming department could not find anyone like Milton Berle, the most popular comedian on early television. Ed Sullivan certainly had no personal performing talent that any of us could discern when we hired him. But he was a newspaper columnist who knew the world of entertainment and he promised that he could produce a good show cheaply. We planned to replace him as soon as we could afford a professional master of ceremonies for the program called *Toast of the Town*.

Ed Sullivan proved his talent as a showman who could attract the best and most timely performers from all four corners of the world of entertainment. His first broadcast of *Toast of the Town* at nine o'clock, Sunday evening, June 20, 1948, was a broadcasting phenomenon. The great Broadway team of Richard Rodgers and Oscar Hammerstein II performed on that first show along with a little-known comedy duo making its first television appearance, Dean Martin and Jerry Lewis. The list of performers who made their television debuts on subsequent Sullivan shows is truly outstanding, a tribute to Sullivan himself: Louis Armstrong, Fred Astaire, Lionel Barrymore, Humphrey Bogart, James Cagney, Gary Cooper, Henry Fonda, Jackie Gleason, Bob Hope, Burt Lancaster, Phil Silvers. *Toast of the Town* also introduced Julie Andrews, Maurice Chevalier, Noel Coward and the Beatles to American television audiences. Sullivan was always timely in presenting public personalities at the height of their prominence. His programs appealed to every level of taste. Yet, his popularity was magical—beyond explanation. He himself could not perform in any way. He never tried. All he had to do was talk, and he did very little of that.

The heart and hotseat of CBS Television has always been our programming department, where the ultimate decisions are made as to which programs get on the air, on what day of the week and at what time. From the start, we have been fortunate at CBS to have attracted some of the most outstanding men in this very specialized business. Our own pioneers of programming were Worthington C. Miner and Gilbert Seldes, who were the first to develop CBS television programs of the forties. They were followed by two of the most talented men in the business, Hubbell Robinson and Harry S. Ackerman, both of whom left the Young & Rubicam ad agency to join CBS Television in 1947 and

1948. Ackerman headed our Hollywood productions and Robinson was executive vice-president in charge of programs in New York.

Ackerman proved to be excellent—one of the best in the business for situation comedy. Robinson, an attractive man, well-educated and personable, became the all-around man in our programming department. He spoke quietly and with a literary flair. Culturally, his interests were levels above many of his colleagues. At times, he may have lacked the common touch. His special flair was for high-quality programming, which he liked to call "mass with class." Dapper, small and self-confident, he did not suffer fools easily, and some people considered him arrogant. I worked well with him and always appreciated what he brought to CBS.

Studio One, broadcast live, was Worthington C. Miner's classic creation. The series remained in New York until January 1958, when it moved West and became *Studio One in Hollywood;* nine months later it went off the air. But for ten years it was a jewel. *Studio One* was the television starting ground for some of the great American directors and producers, such as John Frankenheimer, Franklin Schaffner, Felix Jackson and Martin Manulis. Even the BBC sent a team to New York to study its innovative production techniques.

For similar reasons I can't forget *Playhouse 90,* organized by Hubbell Robinson, which began in 1956 and lasted until 1961. One of the best of the anthology drama shows, it was an ambitious series that presented a ninety-minute drama every week, employing the best writers, directors and actors available. Perhaps some will remember *Requiem for a Heavyweight, A Sound of Different Drummers, The Miracle Worker* and *Judgment at Nuremberg.* Despite the inherent disadvantage of the anthology concept (its lack of continuity) on television, *Playhouse 90* was quite successful.

If you look at tapes of these programs today, they seem rather old-fashioned. Of course the writing and acting talent in them is timeless, but given that same talent today we could make much better programs. There is a temptation to regard those days through a nostalgic fog and think, "Ah, *Studio One* and *Playhouse 90* have never been matched," but when you see the actual programs, you find that it just isn't true. A lot has been learned since then. The alumni of both *Studio One* and *Playhouse 90* consist of writers like Reginald Rose, A. E. Hotchner, Rod Serling, Merle Miller, Arthur Hailey and Abby Mann, and young actors like Walter Matthau, Jack Lemmon, Charlton Heston, Paul Newman and James Dean. These two series, along with NBC's *Philco Television Playhouse*, probably did more for the art of American television than any other group effort.

On Sunday afternoon, November 9, 1952, we introduced *Omnibus*, which we heralded as "the largest and most ambitious entertainment and informational series of programs in television history." The claim was not extravagant: television history covered only a few years up to then, and it would be difficult to point to a higher plateau of consistent program quality to date. *Omnibus* presented Leonard Bernstein explaining music; Joseph Welch discussing the law; Helen Hayes reading fairy tales; E. Power Biggs explaining the organ; and original drama by distinguished playwrights in productions performed by first-rate actors. There were film essays, interviews with all sorts of people and scores of other features over a wide range of forms and subjects. The series was produced in an unusual manner, perhaps unique in commercial television. It was created and financed by the TV-Radio Workshop of the Ford Foundation. We offered it for sponsorship, and, if sold, the network got its time revenue and the Workshop its production costs. As expected, it appealed only to a minority of the public and did not get high ratings; but it remained on the air for seven years, four on CBS, one on ABC, and two on NBC. It is fitting that its host was Alistair Cooke, and its producer Robert Saudek, now head of the Museum of Broadcasting in New York City. This is an institution I created in 1976 so that the classics of early radio and television would be preserved as a library to be used by scholars, researchers and the *aficionados* of broadcasting.

In those early days I believe CBS quickly established itself as the leading network in program quality. Even discounting the influence of nostalgia, I think it's safe to say that the shows I have just described, regardless of whether they were popular successes, were television classics. For several years we were not the most popular network—NBC was. We were second, while ABC and DuMont were far, far behind. But in the early fifties we slowly began to approach that elusive, fragile, ideal mixture of programming that caters to some of the more specialized, more refined tastes and yet pleases a large part of the mass audience most of the time. Our audience grew to the point where, in 1955, while we still had *Studio One* and *Omnibus*, we also had seven of the top ten programs on television: *The $64,000 Question*, *I Love Lucy*, *Toast of the Town* (renamed *The Ed Sullivan Show* in 1955), *The Jack Benny Program*, *December Bride*, *I've Got a Secret* and the *General Electric Theater*.

In 1955 CBS became by far the leading network in popularity. It would remain number one in the audience ratings for twenty-one years—an incredible record that no one foresaw, guessed, or could have believed back in the beginning. Thus we were preeminent in quality and also led in ratings. Being the most popular network was a nice position to be in, and though we could hardly expect to stay there undisturbed forever, we would always try.

Questions and Answers

Quiz shows became the rage of television in the late fifties—and the outrage of the industry, which learned that it had to police itself. We introduced the first big-money quiz on the air in 1955 called *The $64,000 Question* and within a few weeks it became the most popular program on television, surpassing even *Lucy*. It became the talk of the industry, a bright new format which captured the public's imagination and interest.

The show was produced by an independent production company, owned largely by Louis G. Cowan, a truly creative professional who had a special feel and flair for showmanship. A few weeks after *The $64,000 Question* went on the air, Lou Cowan came to work for CBS as a top adviser at the corporate level on all CBS programs. He severed all operational connections with his own production company when he joined CBS, where his principal task was to evaluate the creative output of the network. He became in effect our creative troubleshooter, and three years later he had so impressed us that we made him president of the television network. And *The $64,000 Question* was still going strong on the air, along with its many imitators.

The show had a starkly simple format: contestants were asked a series of increasingly difficult questions on a topic of their own choosing; each correct answer doubled the previous cash prize, but one incorrect answer lost it all. After each correct answer, the dramatic suspense increased as the contestant was asked to decide: Would he or she play it safe and stop—or take the risk and go on? The excitement mounted and the suspense pulled in the audience each week because *The $64,000 Question* dealt in cash prizes unmatched on television or anywhere else. The show really was based on a popular radio program of the forties called *Take It or Leave It*. Its $64 prize, so innocent in those days, introduced a new idiom to our language: "That's the sixty-four-dollar question."

The $64,000 Question was so successful that the following season we introduced *The $64,000 Challenge,* produced by the same company, in which the winners in the *Question* show could compete in the *Challenge*. Robert Strom, an eleven-year-old whose category was electronics, won a total of $224,000. But the all-time record was set by Teddy Nadler, a forty-nine-year-old former civil servant from St. Louis who had never earned more than $70 a week in his life. He won $252,000 on *The $64,000 Challenge*.

The big-money quizzes, including *Twenty-One* and *The $100,000 Big Surprise* on NBC, were a bonanza for everyone involved—contestants, networks, production companies and sponsors. Revlon, the sponsor of *The $64,000 Question,* increased its cosmetics sales by more than 50 per cent in a year's time. Quiz shows spread to daytime programming. They became so popular they attracted established celebrities—Vincent Price, Peter Ustinov, Boris Karloff, Edward G. Robinson—as contestants. Dr. Joyce Brothers, a psychologist, and Charles Van Doren, an instructor at Columbia University, became television personalities.

Then in the summer of 1958 like a house of cards it all collapsed in the worst scandal ever to hit television. One week in August a standby contestant for the daytime quiz show, *Dotto,* on CBS, accused another contestant of having been given the answers to the questions she would be asked on the show. We had a

CBS attorney investigate that situation on *Dotto* and on all the other quiz shows appearing on CBS television. A flurry of investigations followed, including one by the district attorney of New York. But before those other investigations were well under way, our own attorney reported to us that indeed *Dotto, The $64,000 Question,* and several other CBS quiz shows, but not all, had been rigged.

The quiz shows had been put together and produced by outside production companies. Nevertheless, we had broadcast them and we were ultimately responsible for what went out on the air. Our attorney reported to Frank Stanton and he brought me into the picture. The situation, as we learned it, was that in order to keep audience interest high, some producers had plotted out the action as carefully as if the quizzes were dramatic shows. These producers decided who, on the basis of personality and audience appeal, should win each game; answers were supplied to these contestants and, even further, the contestants were instructed on how to act perplexed before giving their answers. The producers had not only deceived us, they had fooled some of the major banks of New York where the answers were kept before show-time in locked vaults to guard their integrity.

CBS made as thorough an investigation as possible and found that not all the facts were clear-cut. Some shows were unquestionably fraudulent, some used borderline practices, some were clearly innocent. Our in-house investigation, I must say, was particularly vigorous, for we were not at all happy over the situation. As soon as enough evidence seemed certain to us, we met and decided to act with vigor. Rather than pick and choose or delay our decision or make further excuses, we canceled the big-money quiz shows on CBS. From NBC and elsewhere, there were suggestions that with careful policing and safeguards in the future, the quiz-show form could be continued. At CBS we had seven big quiz shows on the air per week and we canceled them all.

The scandal did irreparable damage to the reputation and careers of those who had assisted in perpetrating the fraud. A heavy cloud of suspicion hung over those whose involvement had been innocent. Lou Cowan bore much of the public's suspicion and was being smeared rather badly over the scandal. But he steadfastly proclaimed his innocence, insisting that he knew nothing at all about the rigging that had been going on, and we believed him. He had served in the OWI with Stanton* during World War II and the two men had known each other for years. Stanton had every reason to trust the man's integrity. Certainly our investigation turned up absolutely no proof of his involvement. Because of the scandal, he was called to testify before a House investigating subcommittee. Under considerable tension, Cowan suffered an attack of thrombophlebitis and was hospitalized for six weeks and unable to testify. He was suspected openly of faking an illness to stall his appearance before the investigators. This just was not true. However, there was no getting around the charge that even if he was innocent of any rigging, as head of the network he should have known what had been going on for so many years. In December 1959, with some understandable but short-lived bitterness, Lou Cowan resigned as president of the network.

Neither Stanton nor I had known about the rigging, but of course this was no defense for CBS and we recognized that. We were, to be sure, troubled over the whole affair and chagrined that we had been duped. Moreover, we had had warnings but had failed to heed them. There had been rumors afloat for quite a while that the quiz shows were rigged or at least suspect. But there are almost always rumors, planted stories and downright lies about successful shows or performers in this industry. We had given very little attention to the quiz shows because they were so successful and problem-free and thus did not require the attention of top management. In the aftermath, this was no ex-

* Frank Stanton was a man of remarkable energy and devotion to work. During World War II, working seven days a week, he served as a consultant to OWI and to the War Department in Washington, D.C., for half of the week while carrying a full workload the rest of the week with CBS in New York.

cuse. The public held CBS responsible for everything that we broadcast, including programs produced by independent outside companies, as these quiz shows had been.

Before the year was out Stanton made a pledge on behalf of CBS in a famous speech to the Radio-Television News Directors Association in New Orleans: "We accept the responsibility for content and quality and for assurance to the American people that what they see and hear on CBS programs is exactly what it purports to be." This applied to all programs, not just quizzes. We developed and instituted new rules at CBS requiring such now-familiar announcements as "This program was pre-recorded" and "Participants in this program were selected and interviewed in advance." We created a Program Practices Department to see that the rules were followed.

When the quiz-show scandal finally died away it was clear that all of broadcasting had been injured. The public had a little less confidence in everything it saw and heard on the air. But some good did come out of all this. On our part, we learned painfully the need to be fully cognizant of the content and the production background of every program broadcast by CBS. We—and the other networks—set forth new policies which gave us much closer supervision and controls over what went out on the air.

Some critics in the government and in the industry complained that this new development gave too much control over programs to the networks. And this argument has never been fully resolved. Perhaps it never will be. On the one hand, the government and the public holds us responsible for what our stations broadcast; yet, as we try to exercise the responsibility, they say that we have too much control. If we do not practice control, we are accused of irresponsibility; if we take over the broadcasts, we are accused of being arbitrary over tastes and being monopolistic. All that has led not only to certain litigation and regulatory proceedings but also to a built-in tension that network broadcasters have to live with daily.

Another outcome of the scandal was that at CBS we felt that in addition to replacing the canceled quiz shows we should find some way to redeem our credibility as a network which recognized its responsibilities to the public interest. More than canceling shows and making public announcements of new program practices had to be done. That was the consensus of the innumerable conferences held on this subject. We decided to ask our News Division to gear up for a number of prime-time documentaries and to expand the *CBS Reports* programs. Our newsmen had always asked for a bigger share of the nighttime schedule. Now, more time was set aside for prime-time hour-long documentaries.

While the quiz-show scandals were still alive and kicking, in the spring of 1959, I got the first intimations of my own mortality. It started with a bad chest cold that cut short a wonderful golfing party at the beautiful National Golf Links in Southampton, New York. When I returned home my family doctor told me his X-ray showed a shadow which indicated the possibility of a tumor on one of my lungs. I knew what that meant. I had smoked quite a bit over the years: cigars as a young man in my father's cigar factory and cigarettes ever since I had turned into a "smart New Yorker" some thirty years before.

Babe and I decided I should go to New York Hospital for a full and complete examination. A specialist at the hospital did a bronchoscopy on me—putting a lighted instrument down my throat for a look at my bronchi and lungs—and informed me that my lungs were dark purple and the texture of velvet instead of being smooth, pink and glistening. We discussed my cigarette smoking and he asked, "How many do you smoke, usually, a day?"

So I had to tell him. "Four or five packs a day."

He gave me a stern lecture, which was not surprising. "Mr. Paley," he concluded, "if you saw your lungs, you would never smoke a cigarette again."

I raised my hand and said, "See this cigarette?"

"My God," he exclaimed, "you had a cigarette concealed in your hand all the time I was talking to you?"

"Yes," I said, "and it's the last one I will ever smoke."

He shrugged and said, "I've heard that before."

I dropped the cigarette into a nearby bowl of gushing water and when I met Babe, who was waiting for me in my room in the hospital, I announced, "I've stopped smoking." And she agreed with the doctor. "Oh, for God's sake, you'll never quit." Their disbelief made me furious and I resolved truly there and then, "I'll never smoke again, I promise you."

And I never did.

Among the several specialists who examined me, opinion was divided on whether or not I had a growth on my lungs, but the consensus among the doctors finally was that to play it safe I ought to undergo exploratory surgery. So, with considerable trepidation, I submitted myself to a major operation and awoke in the intensive-care ward to find out that I did not have lung cancer or a tumor or anything wrong with me other than a peculiar diaphragm which had pushed my right lung out of its proper position, causing it to cast an X-ray shadow.

One might expect that I would be happily relieved by the outcome, but I was depressed. Something had happened to me in mind as well as body. For a year afterward, I was in a very bad state. The doctors said they had seen that happen to people who escaped unscathed from severe automobile accidents. The reaction, the doctors thought, might come from the vivid realization of how close to death a person had come. I don't know what it was with me.

Nearly three months passed between the bad cold and the operation and hospital recovery, and then Babe and I went to Biarritz for about a month as part of my convalescence. I played golf and tried to be sociable at lunch and dinner with people we knew there. But I still felt low and unhappy, and I suppose I was disagreeable. Babe said I was not easy to live with. I did not get much fun out of anything. I would be myself for a while and then a blanket of gloom would come over me. The only excuse I could offer Babe in expiation was that there were two Williams: William and Guillaume (French for William). William was me

249

when I was myself. Guillaume was whoever I was when I was depressed. My surgery and slow recovery must have been very difficult for Babe, but she saw me through it with her good humor, spiced with her own direct frankness whenever I was feeling too sorry for myself.

Many good friends were concerned over my health and well-being and they tried to cheer me up, but none more than Michael Tree from London, who has called me "Dads" ever since we became close friends many years ago. In November 1959, he wrote me in his own inimitable way:

"You must not sit in draughts and always wear a muffler or overcoat even in the summer. You must be helped from your car and take a long time in your movements in case your heart reacts to the strain. Now be sure to take digitalis, go to bed at ten and have breakfast in bed and above all avoid fats in case your cholesterol goes up.

"I think you had better cut out swimming and golf—they are things for more active and much younger men to indulge in.

"I feel if you take my advice you have a good chance of reaching sixty. Anyhow it's worth trying."

I had just turned fifty-eight. Nice boy.

Returning to work fully recovered physically, I found that I had lost a good deal of the drive I had had before the operation. I slipped into a rather passive role at CBS and did not mind it at all. Even after resuming my usual hours, I simply lacked my former zest. It was easy for me to pass problems that reached my desk on to others, particularly to Stanton. When I had left for the hospital, I had delegated my authority to him and now that I was back—or half back—it was very simple to go along with decisions that had worked their way up the chain of command to my desk. After a while, however, my strength and energy returned and I dove back into the maelstrom of everyday network and company activities.

I have been told that this caused some strain on Stanton: he had done a superb job during my absence and did not particularly enjoy passing back the final executive authority. However, he never suggested to me that he had such feelings.

We had no disagreement whatever on the appointment of James T. Aubrey, Jr., in December 1959, as president of the CBS Television Network, to succeed Louis Cowan. Eighteen months before, we had hired Aubrey who had been working for ABC as vice-president in charge of programming and talent. He worked for us at the corporate level as Cowan had done when he first came to CBS. Aubrey was just turning forty-one when we made him network president, which was fairly young for that kind of responsibility. But he was bright, aggressive, good-looking, and he had a sophisticated charm when he chose to use it. Above all, he showed us that he had a sure, self-confident instinct for the kind of television programs that would appeal to a mass audience. He also had a good sense of business and administration. He was a hard-driving man, tenacious and goal-oriented and over the next five years he gained a reputation throughout the industry as the most efficient, talented executive in television. CBS had been number one in the ratings when he arrived, but in the years of his tenure, he increased our lead, he increased our profits. In addition to all that, he had his own instinctive touch for finding new talent and new programs for the little screen. Aubrey held success in the palm of his hand. There was no question within CBS that he was in line to become my successor. He was young and time was on his side.

And yet his regime ended in tragedy.

Over the long pull, he could not handle his own success: power went to his head and bedazzled his common sense. He became more and more arbitrary and autocratic. He made many enemies. The industry seethed with rumors about him, about his handling of certain business affairs and about his personal life. I myself never saw any of this in my own dealings with him. Whenever we met, he was courteous, bright, and devoted to his work. So I paid no particular attention to the rumors, for, as I have said, in this highly visible business, rumors were always flying about. Then Stanton told me that on several occasions Aubrey had telephoned him at all hours of the night and had carried on wildly, saying some very abusive things to him—for which I would have fired him on the spot had he telephoned me in such a manner. However, this to me was direct evidence, much more than were the rumors.

Both Stanton and I began to take a closer look at this man whom we both had admired. I began to think that perhaps I had made a misjudgment in the first place or that the man had changed. After all, he *was* called behind his back "The Smiling Cobra." Then late one Friday afternoon in February 1965, the thought came to me: If anything happened to me and to Frank Stanton at the same time, would Aubrey be qualified to run CBS? I knew the answer by instinct. So I walked down the hall, opened the door and said, "Frank, he's got to go." Stanton did not have to ask who "he" was.

He telephoned Aubrey who was then in Miami, and asked him to return to New York at once. In his office, he told Aubrey that he was out and that I wanted to see him.

Aubrey, I must say, was magnificent in defeat. He came to see me at the Regency Hotel, where Babe and I were staying while our new apartment was being furnished. At the time, I was in bed in traction with a bad back. Aubrey, standing there tall, physically fit, and handsome, apologized forthrightly. "I know I've made a mess of things," he said. He knew of course that the final decision had been mine. "I want to ask you for another chance and tell you that I would never let these things happen again, but I know you won't do it; I know I don't deserve another chance. And, I want you to know that I understand your actions and will never say or do anything to hurt the company." In my eyes, he was a strong, well-disciplined man, despite his excesses, and I wished him well. Some time afterward, I received a call from an executive at Metro-Goldwyn-Mayer about Jim Aubrey and I gave him a full recommendation in regard to his abilities, adding that I believed he had learned from his mistakes at CBS. He was made president of MGM.

Jim Aubrey, during his reign as network president, was given almost complete credit for every program that appeared on CBS from 1960 to 1965 and he deserves much of that credit. Yet, unseen by the public are the many men in the programming department of the Television Division and also the very important programming committee, which consists of the heads of the programming department, members of our research department, the network president, the president and the chairman of the corporation. Every single program that appears on the air and where and when it appears on the air is decided by consensus of the programming committee. Strategy and tactics play a large part in our decisions of what type or what specific program should come off the air and which should go on the air. Everyone has an equal opportunity to express his opinion and just about everyone does. We are in theory all equal, but some, as the saying goes, are more equal than others. Aubrey, as network president with a well-rounded background in television programming, held a firm grip upon what shows and what performers went on the air over CBS. And, as head of the company, also with a background in programming, my views carried more weight than others. Sometimes, honest differences of opinion were debated heatedly, but in the end we arrived at a general agreement. At times I have muted my views in order to avoid even the appearance of dictating to the others. On rarer occasions I have pushed for certain programs that the majority of the programming committee did not want. Very rarely has a program been chosen or a schedule changed without my approval.

Deciding what goes on the CBS network is an ongoing process throughout the year. In August 1960, when Aubrey set forth his plans for entertainment specials for his first full season, I wrote him a long memo, which I record in part here because it indicates in a general way my own programming philosophy which, at the time, I wanted to share with him. Asserting that "I am frankly disappointed in what I see," I reminded him that we had discussed ideas for some outstanding cultural shows, including a Shakespearean play with Orson Welles, a special with Laurence Olivier, an unusual painting explained by Picasso or some other artist, a ballet special by Balanchine, an opera by Menotti. His staff was supposed to be "hot on the trail of five or six" such properties but I saw none of them on his list of specials for the 1960–61 season. Nor did I see any original drama which we had discussed as four or five special *Playhouse 90's*. My memo concluded with this general statement on programming:

One of the important things to bear in mind in developing the creative output of a mass medium is balance as between various levels of creative quality. CBS for years was able to maintain the kind of balance which, on the one hand, gave most of the people what they wanted and enjoyed most of the time while, at the same time, producing enough product of outstanding merit to gain for itself a reputation of quality, responsibility, etc. I know that this year we are doing more than ever before in the public affairs and news field, for which I am sure we will gain much credit, although NBC competition in these areas will be breathing down our necks hotter than ever before. On the other hand, I think we are leaving ourselves too inactive in the cultural and dramatic fields. Even though some of the things listed for the coming season done by outside organizations might get good attention and bring us some important award recognition, I am just afraid that . . . when people come to look upon the season as a whole, we will not have the same level of success in this quality field as we have had in past years.

I would like to discuss the above with you at the earliest opportunity.

In time, as the sixties rolled on, we did come through with a heavy schedule of outstanding cultural specials, often forty or fifty of them a year. Many of them brought great credit and public acclaim to CBS, including Arthur Miller's *Death of a Salesman* with Lee J. Cobb and Mildred Dunnock in their original Broadway roles; *The Crucible, A Midsummer Night's Dream* performed by the Royal Shakespeare Company; *Vladimir Horowitz at Carnegie Hall* (his first television recital); specials produced in cooperation with the National Geographic Society and a number of plays written and produced especially for television on the *CBS Playhouse* series.

But the sixties were known far and wide not for these specials but for the predominance of television comedies, and CBS led the pack, We seemed very skilled at finding good comedy and comedy stars. In the 1962–63 season, for instance, CBS had eight of its programs in the top ten, and seven of them were comedies. In that same year, NBC and ABC together had two programs in the top ten, neither of which was a comedy. As the decade ended, the pattern remained the same: in the 1969–70 season, CBS had six of its programs in the top ten, and five of them were comedies. That year NBC and ABC together had four programs in the top ten, only one of which was a comedy. The success of CBS programming obviously was built upon a foundation of comedy. And yet, as I think back now, I know that the heavy schedule of comedy was not part of any conscious plan. We did not decide: "Let's emphasize comedy for all of the sixties." The comedy shows just seemed to come to us and when they were good we put them on the air. Ever since the so-called Paley Raids, which brought *Amos 'n' Andy,* Jack Benny, George Burns, and Red Skelton to us, other comedians, such as Jackie Gleason and Dick Van Dyke, gravitated to CBS.

The most dominant comedies on CBS were the situation comedies with a rural setting, which seemed just naturally to follow the Westerns that had begun to fade in popularity in the early sixties. A good example of this new type of comedy was *The Andy Griffith Show,* which we put on in 1960. It was a gentle, relaxed program about a likable small-town sheriff. It was not much noticed in the critiques, nor was it viewed as a particularly outstanding program. Yet everyone seemed to enjoy it. It rose almost immediately to the top ten and never left it during the sixties. When Andy Griffith left the show in 1968, we changed the name of it to *Mayberry R.F.D.*, continued the locale and most of the same characters, and it remained in the top ten. The *Griffith* show was the precursor of all the rural type of comedies. *The Beverly Hillbillies* was introduced in 1962 and within one month became the most popular program of that season and the next. It had a long, long run in the top ten. Certain television critics and some of my highbrow friends criticized *The Beverly Hillbillies* as representative of what they called the cheap programs television brought into homes to attract the mass audience. When confronted with this sort of attack, I insisted that I personally liked that program, and I did. The reason was simple, as I would tell them: "I like it because it is very funny. It's a slapstick comedy—a form of entertainment that amuses me and many other people of low and high taste in other matters." It was well done and I and a vast majority of television viewers enjoyed that show, which is why it was so successful on television.

The popularity of the *Hillbillies* and the *Griffith* show gave rise to *Petticoat Junction, Green Acres,* and such rural-type variety programs as *The Glen Campbell Goodtime Hour* and *Hee Haw.* But we were not devoted to a single form. CBS also had its share of doctor shows, spy shows, and police dramas. But comedy—and especially rural comedies—dominated our program schedule.

Successful programming, however, does not consist merely of giving the mass audience what it wants at any given moment. The true art is to discern what the public will want or will accept in the years ahead. The challenge is to know what the public is seeking before the public even knows it is looking for something else. In the mid-sixties—in fact, it was in 1965—I first began to worry about our successful rural comedies. They were attracting an older age group of the population to CBS, while the other communication media were beginning to describe the rise of a new youth movement in America, especially in the cities. So, I sat down to talk about this with the new president of the CBS Television Network, Jack Schneider, who had just succeeded Jim Aubrey in that post.

Entertaining You

Programming is the heart and bloodstream of network broadcasting. It is also my special love. Over my long years in this industry, I have listened to and looked at just about every kind of program that has been put on the air by all three networks. And I have learned from what I have seen, building up a storehouse of knowledge about what has succeeded and what has failed in the past—and why. So, I have had as much *experience* in programming as any other man in the business. But, more than that, a good programmer must also keep in close contact with new ideas and trends in all forms of entertainment and with the current mores, customs, and changing values of the society we live in. Everything counts.

Experience and knowledge alone, however, are not enough: a good programmer must possess or develop special, indescribable instincts—*gut reactions*. They will tell you sometimes in a loud clear voice or sometimes in a whisper what the unseen mass audience will accept, what it will particularly enjoy, what it will become engrossed in and faithful to, and, equally, what programs most viewers will find boring or too complex or too out of the ordinary to accept. Sometimes gut reactions are right and can be trusted, sometimes not; they are not infallible. And some people have better instincts than others. But this instinctual ability among professionals is based on many things—their experiences in the industry, and in life, and their knowledge of the outside world.

In choosing which entertainment programs deserve to go on the air, the television programmer selects those which he believes will appeal to the mass audience. For it is the public which chooses ultimately which programs will be tuned in and which tuned out. When I look at pilots of new programs, I ask myself, "Do I like it?" But that is not enough. I also ask, "Will the television viewer at home like it?" Oftentimes, the two judgments are the same; sometimes not. Nor do those questions always draw an either-or answer. The answer is usually a matter of degree: How *much* do I like it? How *much* will the mass audience like it? This is another way of asking: "Will this program be a clear-cut winner? Will it gain a modest but adequate audience to keep it on the air? Does it have a chance?" The hopeless cases are easy to dismiss. All the others demand judgment, instinct and the courage to take a risk. Then there are the programs which appear to promise success on the air but are in poor taste and, in my opinion, unworthy of appearing on CBS Television. I vote against them.

Television entertainment makes a valuable contribution to American life simply by bringing enjoyment and relaxation into the home. Every good programmer also is aware that he has the opportunity and responsibility to try to elevate the tastes and knowledge of the viewing audience by providing more serious, uplifting cultural programs. But these programs must be interesting enough in themselves to capture the audience's attention. Today's television does offer such fare on the commercial and the public television channels—more than any other mass medium I know—but not as much as it could if the size of audiences were not so important. The cultural, artistic, and educational programs are there, but they almost always attract only small audiences. I sometimes suspect that even the so-called highbrow critics, who complain of ordinary TV fare, seldom tune in the more cultural programs which are offered.

The best of all worlds is a combination of high quality and popularity, a program that is enjoyed by the mass audience and has a quality feel to it, one that the audience recognizes and enjoys as something rather special. That is when the programmer hits the jackpot. At all three networks programmers are competing avidly for such programs. Where are these programs? They have to be written, cast, directed, and produced; costumes have to be made and sets designed, all of which demands many different skills working together. The truth is that there is a dearth of such skills. As chairman of CBS, I cannot say, "I want this particular kind of program. Get me the best writer, the best director, the best production team." I can say it; but I can't get it. We have to look around, see what is available, and take chances.

How does a television series come into being? The beginning is always the same: someone comes to us with an idea. It could be one of the big motion-picture companies that now has special units making television programs—Universal, Warner Brothers, Columbia, or Twentieth Century–Fox. Or it could be an independent producer such as Grant Tinker, Norman Lear, or Quinn Martin. Sometimes it is an experienced director or writer, or someone else who has never produced a show. Sometimes it is a member of our own staff. Any one of these people might come into our program development group in Hollywood or New York to discuss the idea, or he can submit a written proposal.

We ask the producer or creator to refine his concept by telling us more about the characters, where they will live, what they will do, and what their relationships will be with each other; and we want to know who is going to write, produce, direct, and star in the show. Our aim is to have a show that is better than anyone else's. The execution rather than the idea itself is often what makes a show successful. That is why I want to know who the producer intends to use in making the show—especially which writers. They are the most important ingredient. You can never be sure if you'll like a show until you actually see it; but we

259

check the records of the people whose names the producer brings us in order to estimate how good the effort might be. We hope that once in a while he will come up with somebody who's brand-new and say, "Listen, I've got great faith in this young fellow. He hasn't written anything that's been successful yet, but I'd like to use him. Here's a sample of his work." We are, of course, always looking for new people.

Because writers are the first important element in the making of a good show, our programmers will sit down and discuss ideas with them. They might ask them for brief outlines of several shows. "What are you going to do for the next ten shows?" we might ask a writer. "Just give us short paragraphs so we can get a feel for the basic concept of your proposed series." Later, we might say, "Okay, do four scripts." What we really want to find out is how well the writer can handle his material over the long run. Consistently good writers are as scarce as precious stones and their prices are not dissimilar.

Over the past ten years, the process of selecting proposals, scripts and pilots for our new programs has grown into a large operation, primarily because so many small independent producers are trying to hit it big with a new series. Ten years ago, our program development group consisted of just one man and two assistants, and they handled eight hundred or so proposals or treatments for new series. Today, more than eighteen hundred official submissions of ideas, treatments, and proposals are received from professional sources, and they are logged in and registered at our program development group. This does not count another thousand or so ideas that come up informally in conversations with producers, writers, actors, and our staff every year. To handle all these new ideas for shows and to winnow out the potential winners our program development group has been divided into three separate, specialized units on the West Coast: Comedy, Drama, Variety, each headed by a vice-president with three or four assistants. A separate unit in New York handles all the ideas and proposals that flow in from the East Coast.

We ordered only thirty-seven full scripts for the 1969–70 season and made thirteen pilots, while for this past season of 1978–79 we ordered more than two hundred scripts and from them we had about forty pilots made. Our creative development and programming people work with the producers and writers of these scripts from conception to final draft. If a script does not measure up to expectations, we may reject the whole project at that stage, or we may ask for further revisions or we may order an entirely new script. If we do like a script, we may order four to six more scripts in order to get a better idea of the series before going on. Once in a while, we commission a presentation film—a ten- or fifteen-minute film showing the cast, the locations, the sets, and the flavor of the program. When fully satisfied, the head of our Entertainment Division in Hollywood, in consultation with his programming department, will make the final decision in ordering a pilot for the proposed series. This process goes on throughout the year.

The completed pilots are sent to New York in video cassettes where I and others at CBS can see them. We once used to meet to review our new pilots on a large screen set up in a conference room. But since the advent of cassettes, I prefer to see new pilots on my own television set at the office or at home. In that way, I am seeing the program as the average viewer would in his home and I can judge the quality of the production, the cast and the story line as they would appear on the home television screen. Making notes about the writing, directing, casting, acting, and other points of production, I try to determine to whom the show would appeal. I write down my own estimate of how good a chance the proposed series has of making it into our schedule. A small group in New York do the same thing in preparation for our final programming meeting to determine the new schedule of shows.

The final winnowing of projects and the ordering of pilots goes on during the late fall and winter. Then in the early spring, usually around mid-March, the top people concerned come together either at our Television City studios in Hollywood or at CBS headquarters in New York for final programming meetings to set our schedule for the following September. By this time, everyone involved has seen all the pilots under consideration. The president of our Entertainment Division and the programming chief in Hollywood have worked out a rough outline of which new shows will work best and in what specific time periods for the new schedule. Each of the pilots has gone through our research and analysis department, which pre-tests them in front of a carefully selected group representing a cross section of the national viewing audience. The pilots are also reviewed by a small group from our programming department in New York, men with certain special areas of expertise, as well as the president of the corporation and myself as chairman.

In our full programming meeting, which decided our final line-up for the 1978–79 season, fourteen of us met in a conference room of the programming department on the thirty-fourth floor of our New York headquarters. Like all such meetings, this one was long, agonizing, painful, ego-bruising, and extremely stimulating. It went on for five days! Lunch was brought in. Telephone calls were held. Outside interruptions were rare. Each pilot was taken up in turn, presented by its advocate, and criticized by some, condemned by some, and praised by others. Some pilots were easily discarded by majority opinion, but the more we narrowed the field down, the more intense became the debate. The meeting was open and frank; disagreements were expressed quite strongly; running debates raged. Men who had spent the past year guiding their projects to this critical point found some of their favorite projects rejected as unsuitable. But it was understood that the pilots, the projects, and a man's opinions were wide open to criticism, not the man himself.

Outside the room, there were hundreds of producers, directors, actors, and others, whose careers, livelihood, and well-being depended upon our decisions. Above all, the well-being of CBS Television and CBS as a whole rested upon decisions made in that room. People may scoff at the importance of program ratings; but our network advertising revenues, our financial resources, our plans for future projects, all depend upon how well we do the next season. We must pick and choose our programs and then schedule them for the prime time of the following television season or during the year as replacements for shows that fail. The pilots which do not make the fall schedule are set aside as possible replacements for those programs which do not work out on the air. We go through this same process again after the start of the fall season when we choose new shows for mid-season sometime in January or February. In fact, lately, we have become even more flexible and are ready to make changes at any time, substituting a new show for a failing one no matter what time of the year it may be necessary.

In all of our programming meetings, I like to see healthy differences of opinion. I like to see all possible alternatives and I encourage full, open discussions because such give-and-take often will produce new or clearer ideas of what we should do. There is never any playing of politics or running for higher positions in these meetings that I can discern. What I do observe is an honest respect for the opinions of others. Each one there had earned his right to be at this crucial meeting and no matter how strongly one disagreed with a colleague, no matter how hard one fought for one's own favorite show, it was understood that out of it all would come a consensus which all of us would ultimately support. Aside from the tension and some rubbing of raw nerves, I enjoyed the interplay of strong minds in that room, as I remembered the fierce battles that had gone on in programming meetings before.

The most momentous programming meetings of CBS Television were those which scheduled our 1970–71 season. Bob Wood, who had become president of the network only about a year before, took the position that we would have to change the entire design of our prime-time schedule. It was an audacious stand for a man so new in the job, but then Bob Wood was a man of courage and conviction. He proposed that CBS cancel some of its most popular programs and go into something entirely different.

The problem, as he saw it, was that we had become the prisoner of our own tremendous success as the number-one network throughout the sixties. The longer our top-rated series lasted, the older our audiences became. At the same time, as the sixties drew to a close, advertisers began to use more sophisticated demographic data to make their time-buying decisions. They became interested not only in the size but in the age and economic status of the audience. Specifically, most advertisers wanted to reach an audience between the ages of eighteen and forty-nine. The statistics were saying to us, in effect: the percentage of older people in your audience is too large . . . you are not building a base in the new and younger audience . . . you need to attract a larger proportion of younger people. I saw the beginning of that problem as early as 1965, when I wrote a memo about the make-up of our audience to Frank Stanton.

But Bob Wood was the man who took the idea and implemented it with a proposal of what CBS Television should do next. The change he recommended for attracting a younger audience was simple and basic: abandon fantasy for realism and abandon rural settings for urban ones.

Not everyone, to say the least, approved of this proposal. It meant canceling some of our most popular and successful programs and risking new and untried ones in their place. At our programming meeting, a man from the research department actually started to cry. "You don't know what you're doing," he exclaimed. "You're throwing away millions and millions of viewers. If you do this, a year from today you'll all be sitting around here scratching your heads and wondering why in hell you were such goddamned fools."

But for the long-range view the handwriting was on the wall. Some of our favorite old shows were running their course and getting a little tired. And on the outside, it was a time of youth's uprisings in the ghettos and on college campuses. The action was in the streets of our major cities, not in bygone rural settings. I agreed with Bob Wood's diagnosis and admired him for looking so far ahead. In my mind, a good programmer always tries to stay ahead of his audience's tastes, rather than follow them blindly.

We started the transition in our schedule for the 1970–71 season. The new concepts of realism and relevance were represented, for example, by the story of a single woman working for a Minneapolis-St. Paul television station—the now classic *Mary Tyler Moore Show;* by *Arnie,* a loading-dock worker promoted to a front-office executive; and by *The Interns,* the story of a small group of young doctors in a large hospital. In this transition, we kept such old favorites as *The Beverly Hillbillies* and *Green Acres.*

In June 1970, a few months before this new schedule went on the air, Mike Dann resigned as head of our programming department for reasons of health. On his doctor's advice that he seek something less strenuous and nerve-wracking, he joined the Children's Television Workshop, a non-profit corporation which produces *Sesame Street.* He had been our chief programmer for seven years, a volatile and perceptive man with strong opinions, who really stirred things up and was a good catalyst for generating new ideas.

In choosing a replacement for Dann, we picked one of the youngest men on our program staff, the vice-president for Program Planning and Development: Fred Silverman. From time to time I had noticed Silverman's sharp perception about programming and scheduling. Soon after Silverman took over Dann's job we grouped the older rural-type programs together on Tuesday night and put the newer, youth-oriented programs together on Wednesday and Saturday nights. Silverman left us in 1975 for the top programming job at ABC, where he had been offered extremely generous financial terms plus the challenge of turning the lowest-rated network into the highest one. I was surprised when he left, for I had not known he was even considering it. I was told by mutual associates at CBS that the challenge involved played a big part in his decision to leave CBS. In 1978, Silverman was offered and accepted the presidency of NBC, an important and prestigious advance in his career as he took over the network which had become the lowest-rated.

The biggest break with the past came in the middle of the

1970–71 season, when we put on *All in the Family*. This was the story of an exceedingly boisterous and bigoted middle-class man; his fluttery, plain-speaking, and honest wife; and his liberal daughter and son-in-law. Bob Wood presented the pilot to us for our consideration and we all recognized it as an outstanding program well produced in every respect. But, equally, all of us realized the tremendous risk involved in putting such a different kind of program on the air. After long discussions and much agonizing and considerable trepidation, we agreed to go ahead with it.

For the first time, we allowed an entertainment program to deal in a real way with ordinary subjects, using the kind of conversations that one might hear in any household—ethnic attitudes and all. We came out and said, in effect, we'll do it the way it is and not be afraid of the complaints we expected. Some would say that white people do not have black people coming into their houses, and if you, Mr. CBS, think they do, you're mistaken, and we're not going to listen to your network any more. That would have been, I think, the kind of reaction we would have received ten years earlier. But we felt the time had come to catch up with some of the developments that had taken place in the United States.

We also felt that there were many situations where whites and blacks mix and where they like each other on the surface and don't like each other underneath. As a result, we developed *The Jeffersons* as a spin-off about the black neighbors of Archie Bunker. In *All in the Family*, the racist Archie Bunker cannot abide George Jefferson because he is black, and Mr. Jefferson cannot stand Mr. Bunker because he is such a racist. Yet, the two wives become good friends. In the spin-off, we made Mr. Jefferson a prosperous owner of a dry-cleaning business who flaunts his success by moving into a luxury apartment house in a white neighborhood. So, in *The Jeffersons*, we depict this proud black man who is angry with whites, showing off his wealth and status and at the same time wants to be accepted by his white neighbors. He was a new kind of character for television, which reflected, we thought, a change in the social customs of the country. And we decided to use it as a basis for entertainment.

All in the Family and *The Jeffersons* represented a tremendous change. Norman Lear, who developed both programs, deserves full credit for having created them and we should get the credit for putting them on the network for everyone to see and to absorb. When Lear brought *All in the Family* to CBS, we in effect decided: this is a daring thing to do, but let's try it for thirteen weeks. The show did not do very well in its preview testings before an audience. But we put it on in the middle of the 1970–71 season at 9:30 P.M. Tuesday nights, opposite NBC's *Tuesday Night at the Movies* and ABC's *Movie of the Week*. We hoped for the best. In the beginning, its ratings were low and not encouraging. Nevertheless, we kept it on the air until it found its own true level. Then by word of mouth it started to grow in popularity. It became a historic breakthrough. The next season we became bold enough to schedule it for Saturday in the 8 P.M. slot, where it could make or break the evening for us. There, it became the number-one show on television.

For the next season, 1971–72, we canceled other old standbys and replaced them with a Western (*Cade's County*), two detective series (*Cannon* and *O'Hara, United States Treasury*) and three situation comedies (*The Chicago Teddy Bears, Funny Face,* and *The New Dick Van Dyke Show*); only the Western did not have an urban setting. All in all, the 1971 fall schedule represented the most drastic overhaul in CBS history. That season, we eliminated fourteen programs, introduced eight new series, and rescheduled eleven series in new time periods. Only four time periods out of twenty-nine remained unchanged from our previous fall season.

Our changes worked. The composition of our audience did change—just as we had hoped.

CBS Television continued to rank first in the ratings year after year. Then suddenly, in the fall of 1975, the early ratings indicated that our status as number one was in real trouble. Even before we got the bad news in late September, I had planned a trip to network headquarters in Hollywood.

On a Sunday in mid-October 1975, I flew out to Hollywood, along with Jack Schneider and our top program people from New York. Bob Wood was already there. The next morning in Television City we met with members of the Hollywood staff, about fifteen of us in all. Two big jobs were at hand: first, rearranging the existing programs so that they might become more successful in new time slots; and second, choosing new shows to replace the ones that were failing. Our goal was to have a complete new schedule in place by mid-season, which meant sometime in January.

At the time, we lacked sufficient inventory. We had no series ready for immediate broadcast. So after canceling three failing shows, we filled their time slots with specials and reruns for the several weeks until the replacements were ready. Marginal programs that we might have canceled in other years we left alone because we could not replace them with anything better. We decided at the meeting to put in three replacement series from the small inventory available: *The Blue Knight, Sara,* and *One Day at a Time,* a Norman Lear production. By mid-season all three were on the air as part of the rearranged schedule.

The ratings *did* turn around, and when the 1975–76 season ended, CBS was again on top, for the twenty-first consecutive year. But that was the end of our unbroken chain of seasons in that position.

Early in the next season we found that there was still a lack in our inventory and no time to make up for past lapses. We had several backup projects, but they were mediocre or just plain useless. This time we could not make satisfactory repairs and we finished the 1976–77 season in second place, after ABC.

Being second in the ratings, we brought ten new shows into our prime-time schedule for the 1977–78 season. These were the most changes we had ever made for a new fall season. And many of those shows failed. We made three changes in November, four in December, four more in January, and by the time the season was over, we had canceled and replaced eighteen programs on our prime-time schedule. We also shuffled other programs to new time slots during the year. Despite our efforts we did not regain first place.

Thus the stage was set for programming for the 1978–79 season, when I found that many of our people were quite ready to sacrifice quality and realism, where necessary, to try to gain maximum popular appeal. We had about twenty-five pilots still under consideration for six, seven, or possibly eight open time slots, depending upon how many previous shows we decided to cancel. In going over those pilots, I had some favorites which I thought deserved to get on our schedule; others I considered marginal, and some I thought unworthy of CBS.

Over the years I have learned to judge new programs by certain benchmarks which have characterized previously successful programs. These qualities do not guarantee the acceptance and popularity of a program, but without them a program has a very slender chance of success. I believe the most important and virtually unfailing indication of a good program—over and above basic good writing, direction, casting, costumes, and sets—is likable, intriguing characters who capture the imagination, interest, or concern of the audience. The best of them take on the aspects of real people to such an extent that the audience wants to know from week to week what happens to them. Television has brought into the American home screen characters who have become as familiar as the neighbors down the block. Their personalities and idiosyncrasies are probably better-known to the average family than are those of their nearest neighbors. We all "know" Jack Benny, Lucille Ball, Dick Van Dyke, Mary Tyler Moore, and we "know" all the characters in *The Honeymooners* and *The Beverly Hillbillies* and *All in the Family*. Then there is James Arness as Matt Dillon, in *Gunsmoke*, Richard Thomas as John-Boy in *The Waltons*, Raymond Burr, as Perry Mason, William Conrad as Cannon, and Telly Savalas as Kojak, and, of course, Lassie as Lassie. Superstars like Jackie Gleason, Carol Burnett, and others used their variety-format programs to develop several different characters whom they played with such aplomb that each character became a familiar and likable person. These characters are drawn in considerable depth and they are unfailingly consistent as themselves and in their relationships with the other characters in their shows, whether in comedy or drama.

The other benchmark I continually seek out is believability. In drama, casting is very important for this trait. The story line must be close to real life or, in short, believable. Comedy can go beyond real life but not too far. There is a fine line here. In any case, a program should reflect life through realism, exaggeration, or satire. But the best programs will, however slightly or subtly, be making a clear statement that gives you truly a slice of life.

My personal favorite among all the proposed new shows for the 1978–79 season was *The Paper Chase*, a top-quality adaptation from the motion picture, starring John Houseman in his Academy Award–winning role as the stern Ivy League law school professor who has such an impact upon his first-year law students. This was clearly an outstanding program in every way, serious and yet witty, pertinent to our times, heartwarming, mature, *believable*, with a number of realistic interesting characters. Some thought the trials and tribulations of law school students and their professor would not appeal to the mass audience. As a result, they argued, we would lose out in the battle for ratings and jeopardize our chances of regaining the number-one position among the competing networks.

We had a running battle over *The Paper Chase* versus several other pilots which promised greater popular appeal. The debate was much more concerned with programming philosophy than over the merits of the individual programs. There are some people within CBS and on the outside who believe that I dominate our programming meetings. After one meeting awhile ago, someone sighed with exhaustion and remarked, "We sit around here arguing for days and in the end we do what Paley says." He may have thought so, but it was not true. Our programming chiefs and network presidents have not been weak men. Certainly, Robert A. Daly, president of our Entertainment Division, is known for his outspokenness as much as for his acumen in picking and choosing programs, talent and staff. We argued back and forth on *The Paper Chase*, even though we both agreed the program was of outstanding quality but that it had virtually no chance of making it into the Top Ten. Where we disagreed was whether the program had any chance at all of lasting out the season and what its influence would be on our overall audience ratings. I argued that the quality of the program warranted giving *The Paper Chase* the chance it deserved. It was television at its finest. CBS had a responsibility to put it on the air even if it did fail. And, finally, I argued that the program just might possibly draw an audience which would surprise us all. I do not want to give the impression that I was the only one who felt this way about *The Paper Chase*. Others agreed with me.

I do have a reputation for possessing rather special instincts about programming and the public's tastes and I am often asked, "How do you do it?" I don't know how I do it. There may be an expressible, intellectual side to programming, but for me there is also a deeper, instinctive side that can never be fully explained. Because I usually work in groups seeking consensus, rather than alone, my opinions on television programs often have been influenced by interaction with others; although, I suppose, in my position, mine often may have carried more individual weight.

By the end of our five-day programming meeting for the 1978–79 season, the fourteen men in the room, like a jury on a difficult and controversial case, had reached a unanimous decision on introducing eight new shows into the fall schedule. *The Paper Chase* was among those chosen. The critics acclaimed it as the best of all the new programs on the air and, with equal unanimity, they predicted it would fail and not last out the season. But the public will make the ultimate decision.

The other half of the art of programming—after we have picked and chosen the dramas, comedies and variety series we want—is what to do with them. That is "scheduling" or the plac-

ing of each new program along with the old ones in a time slot
which would be most advantageous. Scheduling is an art or skill
in itself, once again derived from experience, instinct and philosophy. It is also the precise point of competition with the other
networks. Our scheduling strategy is worked out by our programming committee on a standing magnetic board, five feet long by
four feet high, marked for all the prime-time half hours in the
broadcasting week. As we plan our strategy, we move around
different-colored plaques representing our programs in competition with the NBC and ABC expected programs. Such is the
importance of that magnetic scheduling board that during pre-
season planning not only do we keep the doors of the room se-
curely locked, but the board itself, when not in use, is covered
with locked steel doors. One might, as some have, think of it as
the top-secret room of network television. The reputation, the
ratings, and the financial well-being of the network depend upon
the judgments made in that room.

There are two basic strategies to scheduling: scattering your
strongest shows through the week, putting each of them against
the strongest shows of your opposition, which is defensive scheduling (for you are trying to reduce your losses). Offensive
scheduling, on the other hand, is placing your best shows together in sequence on certain nights when the competition is not
at its strongest. The idea here is to gain a cumulative effect, so
that each show brings in a large audience which can carry over to
the other programs on that night. In this kind of offensive planning, you might be conceding certain nights to gain the advantage over one, two, or perhaps three other nights. The overall result, if all this works as it is designed, is to give you the highest
ratings for the week as a whole.

The scheduling of a program can spell the difference between
success and failure. *The Dick Van Dyke Show* was introduced on
CBS October 3, 1961, and ran for three months from 8:00 to
8:30 Tuesday nights, following a rerun of *Gunsmoke*. It was not
even in the top seventy for that period. But we had faith in
Dick Van Dyke and his co-star, Mary Tyler Moore, and we

rescheduled it for a later time slot, 9:30 to 10:00 on Wednesday nights, following *Checkmate*, with a so-so rating. Then we replaced *Checkmate* with *The Beverly Hillbillies* that September and *The Dick Van Dyke Show* rose to number nine. The next season it became number three because *The Beverly Hillbillies*, which led into it, had become the number-one program on television. Scheduling and sequence count a great deal.

Gunsmoke itself was so popular that in the 1961–62 season we had reruns of the show aired on Tuesdays while the new episodes ran on Saturday nights. In the 1957–58 season, its third on the air, *Gunsmoke* became the number-one show on television and stayed in the top position for the following three years until the 1961–62 season. Then it began to slip more and more each year until in the 1966–67 season, it was down to being the 34th-ranked show. Our program department decided to cancel the well-worn Western. Not only was it losing its popularity, but the demographics were against it: it did not attract young people. And yet, it was such a good, well-written program that I suggested perhaps it ought to be given another chance in a different time slot. So, *Gunsmoke,* instead of being canceled, was moved from 10:00 P.M. Saturday nights to 7:30–8:30 P.M. on Monday nights. The simple shift worked wonders. *Gunsmoke* rose from 34th to 4th in rank the next season and it stayed in the Top Ten for five more years, finally succumbing two years later at the end of the 1974–75 season. It was truly, however, a "born again" program with eight more years of life in it, all because it had been rescheduled to a more appropriate time slot.

The daytime and late-night hours also must be programmed and scheduled in similar fashion and beyond our prime-time series, we also have to plan with great care the short mini-series and the motion pictures we put on the air. We also have a separate department which concentrates on broadcasting live sports events. There is fierce competition in all these areas among the networks, for here again ratings and shares of the audience and financial returns depend upon how well we suit the tastes of the audience. So, as part of our 1978–79 season, CBS scheduled such movie classics as *Gone With the Wind*, with Clark Gable and Vivien Leigh, *The Corn Is Green*, with Katharine Hepburn; and such box office hits as *Rocky, Marathon Man, Carrie, Network*, and *Black Sunday*.

Our live sports coverage has generally increased year by year and at an ever-rising expense. I can remember when we first decided in 1956 that CBS should air the National Football League games in competition with college games and the NFL was almost ready to pay us for the privilege. This year, in the twenty-third year with the NFL, CBS will broadcast 107 regular and post-season games. We will also carry about forty professional basketball games, twenty major golf tournaments, the U. S. Open, and other tennis tournaments, as well as auto racing, horse racing, boxing, and skiing. Television has always been particularly well suited for broadcasting live sports events and with close-ups, stop-action, and replays, the TV viewer at home often sees more of the action than if he or she had been at the event itself.

All our programming and scheduling of comedy, drama, and variety series, and our mini-series, specials, movies and sports are designed to give the viewing public what we think it wants to see, what we think it might like to see, what we think is important for it to see. Of course, we strive constantly for quality in everything we do. Although CBS has slipped in the ratings recently, I believe we still maintain our lead in quality. But we do keep one eye on the ratings. It is well enough for outside critics to say, "Don't cater to the mass audience or the majority taste; give them what they ought to have." But a network cannot do that. We must give them very much what they want. Still, at CBS we have always tried to lead the audience to some extent. Over the years I do believe we have broadcast successful programs that broadened audience views about the world we live in. To name but a few: *The Defenders, Playhouse 90, 60 Minutes, The Waltons, All in the Family,* and a long list of documentaries, starting with the broadcasts of Ed Murrow.

Personally, I wish that the ratings were truly a secondary consideration in programming. Television would be much better off and the public better served if the numbers race were not so important. But ratings are terribly important. Advertising revenues depend upon how many viewers the sponsor is reaching with his commercials. So, the financial well-being of each network does depend upon the ratings.

The problem has concerned me for some time. About ten years ago I proposed to the presidents of NBC and ABC that we work out some way in which each network could broadcast a certain number of special cultural, educational, high-quality, serious programs. My proposal did not evoke any interest at that time, but perhaps the time is ripe for the idea now.

What I propose is that representatives of the three major networks meet to work out the feasibility and the details in setting aside a given period of time—say, two hours a week in prime time —for special, high-quality programs that would appeal to educated, sophisticated tastes more than to the mass audience. Each network would take different nights of the week, thus offering the public six hours of high-quality programming each week.

No one network, as a practical matter, can do it alone. If CBS were to broadcast a high-quality cultural or documentary program on a subject which attracted the interest of only a minority of viewers, CBS would lose its normal share of the audience not only in the hour or two of its quality broadcast but very possibly for the whole evening. If, for example, we scheduled such a program at 8:00 P.M., we probably would lose the whole night to the other networks. If we scheduled it for 10:00 P.M., our local affiliated stations might find they were losing their audience for the 11:00 P.M. local news programs. Low audience ratings for an hour or two in order to present special interest programs might be bearable, but forfeiting the whole night through the domino effect would make the cost to the network untenable.

But if all the networks contributed to the objective of increasing the number of high-quality programs put on the air, the losses would be divided among us. I believe such programs would increase in popularity as time went on and the television audience came to appreciate this kind of fare. There would be a point when at least some of them might become income-producing. In any event, the public would get a chance to see programs of greater cultural, educational and informational value and the television industry would be making a fuller and better use of this magic form of communications.

This idea can succeed only if all three networks agree and can persuade their affiliates that it is incumbent upon us all to do something about the paralyzing effect of network competition on high-quality programming. There are innumerable questions to be answered. What is quality programming? Is it only high-minded drama? Good music? Documentaries? Is it an examination of American history? All these are seriously lacking in regular prime-time schedule. Should prime time be limited to that niche we call "the arts"?

These are questions—and there may be others—that men of good will, men who have devoted their careers to broadcasting, can work out. If we must compete, I would like to see the three networks vying to put on the best program of the year in this special category—best in quality, not in audience ratings. It seems to me that the commercial networks should seek out those subjects which are not popular with the mass audience and treat them on the air so that they would be more easily appreciated. It is the exposure of these kinds of subjects which broaden their appeal.

One major stumbling block to this idea might be the U. S. Department of Justice. I understand that the Justice Department could object to any such joint meeting of the three networks as an attempt at collusion in restraint of free competition. This problem could be overcome, I believe, by reviewing the principle with the Justice Department in advance—so long as neither the government nor any of its agencies would have anything to do with the content of TV broadcasting as a result.

My inner feeling is that now the time has arrived when a large part of the American public is asking for a new, major change in television programming. High-quality programs in prime time may be the beginning of such a change.

With my sister, Blanche, and my mother.

Babe with Amanda and Tony.

In Venice.

With my sister-in-law Minnie, Noel Coward, and Babe.

Babe and I posed separately with four of
our children in the same setting.

Christmas 1952 with some of the children.

Babe sketching.

Family portrait at Kiluna.

Jeff.

Amanda.

Kate.

Hilary.

Tony.

Bill.

Amanda's coming-out party.

Hilary's coming-out party.

A favorite picture of Babe.

With Babe and Amanda.

Relaxing.

Sightseeing in Rome with Babe.

A favorite photo I took after the wedding of Tony and Siri, with the newlyweds (upper center) surrounded by family well-wishers at Kiluna in February 1971.

The living room of our Nassau home in the Bahamas.

Posing for portrait painters.

The three Cushing sisters, Minnie (l.), Babe, and Betsey.

With my friend and brother-in-law, Jock Whitney (l.), and my friend Walter N. Thayer.

A Special Niche

Television news began on CBS in 1946 with one regular weekly Saturday night broadcast with Douglas Edwards as our first TV newscaster. Edwards got the job because he was the only experienced newsman on staff willing to make the transition from radio to television. A great many people misjudged the future of television. The program was seen only in New York because no television network existed at the time. But the following year, network cables were extended from New York along the eastern seaboard and television began to be recognized as something more than a toy.

In 1948, both political parties held their presidential-nominating conventions in Philadelphia so that their proceedings and their candidates could be seen on the tiny screen in about 400,000 homes. That year, CBS began a regular nightly newscast at 7:30 P.M. The Korean crisis of 1950 prompted more than one hundred hours of live television coverage of the United Nations debate on the subject. It also produced the first film reports of U.S. troops in Korea. Finally, in 1951, television news came of age when the nation was bound into one single community by microwave relay and a coaxial cable which stretched across the country. Ed Murrow heralded the new age of television on the première of his documentary program *See It Now*. He opened with live pictures of the Atlantic and Pacific oceans on a split screen and declared: "For the first time in the history of man, we are able to look out at both the Atlantic and Pacific coasts of this great country at the same time."

When television started to dominate radio as a medium, it did so in news as well as in entertainment. The shift was basic and Lowell Thomas was as powerless to resist it as Jack Benny. The impact was enormous. The impersonal voice on radio was replaced with a highly individualistic, personal and intimate image of a newscaster, whom the audience could see and hear and relate to with confidence. The newscaster reached into ever-increasing millions of homes each day in all parts of the country. In time surveys would show that more people received their news from television than from any other source and that they also trusted this source of news more than they did all other news publications. This placed upon the newsmen of all networks a grave responsibility.

Even before television, CBS News had occupied a very special and privileged niche within the broadcasting activities of the network. It always has been kept free and distinct from the entertainment side of the business, from the encroachments of commercialism, advertisers, and from the government. From its very conception, the news department was designed and functioned as the public service arm of CBS, supplying objective reports of the news of the day and, as those events became more complicated, supplying analyses and commentaries on those events as well. At its operating level, the News Division is independent. It is governed by the broad policy standards established by Ed Klauber, Paul White and myself and others back in the thirties, and by the traditional tenets of professional journalism. It is a self-policing operation, run by professional people—whether they be newscasters on the air, writers, producers, or the officers of the division.

We believe we have hired the best in the business and they have made CBS News the most respected organization in broadcast journalism. However, we do hold our journalists individually, and CBS News as a whole, responsible for what they put on the air. Whenever it has become necessary for me or other corporate officers to intervene, it has always been on a post-audit basis. We express our views only after a program has been on the air and when a person or a unit fails to live up to CBS policies of objectivity, fairness and balance, and complete honesty, we take appropriate action. Despite government industry regulations, we look upon our news people as members of the Fourth Estate, with all the rights and privileges that the First Amendment to the Constitution gives a free press in this country. As such, one part of a professional journalist's responsibility is traditionally to serve the public as a watchdog, on the lookout for wrongdoing in whatever segment of our society it may occur. But we also expect and have so instructed our newspeople to keep their personal feelings, opinions, and convictions out of CBS news reports and documentaries. That may seem to be contradictory and impossible to accomplish. But it is not. It is only difficult.

Edward R. Murrow accomplished that feat classically in his celebrated television series, *See It Now*. The precursor of present-day television documentaries, *See It Now* was developed by Murrow and Fred W. Friendly from a radio show of theirs called *Hear It Now*, which itself had come from an all-time best-selling phonograph record album they had made of recent historical events called *I Can Hear It Now*. Murrow and Friendly, two of the most gifted producers in television, made no attempt to cover spot news, but instead went behind one or two stories for a half hour each week in search of explanation and meaning, attempting to narrow the focus and give what they called "the little picture." Over the years, their show traveled everywhere, from Las Vegas to India, from the eye of a hurricane to the depths of an ocean, and examined a world of issues. But the most famous *See It Now* broadcast took place on March 9, 1954, when Murrow devoted his whole program to an examination of the most powerful, controversial politician in the country, Joseph R.

McCarthy, the junior senator from Wisconsin. To comprehend what Ed Murrow accomplished and the ramifications involved, it is necessary to recall—and understand—the temper of those times.

No sooner had the victory celebrations died down after the end of World War II than the United States became engrossed in a national debate over whether the Soviet Union had friendly and cooperative intentions toward its former allies or some dark Marxist design to convert the world to Communism. All of the communications media became involved. We saw and reported the Russian takeover of the small nations of Eastern Europe, after the Soviets repudiated treaties calling for free elections there; the Communist coup in democratic Czechoslovakia; the attempts to subvert the governments of Greece and Turkey; the blockade of West Berlin. We saw the imposition of terror and tyranny wherever the Communists went, and finally we saw the "Cold War" turn into a hot war in Korea in 1950. All during these years, a debate raged in this country: Were the Communists trying to do the same thing here, to infiltrate and subvert the government and democratic institutions of the United States? Congressional committees were questioning the loyalty and political affiliations of men and women in government, in the entertainment world, in the colleges and universities. The federal government in fact did indict and convict the leaders of the Communist Party of the United States on conspiracy charges, and then there were espionage trials which seemed to be going on almost all the time. Private crusades were launched against Communists, alleged Communists, and so-called Communist dupes and Communist sympathizers.

In 1950, *Counterattack* which called itself "The News Letter of Facts to Combat Communism" published a much-heralded booklet called *Red Channels: The Report of Communist Influence in Radio and Television*. It listed 151 individuals by name, employed in broadcasting, who were alleged to have Communist affiliations. And there were other lists with other names published by other anti-Communist groups, all of which led to the practice known as blacklisting: the denial of jobs to anyone having suspected present or past left-wing affiliations. The practice infected a wide segment of life in America—business, government, motion pictures, radio and television, newspapers and magazines, and on and on. Those were frightening times.

At CBS, my associates and I felt caught in a dilemma. On the one hand we owed it to the public to assure people that CBS broadcasts were not being influenced by subversives; on the other hand we did not want to do anything that would abridge the rights and freedoms of our own employees. We certainly did not believe anything broadcast by CBS was in fact subversive or influenced by an Communist or left-wing bias. Nor did we want to require a "loyalty oath" from our employees, for in those times demanding an oath of allegiance would signify a doubting or an impugning of the characters of the thousands of men and women who worked for CBS.

After much thought, studies, and consultations, we decided upon an in-house questionnaire, issued to all CBS staff employees, including some performers. The employee was asked if he or she was then or ever had been a member of any organization listed as subversive by the Attorney General of the United States, and the list of organizations, including the Communist Party, U.S.A., was printed on the reverse side of the questionnaire. That system was used to relieve us and our employees of any threatened blackmail, accusations, or pressures by outside crusaders. Only three or four of our employees refused to comply, and one person resigned "as a matter of principle." About fifteen or twenty stated in their replies that they had joined one or more of the listed organizations in the past. They were interviewed and when the circumstances of their past activities seemed absolutely harmless, they were kept on. Four or five employees either had inimical associations or were so ambiguous in explaining their affiliations that employment was terminated.

Neither CBS nor I, nor any combination of organizations, could protect the civil liberties of all performers, writers, or producers. The Cold War ruined many careers in the entertainment field. At that time most of the entertainment programs still were controlled by the advertisers and their advertising agencies and some did bow to blacklisting writers, performers and producers because of their alleged past political affiliations. But in the tight family of CBS staff employees, particularly those who belonged to the News Division, we defended our own all the way down the line. Four people come to mind.

In one case, the charge was so absurd that we refused to even listen to anything of this nature, and that prominent newsman received no instructions of any sort to temper his reporting. Another was an emotional man of great journalistic enterprise who was the special target of the Hearst press. We knew him as a trustworthy and excellent reporter, and nothing was ever said to him. The third newsman explained to us that indeed in the late thirties he had belonged to a Communist cell in the now defunct *Brooklyn Eagle,* and whatever his political opinions had been in the thirties, it was clear that in the fifties he was no Communist. We put our trust in him, kept him on staff, and he went on to a brilliant career. One army general labeled one of our news commentators a "Communist," and he went directly to the Pentagon, demanded a written public apology from the Secretary of the Army, and got it. We let it be known to all our correspondents that if they would gather the news objectively, to the best of their professional abilities, the management of CBS would take the heat.

Only with the passage of years have I learned some of the facts given above. My own feelings for personal privacy are so strong that I am astonished that I could have tolerated the invasion of privacy that even our mild questionnaire required. Yet, the more I reflect on this, the more I see that CBS too was caught in the crosscurrents of fear that swept through the whole country.

One of the more obvious cases in point of those times was that of an Air Force Reserve lieutenant named Milo Radulovich, who had been declared a security risk and asked to resign his commission because his Yugoslavian-born father and his sister subscribed to a Serbian-language newspaper which was alleged to be subversive. He had refused to resign, saying, "Against me, the actual charge against me is that I had maintained a close and continuing relationship with my dad and my sister over the years. . . ." An Air Force Hearing Board had reviewed his case and recommended that he be severed from the Air Force. Ed Murrow focused *See It Now* on that case in October 1953. With the cameras behind him, Ed's reporter went to Radulovich's home town of Dexter, Michigan, and interviewed the Raduloviches, the neighbors who knew them, and the townspeople. There was nothing to be found against that young lieutenant except that his father and sister read a foreign-language newspaper. The program had an impact. Five weeks later, the Secretary of the Air Force, Harold E. Talbott, appeared on *See It Now* and announced his decision "that Radulovich be retained in his present status in the United States Air Force."

The Radulovich case was the first instance, I believe, of such a reversal. Ed Murrow then was being urged by a great number of people, including some of his journalist colleagues, to take on Joe McCarthy. The junior senator from Wisconsin epitomized the excesses of the anti-Communist crusade in this country as he used the power of his office to ferret out unsubstantiated information which he declared proved that there were subversives infiltrating sensitive posts in the government. He rose from obscurity in early 1950 with a single speech in Wheeling, West Virginia, when he held up a piece of paper and announced he had a list of 205 names of people still employed by the State Department who were members of the Communist Party. He never produced the "list" and kept reducing the number of names. He was very clever in his use of words and in his understanding that the press, by its own rules, was obligated to print or broadcast the charges made in public by a United States senator. He was diabolical in accusing anyone of being a Communist sympathizer who disagreed with his brand of anti-Communism. Senator McCarthy made headlines with his startling accusations, and there seemed to be no one of equal stature or force who was prepared to answer him. Ed Murrow held back, not out of any fear, as some people thought, but because of his sensitivity to the fine lines of journalistic integrity. When Ed had returned to the air in 1947, he explained to his listeners in his first radio broadcast that there would be no editorializing in any of his programs. He felt so strongly about objective journalism that he had the no-editorializing policy written into his employment contract with CBS. When the McCarthy issue arose, Ed held back because he believed that a journalist should not give his own personal opinions on a subject, even McCarthyism. *See It Now* was supposed to do no more than allow the public to *see* a subject as it existed, with objectivity and without bias, to the degree that was humanly possible.

When Murrow told me he was doing a broadcast on McCarthy, he asked if I wanted to see it. He had on occasion asked me to preview his work so that he could get the benefit of my opinion and advice—as a friend and colleague.

"Are you sure of your facts?" I asked. "Are you on safe ground?"

"Yes, I am. No question about it," he said.

"In that case, I'll wait until everybody sees it," I said. That was meant as a vote of confidence and was received by him as such. We had discussed the broadcast and both of us were well aware of the wrath it would draw from McCarthy and his supporters. As a matter of fact, with Ed's approval and cooperation, I engaged a law firm to check into Ed's past so that we would be prepared if there were anything there which McCarthy could twist in order to malign Murrow, and we found nothing. In our talks before the broadcast, I did advise him on one point: I recommended that he invite McCarthy to reply. I wanted to be sure that if the senator requested any air time to respond that we had already offered it, and thus rule out any impression that we were succumbing to pressure from the senator. I also had in mind CBS's long-standing news policy of fairness and balance. Ed agreed readily.

The program, when it went on the air, consisted almost entirely of film of Senator McCarthy in action, conducting his investigations and making speeches, with Murrow narrating briefly and attempting to set the record straight. He and Fred Friendly had worked hard gathering CBS film clips which indisputably showed McCarthy's use of twisted sentences, intimations, and innuendoes. Even so, some editorializing crept in, perhaps unavoidably, as Murrow sought to explain and characterize the techniques used by McCarthy.

The broadcast moved millions. Within a week CBS received more than 15,000 letters, more than 14,000 telephone calls and more than 4,000 telegrams. The vast majority of them were favorable. But praise was not universal. McCarthy's supporters launched a virulent attack upon Murrow. McCarthy himself told reporters he had not seen the program. "I never listen to the extreme left-wing, bleeding heart element of radio and television," he declared in his own inimitable manner. But he did accept the offer to reply on CBS.

McCarthy's reply, pre-recorded on film and shown on CBS on April 6, was typical of him: "Now ordinarily I would not take time out from the important work at hand to answer Murrow. However, in this case I feel justified in doing so because Murrow is a symbol, the leader and the cleverest of the jackal pack which is always found at the throat of anyone who dares to expose individual Communists and traitors." He went on to question Murrow's past and impugn his loyalty, saying little about the program to which he was replying.

Ed and I fully anticipated McCarthy's attack and during the weeks between the two broadcasts we met almost every day to discuss the situation and to map out our own strategy. Ed wondered if and how he should respond to the personal attacks McCarthy was making in public speeches and would certainly make on his program. I suggested at one point that he say something to the effect that history would one day decide whether he or McCarthy had served his country better. After McCarthy's broadcast, that same night, Murrow met with reporters and gave them his prepared statement which has so often been quoted: "When the record is finally written, as it will be one day, it will answer the question who has helped the Communist cause and who has served his country better, Senator McCarthy or I? I would like to be remembered by the answer to that question."

A few weeks later McCarthy sent word that he couldn't afford to pay the costs of his April 6 filmed reply. He claimed he did not have the same resources that Murrow had. Without hesitation I said, "Tell him we'll pay." Murrow thought it was going to cost $25,000 and I said, "Okay, we'll pay the $25,000." The actual cost, as it turned out, was $6,336.99.

The ironic thing about the whole episode, as I see it, is that McCarthy did more damage to himself in his reply than Murrow had in the original broadcast. Seeing McCarthy present himself in action in this confrontation convinced many people that he was a true demagogue. That was and still is the true power of television. So it was also in the thirty-six days of televised Army-McCarthy hearings in the spring of 1954. He destroyed himself day by day as the hearings were televised live and summarized every night. When the hearings ended, television had shown the full man, and the American people rejected him once and for all. His peers in the U. S. Senate "condemned" him for his conduct.

In the early days of the Cold War there was a tradition of co-operation between journalists and government agencies concerned with threats to our national security from abroad. In the early 1950s, a representative of the Central Intelligence Agency came to see me and requested the use of my personal foundation, The William S. Paley Foundation, as a conduit for transferring money to another foundation to underwrite a research scholarship. I thought it was my patriotic duty to accede to this request —and I still think so. This was something I did on my own. It had nothing to do with CBS.

From time to time since then, there have been allegations made about the relations of CBS and the CIA, particularly following recent investigations of CIA activities in this country and involving the media. To clear up this matter, I had CBS issue a formal statement in September 1977, reviewing any and all such "cooperation" between CBS and the CIA. That statement tells the story:

In recent months there have been various public references to alleged cooperation between the CIA and the media, including CBS. Following is a recitation of what this "cooperation" involved with respect to CBS.

During the early years of the Cold War, the CIA requested CBS News to cooperate in ways that seemed not only innocuous but patriotic. The Agency asked that CIA representatives be permitted to screen, and in some instances to purchase, certain CBS News films. On occasion, the CIA was permitted to view material which was of interest to the Agency but was not broadcast, such as footage of parades and demonstrations. Agency representatives also were permitted to listen to radio transmissions from some of our overseas correspondents prior to their being edited and actually broadcast.

At the Agency's request, CBS News foreign correspondents, upon their return to the U.S., sometimes met with CIA officials and briefed them on the countries they had covered. And in one instance a CIA lipreader was permitted to observe the Soviet delegation from the CBS Television booth at the United Nations during Nikita Khrushchev's appearance at the U.N. in 1959.

Virtually all these arrangements occurred during the decade of the 1950s and the cooperation was terminated completely in 1961. Since that time we have sold as-broadcast newsfilm to the CIA on the same basis and terms as any other customer of the CBS Newsfilm Library.

There have also been allegations that in three specific instances CBS News personnel were simultaneously in the employ of the CIA and that executives of CBS News were familiar with these covert relationships.

Sam Jaffe, who worked for CBS News from 1956 to 1961, has claimed that he was hired at the behest of the CIA. No one at CBS News recalls any intervention by the CIA on Jaffe's behalf, and an investigation reveals no evidence to support Jaffe's claim. The people who actually hired Jaffe insist that they did so solely on the basis of Jaffe's qualifications and his own efforts to join CBS News.

The second allegation concerns Austin Goodrich, who worked for CBS News as a news writer in New York in 1954 and as a radio stringer in Stockholm in 1951–52, and 1954 and 1955. In February 1976 Sig Mickelson, who was President of CBS News from 1954 until 1961, told an interviewer that Mickelson had met with two representatives of the CIA in William S. Paley's office in October 1954 and had been informed that Goodrich was also in the employ of the CIA. Mr. Paley has no recollection whatsoever of the meeting described by Mickelson. On the other hand, Mr. Paley does recall that at one time, many years ago, he met with Mickelson and CIA representatives to discuss arranging press credentials for a CIA agent to be assigned in an area of key interest to the Agency but of minor interest to CBS News.* This, and the 1959 lipreading incident, referred to previously, were the only two occasions in which Mr. Paley was involved in CBS's cooperation with the CIA.

Finally, Frank Kearns was alleged to have been in the employ of the CIA while working as a stringer for CBS News. When Kearns was being considered for a staff correspondent's job in 1958, Mickelson claims to have discovered the CIA role and to have secured Kearns' resignation from the CIA before approving his new post. Kearns has denied ever having worked for the CIA.

To the best of our knowledge and belief, no CBS News person has ever served as an agent of the CIA or any other intelligence agency while in the employ of CBS. Nor is CBS aware of any ties with the CIA, past or present, other than those described above.

In summary, CBS's cooperation with the CIA during the Cold War years was definitely limited, and it was terminated completely in 1961. Given the tempo of the 1950s, we do not apologize for our actions. We do acknowledge, however,

* No one currently at CBS knows whether these credentials were indeed arranged.

that prior to 1961 we were not as sensitive as we have been since to the compelling need for a distinct and clearcut separation between journalism and government.

We also wrote a formal request to the CIA to make a full disclosure of its relationships with CBS employees that we might not know about. Our request was denied. But we were assured that new CIA regulations prohibited any future relationships between the CIA and American journalists "for the purpose of conducting any intelligence activities." That is all we could find out. CBS itself is not aware of any other ties, past or present, with the CIA.

With hindsight, it is clear now that we and other communications media were not as alert as we might have been to the need for a distinct and clear-cut separation between journalism and government.

The Newsroom

From such a small beginning before World War II—a handful of reporters and writers in this country and one or two in Europe—CBS News has grown to become one of the largest, most respected, most relied-upon news-gathering organizations in the world. More than one thousand men and women today work for CBS News. It is never a one-man operation. Our newsroom works around the clock, tied by cable to some fourteen national and overseas bureaus and augmented by part-time "stringers" who send us news dispatches from remote places. Our highly motivated journalists live intense and competitive lives covering the news events of the world; yet despite their glamour and mellifluous voices, they are human, sensitive, and frail; and so from time to time do make mistakes. But the remarkable feat of CBS News is the high standards of accuracy, honesty, and integrity these journalists achieve in their day-to-day reporting of the thousands of fast-breaking and complex news stories they cover every year.

The true strength of CBS News lies in the caliber of newsmen recruited during the early days of World War II—Winston Burdett, Howard K. Smith, Charles Collingwood and others. Today our staff of reporters and correspondents are the best in their field, supported by about forty producers and associate producers on the "hard news" side of the newsroom and an equal number on the "soft" or documentary side. But of equal importance to the news staff—on the air or off—is the well-knit organization and structure of the news operation itself. With the exception of fast-breaking news that comes in live, every report from the field is checked by a producer or an associate producer before it goes on the air. Matters of more than routine reporting are examined by executive producers, vice-presidents and the president of the CBS News Division. The operation of the newsroom is scrupulously handled within the division itself. When news stories or events or personnel become involved or in conflict with long-range company policy, such situations are reviewed by a special executive committee consisting of the heads of the various broadcasting divisions including CBS News, and the president of the Broadcast Group, and the chairman and president of the corporation. We sit as a kind of board of directors, deciding matters of policy but not getting involved in actual operations.

Corporate management does get directly involved when policies governing news coverage are promulgated by the government. Unlike print journalism, which receives the full protection of free speech and free press under the First Amendment, the broadcast industry is subject to a certain amount of regulation by the federal government via the Federal Communications Commission. The regulatory powers over broadcasting were first enacted back in 1927, during the early days of radio, and were based upon the theory of scarcity; namely, that the airwaves were limited and so radio stations must be licensed and kept on determined wavelengths. At the time, there were only 677 broadcasting stations in the country and 1,949 daily newspapers. Today, however, there are many more radio and television stations than newspapers in America. In any given town or city, people have access to more stations than they do to local newspapers. When it comes to monopoly control, there are far more one-newspaper towns than there are places which can receive only one television or one radio station. Nevertheless, broadcast journalism is regulated—no matter how minimally—by the government to an extent which would not be tolerated if attempted upon newspapers or magazines.

When the government tries to impose its will upon how radio and television should cover stories, it often leads to some very impractical and undesired results. Under the "equal time" provision of Section 315 of the Communications Act, a broadcaster must give "equal opportunities" to all opposing political candidates on the air—a provision that the FCC over the early years of its administration had interpreted broadly enough to include almost any broadcast appearance by any candidate during an election campaign. Thus, in 1952, when CBS wanted to invite Adlai Stevenson, the Democratic candidate for President, to appear on its *Man of the Week* news interview program, it could not do so without also inviting all the other presidential candidates who requested it, including Dwight D. Eisenhower, Homer A. Tomlinson, Fred C. Proehl, Don Du Mont, Edward Longstreet Bodin, and Ellen Linea W. Jensen, as well as the candidates of the Poor Man's Party, the Republimerican Party, the Spiritual Party, the Vegetarian Party, and enough other marginal candidates to monopolize *Man of the Week* for the rest of the year.

In 1959, Congress eased the limitations by exempting certain broadcasts from the equal-time provision of Section 315: newscasts, news interviews, news documentaries, and on-the-spot coverage of news events. But the broadcaster still did not have full discretion as to who legitimately deserved equal time on the air during a political campaign. Furthermore, Congress added the crippling proviso that stations were required to afford reasonable opportunity for the discussion of conflicting views on controversial issues of public importance. This requirement— the so-called Fairness Doctrine—was now not only FCC policy, as it had been before, but law.

The FCC was also upheld by the Supreme Court in its right to compel stations to "give reply time to answer personal attacks and political editorials." While broadcasters have no quarrel with the concepts of fairness and balance, questions arise as to who should decide what is fair in individual cases. Here we believe that broadcasters should be as free as the print media in deciding those questions. We think we perform the same function for the public as do the newspapers and that we deserve the same protection from governmental interference. Actually, at this writing, all these matters are being reviewed by Congress as it attempts to rewrite the 1934 Federal Communications Act.

After Frank Stanton made one of the first of his many brilliant appearances before the FCC in 1948, broadcasters won the right to editorialize on the air. But having won the right, we at CBS could not ourselves devise a formula for editorializing which we thought would be fair and balanced. Many long conferences were held on the subject and finally we concluded that there was no way the network could give editorial opinions on national or international subjects, and have those opinions truly represent the thinking of all the CBS affiliated stations. We did not own those stations and we could not speak for them editorially. They were linked to us only by voluntary ties and across the spectrum of our affiliates there were many differences of opinion on various subjects. So, even having won the right, the CBS network has refrained from editorializing, except in rare cases involving broadcasting. Our wholly owned radio and television stations can and do editorialize regularly but mostly on local issues.

As a matter of internal policy, CBS has strictly forbidden editorializing by our regular newscasters. And this has caused persistent problems over the years about interpreting what is editorializing, commentary, or analysis, even though it is clearly separated from hard news. Editorializing, or something very close to it, has crept into commentaries of even our most punctilious newscasters. Reporters who live and breathe news every day come to feel very strongly about some issues and cannot at times recognize their own biases. I have had heated arguments on the subject with Ed Murrow, Elmer Davis, Eric Sevareid, and Howard K. Smith. I always insisted that when it came to straight reporting, it had to be as objective as possible. I would admit that no one could be purely objective, that everyone has some biases, but my final line on the subject was usually, "If you try hard to be objective, you will come pretty close."

Howard K. Smith, for example, argued time and again that in news analysis and commentary he should have the same license as a newspaper columnist, like James Reston of the New York *Times*. But if we started this, I would reply, we would have to present viewpoints of various persuasions. We have to have fairness and balance. A newspaper does not.

This did not mean that I wanted the medium to have no influence or impact. The public has need of various points of view, presented, of course, as straight, out-and-out opinion. But those should be given not by the broadcasters (who are associated in the mind of the public with hard news or documentaries) but by qualified people on the outside, with no restraints placed on them, except those of the laws of decency and libel.

I was asked to talk to Howard Smith about this when the matter came to a head, and one day at lunch in 1962, he explained how much he liked to editorialize, how important it was for the public's understanding of the issues. I told him I recognized his abilities in that direction and understood his keen desire to voice his opinions.

"The only trouble is," I said, "if you want to do it, you can't do it on CBS and still remain a staff newscaster. If you want to do it, you have to do it someplace else." And so, before long, he left us for ABC. I liked Howard and admired his work very much, and I missed him. He was one of our best men, but he had a passion for expressing a point of view on the news which was incompatible with our policy.

Ed Murrow also had his disputes with CBS from time to time over news policies, and I believe after a while he did become dissatisfied with the amount of time he was getting on the air. But these disputes were momentary ones and to be expected in the regular course of our business. In 1956, after a *See It Now* broadcast called "The Farm Problem: Crisis of Abundance," CBS gave air time to Secretary of Agriculture Ezra Benson for his reply. This infuriated Murrow, who believed that no time should have been given and, in any event, he should have been consulted first.

In 1958, speaking before the Radio and Television News Directors Association in Chicago, Murrow blasted the whole television industry. He predicted that future historians who examined kinescopes of current television would find "evidence of decadence, escapism, and insulation from the realities of the world in which we live." He went on to say: "I invite your attention to the television schedules of all networks between the hours of 8:00 and 11:00 P.M. Eastern Time. Here you will find only fleeting and spasmodic reference to the fact that this nation is in mortal danger."

I did not believe television was overlooking any "mortal danger" and I didn't agree with Murrow's gloomy thesis at all. I wished he had come to talk to me about it. How much time should be given to news and documentaries in the prime evening hours has always been one of the thorniest questions in broadcasting. News people always want more prime time and the entertainment people want to give them less. CBS has broadcast hundreds of documentaries over the years, more than any other network.

In mid-1959 Murrow left on a year-long sabbatical, and that fall, while he was away, in the wake of the quiz-show scandals, Frank Stanton declared publicly that henceforth "what [the American people] see and hear on CBS programs is exactly what it purports to be." Later, while talking to Jack Gould of the New York *Times*, Stanton mentioned Murrow's *Person to Person* interview program as an example of what would no longer be allowed on CBS, namely not informing the public that the on-camera interviews in celebrities' homes were rehearsed to some extent beforehand. Murrow was furious and issued his reply from London: "Dr. Stanton has finally revealed his ignorance both of news and of requirements of television production. . . . Surely Stanton must know that cameras, lights and microphones do not just wander around a home. The alternative would be chaos. I am sorry Dr. Stanton feels that I have participated in perpetrating a fraud upon the public. My conscience is clear. His seems to be bothering him."

Stanton's criticism of the *Person to Person* show was technically correct, but I did not like the way he went about criticizing Murrow in the context of the quiz scandals. The situations were not at all the same. I could understand Murrow's wrath, but I was caught in the middle. I could not stand by silently and allow Murrow or anybody else to attack a CBS president in such a way. And so I sent an intermediary to London to try to persuade Murrow to retract his attack on Stanton. He refused. And I let it be, hoping that time would take care of the situation, and it did. The heat of tempers subsided. But this incident reflected the animosity that existed between Murrow and Stanton. I never discussed Stanton with Murrow or Murrow with Stanton except in a formal way on operational matters.

When in early 1961 Murrow was offered the position of director of the U. S. Information Agency in the new Kennedy administration, I think he might have seen a chance not only to escape the dissatisfactions he had with his work, but also to do public service. He was enamored of Kennedy. He never really complained to me about his work, but then he was not the kind of man who would have. He came to ask me what I thought he ought to do, and I said, "Well, you know you have a home here as long as you want one, but if you decide to take it, I have some advice on the job and the conditions you should insist upon." I suggested that he make it a condition of taking the job that he be a member of the President's inner circle, attending all meetings with the Cabinet, National Security Council, and other discussions of serious consequence. Ed agreed, and he took the job. Shortly after he went to Washington, he sent me this letter:

February 8, 1961

Dear Bill,

This is the first letter written from this ancient building in which I now work. I write primarily to say that had it not been for our last conversation I doubt that I would have had the equanimity, peace of mind, or courage to undertake this task. Perhaps all three will soon fade, but I wanted you to know of my gratitude and abiding affection.

The operation here has been set up in a fashion that makes it possible for a job to be done, and we have had plenty of indications that many people are willing to help.

I send you my best salute and remind you that if I get into serious trouble, I will be knocking on your door.

As ever,

> Yours,
> [signed] Ed

Ed and I met frequently while he was in Washington and at one point I heard about his disappointment. Kennedy had agreed to bring him into the inner circle, but there had been slippage on this promise and Murrow had come to feel that he was not part of the inner team. Nevertheless, he did not resign. He stayed on and made the best of it. It was like him to swallow the disappointment. When he left the USIA three years later, in January 1964, he was already suffering from lung cancer, and fifteen months later he was dead. I remained close to him until the end, visiting him and Janet in their rented house in La Jolla, California, where it was so obvious that he was dying.

Murrow would not have been Murrow nor I myself if we had not had differences of opinion during our long professional and personal relationship. These differences and their meaning have been distorted by careless writers who interpret disputes as estrangement. Sometimes our differences were in fact very strong. In his 1958 speech, attacking television, Murrow showed his concern with the relationship of "show business, advertising, and news." I was extremely hurt by it but never discussed the speech itself with him. We continued our meetings, our discussions over a wide range of subjects, and our friendship. His widow, Janet, after reading a rather critical account of our relations, wrote me a letter about it which, with her permission, I quote here:

> 12, April, 1976

Dear Bill,

This letter is, I think, about four months overdue. But, though I dislike thinking about it, I want to tell you how I deplore the articles which appeared in the Atlantic Monthly in January and February [by David Halberstam]. . . . To go back to that dratted article: I find it painful to think of; you must find it more so. I remember that you and Ed went through so much together over a long period of years. You both knew each other's weaknesses and each other's strengths. I know that Ed thought of you with love and understanding and compassion. I feel that you reciprocated these sentiments.

It's a pity to see the difficult moments blown up out (of) proportion and woven together in an unnecessarily unpleasant way—I'm sorry about that.

All best wishes and my love to you and Babe.

[signed] Janet

CBS News, after Ed Murrow went back on the air, was run by a series of men—Wells Church, Edmund Chester, Davidson Taylor, and Sig Mickelson—who routinely reported directly to Stanton and myself. Policy decisions were made by an editorial board which we formalized in 1960 under the name CNEC (CBS News Executive Committee) which was composed of Stanton and myself and the president of each of the CBS broadcasting divisions. The guard changed in 1961 when Richard Salant succeeded Sig Mickelson, and again in 1964 when Salant was succeeded by Fred Friendly. Friendly also had direct personal contact with Stanton and me.

By 1966, CBS had grown to such an extent that in the interest of efficiency, we reorganized the company into two separate groups, broadcasting and non-broadcasting, each headed by a president who would handle the day-to-day decisions and report to us. We appointed Jack Schneider, our young president of the television network, as president of the Broadcast Group, with all broadcast divisions reporting to him, including the News Division. Fred Friendly, as president of CBS News, took great exception to this. On the day the change was announced, February 9, he sent me a memo: "Two years ago when I was asked to head the News Division, I was told that my responsibility would be directly to the Chairman and the President. I gather from today's announcement that this is no longer so. Because of the seriousness with which I regard this matter, I would like to see you at your first convenience."

Fred was a big, enthusiastic, volatile man of enormous energy and talent who had started with CBS in 1950 as the co-producer with Ed Murrow of *Hear It Now,* which was succeeded the following year by *See It Now.* Seeing him in my office the next day, I heard him out as he pleaded for the privilege of bypassing Jack Schneider and reporting directly to Stanton or myself. I told him I had no recollection of ever promising anything about to whom he would report. I tried to explain that Stanton and I needed help in running the company and we had to divide some of the responsibilities.

"I'm sorry, Fred, the logic calls for putting all broadcasting activities under the supervision of one man," I told him.

"Well, I don't know if I can stay under those circumstances," he replied. "It would be degrading the importance of News and I won't have the opportunity of discussing things with you and this will just separate the two of us."

"I'm very, very sorry, Fred, but progress is progress," I said, adding, "I hope this will all work out. You're making a mountain out of a molehill. And I just don't know any other way to handle the enormous workload here, except by making group presidents."

When Friendly complained about Schneider's lack of experience in news, he mentioned in passing that Schneider had just denied his request that we broadcast a third day of the Vietnam war hearings before the Senate Foreign Relations Committee, at which George Kennan, a former diplomat, was due to testify. I asked him to bear with Jack, to work with him and to have faith that Jack would find his way with news judgment as he had in the other phases of broadcasting. (Schneider had been very successful in radio time sales, as manager of our Philadelphia and New York stations and then as president of the television network. He did lack experience in news, but I was not about to overrule his very first decision as president of the Broadcast Group.) But Friendly continually demurred, repeating that he just might have to resign rather than report to anyone except top management.

"Fred, you sound as though you're not going to stick around with these new conditions and there's nothing I can do about that," I said. "But if you do decide to leave—and I hope you don't —for goodness sake, let's part in a civilized way."

"I agree with you absolutely. I love CBS and CBS News," he declared. "The farthest thing from my mind would be to do anything that would be detrimental to the best interests of CBS or CBS News. And I hope CBS will be fair-minded about me."

I really did not know if Friendly was serious in his threat to resign or if he was just bluffing in an attempt to persuade us to change our minds about the chain of command.

The very next week, when I had just started a vacation in Nassau, I received a phone call from Stanton. He told me Fred had just resigned and left with him a long, vitriolic letter of resignation castigating CBS management for its decision to broadcast reruns of *I Love Lucy* and *The Real McCoys* rather than the Vietnam hearings. Stanton read me the letter, in which Friendly quoted Ed Murrow and John F. Kennedy's *Profiles in Courage* as justification for his quitting. It was quite a blast.

When Fred telephoned me and said how sorry he was that he had to resign, I reminded him of his promise not to hurt CBS News. I told him Stanton had read his letter to me and asked him if he had released it. He hesitated and said no and hesitated and then said, "Well, to only one person." I said to whom, and he replied, "Jack Gould." That's when I blew my stack and told him he had broken his word to me, that I regarded his letter not only to be vituperative and full of rancor but designed to cause CBS and CBS News great damage. Only one copy, but to the head radio and television critic of the New York *Times*! I could not believe that Fred Friendly, after sixteen years with CBS, had resigned over a single decision on whether or not to pre-empt our schedule for a news story. Those decisions crop up all the time.

Babe and I met Chou En-lai in China.

A visit with Chinese youngsters.

At the Whitney plantation in Thomasville, Georgia, with Babe, the Whitneys, and Roy Atwood.

Mr. and Mrs. Robert Sherwood.

Babe with Picasso at his home in southern France.

Jack Baragwanath with Dominguin, the matador.

With Picasso.

The Loel Guinnesses.

The Guinness yacht, the *Sarina*.

The Earl and Countess of Avon (the Anthony Edens).

Michael and Lady Anne Tree.

Lord Beaverbrook (l.) with Babe
and John Minary.

Lord Victor Rothschild.

Photo by Arnold Newman

Starting a walk after lunch with Queen Elizabeth, Prince Philip, and party.

Lord Mountbatten.

The David Somersets.

A family gathering on the terrace at Kiluna.

Babe with Randolph Churchill at Kiluna.

Jeremy Tree.   Babe and our son Bill with guide in Leningrad.

Babe in Venice.

I try for salmon in Canada.

In fact, CBS carried the fourth and fifth day of the Vietnam war hearings. But that is the way the press ran the story of his resignation—that he had quit over the principle of who was to judge the value of a news story at CBS. So, Dick Salant returned as president of CBS News and has continued to serve there admirably ever since. Upon Salant's retirement at age sixty-five in 1979, William A. Leonard, a veteran CBS newscaster, is scheduled to become the next head of CBS News.

During the early sixties we continued to expand the news in the television schedule. From 1959 (when separate figures were first kept) to 1978, the staff has more than doubled (from 450 to more than 1,000) and the budget has increased more than sixfold. In September 1963, we added a half-hour morning newscast and the evening newscast was extended from fifteen minutes to a half hour. We were the first network to do so. By the end of the year, about 15 per cent of the CBS Television schedule was being produced by CBS News, a proportion that has remained generally constant ever since. In March 1969, the *CBS Morning News* was expanded again to become network television's first one-hour news program.

The stalwart kingpin of CBS News over the past sixteen years has been Walter Cronkite, who has earned for himself and in turn for CBS that which we have wanted from the very start of our News Division: the highest degree of credibility in the world of journalism. Walter earned that credibility along with the respect of his peers by sheer hard work, attention to detail, and a sense of journalistic honesty, integrity, and fairness that has marked his twenty-eight-year career with CBS. He is not just a man reciting the evening news, he is the managing editor who has a strong voice in selecting the stories and the treatment of them on the *CBS Evening News*. Walter is so objective, careful, and fair in his presentation of news that he has been characterized—if not immortalized—with the oft-heard line: "If Walter says it, it must be so." Five nights a week, he has an average audience of 18.5 million people. On

special or extraordinary news events, many more millions, perhaps a majority of the American people, turn to CBS and to
Walter Cronkite to follow the happenings. Walter is there for
the political conventions, the presidential campaigns, the election nights, the assassination of a President, the flights into
space and man's first landing on the moon. In my mind, he is
to today's news what Ed Murrow was to yesteryear's "blitz"
of London—a fair representative of us all.

In similar fashion and with similar attributes, Eric Sevareid before his retirement in 1977 had become the most respected analyst of the news in the industry. Like Walter, he earned that
respect and credibility over the thirty-eight years he was with
CBS News because people found they could trust his commentaries and analyses to be fair, honest, and well-founded. I could
go on and on naming CBS newscasters, but everyone can see
and judge them for himself by watching their CBS newscasts
every day of the week.

Ever since the first *See It Now* program in 1951, CBS has led
the industry in the quality and quantity of its news documentaries through the years. *CBS Reports* is noted for the breadth
and scope and impact of its documentaries on important and
controversial subjects.

The crowning achievement of the documentary units of CBS
News, in recent years however, has been *60 Minutes*. Don
Hewitt, one of the all-time great producers of CBS, introduced
the magazine format of *60 Minutes* in 1968 and has supervised
the program with loving care ever since. Because of the quality
of the program, we stuck with it during its first struggling years
of low ratings and watched it become the first documentary series
in history to rise to the magic circle of the ten most popular
programs on television in the 1977–78 season. Since its start,
60 Minutes has won virtually every major award in television
news reporting. Every week, that news program reaches some
32.6 million Americans. Its hard-hitting investigative newscasters,
each an outstanding veteran newsman at CBS, are today among
the best-known journalists in the world: Mike Wallace, Morley

Safer, Dan Rather, and this past year they have been joined by one other fine journalist, Harry Reasoner, a past news anchorman who left us for a while and then came "home" again.

But the News Division did not develop without problems. One of Howard K. Smith's criticisms of the strictness of our rule on objectivity in the news, for example, was that it was not then consistently administered. For one thing, he had said, "it applies almost not at all to foreign correspondents." I think he was right at the time and for some time afterward. The worst instance of such license and the worst blot on the record of CBS News was Daniel Schorr's broadcast from Germany on the eve of the 1964 Republican Convention in San Francisco where Senator Barry Goldwater was about to become the Republican candidate for President. In a *World News Roundup* program on radio on Friday, July 10, 1964, and on television the following day, Schorr reported from Munich that Goldwater intended to take a vacation in Germany and would stay in Berchtesgaden, Hitler's former retreat. Schorr reported that Goldwater had tentatively agreed to speak at a seminar in Bavaria, and that "This is only the start of a move to link up with German rightists. . . ." Senator Goldwater denounced the report as "the damndest lie I ever heard," and canceled the vacation he had planned to take in Germany.

I was at the convention with Fred Friendly, who was then new at the job of running CBS News, when he telephoned Schorr to question him about the broadcast. Schorr was unable to support the statement he had made on the air. I was shocked and Friendly was furious. He screamed at Schorr on the telephone and then he cabled him a reprimand. Friendly noted that the New York desk should not have carried the story. Schorr cabled back acknowledging that he had no evidence for what he had said about Goldwater, that it was a hurried and sloppy script which he regretted and that what he had actually observed was what he called a "tendency of Goldwater and German right-wingers to gravitate towards each other."

Six days after the first broadcast, Schorr then went back on radio with a purported clarification of the Goldwater broadcast (which he repeated two days later on television) and announced, "In that connection, may I say that in speaking the other day of a move by Goldwater to link up with these forces, I did not mean to suggest a conscious effort on his part, of which there is no proof here, but meant more a process of gravitation which is visible here." Gravitation!

The events of the sixties themselves imposed new problems for television news coverage. Some of the civil rights protests and marches seemed to be planned with one eye on the TV camera. In 1967 Frank Stanton noted: "There seems to be a tendency on the part of persons who are setting up demonstrations to accommodate the networks to reap the most publicity and exposure." City officials in Toledo and Newark charged that television coverage had provoked riots in their cities. In 1960, Buford Ellington, governor of Tennessee, even charged that "the sit-in demonstration by Negro students in downtown Nashville today was instigated and planned by, and staged for, the convenience of the Columbia Broadcasting System."

The charge was groundless but it illustrated the difficulty of the problem. We tried to meet it with a combination of precaution and discretion, using unmarked cars, avoiding the use of bright lights and declining to promise TV coverage of future protests. Our newsmen were instructed that "the best coverage is not necessarily the one with the best pictures and most dramatic action."

The war in Vietnam presented new and perhaps the most vexing problems of all. It was the first war involving Americans that television had the ability to report fully and regularly and there were few precedents to follow. In 1961, CBS carried the first combat footage showing Vietnamese troops in action. In March 1964, when Secretary of Defense Robert McNamara went on a mission there, and again in August, following the Gulf of Tonkin episode, CBS News sent special task forces of news and cameramen to Vietnam. Then, in 1965, when the war was escalated and American involvement grew enormously, television news brought the war into American living rooms almost every night. The war became a central experience in American life. It continued to be that for eight years and CBS News increased its coverage accordingly.

The news reports of the war were often controversial, perhaps never more so than in 1965, when Morley Safer reported that U. S. Marines had set fire to the Vietnamese village of Cam Ne with their cigarette lighters. People could hardly believe it. The Pentagon denied the story until Safer's film arrived in this country, confirming his report with pictures showing what had occurred.

Other reports frequently touched on American emotions and sensibilities. *Saigon,* a 1967 special, was rejected by some affiliates on the grounds that it failed "to tell of the good work our troops are doing for the people of that city." Some viewers objected to reports of brutality; some objected to coverage of student uprisings in this country; some objected to coverage of the My Lai story; and some objected to pictures of American soldiers smoking marijuana. In the emotional atmosphere generated by the war, television was often blamed for what it reported. Through it all, however, our policy was to cover every element of the war in Vietnam and the whole spectrum of opinion about it at home. Those were times of upheaval. The civil rights struggle and the riots that sometimes accompanied it, the war and the protests against it, the assassinations of John Kennedy, Robert Kennedy and Martin Luther King—all stirred powerful emotions. Yet, in covering them, television proved its unique value: the whole country became witness to the true trauma of the times. During the sixties, television became the country's main source of news, surpassing newspapers. Surveys indicated that television also had become the most believable source of news of all media and by a wide margin. Our responsibilities obviously increased.

The constitutional rights of broadcasters have always been compromised to some extent by Section 315 of the Communications Act. Since 1969, however, these freedoms have been attacked and threatened in new ways and with such vigor that broadcast journalism seems to have entered a new era of difficulties. The administration of Richard Nixon tried to control the news media and in the midst of that struggle we were attacked by a congressional committee which decided to judge the fairness of a CBS documentary, *The Selling of the Pentagon*. On February 23, 1971, the program examined the huge public relations organization of the Defense Department and investigated charges that the Pentagon used its "public relations funds not merely to inform but to convince and persuade the public on vital issues of war and peace." The narrator noted: "We sought no secret files, no politicians pleading special causes, no access to classified documents. We looked only at what is being done for the public—in public."

Reaction by mail, telephone, and telegram was unusually high and predominantly favorable. The program won a Peabody Award. But it was also loudly denounced, especially in the government and particularly by F. Edward Hébert, chairman of the House Armed Services Committee. He called it "the most horrible thing I've seen in years . . . a splendid professional hatchet job . . . one of the most un-American things I've ever seen on a screen." Vice-President Spiro Agnew denounced it as "a subtle but vicious broadside against the nation's defense establishment." Defending the film for CBS, Dick Salant commented, "No one has refuted the essential accuracy of *The Selling of the Pentagon*." There was, however, a flaw in the film which our adversaries were quick to take advantage of: an interview in the film was edited in such a way that parts of different answers appeared to be in response to the same question. Dick Salant rightly maintained that the validity of the broadcast as a whole was unscathed and that the editing did not change the essential meaning of the interview. It had been done for convenience.

On April 7, 1971, the Special Subcommittee on Investigations of the House Interstate and Foreign Commerce Committee issued a subpoena to Frank Stanton in his capacity as president and customary representative of CBS in important matters in Washington. It commanded him to turn over an array of materials connected with the broadcast, including "all film, work-prints, outtakes." Stanton replied by going straight to the real point of issue:

> The sole purpose of this subpoena, so far as we can ascertain it, is to obtain materials which will aid the Committee in subjecting to legislative surveillance the news judgment of CBS in preparing *The Selling of the Pentagon.* The fact that television and radio stations are licensed by the government does not deprive the broadcast press of First Amendment protection, and the courts have so held. That protection does not depend upon whether the government believes we are right or wrong in our news judgments. We will respectfully decline to furnish to the Committee the outtakes and other materials used in connection with preparing the broadcasts, but not actually broadcast.

The subcommittee rescinded the subpoena and issued a new one on May 26, demanding much less material than had the first, but still requiring "all film, workprints, outtakes." But the committee this time summoned a personal appearance by Stanton. He went before the subcommittee on June 24 and again declined to hand over the materials. Five days later the subcommittee recommended that the president of CBS be cited for contempt of Congress; two days later the full committee voted to cite both Stanton and CBS.

On July 9, 1971, I informed the CBS organization of our position in a memo:

> . . . Yielding to the demands could very clearly obstruct freedom of the press. Therefore, resistance to them is a matter of our duty as responsible citizens. . . .

> To lose this fight would be a serious setback to free speech in this country. It would also go against every principle that CBS has stood for and fought for since its founding. The issue is as grave as that.

On July 13 the full House rejected its committee's recommendation and voted to recommit the contempt citations to committee, and there the matter ended. No workprints or outtakes were ever turned over to the committee. Our having blocked government intervention, however, was only half the story. I have said again and again in claiming a constitutional freedom from government interference, CBS must adhere to our own code of editorial correctness and fairness in the best traditions of American journalism. Personally, I did not approve of the editing which had been done. The misplaced questions and answers occupied only a small part of the film. Nevertheless, any such editing could always invite doubt about our news reports.

We had an internal conflict over that one. At the same time that we were defending our position against Congress and not giving an inch, I told the members of our news policy committee (CNEC), "I don't like this kind of editing. Technically, it might be easier to do it that way, but it is not what it purports to be on the air, and it is not living up to the guidelines of our news policies." Taking the answer to one question and adding it to the answer of another question was simply not right, even when the intended meaning was not changed. Actually we had been struggling with the problem of establishing standards for editing for many years. These discussions got results. A few months after the broadcast of *The Selling of the Pentagon*, we issued a new set of rules to our newsmen governing documentary broadcasts:

> In interviews, if an answer is used out of context in any way for broadcast, it must be so indicated on the air; if more than one excerpt from a speech or a statement is broadcast, the order of the excerpts must not be changed, unless indicated on the air; and, transcripts of the entire interview will be made available to the interviewee, upon request, after the broadcast.

After mulling over this new policy for a while, I decided that the rules for documentaries should apply to hard news as well. It was pointed out to me that this might at times necessitate using two cameras instead of one for interviews. But I insisted: "If it costs more money or you have to have a second camera, no matter, let's do it. We're not going to have anything on the air that isn't what it purports to be." And so, out of experience and learning, we developed a new policy for our News Division:

> "Effective today CND will no longer permit composite answers on hard news interviews, unless appropriate narration indicates to the contrary."

Headlines
and Headaches

Ever since the administration of George Washington, Presidents of the United States have complained privately or in public that they have been misunderstood, misinterpreted, or unfairly criticized by the press. George Washington always referred to one critical newspaper editor as "that rascal Freneau." But then Philip Freneau of the *National Gazette* referred to Washington as King George. The point is that all our Presidents have felt at one time or another that they were being treated unfairly by the press. It is only natural for any man to prefer praise to criticism. The conflict in interests and outlook between the government and the press is built into our democratic system, and quite deliberately so. But through the years each President has handled his complaints against the press differently. All this always has been understood by experienced newsmen. But it was not until the beleaguered administration of Richard Nixon that the news media, particularly broadcasting, were seriously threatened by the Executive Branch of the government.

Among the Presidents of the United States I have known personally, I do not recall much if any pressure from Franklin D. Roosevelt to influence our reporting on his administration. Roosevelt had a natural affinity with broadcasting and from the earliest days he used radio more effectively than any President has ever since.

I do not remember Harry Truman or his people ever voicing any objections directly to me or to CBS. When Truman complained, he complained publicly in a loud, clear voice.

Dwight D. Eisenhower just did not seem to care about press criticism, or at least, he never let it be known. If he decided a publication was against him, he simply stopped reading it. Sometime during his two terms in office, I understand, he stopped reading the New York *Times*.

I knew Eisenhower best, having worked under him in World War II. When he was president of Columbia University in New York, I accepted his invitation to serve as a trustee there and was a trustee of Columbia for twenty-three years. I continued to see him and correspond with him during and after his stay in the White House. We were frequent golfing companions and occasionally I visited him at his home in Gettysburg, Pennsylvania. I served as his special ambassador to the Republic of the Congo for the ceremonies marking the independence of that country in 1960. During all that time, he never voiced any disapproval about broadcasting or its coverage of his news conferences or of his administration. He was the first President to allow television cameras into his press conferences but, in fear of making a slip of the tongue, he insisted upon the right of his staff to review the film before it was released. In 1963, after his retirement, Eisenhower acceded to my request to make a *CBS Reports* special with Walter Cronkite commemorating D-Day called *D-Day Plus 20 Years: Eisenhower Returns to Normandy*. I went along to watch and to tour landmarks of the war with him. We reminisced about that marvelous trip six years later when he lay dying in Walter Reed Army Hospital. I remember him, so pale and thin, inhaling oxygen, and shooing the nurse away when she tried to get me to leave the room. So near the end, he was in a cheery mood, his mind as acute as ever.

On handling the press, the Kennedys were different. Both the

President and his brother Bobby believed in the direct, personal complaint, and they thought that the harder they attacked, the better break they would get. I remember Frank Stanton coming in to tell me one day that President Kennedy had telephoned and bawled him out for something that had been on the air which he thought was unfair. But publicly, the Kennedys never, as far as I can recall, attacked the media or broadcasting in the general way the Nixon administration did later—one or two newspapers, yes, like the New York *Herald Tribune*, but never all the press. Kennedy was the first President to allow his press conferences to be televised live without White House editing, but then, he was a master of the medium. Kennedy was the first President to recognize the full importance of television in politics and government. At a small dinner party given by columnist Joseph Alsop shortly after his election, Kennedy asked me if I could give him any advice on the use of our medium. I told him I thought the President who used broadcasting most effectively had been Franklin D. Roosevelt because he used it so sparingly and only when he had something very important to say. He did not want his broadcast to become commonplace. Thus, every time he went on the air, it was an important event. Kennedy nodded in agreement and thanked me.

Neither did Lyndon B. Johnson attack the press—not publicly. I had known Johnson since the early forties, when he had been a congressman, and had introduced him to Stanton when Frank took over our Washington beat, and the two of them became close friends. Johnson, a volatile Texan in the old tradition, never seemed to hesitate in telephoning his salty complaints to whoever he thought could help him. He phoned reporters, columnists, Sevareid, Stanton, me at any time of the day or night. But they were usually spur-of-the-moment outbursts and he never seemed to hold a grudge when his requests were heard and ignored.

And then came Richard Nixon. I knew him from his days as Vice-President under Eisenhower. I even made a contribution to his 1960 campaign for President, for I was raised as a Republican, although I often crossed party lines in my voting. Lest anyone jump to quick conclusions, I never allowed partisanship to have anything to do with what CBS did on the air. In 1968, I was as astonished as everyone at Nixon's political resurrection and I went to the Republican Convention with Nelson Rockefeller as my personal choice. But Nelson failed to take the convention by storm and Nixon had the delegates lined up behind him. After that election, I decided that broadcasting had become so closely tied to the electoral process that I had better end any personal associations with presidential candidates and campaigns. After 1970, I decided to stay clear of local politics as well, and since then I have not participated in or contributed to any political campaign.

On one of the rare occasions when I visited the Nixon White House, along with four or five other CBS executives, Nixon, addressing me as "Bill," remarked that he realized I was trying to protect broadcasting against any government encroachment. "You keep your medium free," he said. "It's most important." I thanked him and told him I appreciated those sentiments on his part. At the time, I was comforted by his advice and encouragement. Later I learned that while this exchange was taking place in the Oval Office, other men in the White House were plotting on his behalf against us and the other networks.

The White House fired its first major salvo at the press just a year after Nixon's election. On November 13, 1969, in Des Moines, in a major address carried live by all three networks, Vice-President Spiro Agnew attacked the news organizations of all the networks. "Is it not fair and relevant to question its [power] concentration in the hands of a tiny, enclosed fraternity of privileged men elected by no one and enjoying a monopoly sanctioned and licensed by government?" Further along, he declared: "As with other American institutions, perhaps it is time that the networks were made more responsive to the views of the nation and more responsible to the people they serve."

The message was clear, the threat unmistakable. The Nixon administration was reminding all broadcasters that we were licensed by the government and regulated by one of its agencies,

313

the FCC, which they thought had the power to make us "more responsive" to the views of the man elected to the White House. Nor was this the first of the implied threats from the Nixon administration.

After one televised speech on Vietnam by the President, FCC Chairman Dean Burch had telephoned executives of all three networks—Stanton at CBS—and asked for transcripts of their commentators' remarks after Nixon's speech. He could have obtained a transcript routinely, but instead he had called top network executives. The meaning was loud and clear: the White House wanted us to know they were watching.

In mid-October of 1969, White House aide Jeb Stuart Magruder had written a memo to H. R. Haldeman, the President's chief of staff, on what he called "unfair coverage." Although we do not know the extent to which his recommendations were followed, that memo, which was revealed during the Watergate hearings, stands as an example of how the government could try to control the media. It also illustrates the differences in attitude between the Nixon administration and all of its predecessors. Calling his memo "The Shot-gun versus the Rifle," Magruder recommended that instead of taking diverse case-by-case action, the White House "should begin concentrated efforts in a number of major areas that will have much more impact on the media and other anti-administration spokesmen and will do more good in the long run." Here are some of his suggestions:

1. Begin an official monitoring system through the FCC as soon as Dean Burch is officially on board as Chairman. If the monitoring system proves our point, we have then legitimate and legal rights to go to the networks, etc., and make official complaints from the FCC. . . .

2. Utilize the anti-trust division to investigate various media relating to anti-trust violations. Even the possible threat of anti-trust action I think would be effective in changing their views in the above matter.

3. Utilizing the Internal Revenue Service as a method to look into the various organizations that we are most con-

cerned about. Just a threat of an IRS investigation will probably turn their approach.

In May 1970 the White House leaked a story to syndicated columnist Jack Anderson that a film report seen on the *CBS Evening News with Walter Cronkite* the previous November had been faked. The film showed a South Vietnamese soldier stabbing to death a North Vietnamese prisoner. The Pentagon suggested that the prisoner might already have been dead. CBS responded with a rebroadcast of the film which served to magnify certain substantive details, and we found the South Vietnamese soldier, who admitted to the killing on film. Walter Cronkite opened that story by saying, "What follows is unusual for the *CBS Evening News*," and continued, "For reasons not entirely clear, the White House has engaged in an undercover campaign to discredit CBS News by alleging the story was faked." Referring to the original broadcast, he said, "What has happened since then tells something about the government and its relations with news media which carry stories the government finds 'disagreeable.'"

Over the next three years, as President Nixon became more and more embroiled in controversial speeches, at CBS we faced the problem of how best to be fair to those who wanted to reply to the President, particularly the Democrats and the increasing number of responsible people who opposed the Vietnam war. We gave them time on our regular news broadcasts, but those were only brief interviews and did not really suffice. CNEC discussed the difficult and complex matter many times—eighteen times, in fact. We tried the idea of "Loyal Opposition" broadcasts; but after the very first broadcast, the Republican National Committee asked for time to reply. Since the first broadcast had itself been a reply to President Nixon, we refused. The Republicans appealed to the FCC, which ruled that we had to give them time. CBS then appealed that ruling but by the time we won our court case, sixteen months had passed since the initial broadcast and we had developed a new and broader policy at CBS: whenever the President spoke on matters of controversial national policy, CBS would invite proponents of differing views to reply as soon as possible, and the choice of a speaker would be based upon the issues involved, and not upon the politics or party line disagreements.

We also took up the problem, which I considered secondary in importance, of whether or not it was fair to have our newsmen given an "instant analysis" directly after a presidential speech. When our analysts had no advance time to truly analyze a Nixon speech, the "instant analysis" was often of little value.

Eric Sevareid, who gave most of our instant analyses, had strong reservations about them. He personally wanted more time to consider a speech rather than give a quick, improvised reaction. The advantage of an immediate analysis was that it reached the same audience that had just heard the speech. But the disadvantages seemed to us to outweigh the advantages. We decided to eliminate instant analysis and give our commentaries on the next morning's news or on the Cronkite broadcast the following evening. We held the matter up to see whether the other networks were interested in joining our announcement of the basic presidential reply policy, but nothing came of that and we decided to go ahead anyway.

When CBS announced our decision in early June 1973, the whole CNEC group, myself included, was surprised at the press coverage. We considered the important news to be that CBS was going to offer air time to the President's opposition. Instead, the headlines emphasized the abandoning of our "instant analysis" along with allegations that CBS did so because of pressure from the Nixon administration. It created a flurry of controversy in and by itself. Some CBS newsmen expressed disapproval of the new policy, others supported it, including Sevareid and Dan Rather. I was obliged to write a memo to the whole CBS organization on the subject, although I thought it was rather obvious we were not bowing to Nixon's complaints on press coverage. We were, after all, giving air time to Nixon's opponents to reply to his speeches. Nevertheless, I explained: "The sole reason for the decision was to furnish better, fairer, more balanced and more thorough coverage of presidential broadcasts. There was no other motive."

But I have seldom been so wrong in measuring public interest as I had been in thinking those instant analyses were not particularly useful or interesting. Five months after stopping our instant analyses, we changed our minds and started them again. I had admitted to CNEC, "Fellows, it isn't working. I think people expect some reaction right after the President's speech, and I think we have to change that policy again." Accordingly, on November 12, we announced we would resume "instant analysis" of presidential speeches whenever it "seems desirable and adequate preparation is feasible."

During those tumultuous Nixon years, when his administration was troubled, among other things, by the war in Vietnam, the anti-war demonstrations throughout America, and finally by the Watergate scandal, CBS more than any other network was denounced by the Nixon people and his supporters for our coverage of his administration. Yet other critics thought we were too "soft" on the Nixon administration, and each side would quote statistics or particular broadcasts—usually inaccurately—in an attempt to prove their case on one side or the other. Actually, such diverse criticism should demonstrate that CBS News was diligent in its coverage and as impartial as was humanly possible, considering the mood of the times. There was no policy decision to be either "tough" or "soft" in covering President Nixon. The news of his administration was reported on a day-to-day basis, and, when events warranted, they were put on the air according to the best journalistic judgments made on the spot and at the time.

Only when it was all over could we count the number of hours CBS devoted to Watergate and the downfall of the Nixon administration.

In the seven-week period before the presidential election, during which most news organizations gave the story only cursory coverage, the CBS Television Network devoted almost twice as much air time to Watergate as did any of the other networks. From the break-in on June 17, 1972, to President Nixon's resignation on August 9, 1974, we gave a total of more than ninety-two hours on our regular newscasts. In addition, our Watergate "specials," documentaries and *60 Minutes* segments equaled more than fifty hours of air time. We also carried live twenty-eight days of the Watergate hearings before Congress, which was our portion of a rotating arrangement with the other networks.

Before Watergate and afterward, my role as the head of CBS was to protect the integrity and independence of our newsroom from outside criticisms, pressures, or threats. At the same time my job was also to keep watch over our policy of fairness and balance, which was the best defense against criticism from outside sources. Frank Stanton, as president of CBS, fully shared that dual role with me. Critics of CBS have sometimes not understood this position we adopted for ourselves at the top management level of CBS. One incident—and only one—out of all the Watergate news coverage has become a *cause célèbre* in the industry. I am accused—and quite inaccurately—of having interfered with the content of a news broadcast. I am said to have ordered one *CBS Evening News* broadcast—out of more than a hundred hours devoted to the subject—edited and cut as it related to Watergate. It is worthwhile to relate the details of this incident not just to deny what I have denied before, but in order to illustrate how things work vis-à-vis corporate management and our newsroom.

The day was Friday, October 27, 1972, eleven days before the presidential election, when shortly before I left the office, Stanton telephoned to tell me to watch the Walter Cronkite news broadcast that night. So I made sure that I reached Kiluna in time to seat myself in front of my television set for the *CBS Evening News*.

About two thirds of the entire broadcast was devoted to Watergate. And I did not like it. The news summary seemed to be seriously out of balance—about 65 per cent of it devoted to Watergate—and furthermore, it seemed to me that the allegations being made were not adequately separated from known facts. There was one comment made about the difference but it seemed that the two were run together to such an extent that the distinction was rather difficult. The broadcast troubled me. It just did not seem in keeping with Cronkite's usual objectivity. Later that night or perhaps early the following morning, I phoned Stanton to discuss it and found that both of us were disturbed about the broadcast. So I decided to have a meeting to review it on Monday morning in the office and I asked him to invite Dick Salant, the president of CBS News; Arthur Taylor, the new president of CBS; and Jack Schneider, the president of the Broadcast Group.

A later line-by-line analysis of that broadcast confirmed my instincts about it: many of the allegations had been based upon accounts from reputable publications, particularly the Washington *Post*, and had not been independently found or checked by our own reporters. I had no way of knowing this at the time and it must be remembered that in the early days of Watergate, prior to the election, not many newspapers carried the story in any great detail. In fact, I have since learned that the editors of the Washington *Post* were extremely nervous about doing it alone. Since other newspapers did not pick up the *Post*'s stories, as was the usual practice, they were greatly relieved when CBS finally went into the matter. Here were the Washington *Post* and CBS reporting a story of major consequence which at that early stage still was based largely upon allegations and conjecture.

The broadcast was unique in one other way, which contributed to the controversy over it: it was only the first of a two-part wrap-up on Watergate, the second part promised for the Cronkite broadcast Monday evening. The waters were muddied further by a phone call I received the next day, Saturday morning, from Charles W. Colson, the Nixon White House trouble-shooter. This later led to the charge that I called the Monday meeting at CBS and that I made changes in the second broadcast all because I was intimidated by Chuck Colson and pressure from the White House.

Colson and I had met in Washington and before his Saturday telephone call, he had been to my office twice—in September 1970 and again in September 1972—each time to complain about our news broadcasts. At those meetings I thought we had all been well mannered. He did not make any threats or intimidating comments as far as I could discern. He tried to show me that our broadcasts were politically unfair to Nixon; and I tried to explain CBS policies on news to him and that we were covering the news fairly, with no political intent at all, one way or the other. Subsequently, I learned that Colson had written a memo to H. R. Haldeman on that first meeting describing how well he had threatened and intimidated the heads of all three networks. I can only surmise that he was trying to impress his boss, for there were no such threats or intimidations that I recognized at our meeting.

On his Saturday phone call to me, Colson brought up a number of complaints. After that call, I made careful notes of what had been said:

Colson had told me that he had heard that CBS had offered a Watergate "special" for sponsorship and that a sponsor had turned it down. He complained that CBS had completely overblown the Watergate affair and had reported very little of a derogatory nature about the Democrats or about their "incorrect behavior." Colson charged that Watergate had taken up too large a part of the Cronkite show Friday night, and was mostly a rehash of things we had reported before. He asked about the broadcast announced at the end of the Cronkite show to deal further with the matter. He complained too about the three-part CBS series concerning the Nixon administration's sale of wheat to the Soviet Union which had resulted in a windfall for some dealers. He insisted that we had broadcast very little that was negative about McGovern, particularly about what he said was the support McGovern was getting from rich backers.

Along about here Colson put in a barb, saying that if the President were re-elected, which he thought very likely, it would be difficult for them to establish good relations with us. He wondered whether the Watergate broadcast was the result of annoyance because the President had refused Cronkite's request for an interview; he said that he had heard on Thursday from some gossip chain that Cronkite was "going to zing the President the next night."

Colson proceeded along the same line—that we were discriminating against the Administration in favor of McGovern—and he questioned why we did not try to get comments from White House spokesmen as part of the wrap-up on Friday night.

For a long, long time, I have listened to complaints from on high and from the man in the street, and in this spirit I listened to Colson. Much of what he said I had good reason to dismiss out of hand; on some points, I said I would check into; and some of his complaints I recognized as similar to my own reactions to the broadcast.

I told Colson that from my own observations and knowledge, Cronkite was a thoroughgoing journalist and that I was sure that in no way would he allow his feelings or emotions to influence his selection of news or how he reported it. I said I doubted that we made an offer of a special Watergate broadcast to an advertiser. It was not our method of selling. Our sales department was completely separate from the News Division. Whether or not a news or public affairs broadcast went on the air had nothing to do with finding a sponsor. I asked him for the sources of his information. I tried to explain that I was more concerned about whether we had been fair and objective in light of all the facts than in the effect our broadcasts had on political parties or the election. I said in effect that foremost in my mind, overriding everything else, was the maintenance of our policies governing news and public affairs and the integrity of our news operation.

So I was annoyed with CBS News for a broadcast I did not think was in keeping with our policies, and at the same time I was angry with Colson for his free-wheeling accusations.

After talking with Colson, I again called Stanton and gave him a rundown on the Colson call and asked him to make a few checks. Stanton reported back later that he found no evidence that we had tried to sell the Watergate wrap-up as a special. He also said that our news department had made numerous requests for an administration spokesman to participate in the broadcast and had been turned down.

At the Monday morning meeting, I spelled out my criticism and my dissatisfaction with that first Watergate broadcast. I did not tell Salant about the telephone call from Colson; I did not mention it at all. That was normal procedure for us. It was basic that neither Stanton nor I would ever relay to the News Division anything that could be interpreted as pressure. Nor did I or anyone else there tell Salant how he should handle the second broadcast scheduled for that night.

As it happened, Salant and others in the newsroom decided to postpone the second part from Monday to Tuesday evening and he had it cut and edited from fourteen minutes down to about seven or eight minutes. When I saw the second broadcast on Tuesday, I still did not think it came up to our standards of fairness and balance. So, on Wednesday, the day *after* the second broadcast, I sent Salant a memo expressing my post-audit views on both broadcasts and, at this late date, I consider that memo the best evidence of my thinking and of my action at that time. This is the complete memo:

From: William S. Paley   CONFIDENTIAL
To: MR. SALANT
Date: November 1, 1972/c

On Monday (30), at a meeting attended by Dr. Stanton, Mr. Taylor, Mr. Schneider, you and me, I expressed on behalf of Dr. Stanton and myself a serious uneasiness at the devotion of some two-thirds of the Evening News broadcast on Friday night to the Watergate affair—an extraordinary length of time for a hard news broadcast and one seldom, if ever, done before. Our objection also was that it departed from our basic news policy of fairness and balance in that, by dealing with a mixture of allegations and facts without the distinction always being clear, it seemed to be showing a distinct bias against one of the Presidential candidates.

I pointed out that, although the commentary specified at the outset that some of the contents of this long segment was still allegation, this caveat was inevitably lost sight of by the audience in view of the emphasis given the story by the length of time devoted to it and would, in any case, be apt to be forgotten in the long list of charges that followed in such a way as to leave the impression that they were substantiated facts.

Again last night, just a week before the election, the same situation arose. Some seven minutes—a third of the news content of the broadcast—were devoted to a similar mixture of allegations and facts. The use of names and pictures in this context left a strong impression of guilt. This impression was intensified by our clear refusal to accept any of the denials already made because they were not made to CBS News— even though CBS News was not the original source of the allegations. Making this kind of a demand and obscuring the distinction between facts and allegations, even if unintentional, seems to me unworthy of our fine traditions and ought not to be practiced. I hope very much that it will not be repeated.

My memo to Dick Salant and the Monday meeting were, of course, confidential, and I suppose I can now understand, but not appreciate, how that meeting could be misunderstood by those who had *not* been there but talked about it and wrote about it. They would hear that the president of CBS News had been summoned to a meeting with the chairman of the board (and others); they would learn that afterward Salant had the second broadcast cut to seven or eight minutes; and they would jump to the conclusion, as the rumor mill generally exaggerates any story, that I had flown into a rage and/or succumbed to White House pressure and ordered Salant to cut that second broadcast. It may seem logical to those who take a cynical view of broadcasting management but it is simply not true. It has been repeated by writers ever since with ever-increasing inaccuracies added to the story. They were relying upon secondhand stories and assumptions. Two years after the event, on December 4, 1974, *Variety,* the trade newspaper for broadcasting, printed a story about "the order" from me to cut our second broadcast, and referred to reports that the "the order" had come after a telephone call from

Colson. Dick Salant, who *was* there, took the occasion to set the record straight, in a letter to *Variety:*

New York

Editor, *Variety:*

Your piece at page 39 of *Variety* (Dec. 4), relating to our two-parter on Watergate on the CBS Evening News in October, 1972, proves once again that old myths not only never die but do not even fade away. They have simply learned the secret of perpetual, though thoroughly unjustified life.

The *Variety* piece refers to an "order" from William S. Paley "to cut the second part" of our Watergate report. This is a flat-out factual error and does an immense disservice to Bill Paley, who has never in his life issued an order to me or to CBS News in matters of news judgment or news content and it does an immense disservice to me and to the CBS News Division. The relationship between news publisher or owner on the one hand, and news editors and reporters on the other, is a difficult and delicate one, calling for immense restraint and understanding on both sides, and, if I may say, particularly on the side of the publisher or owner. The publisher or owner does, after all, have the ultimate organizational responsibility for what the news people do. In the final analysis, it is the publisher and owner who must be ultimately accountable. Yet there must be, if a news organization is to maintain its integrity, maximum freedom for the news editors and reporters in the area of news judgments and news content.

The problem is an old one and a perpetual one. The precise definition of where the line should be drawn has never been successfully and definitively mapped. But in the eleven years in which I have been president of the News Division, I have never—repeat never—experienced any improper or undue interference by Mr. Paley, or anybody else in CBS senior management, with our news judgments or our news content. Of course, Bill Paley, who after all was the founder of CBS News, played an immense role in establishing it and in setting the basic policies governing it and has a deep interest in

CBS News and what it does. That interest has provided the support and the climate which has made it possible to achieve whatever we have been able to achieve, and we are the better for it.

In the case of our Watergate two-parter, Mr. Paley did express to me a specific concern about the fairness aspect of the first broadcast and, again, concern after the second broadcast. After all, fairness is, and always has been, the cornerstone of basic CBS policy for which, of course, the chairman of the board, and other senior CBS management, is ultimately accountable. Further, we had devoted more than half of our news hole, in aggregate, to a single story on those two nights, thus necessarily having to neglect other stories. It was made clear to me that I was free to do whatever my independent judgment indicated. In exercising this judgment, I discussed with my people whether we ought now shorten the second part by omitting portions which were simply repetitious of reports we had made only a short time before—particularly in an August 1972 special documentary we did entitle "A Matter of Money." In consultation with my associates, the second part was tightened and many of my associates felt it was a better piece for it. But the important point was that nothing was done by me under orders from Mr. Paley or anybody else. I did it all with my own little hatchet. Mr. Paley and I, at lunch, discussed the matter some days after the broadcast, but only from the standpoint of our basic policies. Mr. Paley understood that I had taken full responsibility if indeed there had been a breach of those policies, and he made it clear that he had confidence in my judgment and the right to apply it as I saw fit in the light of my authority as president of CBS News—as I did. I am still here—happy as a clam about the freedom and the support, which I immensely enjoy. Would that all publishers or owners, or even more than a handful of them, be like Bill Paley.

And, by the way, I had no indication whatever, and I do not believe, that Mr. Paley's criticism and suggestions were anything other than the product of his own convictions and beliefs or that they were in response to pressures or communications from anyone.

Finally, one far smaller point: The piece is wrong in stating that "Paley announced during the end of a speech" that immediate analysis was being dropped. It was announced in a release which principally established the CBS policy of providing equivalent time to voices of significant opposition when the President of the United States, in a broadcast address, dealt with issues of national importance on which there is significant disagreement. I actively participated in the decisions both to drop immediate analysis and to restore it; the question of restoring immediate analysis was introduced by Mr. Paley and the decision was made simply on the ground that we had made a mistake in eliminating such analysis. The implication that analysis was dropped and then restored because of some relationship to the White House, or any other, pressure is simply and plainly wrong.

> Richard Salant
> President, CBS News

The actual story is simple. All I conveyed to Salant was what I have recounted in my memo to him—that is, strong criticism of the first broadcast *after* it took place and strong criticism of the second broadcast *after* it took place. I gave no orders, direct or indirect. And, as a matter of fact, Salant went on with the second part of the program as he chose to and as it was his privilege to do.*

---

* One of the worst and most disturbing misrepresentations of these events occurred in Daniel Schorr's 1977 book *Clearing the Air*, in which Schorr misquotes Frank Stanton as having told him in an interview that I did not actually have to insist that Salant do something about the second broadcast because if I just said I did not like the first part and asked how long was the second part, the message would be clear. Both men taped the interview, and afterward, when Schorr's book came out, Stanton wrote me that he had been misquoted. I was shocked when I listened to Stanton's tape recording, for it was clear that the voice that made the above assumption was the voice of Daniel Schorr asking the question, not that of Frank Stanton giving an answer.

With perfect hindsight, it seems clear to me now that our wrap-up of the Watergate situation, coming before the 1972 election, should have been a CBS special, so that allegations and established facts would be more clearly separated. It makes no difference really that the allegations made at the time turned out to be true. I still think it was bad news judgment, unbalanced, and contrary to CBS established news policies. I still think it was my duty as head of the company to tell the head of one of our divisions, any division, what I thought of his work or that of his division.

Since Watergate, news about news has heightened. Universities all over America have made news coverage the subject of academic study both on the undergraduate and graduate level. Scholarly theses appear every year which treat news media as profoundly as scientific analyses. Our actions are watched by non-academicians and the ordinary public with increasingly healthy skepticism, and that's the way it should be.

As the long-time chief executive of CBS I am proud of the accomplishments of CBS News. Who wouldn't be? Its excellence often has been revealed in spectacular ways in war and in peace —from Murrow's rooftop broadcasts of the bombings of London to the most intensive treatment of Watergate on the air. It is essential to its function that CBS News be prepared to meet all such crises. But its reputation rests on more than that. Day by day, round the clock, CBS News has demonstrated its preeminence by broadcasting to the American people the many dimensions of life—events that are not always so spectacular, but the way life is most of the time. This broad coverage is what has made our news operation a staple for so many millions of people.

CBS Inc.

From the time I came to CBS, in September 1928, I was always involved with the particulars, the day-to-day worries of the business. Whether changing Paul Whiteman's mind about radio or making mid-season revisions in a prime-time television schedule, selling an idea to George Washington Hill or watching a pilot for next fall, matters of immediate concern were always a large part of my job. But they were not all of it.

As the chief executive I also had to take the time to pause, to step back and take the long view of CBS. Instead of looking at tomorrow, I would try to look years ahead, and ask myself: are we conducting our business properly for the long run? Is the balance right between broadcasting and other activities? Is the company itself properly organized?

There is a certain excitement in looking at a company this way, for decisions on this level are designed for long-lasting effects. It is often years before one can say if he has been right or wrong. At CBS, many of our most important decisions have been made after pausing to take this long-range corporate view, which is uniquely the responsibility of the chief executive.

Although CBS is associated in the public's mind with

broadcasting, which is our primary business, CBS almost from its very beginning has been involved in other ventures. Over the past fifty years, CBS has acquired more than forty other companies in what I like to think has been, more or less, a natural progression in the field of communications. We went from radio to a talent agency, to records and then to manufacturing records and then television sets, musical instruments, to books and magazines and we also took a flier into sports when we acquired the New York Yankees.

It was not until I was physically away from CBS during World War II that I could look back and ahead and comtemplate the company as a whole and think about how much of CBS should be devoted to broadcasting, which was regulated by the government, and how much of company activities should be in fields beyond broadcasting. Before the war the outside ventures of CBS came about mostly by happenstance. I saw an opportunity or a need, and I acted. It was then a matter, one might say, of tactics. After the war, I engaged my associates at CBS in some strategic thinking of how CBS could best be served over the long run. But before the war it was different.

In the depths of the Great Depression, a man named Milton Diamond, who was the head of the Music Producing Managers Association, came to me and pleaded for help. Concert attendance was very low, concert managers were going broke, the whole structure and organization of booking and producing concerts was in jeopardy. So, at his urging, in December of 1930, I helped merge the seven leading concert bureaus in the country into the Columbia Concerts Corporation. In one fell swoop, we represented about 125 of the best concert singers, soloists and musicians of the nation. Among them were Jascha Heifetz, Ezio Pinza, Lily Pons, Lotte Lehmann, Paul Robeson, Yehudi Menuhin, Mischa Elman, Vladimir Horowitz, Nathan Milstein and Serge Prokofieff. Columbia Concerts was not made a part of CBS. It was a new company with most of its stock owned by CBS. I was named chairman of the board, and its president and chief operating officer was Arthur Judson, who at the time had headed two of the seven bureaus involved in the merger. He also managed both the New York Philharmonic-Symphony and the Philadelphia Symphony Orchestras. Our move to consolidate the leading concert management companies of the time was hailed in the press and elsewhere as a master stroke. The New York *Sun* said editorially: "Columbia's merger with the concert offices is regarded as the outstanding step forward taken by broadcasting in the last year." Our purpose was to step into the breach and to save concert management during the Depression rather than any great hope for a profitable business. We did indeed sustain some losses for a while but ended up making a modest profit.

We formed the Columbia Artists Bureau at about the same time because it seemed to be a natural outgrowth of our own business. Columbia Artists was a talent-management agency which arranged theater and movie-house bookings for popular radio performers like Bing Crosby, the Mills Brothers, and others. Its earnings for CBS were rather insignificant, since Columbia Artists was operated more than anything else as a service for our own family of performers. These talent businesses, however, came to be seen as a conflict of interest for CBS. In 1941, the FCC noted that CBS was in the business of both buying and selling talent. So, that year we sold our controlling shares of Columbia Concerts, some to the original owners of the various bureaus we had merged together, and we sold Columbia Artists to the Music Corporation of America, which helped MCA on its way to becoming the largest talent agency in the world. Ironically, Jules Stein, the head of MCA, almost walked away from the deal, thinking he was overpaying us.

In the same vein, many people thought I was overpaying when CBS bought the American Record Corporation, whose chief asset was the Columbia Phonograph Company, for about $700,000 in 1938. Some people at the time may have attributed our purchase to sentiment, for the same Columbia Phonograph Company had been the largest stockholder in CBS for a short time back in 1927. But sentiment had nothing to do with it. The whole recording industry had been in a slump during the Depression years and yet I felt bullish about its future. Radio had introduced a great many people to the enjoyment of music and with radio then starting to turn to variety, drama, and comedy programs in place of music, I felt the record business was on its way to making a comeback. Negotiating the purchase was not difficult at all. The owner of American Record thought he had a lemon on his hands, a company that was draining him and, I think, he was happy at the time to get rid of it at that price.

It turned out to be the best deal I ever made, except for buying CBS itself. We gave the company a new name, Columbia Recording Corporation, and it has evolved into what is known today as Columbia Records, which is part of our CBS/Records Group. In its first full year as part of CBS, the new company lost $73,000, and from that tiny operation in red ink in 1939, we developed it into one of the largest record companies in the world, as well as CBS's largest non-broadcasting operation.

At the very start, we engaged Edward Wallerstein, who had then been the general manager of Victor, the record division of RCA, as the first president of Columbia Records. Later in that first year, we hired a young, struggling composer, as the assistant to the director of the Masterworks Division of Columbia Records at $50 a week. That was Goddard Lieberson, the son of an English manufacturer and a graduate of the Eastman School of Music, who rose to become the brilliant president of Columbia Records and a legend in his time. Working closely with Wallerstein in the beginning, it occurred to me that to get Columbia Records off the ground, we would have to do something special. So, I put it to him: how many more classical records would we have to sell at a dollar each to make as much money as we were then making on these records that were being sold at two dollars each? In a few weeks Wallerstein came back and said, "I think, seven or eight times as many." So, having a strong belief in the price factor, I asked him to do it—put out classical records at a dollar each.

At that time, RCA was far ahead of us with their Victor label.

When we cut our price, RCA was absolutely thrown. They thought it was the silliest thing that ever happened and were outraged, I learned. They were doing a big business and of course they did not appreciate having to meet competition that was selling records at half the going price. This move, however, gave us a tremendous boost in the classical music field. RCA then reduced their records to a dollar too—after they concluded they couldn't stand the price difference. At the end of six months, I think RCA would have built a monument in my honor: not only did our record business soar, but RCA's did also. We made more money. RCA made more money. And the public got a lot more music.

The outbreak of World War II cut off our European market and severely reduced the amount of shellac available for manufacturing records. But the end of the war revived the industry. Our business jumped from $7.7 million in 1944 to $25.4 million in 1947. By then we had exclusive recording contracts with the New York Philharmonic-Symphony and the Philadelphia Orchestra; with conductors Eugene Ormandy, Fritz Reiner, and Bruno Walter, pianists Rudolf Serkin and Robert Casadesus, and violinists Isaac Stern and Nathan Milstein; and with such popular performers as Frank Sinatra, Doris Day, Pearl Bailey, Dinah Shore, and the Les Brown, Duke Ellington, and Harry James orchestras. And in 1947 we added the Metropolitan Opera to our classical roster.

In June of 1948 came the revolution. We introduced the long-playing record. Previous recordings had been made on shellac discs. Spinning at a speed of seventy-eight revolutions per minute (rpm), they provided about four minutes of sound per side; a symphony had to be sold as a bulky album of four-minute sections. Shellac records were thick and heavy; when dropped, they shattered. They sounded scratchy with "surface noise" and had poor fidelity.

The long-playing record, developed by CBS Laboratories, headed by Peter Goldmark, with the help of William Bachman, director of research for Columbia Records, suffered from none of these drawbacks. Because it turned at only 33⅓ rpm and had three times more grooves per inch than the old seventy-eights— new grooves that were as thin as a human hair—it could play about twenty-five minutes of music per side. Most symphonies could be contained on a single LP record with the only breaks occurring, when necessary, between movements. Made of light, almost unbreakable Vinylite, the LP produced a far greater fidelity of sound with far less surface noise than the old shellac records. Vinylite was more expensive than shellac, but because it had become possible for a customer to buy a piece of music on one record instead of several, the cost of a music library actually dropped.

The new record shook up the whole industry. New equipment was needed on which to play it. Philco, with our help, brought out a player that could be attached to any existing radio, phonograph, or television set; soon more than a dozen manufacturers were adding the 33⅓ speed and the special lightweight tone arm to their equipment. Within eight months nearly 600,000 players had been sold, along with more than 2 million LP records—the equivalent of more than 10 million 78s.

We were remarkably well prepared for the revolution. Wallerstein—who with his colleagues in CBS foresaw the LP revolution —had all our classical performances recorded on special high fidelity 33⅓ rpm master discs, as well as on the usual 78s. We had begun our research on the LP in 1939 and were gambling that the research would succeed. Nine years later, it did. When the LP was perfected, we did not need to make new recordings. We had a full catalogue ready to press and sell.

When RCA declined my offer to adopt the LP and came out with the 45 rpm record, which was better suited for single popular songs, there was confusion in the market for a time because the LP was far superior for longer classical music and for albums of popular music. We both wound up using both systems. Columbia introduced the LP in June 1948 and RCA did not bring out its first long-playing record (a jazz album) until 1950, which gave Columbia a marketing lead in long-playing records. RCA announced its 45 rpm record in January 1949 and Columbia started making them shortly afterward. Ed Wallerstein presided over the introduction and early success of the LP. In 1951 he left and we put in James B. Conkling, who had been in charge of repertoire at Capitol Records. He continued the growth of Columbia Records until he left us in 1956, when Goddard Lieberson took over as our leading records executive and remained so under various titles until 1971, when he became a senior vice-president of CBS.

Columbia Records soared during all those years as Lieberson, a devotee and composer of classical music, attracted to the Columbia label the very best symphony orchestras, conductors, soloists and performers throughout the United States and abroad. Lieberson adored Broadway musicals and was first and foremost in recording the very best of them with their original casts. He also had a prescient taste for popular music of all kinds. He discovered, for example, Barbra Streisand in a Broadway musical and signed her to Columbia Records as a solo singer. He was an extraordinary human being, a brilliant executive, who supervised many major recordings made at Columbia and gave his personal touch to the many artists who came to record at Columbia. A handsome, elegant, dapper, and meticulous man, he left behind him at Columbia Records a tradition and sense of good taste that is with us yet. He retired in 1975 to write more books and compose more music and died in 1977 at the age of only sixty-six.

While Lieberson concentrated upon classical music, John Hammond, who became our vice-president of talent acquisition, toured the country in search of outstanding performers in popular music. His career spanned his rediscovery of Bessie Smith in a Philadelphia speakeasy, his discovery of Billie Holiday singing in a Harlem speakeasy and of Count Basie performing in an out-of-the-way nightclub in Kansas City, to Bob Dylan, the outstanding vocalist of the sixties, and Aretha Franklin, the gospel and rhythm-and-blues singer, to Bruce Springsteen, the biggest rock and folk singer of the seventies. Mitch Miller, the bandleader, worked for Lieberson, handling the recording of popular

334

vocalists whom he brought to Columbia, including Rosemary Clooney, Frankie Laine and many others.

In 1955, taking advantage of the LP's light weight and durability, we organized the Columbia Record Club and began selling records by mail. The idea had come to me at the very start of our purchase of Columbia Records, but then the weight and the fragility of the old shellac records made it impractical. But with the LP it became feasible. The Columbia Record Club became popular, and today, with more than four million members, it is the largest record club in the world. In four years, the club helped Columbia Records pass RCA's Victor in sales. In the early fifties, Columbia Records began establishing record companies in foreign countries. As distinct from licensees, which would simply distribute Columbia's records, these CBS companies abroad started with our catalogue of American artists and then slowly added their own native artists. Today there are twenty-seven of these subsidiary companies around the world, along with nineteen licensees.

Goddard Lieberson also brought CBS to Broadway and Broadway to CBS. In the late forties, he purchased for CBS the recording rights to a Broadway musical long before it opened simply by reading the Cole Porter score based upon a Shakespearean play. It was *Kiss Me, Kate,* a smash hit on Broadway and as a Columbia LP record. In the summer of 1955, he went one step further. He brought producer Herman Levin to my office with a proposition that CBS become a backer of a new musical based on George Bernard Shaw's *Pygmalion.* Along with them was Alan Jay Lerner, the author and lyricist of the show, which I think they planned to call *London Bridge.* Discussing the idea of the show, I learned that Rex Harrison, one of my favorite actors, had agreed to play the male lead and that Moss Hart, one of our country's leading playwrights and a friend of mine, would direct it. On that basis, I agreed on CBS's behalf to put up all the money sought from outside backers, which gave us 40 per cent ownership of the musical plus recording rights. Our investment came to $360,000.

335

That musical opened on Broadway as *My Fair Lady* in 1956 and with Rex Harrison and Julie Andrews as its stars went on to become the biggest musical phenomenon Broadway had yet seen. It ran for more than six years—2,717 performances—making it the longest-running musical in Broadway history up to that time. The original cast recording, put out by Columbia, sold more than six million albums, one of the best-selling albums of all time. In 1959 I bought out Lerner and Loewe's interests in the company that had been formed to produce the show, and in 1961 bought Moss Hart's interest. CBS also owned the rights to stock and foreign productions and other commercial rights, as well as the movie rights. I think the deal I made with Harry Warner of Warner Brothers set a record for the movie rights to a musical: Warner paid $5.5 million plus 50 per cent of the distributor's gross above $20 million. This was an unusual arrangement at the time because most such deals were based upon a division of net profits. Since I had misgivings about computing net profits, I insisted upon sharing gross receipts. Most unusual of all, at the end of the term of the contract, all rights in the picture, including the negative of the film itself, became the property of CBS. As one of the most delightful and timeless musical productions, it has been a continuing source of substantial income. In all, up to this time, CBS had earned more than $33 million from its investments in *My Fair Lady*.

Since *My Fair Lady*, CBS has invested in more than forty theatrical productions, nearly all of them Broadway shows—a risky business indeed—and we have had to date eleven winners and more than three times that many losers. But not even counting *My Fair Lady*, CBS has made far more money on its successes than it has lost on its failures. We backed *Camelot, Mame, Cabaret* and *Bye Bye, Birdie*, to name a few well-known musicals; we also invested in *Here's Love, We Take the Town, Dear World*, and *Bravo Giovanni*, which are best not remembered at all. I must admit, too, that I turned down a chance for CBS to invest in *Fiddler on the Roof* because I did not like the ending.

In 1967, Lieberson, who was then the president of the CBS/

Columbia Group, proposed making Clive Davis, an associate of his, the president of the Columbia Records Division, and I approved. Davis had risen quickly through the executive ranks and developed a well-organized position in the industry. He was a hard worker with unusually good instincts for popular and rock music. He became president of the CBS/Records Group when it was formed in 1971. It was a blow when, in 1973, as a result of a federal grand jury investigation in Newark, documents were discovered indicating that CBS funds had been used to pay for certain of Davis' personal expenses. We confronted Davis with this information, thought his explanations satisfactory at first but after further examination we found them inadequate and severed relations with him.

We were fortunate to have Goddard Lieberson who had become a senior vice-president at the corporate level, return to his old job as head of the CBS/Records Group. He remained in that position until his retirement two years later in May 1975. Then Walter Yetnikoff, who had led the CBS Records International Division since 1971 through an extraordinary period of growth, took over. Yetnikoff, a brilliant attorney and businessman with a taste for the musical arts, had joined CBS in 1961. The great success of Columbia Records through the years rests upon its well-deserved reputation for creative feel and marketing expertise. It can attract the very best talent in all forms of popular music, including jazz, rock and roll and country because of its philosophy of developing the long-term careers of its artists rather than pursuing the one-shot hits that come and go in popular music.

Starting in 1962, we at the top management level of CBS along with the board of directors began to study and to devise a broad policy of business diversification. Economic forces in the early sixties, plus CBS's internal growth, and increased cash on hand made planned diversification the logical course for us. Economically and strategically it made good sense to broaden the base of the corporation and particularly to extend ourselves beyond broadcasting activities, which were subject to possible government regulation. We hired a specialist in company acquisitions and engaged the services of various business consulting firms to advise us on the economic prospects in various other industries. We looked at study after study and gradually came to the conclusion that CBS would best venture into activities that were associated with or related to the kind of business we knew best—communications, entertainment, education, and the like.

In 1964 Dan Topping and Del Webb, as co-owners, offered to sell us 80 per cent ownership of the New York Yankees and to stay on and run the powerhouse, which in its forty-two-year history had won twenty-eight American League pennants and twenty World Series. We figured that by owning a professional baseball team we would gain a deeper insight into the world of professional sports, upon which we were spending millions in television rights each year. We bought the Yankees, paying $11.2 million for the 80 per cent interest and over the next two years we bought the remaining 20 per cent of the club for another $2 million.

Unfortunately, for the next eight seasons that we owned the team, the Yankees finished second once and fourth or worse the rest of the time. And that was just the beginning of our problems. Baseball itself began losing its popularity to the faster-paced professional football. In six of those eight years, the Yankees operated at a small loss: it costs just as much to run a losing team as a winning one and the income is far less. Finally convinced it did not really fit into the CBS complex, we sold the club early in 1973 to a group headed by George Steinbrenner for $10 million. Because we amortized our investment over the years of our ownership, the sale caused us to show a profit of around $5.4 million after taxes on the books.

A logical business for CBS to pursue in its diversification effort was publishing. Like broadcasters, publishers communicate with the public in the fields of both entertainment and education, and depend for success on creative talent and judgment.

We acquired Holt, Rinehart and Winston in 1966–67, and

with that one purchase became a leading publisher of elementary, high school, and college textbooks as well as trade books for the general public. The Holt purchase led us in 1968 to buy W. B. Saunders Company, the world's leading publisher of medical textbooks. That led us further to a Mexican company, Editorial Interamericana S.A., which was the world's leading publisher of scientific and medical books in Spanish and Portuguese. With the Holt purchase came *Field & Stream* magazine. We then branched out to other special-interest magazines, including *Road & Track, Cycle World, Sea, Pickup Van & 4WD,* and *World Tennis*. We became a publisher of paperbacks, especially novels and reference works when we acquired Popular Library, Inc., in 1971. In January 1977 we bought Fawcett Publications, a leading publisher of mass-market paperbacks and acquired with that purchase *Rudder* magazine, *Mechanix Illustrated,* and *Woman's Day* magazine with its circulation of more than eight million. In December 1977, we bought 80 per cent of Doin Editeurs, a medical and science textbook publisher in France. All these acquisitions gave us a good, sizable position in the industry. Our publishing operations began making substantial contributions to our overall sales and profits and have given us a more rounded picture as a corporation.

In 1966, we entered into another phase of diversification with the purchase of Creative Playthings, a manufacturer of high-quality educational toys. In 1976 we purchased Wonder Products, manufacturer of the popular Wonder Horse riding toys, and joined it to Creative Playthings.* In the summer of 1978 we went further and acquired Gabriel Industries, a large toy company, which gave CBS a respectable share of the toy industry market.

---

* Also in education, in addition to the publishing, we have bought Bailey Films, Inc. and Film Associates of California, both outstanding producers and distributors of educational films and filmstrips for schools, colleges, and libraries, which we combined into a unit known as BFA Educational Media that sells filmstrips, other audio-visual teaching aids, and printed materials to schools around the country; we also own five small private technical and business schools.

We also became movie makers for a few years. Our idea was to produce ten full-length feature films a year for theatrical release around the world. We signed up top people—the producer Hal Prince, the director Howard Hawks, and such performers as Doris Day, Steve McQueen, Jack Lemmon, and Charlton Heston —and we had some big hits: *A Man Called Horse, Little Big Man, The Reivers.* But the venture as a whole was not working well and so we closed the production end but continued to license the movies we had made. It is astonishing that these films are still returning sizable sums of money and in time may well make up all the losses initially involved.

Today CBS is the second-largest maker of musical instruments in America. We own a number of musical instrument companies, some of them large, some small, each of them characterized by the widely recognized quality of its products. Entering the industry in early 1965, we bought Fender, the company that introduced shortly after World War II the solid-body electric guitar which gave the guitar a new role in popular music. As a lead instrument playing the melody, it has become the standard lead instrument in rock and popular music. Many companies now make electric guitars, but the Fender instruments, I think, are still recognized as the best: more than 40,000 of them are sold every year. CBS went on to buy V. C. Squier Company, which makes guitar strings sold under the Fender name; Rogers Drums, maker of high-quality drums and tympani; Electro Music, which manufactures tone cabinets and speaker systems (under the Leslie name), and Gulbransen, which makes electric organs.

In 1972 we acquired Steinway & Sons, the famed piano company. There has been no change in the Steinway instrument since we purchased the company. Three of the Steinway brothers are still there, directly involved in management, and quality remains the paramount concern. There is always a backlog of orders in this country and in our Steinway operations in Germany. We acquired the Gemeinhardt Corporation of Elkhart, Indiana, a leading maker of flutes and piccolos, and Lyon & Healy, which manufactures harps recognized as the best in the world. Our most recent acquisition in the field is the Rodgers Organ Company, makers of electronic organs for churches and auditoriums, including the unique five-manual organ in Carnegie Hall.

As an operator of retail stores, CBS has had a mixed experience. Discount Records, a national chain, began to suffer losses in 1972, and in 1975, after seven years of ownership, we sold it. On the other hand, the Pacific Stereo chain, acquired in 1972, has been a great success. Enjoying unusually good management and employing knowledgeable and thoroughly trained salesmen, it sold high-quality audio equipment through stores in the West. Since we bought it we have expanded it into the Midwest and, recently, Texas. It is profitable and growing fast.†

It has been the source of considerable satisfaction at CBS that our diversification program has succeeded so well in fulfilling its original purpose. For the past seven years, starting in 1971, more than half of all CBS sales have come from non-broadcasting businesses. About 40 per cent of our net income is now produced by non-broadcasting activities and that division would be closer to fifty-fifty were it not for the happy fact that broadcasting itself has experienced such robust growth in the past decade.

As 1978 ended, CBS was in solid shape. Sales surpassed $3 billion for the first time and profits reached an all-time high in the history of the company. Each of our businesses was performing well and poised to move ahead in the years to come. In broadcasting, despite tough competitive problems, sales and profits continue to rise. Recorded music had explosive growth in 1978; new pressing plants were under construction in the United States and abroad to handle increased production and our roster of talented artists was growing daily. The Columbia Group was also expanding rapidly on every front. Its record and tape club was adding hundreds of thousands of new members annually.

† At one point, CBS acquired cable television interests in Canada, but after the purchase, Canadian law required non-Canadian interests to limit ownership in Canada to no more than 20 per cent; as a result we disposed of 80 per cent of our interests there. We also had a very large ownership position in cable TV in the United States; but by FCC decree we were forced to divest ourselves of these properties.

Musical-instrument sales had never been higher. The chain of Pacific Stereo audio product stores was moving steadily into new markets and was already a leader in its field. And in the toy business, with the 1978 acquisition of Gabriel, CBS attained a market position that would allow for meaningful growth in this exciting industry. In publishing, sales and profits also reached new record-high levels with creative and informative new publications under development for virtually every segment of the reading public.

Even before we got into full diversification, by the late 1950s CBS had grown to such an extent that Frank Stanton and I began discussing our need to move from 485 Madison Avenue, which we had occupied since 1929, to larger quarters. CBS was spread out in dozens of buildings around the city. When we finally decided the time had come to move, we also agreed that the time had come to build our own headquarters, and so we initiated discussions with some of the leading architects around the country. We also set about looking for a suitable location. I think we were by instinct determined that if we went ahead on our own building for CBS, it would have to be of the highest aesthetic quality obtainable. We never discussed it in so many words; we knew what we wanted and we realized that we were embarking upon a major undertaking. We considered Park Avenue and concluded that it had too cold a feeling. Madison Avenue was too narrow to display good architecture. No suitable location was available on Fifth Avenue. But on Sixth Avenue—formally known as the Avenue of the Americas—we found a marvelous site, assembled by the master real estate developer William Zeckendorf, on the east side of the broad avenue running from Fifty-second to Fifty-third streets. It was close to Rockefeller Center, in a location that was emerging as the newest important business area in midtown New York. It was just two city blocks west of our old location. So, we bought it.

Of all top architects we interviewed and consulted, we chose Eero Saarinen, a truly remarkable man in so many respects beyond his professionalism. Not only was he one of this country's outstanding architects, he was also a creative artist in the deepest sense, and he won us over by the force of his personality, imagination and practicality. In our preliminary discussions, Saarinen always spoke of his concept for a CBS building as one which would "soar" out of the ground, reaching for the sky. By March 1961, he had a design, which he described to us in a letter:

> I think I now have a really good scheme for C.B.S. The design is the simplest conceivable rectangular free-standing sheer tower. The verticality of the tower is emphasized by the relief made by the triangular piers between the windows. These piers start at the pavement and soar up 424 feet. Its beauty will be, I believe, that it will be the simplest skyscraper statement in New York.

We flew to Detroit to see a mock-up he had made. Seeing it for the first time I was very disappointed. We examined a small part of the building, full-sized, made out of plywood or something of that kind. Because I didn't embrace it immediately he started to work on other designs. But then I went to see it again and changed my mind; I saw what I had first thought of as austerity really came through as strong, exquisite, ageless beauty. In July 1961, I decided to go ahead with Saarinen.

However, not very long after our decision, Saarinen died unexpectedly. It came as a terrible shock—he was only fifty-one. His associates immediately wrote us, telling us how enthusiastic he had been about this design for CBS and how the challenge of a skyscraper in New York had actually absorbed him for years. They promised to carry on his work efficiently and loyally if we would continue with the Saarinen firm.

We faced a big decision—to stay with the Saarinen organization or transfer to some other architect. I had become acquainted with Kevin Roche, who was Saarinen's chief designer, and had developed a confidence in him. I liked the way he handled himself. I liked his tastes and his approach, so I decided we'd stay with the Saarinen firm.

We built a mock-up of the building in New Rochelle, New

York, and when Roche, Stanton and I went out to look at it, we realized that the difference between the window area and the column area was not right. Your eye could tell you that. We started then to change it. We got down to talking about a quarter of an inch or a sixteenth of an inch. We must have put up five or six different-sized mock-ups before we finally got it right. In the process I must have gone out to New Rochelle at least thirty times to study the various mock-ups. Anyone who has ever become involved in building his own custom home will understand the agonies, the indecisions and the decisions involved.

Saarinen had envisioned the building in dark masonry, and we considered several different materials for a dark-colored building. After inspecting various modern synthetic materials, we decided to use real granite for the shell of the building. It was more expensive than the other materials, but in the long run it would be worth it. The building would be built to last a hundred years. Granite would retain its beauty as long as the building stood.

The task then was to find the granite—of the right color and the right texture. We wanted a dark shade but we did not want it polished or to look like marble. We wanted it to be rugged and strong—and graceful. So, we had people sending us pieces of granite from all over the world, from Africa, Japan, Norway, Sweden, Germany, France, Spain, Portugal, Canada, and the United States. We gathered a collection of at least fifty varieties of granite. When I toured Europe and saw a new and different-looking granite, I'd stop and find out the name of the architect and search out where the granite came from and who processed it. Stanton visited quarries in Norway and in other places. I took one trip to San Francisco just for one hour to look at a new building that had been made with a certain kind of granite that came from Minnesota. Finally, we came upon the Canadian Black granite from the quarry of the Robitaille family in Alma, Quebec, about 150 miles north of Quebec City, and that was it. It was a beautiful dark color. That is why the building has come to be known familiarly as "Black Rock."

The CBS staff began moving in at the end of 1964, six years after Stanton and I had first discussed the project with Saarinen over lunch on November 21, 1958.

In the fourteen years since Black Rock has been up and occupied it has been recognized as a landmark in architecture and has won awards from the American Institute of Architects, the New York Chapter of the AIA, the New York Board of Trade, and the Municipal Art Society of New York. It is said to be one of the two or three best buildings in New York City. Participating in the creation of Black Rock was one of the great sources of satisfaction of my life, not to speak of the pleasure I share with others working there.

Once we were ensconced in Black Rock we began to deal with the very real problem of how to reorganize the structure of a burgeoning CBS for greater efficiency. Our new diversification and acquisitions program on top of the very rapid rate of growth we were enjoying in broadcasting and in phonograph records made it essential that we restructure our organization of top management.

In the beginning, when I first came into CBS, there was absolutely nothing in the way of organization. I had to construct the business from the ground up. I was in effect the program manager, sales manager, and financial officer—you name it, I was it. I worked with others, of course, but the responsibility for all those activities was mine. As CBS grew and diversified through the years, my work habits changed and I began to delegate work and authority to more and more people. Nevertheless, for some time the organization of CBS remained the same, not unlike that of a much smaller company. Our management was centralized in myself as top man, aided and backed up by one chief-lieutenant—Klauber, Kesten, and then Stanton. Stanton became CBS's first president and chief operating officer other than myself in 1946. Five years later, with television growing at an enormous rate and as we were about to enter manufacturing, we reorganized the company into six autonomous divisions, each operating like a sep-

arate company with its own president and staff, each encouraged
to compete with the other divisions.‡

The plan worked fairly well for fifteen years, but the divisions
grew bigger and more numerous so that by 1966 we had ten large
divisions, all reporting directly to Stanton and me. After consultations with two management consulting firms and after numerous studies, we proposed to the board of directors a major
reorganization of CBS. At the February 1966 meeting of the
Board we divided the company into two basic groups—broadcasting and non-broadcasting activities. John A. Schneider at age
thirty-nine was promoted to president of the CBS/Broadcast
Group with the tacit understanding that he would then be the
number-three man in the corporation, destined to succeed Stanton
and me. In June of that year, we made Goddard Lieberson the
president of all the non-broadcasting activities, which we called
CBS/Columbia.

At the February meeting, upon a motion of Joseph A. W.
Iglehart, the Board voted unanimously that I "be requested and
urged" to continue as chairman of the board, and I agreed to continue beyond my sixty-fifth birthday, which would occur that
September. It was the first and only exception to the company's
mandatory retirement policy, which was introduced by Stanton
through the company's personnel office in 1959.

As CBS continued to grow and to diversify, all of the non-
broadcasting activities became too burdensome for one group
president and so we evolved the structure of CBS into its present form of sixteen separate divisions reporting to four group
presidents—of broadcasting, records, publishing and Columbia.*

‡ The six divisions were CBS Television, CBS Radio, CBS Laboratories,
Columbia Records, Hytron Radio & Electronics, and CBS-Columbia.
* The Broadcast Group includes six divisions: CBS Television Network,
CBS Entertainment, CBS Sports, CBS Television Stations, CBS News and
CBS Radio. The Records Group is made up of the CBS Records Division
and the CBS Records International Division. The Publishing Group in-
cludes the CBS Educational Publishing Division, CBS Consumer Publish-
ing Division, CBS Professional Publishing Division and the CBS Inter-
national Publishing Division. The Columbia Group consists of the Columbia
House, CBS Musical Instruments, Retail Stores and Toys Divisions.

This reorganization was an ongoing process starting in the last half of the 1960s. It was a complex task, for we needed men for their specific expertise and at the same time we needed men who could span the creative, business and administrative requirements of the various parts of the company.

Once we had Jack Schneider in place in the line of succession, there came a time when Frank Stanton and I discussed the prospect of his succeeding both of us. Stanton and I together had run CBS by that time for more than twenty years. Although we were quite different in personality and disposition, we did make a good team. Stanton was cool, analytical, precise, possessed a high sense of standards and style, and had become known as "the statesman of broadcasting" because of his frequent public appearances before the industry, congressional committees, and the FCC. He was much more than a lobbyist in his public role, for Frank prepared long and hard for each of his public appearances. He spoke from deep knowledge and keen insight upon virtually all aspects of broadcasting and its role in a free society. He was outstanding in maintaining good relations with our affiliated stations, the sinew and backbone of network broadcasting, keeping them informed of network activities as he absorbed their views and needs.

I focused my activities upon the business affairs of the company, particularly in planning and developing, which in the sixties were becoming more and more significant. I also gave much of my time to programming, talent and personnel in the important entertainment sections of our broadcasting division. Of course, I reviewed and passed on all policy and important operational decisions of the company as chief executive officer. On most of the problems which confronted CBS, Frank and I saw eye-to-eye and worked together for the good of the company. We had our differences, of course, but we worked them out.

And yet, a strong personal friendship never developed between us. Our bond was business and it never seemed to go beyond that. We shared no outside activity. We never grew close. In fact, as the years went on, we seemed to grow further and further apart. When we came to reorganizing the company in the mid-sixties, I seriously considered for a while the prospect of relieving my own burdens by stepping down as chief executive officer. We tried at one point to work out an arrangement whereby Frank would become chief executive officer of the company as well as president and I would continue as chairman of the board. But that did not work out. I exercised my prerogative to continue on in my own role and despite my age, frankly, I felt just fine, years younger than my age. No doubt, Frank was disappointed. I don't know to what extent, because he was a reticent man and never told me. A year later, Frank signed a new five-year contract with CBS which contained provisions for his consulting services for another sixteen years beyond his own retirement. We continued to work together as we had before, and when the time approached for Frank's retirement, he was instrumental in helping me choose his own successor.

Trying to promote from within, we had moved Jack Schneider up the ladder to executive vice-president of CBS in February, 1969. But that just did not work out. Jack's expertise and fund of knowledge was in broadcasting and he found it difficult to cope with the intricate business and financial decisions incumbent upon anyone involved in running a complex corporation, which CBS was fast becoming. We concluded that what CBS truly needed at the helm was not necessarily a broadcaster but rather someone who was a professional business manager, experienced in handling a multidivisional, diversified corporation like CBS. The outstanding men at CBS had always been broadcasters, for in years past that is what CBS was primarily involved in. Stanton himself was a victim of the CBS transition. I had come by business instincts and know-how at my father's knee and at the Paley family dinner table. So, without fully realizing it, I had developed certain instincts and techniques which served me well in the intricacies of business decisions. In short, both Frank and I came to the conclusion that there was no one else in CBS who could be moved up and that we needed to go to the outside to find a man to replace him as president and me eventually as chairman and chief executive officer of CBS.

The waterfall at Paley Park, New York City.

With Carter Burden and Jeff, Brooke and Hilary Byers at the opening of Paley Park.

Ed Sullivan with Ella Fitzgerald.

With Joe Iglehart (l.) and Arthur B. Tourtellot at the Paley Park opening.

Election Night 1972 with Frank Stanton and Dick Salant.

With Walter Cronkite while working on our fiftieth-anniversary program.

Visiting President Nixon at the White House with (l. to r.) Bob Wood, Dick Jencks, Frank Stanton, and Jack Schneider.

Speaking at the Museum of Modern Art.

Cutting the *60 Minutes* tenth-birthday cake.

Mary Tyler Moore.

Alan Alda and Mike Farrell
of *M*A*S*H*.

Carroll O'Connor and Jean Stapleton of
All in the Family.

Consul General Trexler making me a
Commander of Italy's Order of Merit.

With the Television Academy's
Governors Award Emmy in 1978.

Looking at model of the Paley Art Center in Jerusalem, established in honor of my mother.

At the opening of the Museum of Broadcasting.

Using the camera—one of my delights.

With Bob Saudek at a Museum of
Broadcasting carrel.

At the 1977 Annual Meeting, with John D. Backe.

Working very closely on the problem, we agreed that we had better find his successor at least a year before his retirement. We wanted the incoming president to get the benefit of Frank's knowledge, experience and guidance. So, in 1971, after some looking around, we hired a top executive search firm to find us a new president for CBS. We spelled out the specifications of the type of man we wanted, and Frank handled most of the preliminary interviews of the candidates brought to us.

He found the man he liked while I was off in Europe, and so the candidate flew over to meet me. This was Charles T. Ireland, Jr., who had had a colorful business career as secretary of the New York Central Railroad Company, president of Allegheny Corporation, chairman of the board of Investors Diversified Services and for the previous four years had served as a right-hand man to Harold S. Geneen of International Telephone and Telegraph, the largest conglomerate in the United States. Chick Ireland was an expert in diversification and acquisitions, and I could see that he was a strong executive of the kind we needed. We talked at great length and agreed that as successful as CBS had been through the years, it also had been rather loosely run. It did not have the controls and checks and balances that modern management requires of a large, diversified company. We had grown so fast, we had not had a chance to fine-tune the operation.

I was impressed with Ireland and told him so, but also said that I could not make a decision on the basis of one meeting and that I could not take the responsibility of his passing up another job that had been offered to him. I could not guarantee that we would hire him until I had had a chance to look into the situation further. He said he was eager to be a contender for the CBS position and would wait for our decision and take his chances.

Upon the recommendation of Stanton and myself, Ireland was elected by the Board as the new president of CBS in September 1971, and started on the job October 1. Stanton was moved up to vice-chairman. Jack Schneider was moved back to his old position as president of the Broadcast Group. Chick Ireland, even though he was still working under the guidance of Stanton, soon demonstrated all the skills of a very well-trained, hard-driving manager. He was a strong, no-nonsense leader who brought about better financial controls, a better flow of information within the executive ranks and better analyses and predictions of what we could expect at CBS. There was some grumbling in CBS ranks as he pushed people rather hard to institute new management controls, but he was doing precisely what was needed at CBS, what we wanted and what he promised to do.

Unfortunately, about six months after he had started on the job, Ireland suffered a heart attack. He was out for five or six weeks and then returned to work, building up his work schedule gradually as he worked one hour a day the first week, then two and gradually to a full schedule. One afternoon, quite late, he came into my office with the good news that his doctor had pronounced him fully recovered: he could take on a full workload at CBS with no restrictions and could even return to playing tennis. I congratulated him. The next morning I received word: Ireland had died of a heart attack in his sleep that night. He had been only fifty-one years of age.

When we recovered from the shock of losing Ireland, we turned to the same executive search firm and asked them to find us another man as quickly as possible. We interviewed quite a few promising candidates and, within one month, Frank and I settled on Arthur R. Taylor, a financial wizard who had risen fast to the position of executive vice-president and chief financial officer of International Paper. He was only thirty-seven years old, tall, good-looking, and extremely articulate, and, above all, it was immediately obvious that here was a man with a very quick mind and a tremendous amount of energy and vitality. We offered the job and Taylor quickly accepted it and won the approval of the CBS Board in July 1972.

There was much surprise and some resentment within the ranks of CBS when Taylor took over as president, particularly because of his age. But I defended him vigorously, pointing out

time and again that I had been twenty-six when I took over CBS
and Stanton became president when he was thirty-seven. Arthur
Taylor represented to me the promise of a long reign at CBS.

Frank worked with Taylor for about eight months before he retired as vice-chairman of CBS on March 31, 1973,
which was the last day of the month in which he reached age
sixty-five. I had suggested that we give a dinner to salute Frank's
achievements and long service to CBS, but he preferred not to
have any embellishments added to his retirement. At the Board
meeting prior to his retirement, we expressed our sentiments of
gratitude for his long service and I presented him with a small
Henry Moore sculpture with an inscribed base. He retired from
active, everyday duty but served for five more years on the board
of directors and continues to serve as a consultant to CBS.

As time went on, it became more and more apparent to me
that while Arthur Taylor was indeed brilliant and the company's
earnings were at an all-time high, he did not have all of the essential qualities to become my successor. I discussed my analysis
of the situation with the outside directors of CBS, singly and then
as a group, and they all agreed that Taylor should be replaced so
that someone else could be in the position to take over as the
chief executive officer of the company.

Once that decision was made, I acted quickly. In preparation I
had already looked around for a possible replacement and found
the right man with all the qualifications we sought and he was already within the CBS organization. So, on the morning of our
scheduled board of directors meeting in October 1976, a little
more than four years after Taylor had joined CBS, I summoned
him into my office, and in the presence of two Board members, I
explained the situation to him and asked for his immediate resignation.

I took his resignation before the Board and proposed a new
realignment of management at CBS: I would relinquish my post
as chief executive officer of the company after the next stockholders' meeting but would continue as chairman, and as the new

351

president and the next chief executive officer of CBS I proposed John D. Backe, age forty-four, the head of the CBS/Publishing Group.

I had had my eye on John Backe for some time. From the day he came to CBS, I had been impressed with the caliber of his work and, seeing him several times a week in various meetings and conferences, I came to like and admire him personally. I had noted that he thought before he spoke at meetings, was well-prepared, and never overstated his presentations, proposals or estimates. He had a sure hand in everything he did. In one instance he negotiated the acquisition of a company for CBS at several million dollars *less* than the price he had been authorized to pay, a most unusual feat in these times. So, when I realized I needed a good man to replace Arthur Taylor, I settled upon John Backe. I was convinced that in him I had found not only an outstanding business executive but also a good "generalist," a man who could apply his experience, acumen and common sense to a multiplicity of business affairs.

Backe had a master's degree in business administration and, like Ireland and Taylor before him, was a professional business manager with a brilliant career behind him. He got his early training in management at General Electric in Cincinnati, then joined Silver Burdett, the textbook-publishing unit of the General Learning Corporation, a joint venture between General Electric and Time Inc., and within three years became the president of General Learning. He came to CBS as the president of our Publishing Group in 1973, and in the next three years he reorganized that group brilliantly so that its sales increased by about one-third and its profits increased dramatically.

As chief executive officer of CBS since I stepped down after the April stockholders meeting in 1977, Backe has proved himself a strong leader with outstanding skills in managing a multidivisional company. A straightforward man of great integrity, he has been well received by people within and outside CBS, for in addition to his professional qualities, he has a sensitivity for and understanding of the people with whom he works at CBS.

He has instituted several innovative practices at our regular corporate planning meetings and our inter-group conferences. Our group presidents can now share their problems and successes with one another on a regular basis. New checks and balances and reporting procedures and corporate strategy sessions have been established under Backe's administration, making for a tighter-knit organization at CBS.

I feel we have made a wise choice in John Backe. He and I have been working well together ever since he took over the active management of CBS. I have stayed on as chairman of the board, in order to make myself available and as helpful as I can be in achieving a smooth transition of executive management, especially in the creative and long-range policy areas. I seem to be working as hard as ever, but now with a feeling of pleasure and comfort because my successor is in place.

...And Beyond

S everal years ago, I was in Chicago for a day on business when a craving came over me to revisit the old neighborhood where I had spent my childhood. In a borrowed car I drove alone to Marshfield Avenue and had no trouble finding the first house I can remember living in, when I was about ten. It was not the large, grand home I had always pictured in my mind. It stood no more than twenty feet across and, almost a half century later, the corner lot next to the house, which my father could not afford but had wanted to buy in order to protect his property, still was vacant, except now it was strewn with rubbish. The neighborhood as well as the old Paley house was unmistakably rundown. I rang the bell, and the woman who lived there in one of the apartments into which the house had been divided, invited me in. Because she spoke no English, there was little I could learn of the house, the neighborhood or old friends.

The public school I had attended offered me no renewed memories. At the apartment building on Logan Boulevard where we had lived, I rang the bell of our old apartment, and asked the woman who answered the door if I could look around where I once had lived. "You tell that goddamn landlord she ain't goin' to get me out of here with tricks of this kind," she yelled, and slammed the door in my face.

Somewhat disheartened, I tried the apartment of the landlord-owner of the building and explained once again that I used to live in the building and would like very much to see where I had lived. She looked at me closely and asked my name and when I told her, she screamed out, "Oh, little Willie Paley is here." Her husband and children came running to the door. I was invited in, and within ten minutes the apartment was filled with people who remembered my parents, my sister, and me. Over tea and cookies we reminisced, and though they had followed my career at CBS, they were much more interested in me as "little Willie Paley" and in my family life. It was a lovely, warm meeting.

That afternoon in Chicago remains fondly in my memory because of its contrast to my everyday life in New York. Every once in a while someone will marvel out loud upon my accomplishments, saying in one way or another that it must feel awfully good personally to have started from scratch and now to see this great big empire I have built at CBS. And I never know quite how to answer. The point is that I never do sit back and say to myself, isn't it wonderful! Either I never find the time or inclination, or perhaps the growth of CBS seems to me to be just a matter of development. I have no conscious feeling of "God, how wonderful it is!" I know I have led an exciting, fulfilling, and satisfying life, and for some time now there has been very little I could not do, if I wanted to do it. Yet, the happiest years of my life, from the standpoint of my work, would have to be back at the beginning—in the early years of CBS when things were not so complicated.

In those days, I seemed to have a closer relationship with everything that was happening. I would pick up the telephone and say, drop that and do this. You were either right or wrong. You could correct a mistake pretty quickly in those days, and if you were right, you had the satisfaction of seeing something work

355

out better than it would have otherwise, all because of your own instincts.

Then, as CBS grew larger and larger, I had to delegate more and more authority to more and more people. The company had to be organized and structured again and again for the most efficient operations; the larger and more diversified CBS became, the further back I had to push myself from the actual day-by-day work involved. There simply was not enough time for me to participate directly in the complexities of so many varied operations that were part of CBS. At times I came to feel like a titular head of a large corporation, except when there was trouble or a question of company policy or a matter of overriding economic importance to the company. Reports from our operating divisions, from outside consultants, from study groups flow across my desk and keep me abreast of what is going on, and, of course, I attend important meetings and conferences regularly, and I do make my feelings and opinions known. Nevertheless, it is no longer the same as it was in those early days.

There is no question about the success of CBS over the years. Measured by size or sales, the company grew from a small, struggling outfit in 1928 to a diversified corporation with more than $3 billion dollars in revenues fifty years later; from a handful of employees to some thirty-seven thousand. But size and joy do not necessarily go together; sometimes as one goes up, the other goes down. It is quite amazing to me now when I look back and see just how small CBS used to be and how seriously we took our problems then and how hard I worked, as though everything were a matter of life and death. Now, those same things would take none of my time at all—they would be considered too unimportant for the chairman of the board.

Nevertheless, it was precisely those small things, that slow building-up process during those early years, which enabled CBS to go on and to grow and to do bigger and better things. If we had not established a very solid foundation of good principles and concepts at the beginning, I think, we would not have gone as far as we have gone over the years. We developed traditions that have been followed as a matter of course, beyond anything put down formally in writing as rules and regulations. The progress and development really has been steady and solid. The success of CBS has been based upon three fundamental principles agreed upon right at the beginning and from which I believe our management has never deviated: one, all CBS products would be of the best quality obtainable, for in the long run quality merchandise and profits go hand in hand; two, CBS would never be better than its own employees and thus must seek out men and women of the highest character and integrity over and beyond competence or superior ability; and three, we would trust these people with the full authority and responsibility of the positions they occupy so that they could achieve the pride and self-satisfaction of a job well-done.

The reputation and image of CBS as a quality organization has been earned day by day over these past fifty years. It permeates the organization and can be seen everywhere: we spared no effort, no amount of money to produce the best of which we were capable, from our news programs to our entertainment shows, whether they were serious drama or the lightest slapstick comedy designed for pure enjoyment. The quality is there, as it is in the design of our every product from records and books to toys for children. Quality is an ingredient which one recognizes subliminally; it is either there or it is not there, and yet it is even more difficult to describe than it is to achieve.

The quality of a thing or of an activity has always been of particular personal importance to me. I seek it out with an ineffable combination of instinct, experience, and careful thought. I look for it in my own work and activities, in the work of others, in the relationships of business associates and of friends and of those I meet every day. I seek it in the rooms I work in, and in the rooms in which I live. It is true of the food I eat, in the art with which I like to surround myself.

For example, my office at CBS would hardly give the impression of being anything special. At first glance one would imagine it was rather casually put together, a chair here, a table there, a coffee table, a sofa with two overstuffed chairs in a single grouping. The hand of an interior decorator cannot be discerned. In a building decorated with modern and contemporary furnishings, my office is rather traditional. The most important piece of furniture in the room is a rather large round table, which is really a very old *chemin de fer* table I found in Paris many years ago. I use it as my desk and it serves also as a conference table for eight or so people when necessary. I have it placed in a corner of the room, with the light coming in on it from two windows on the east and the north. It looks to be just what it is, a rather old, handsome table of quality, nothing pretentious. Behind it I use a modern desk chair, designed by Eames, simply because it is one of the most comfortable chairs I have ever encountered; it also forces me to exercise my stomach muscles when I bend forward or lean back. The chair does not match my table-desk and yet the two go together.

On one side wall, I have an old architect's table for holding a drawing or a presentation or anything of the sort which is more convenient to inspect standing up rather than seated. Alongside this table is a long wooden antique lounge chair which once was used by the British in India; Babe discovered it in a London shop and gave it to me as a birthday present. It is a beauty in which one can sit up, recline, or swing some wooden attachments over to hold your legs, a book, or a writing tablet. It is a chair to live in, if one so desires. The off-white walls carry some paintings of my personal choice: a large, early abstract by Picasso, a black-and-white abstract by Kline over the black leather sofa, another abstract with subtle gradations of color by Ben Nicholson. On a far wall, opposite my desk, and above a cabinet which holds the television sets from which I can view competing network programs, is a series of paintings—a bright Rouault, a small Derain, an oil by Giacometti, and others. Mixed in with all of this is a thoroughly modern glass-top coffee table in front of the sofa, also given to me by Babe to add that "modern touch" to the room. All in all, it is a room that looks lived in, that *has* been lived in for some time. There are the old radio-station microphones, books, artifacts, and whatnot scattered about. Things are not exactly in place and do not exactly go together. Actually, a great deal of time, thought, and effort have gone into producing this effect. The pieces were personally collected over a long period of time and the first-time visitor might well believe it all came together out of some sort of carelessness, yet everything in my office is where I want it to be.

This studied casualness has been the theme Babe and I used in choosing the decor of our apartment in the city, our home on Long Island, and our winter retreat in Nassau in the Bahamas. Babe and I developed a certain feeling for wanting a room to give a very cozy, warm appearance, without any one spectacular object catching the eye. We loved to have beautiful objects around us but we did not want anything overpowering. Babe worked with decorators in cooperative ventures as she enjoyed the process of making a house, or a room, or a part of a room a reflection of our lives together. In our travels around Europe we almost always took the time to search out the best antique shops, art galleries, and we derived as much fun from finding an item in a recommended secondhand store as in the fanciest shops of London and Paris.

London tailors are noted for that understatement in the men's suits they custom-make with such care. I remember once ordering three suits and when they did not fit quite properly I sent them back to the tailor, paying the bill and saying I would stop in for another fitting on my next visit to London. It was three or four years later before I returned and remembered those suits as I happened to walk past the tailor's shop. I hesitated about bringing up the subject after so many years, but after approaching the shop three times, I finally walked in. There sat a man at a table. He looked up at me over his spectacles and casually shouted to the back of the shop, "Mr. Paley's 'ere for 'is fitting!"

Babe and I usually visited Europe once or twice a year, often stopping off in London or Paris for a day or so, and then going on to tour a region we had not seen before. Over the years we became familiar with many of the cities and towns of Europe, looking at the art, and the gardens, adventuring with new restaurants and good food, and visiting or touring with old friends. Almost every July, I think, we spent with close friends, Loel Guinness, and his wife, Gloria, usually to cruise on their yacht. Loel, as he likes to point out, comes from the other side of the family that went into the brewery business in 1759. He is merely a financier and businessman, but he is so considerate that he installed a special pantry on his yacht, near the stateroom reserved for the Paleys, so that I could enjoy on my own a midnight snack when hunger pangs struck. On these trips we also would stay with the Guinnesses at their beautiful country house, called Piencourt, which is near Deauville in Normandy, France. Quite often we would go on from Piencourt to visit with our friends, the Baroness and Baron Guy de Rothschild, at their nearby country home, Mautry, in Normandy. The British side of the family is headed by my long-time friend Lord Victor Rothschild, who has served as a sort of one-man brain trust to recent British governments. He often flatters me tacitly by asking my advice on important decisions and turning points in his life. On other trips, we would stay with friends who maintained vacation homes in the Greek Islands. Such travel and associations always played an important part in our lives, as we enjoyed not only the leisure but also the fresh points of view on world affairs of our non-American friends. Then there are the Tree brothers, Michael and Jeremy, and David Somerset in England who entertained the Paleys for years with hospitality and warm friendship. It would not be fair to go on about all the friends, dinner companions, and storytellers who helped make our lives —Babe's and mine—so happy through the years because I would be sure to forget someone and be everlastingly embarrassed.

Our favorite form of entertainment was holding weekend parties at Kiluna so that we could enjoy the company of our guests for two or three days at a time. The same was true of our house in Nassau. I love to eat and both Babe and I would enjoy the lively conversation of bright, interesting and entertaining friends and acquaintances. Conversations at the Paley dinner table ranged over the widest conceivable range of subjects, depending on the guests.

One of the most brilliant raconteurs of all time at the Paley dinner table, who became one of my closest friends, was Jack Baragwanath, a mining engineer of Welsh ancestry, who could tell a story, any story, so well that he held his listeners spellbound. A handsome, elegant fellow some years old than I, Baragwanath also happened to be, in my opinion, the funniest humorist in the world. He enjoyed telling seemingly plausible stories of his mining adventures in South America and could lead a listener into flights of fancy far beyond belief.

On one occasion I had a leading American industrialist and his wife for lunch at Kiluna. The lunch was not going particularly well until Jack, at just the right moment, said to the industrialist's wife on his right, "Mrs. L——, would you please take your hand off my knee." His timing was perfect. The industrialist rose in shock and anger from his seat, the wife paused, then luckily saw the joke, and erupted in laughter. Things went well after that, as they so often did with Jack Baragwanath.

He went to great trouble at one period to memorize a particular singing commercial heard on TV and radio and then drove me crazy by singing it, humming it, or just mumbling it for my benefit for days on end. I could not get him to stop. So I then arranged to have a tape recording installed in a locked cabinet in his office, one which, without stop, sang over and over the commercial he had been singing to me, "Chiquita Banana." Finally he came to me, hands held high, saying, "I surrender. Please shut it off . . . I promise no more commercials."

Jack wrote a book of his adventures in South America and persuaded his publisher and friend, Nelson Doubleday, Sr., to have fifty copies of the book made up with different dedication pages, each one appropriate for each of fifty of his friends. Edna Ferber, the novelist, was so touched by Jack's dedication that she kept his book on her coffee table for two years until someone finally explained the joke to her. Then she would not speak to Jack again for years.

Another old friend, Roy Atwood, a stockbroker who was a trifle overweight, used to telephone me regularly each morning. He would moan and complain about his hunger and diet and I would describe in vivid detail what I was having for breakfast that morning, from kippered herring to lamb chops. I figured this gave him great vicarious pleasure and I embarked on great flights of imagination to satisfy a friend.

Away from work, I have relished the enjoyment of life, just as much as I have derived pleasure from plunging into the intricate strategies, the bargaining and the deals, the instinctual decisions and the administration of affairs at CBS. I found it a very creative business, and I have always gone at it hard, full blast, and with utter concentration and focus. But away from work, I have equally sought the enjoyments, pleasures and stimulations of the good life, enjoyed with good friends.

My father suffered his first heart attack—a major one—when he was nearly eighty-three, and, despite his age, it came as a great shock to the whole family. He had always guarded his health so carefully, keeping his weight to within a quarter of a pound of what it was supposed to be, visiting his doctor and his dentist regularly. Up to the time of his attack he had been in excellent health, regularly attending CBS Board meetings as a founding director. When he had survived the initial phase of that heart attack, a group of heart specialists was called in to examine him in a Philadelphia hospital. When the nurse announced their arrival, my father asked, "What time is it?"

"It's just about four-thirty," she said.

"I'm very sorry," said my father. "Turn the television set on, please. I must see *The Edge of Night*. Tell the doctors I cannot see them until five o'clock." The doctors laughed and they waited.

My father was very proud of me and would talk endlessly to anyone who could bear to listen about his son's accomplishments, but he also was a devoted fan of television. When I visited him at home, he would glance every so often at a clock and sometimes say to me, "Son, I feel a little sleepy now. Do you mind if I just take a short nap? Come back in thirty minutes or maybe an hour and see me again." Invariably, as soon as I left the room, he would turn on the television set because there was a show he did not want to miss.

My father lived quietly after that first heart attack, reading, watching television, seeing a few friends and family. He suffered three more heart attacks before he succumbed on March 31, 1963, at the age of eighty-seven.

I wanted to honor the memory of my father in some way that would also be a public service. Long before my father died I had often thought that New York City, unlike London and Paris, lacked places to sit down and relax in the midtown business area. So I settled on the idea of building a small, vest-pocket park somewhere in midtown business area and I began to look for an empty site or a building I could have torn down. But every time I found a house or a small building for sale, it had a tenant in it who did not want to move. Two whole years went by before it came to my attention that the famous Stork Club on Fifty-third Street near Madison Avenue was for sale. The building and site had only one owner and no tenants and so I bought the property from Sherman Billingsley, engaged the services of landscape architect Robert Zion and a year later he came through with the marvelous idea, based upon what he had seen in Mexico, a park in the middle of Manhattan with a superb waterfall at one end.

In about another year, on May 23, 1967, Paley Park was opened to the public when my mother, with members of the family looking on, pressed a button, and the wonderful waterfall began to flow. It was so pleasing that I asked if there were not a way to keep the waterfall going during the winter months and so the water was recycled into an adjacent building, heated there, and returned for re-use in the waterfall. That little park, just forty-two by one hundred feet, has given me great joy and satisfaction. It is being maintained privately by The Willam S. Paley Foundation—in perpetuity, I hope.

My mother lived to within three months of her ninety-sixth birthday. She took up painting at about the age of sixty when a friend who had been left penniless upon her husband's death opened an art school in Philadelphia. My mother took lessons because her friend was too proud to accept financial help. It turned out she had a marvelous talent for primitive realism and she devoted the major part of the next thirty years to painting in a studio built for her on the top floor of her Philadelphia home. I have a three-by-two-foot oil painting of hers hanging in the anteroom to my office. It is a still life of a table laden with fruit—strawberries, peaches and one pineapple—with a cane-backed chair nearby holding half a watermelon. It is most attractive.

When Teddy Kollek, the mayor of Jerusalem, was showing me around the ancient city, it occurred to me that I could honor my mother by building an art school in her name there for Arab and Israeli children in the daytime and for adults at night. Mayor Kollek found a suitable location near the Israel Museum and close to the historic Herod's Gate, at the edge of both Arab and Jewish neighborhoods in eastern Jerusalem. Moshe Safdie, the outstanding Israeli-born architect, designed the air-conditioned building of five studio-classrooms, an auditorium, exhibition space, offices and terraces. I showed the plans to my mother and promised to take her to the opening. Unfortunately, she died in the winter of 1977, before the Paley Art Center was opened on January 23, 1978.

Art and the world of art have played a significant role in my life. Not long after I began collecting, Nelson Rockefeller invited me to become a trustee of the then small and new Museum of Modern Art. The Museum of Modern Art, which chose to specialize in the art of the modern period beginning with Cézanne, had been started in rented quarters in 1929 by Nelson's mother, Mrs. Abby Aldrich Rockefeller, and two of her friends, Miss Lillie P.

Bliss and Mrs. Cornelius J. Sullivan. I was honored to become a trustee of the museum in 1937 but it was not until the 1950s that I became really active in the museum's affairs. It was fascinating and significant work, for after the end of World War II the museum enjoyed a tremendous growth in both acquisitions of art and in public attendance. At the same time I was giving a good deal of my time to the post-war growth of Columbia University, which I had been elected a life trustee of. Thus it came about that in 1968 I was approached informally with two separate, gratifying invitations, of which I felt I could accept only one: would I like to become chairman of the board of trustees of Columbia? or, would I like to become president of the Museum of Modern Art?

Both were very attractive opportunities for worthwhile public service, but it was my long personal interest in art, I think, that became the determining factor. After due consideration, I accepted the invitation to become president of the museum. I was elected to that office and became, in effect, its chief executive officer in September 1968. By that time, the Museum of Modern Art had already become largely what it is today: the most prestigious museum in the United States specializing in modern and contemporary art. More than any other museum, it has had the widest influence, not only upon trends in the art world but also upon the designs, shapes and colors used in thousands of products we see and use every day—from magazine covers to the latest models of automobiles, houses, furniture and kitchen appliances. The museum's scope is international, ranging over painting, sculpture, still photography, motion pictures, architecture and design.

It is a complex organization to run, from its day-to-day operations to special exhibits, from administrative policies to the choices of what art the museum should buy or accept as gifts, and where and when particular pieces should be exhibited. Most of the basic work is done in committees, where the advice of various experts comes into play. For me, it became a fascinating learning process. As an ex-officio member of each of the committees, I came in contact with some of the leading art scholars of this country: William Rubin on painting and sculpture, John Szarkowski on photography, Arthur Drexler on architecture and design, William Lieberman on drawing, Riva Castleman on prints and illustrated books, Ted Perry on classic motion pictures, and, of course, Alfred Barr, Jr., the museum's first director and the acknowledged foremost expert on modern art in the country. My years with the museum have enriched my life, making me much more sophisticated and knowledgeable about art. In return, I hope I have given the museum the benefits of my own experience and my ability to work with creative people of strong minds and opinions and delicate egos. Controversies, arguments and personal peeves are part of the atmosphere behind the scenes in almost all art museums, where the work and the decisions are subjective.

Soon after I became president, it fell upon me to obtain the resignation of the museum's director, a professor of art history who was experienced and able in his own field but not so successful as an administrator. The details no longer matter but there came a point when many of the trustees thought he should go. Since the director had started only a few months before I had become president, I did not feel justified in judging his competence. The older and more experienced trustees, who represented a majority of the executive committee—including David Rockefeller, Blanchette Rockefeller, Eliza Parkinson, William Burden and Nelson Rockefeller (by consultation) who was then governor of New York—met and decided to ask the new director to resign quietly rather than to undergo any publicity about conflicts within the museum's ranks. As president, I was asked implement the decision.

I explained the situation as gently as possible to the director and after some consideration he agreed to write the Board a letter of resignation to which I would reply with a letter of appreciation for his services. That is the way the matter should have ended—without fanfare.

But before the Board could act upon the letter of resignation, the matter leaked and Ralph Colin, a long-time trustee and vice-president of the museum and my personal attorney, objected very strongly to the way the resignation had been handled outside of regular channels. Angry that he himself had not been consulted, he telephoned various trustees, complaining bitterly and accusing me of having acted autocratically.

To at least one trustee, he threatened to resign from the museum in protest to my actions. At the trustees' board meeting, he raised his objections formally, saying he did not object to the director's resignation itself, but rather that the matter had not been brought before the executive committee. I tried to explain that the result would have been a foregone conclusion and that the senior trustees had wanted to handle the resignation in an informal, gentlemanly manner, without publicity, so as to do as little harm as possible to the museum and to the director himself. I became quite upset and angry. He had been my personal attorney for forty years. It seemed to me he could easily have come to me with his complaints and it seemed odd that after so many years he should so misconstrue my motives.

Finally, I called him in and told him that because of all that had happened, I did not feel I could work comfortably with him again and so I was going to find another attorney to handle my own legal business. There is a story extant—very much abbreviated—that Ralph Colin had cried out, "Bill, how can you do this to me—we've been friends for forty years?" and that I supposedly had replied, "You were never my friend, you were my lawyer." That just never happened. What he said, as I remember it, was, "I was close to you and you never asked me about it [the resignation]," and I said, "I couldn't ask everyone and I'm sorry but we wanted to keep the group small and keep this thing as quiet as possible and do as little harm as possible."

In any event, the incident had further repercussions. After I had changed lawyers, the CBS law department recommended changing its outside counsel from the Colin firm to another, larger law firm. The law department for many years had wanted to change its outside counsel, but I had always resisted this action because of our long association with Colin and his firm. This time I did not feel I could oppose them. The result was that CBS changed its outside counsel. Ralph Colin chose to resign from the museum, publicly charging me with autocratic behavior. Since then, we have shaken hands and made up. As I have said, people take their art and their egos very seriously.

Some four years after I had become president, David Rockefeller, Blanchette Rockefeller (Mrs. John D. Rockefeller 3rd) and I agreed to shift roles in the museum because of the extent of our businesses and other activities at the time. David, who for some time had wanted to lighten his workload there as chairman would become vice-chairman; I would become chairman and lessen the demands on my time; and Blanchette Rockefeller, who had given up the post some years before because of other pressing obligations, would resume as president of the museum. In November 1972, the trustees duly elected us to our new posts. Since then, the museum has been pursuing an ingenious new plan to sell its air rights for a condominium apartment tower to be built above a new museum wing. If approved in the courts, it would allow the museum as a non-profit organization to receive the equivalent of real estate taxes on the condominium that ordinarily would have gone to the city. This plan would more than double gallery space and add other new facilities. It would also stabilize its financial future without any cost to the City of New York.

For a very long time, going back even to the early days of radio, I had had an idea that the broadcasting industry should sponsor some sort of museum to preserve and make available the best of its output for students, scholars and any of the public which might be interested. I talked about it with others in the industry then and I talked about it when television came of age, but it was not until the early seventies that I decided to launch the project myself.

After the usual and expected trials and tribulations, financed and supported by The William S. Paley Foundation (the private foundation I use for my philanthropic giving), the Museum of

Broadcasting was opened in 1976 on Fifty-third Street, just east of Fifth Avenue. Students, scholars and the public are offered re-recordings of hundreds of thousands of hours of radio programs and television programs, donated from various sources, including the three networks and the Corporation for Public Broadcasting. The catalogue of historic radio and television broadcasts is constantly growing. The Museum of Broadcasting has been a tremendous success. Its primary problem now is how to expand its facilities to accommodate the people who visit there and must wait so long for their turn on the consoles which allow private listening and viewing of historic and favorite moments in radio and television broadcasting.

In 1973, Babe and I embarked on a very special, exotic trip— our first visit to mainland China. We happily toured cities and towns, inspected historic landmarks and simple schools and factories, and met with several leaders of Chinese government and society, including Chou En-lai. It was toward the end of our stay at the Peace Hotel in Shanghai that Babe woke me up very early one morning, complaining that she was terribly cold. I heaped blankets on her and after a while she said she was much too hot. I took her temperature. It was 102. I ministered to her and then asked that a doctor be called. Babe stubbornly refused his advice that she go to a hospital. When the doctor's medicine did not help and her temperature went up to 104, I took it upon myself to summon, through our interpreter, an ambulance and notify the hospital. There her condition was diagnosed correctly as pneumonia and she was treated with great skill and care. I marveled at the state of world communications as I placed a telephone call from Shanghai, China, to Babe's personal physician in New York and relayed information on her case. Her New York doctor agreed with the procedures taken and the medication being used.

Babe remained in the hospital for two weeks and upon her release, rather than go on to Japan as planned, we flew directly home and I took her to New York Hospital. Doctors there were full of admiration for the fine, up-to-date treatment she had received in China, and asked only that she come in every thirty days or so for a check-up. Two or three months later, X-ray examinations revealed a shadow on her right lung, indicating a tumor and the need for an operation. The tumor was removed successfully but we learned it had been malignant.

Two years later another tumor appeared and another operation was needed. During this time, however, doctors decided to remove the lung entirely and later to begin chemotherapy and some radiation. Everything seemed to be going well for about a year, until in 1976 Babe began losing her strength. Short stays in the hospital for treatment seemed not to help. She decided she wanted to be at home and I brought in round-the-clock nurses and hospital equipment. Blessedly, she suffered little pain. Throughout it all, she maintained her gallant spirit, never acted depressed and almost never talked about her illness. For the longest while, she kept her social contacts by telephone so that few of her friends at first realized how ill she truly was, for she never told them. She conferred with her minister and helped plan her funeral service.

Finally, the end came in the very early morning hours of July 6, 1978, the day after her sixty-third birthday, in our apartment in New York. The family was gathered around her, all the children with whom she had shared her life: Amanda, Hilary and Kate, and Tony, Jeffrey and Billie. Her illness had spanned five long years and yet, when death took her, it came as a terrible blow, an emptying loss . . . leaving a wide gap in our lives, and in mine to an extent I never thought possible. Her life will always be a part of me, for we shared so much together over so many years. As I write this I am still trying to work out a new life style—one without Babe at my side. I find it most difficult. But I am still running fast, keeping myself busy in order to help push away the tendency to fall into a depressed state and also to eliminate the pain that strikes me at odd moments, particularly in the early mornings. My family and friends have been wonderful. They sense my needs and are ever on hand to keep me occupied. I am fairly strong and well disciplined and I am making progress. Although I am sure I will always miss Babe, I know that in time I must find a way back into the normal stream of life.

When I think back—which I do not do too often—I can recall with vivid clarity so many turning points, even the day I first clamped those radio earphones on to hear music carried hundreds of miles through the air. I can relive the sense of fascination over someone unseen communicating with me from afar. Today, we hardly stop to consider the remarkable strides made in communications via radio and television. To me, it still seems miraculous that a human being could walk on the moon and even more astounding to see it happening on our television screens. The great impact of television upon our lives, as with radio before it, is that it can show and tell us events around the world as they happen, it can recount and recapitulate other events soon after they occur. Broadcasting reaches into virtually every home in America. It brings into those homes not only the news of the day but the changing trends in the way we lead our lives. It binds our vast, pluralistic country together as one nation. With television and radio, we can all see and hear the same things together. We see and are exposed to more facets of American life than any generation before us.

Despite its critics, I believe television is better today than it has ever been before, and better than any other television system in the world: it provides programs to satisfy the tastes of a broad spectrum of Americans. I believe, too, that television will continue to improve its home entertainment, and also its delivery of the news, and its public information service, so necessary to the people of a democratic nation who are faced with the need to be informed on all important public issues. One needs only to stop and to consider what the United States and the world would be like today without the communications provided by the broadcasting media.

Over the past fifty years, radio and television have become an integral part of our daily lives, representing a great development in modern America. I have been very fortunate to have been able

371

to take part in its development right from the very beginning. In all, CBS and I have enjoyed a remarkably good and stimulating life together. It has been fascinating. In this book I have tried to the best of my ability to tell it as it happened.

Appendix

HIGHLIGHTS OF CBS NEWS

1930   PAUL W. WHITE joins CBS and is named News Editor.

1931   CBS's experimental television station presented *Bill Schudt's Going to Press,* an interview show with correspondents, columnists, and editors. This was the first regular series of new programs on television and the first regularly scheduled program to be simulcast on radio and television.

1933   PAUL WHITE organized Columbia News Service, the first network news-gathering service.

1938   CBS pioneered the first multiple news roundup from foreign capitals in its coverage of the Nazi invasion of Austria. Edward R. Murrow reported from Vienna, William L. Shirer from London, and other newsmen from Paris, Berlin, and Rome.

             CBS covered the Munich crisis, and as World War II approached, CBS listeners were served by a staff which grew to include, Elmer Davis, Albert Warner, Eric Sevareid, Winston Burdett, Charles Collingwood. Bill Downs, Joseph C. Harsch, Richard C. Hottelet, Quincy Howe, and Howard K. Smith.

1941   On July 1, CBS Television resumed with the first up-to-minute, visualized news service.

CBS station WCBW, went on the air with a nine-hour broadcast on the attack on Pearl Harbor, which was the first television news instant special.

1945   A CBS newsman was the only American broadcaster present at three of the five decisive enemy surrenders to the Allies.

At the war's end, six hundred radio editors selected CBS as the network which had performed the "Best News Job in Radio" in its coverage of V-E Day, V-J Day, the Japanese surrender, and the death of Franklin D. Roosevelt.

PAUL WHITE resigned from CBS and EDWARD R. MURROW was appointed Vice President and Director of Public Affairs.

1946   EDWARD R. MURROW appointed WELLS CHURCH as Director of News Broadcasts encompassing both radio and television.

1947   The creation of the Documentary Unit to give extraordinary research and preparation to special programs dealing with subjects of major public importance and interest was recognized by both critics and listeners as one of the most promising new developments in American radio.

On July 17, EDWARD R. MURROW resigned as Vice President and Director of Public Affairs to resume broadcasts.

1948   EDMUND CHESTER was appointed Director of News, Special Events and Sports for the CBS Television Network.

CBS-TV News with DOUGLAS EDWARDS, the first regularly scheduled television network news program, began on May 3.

In November, CBS presented on television its first full coverage of presidential election returns.

1949   Radio and television public affairs were integrated under DAVIDSON TAYLOR as Vice President and Director of Public Affairs.

Radio and television news and special events were integrated under Edmund Chester as Director of CBS News.

SIG MICKELSON was appointed Director of the CBS Division of Discussion.

Foreign correspondents were equipped, by means of portable newsreel cameras, to add film to their tape commentaries.

CBS was granted exclusive television rights to the sessions of the United Nations General Assembly at Flushing Meadow and televised the deliberations for three hours a day from November 7 until early December.

1951   Radio and television news operations were separated into distinct departments: television network news and public events headed by Sig Mickelson, and its radio counterpart headed by Edmund Chester.

On November 18, *See It Now*, hosted by Edward R. Murrow, premièred featuring the first coast-to-coast transmission between New York and San Francisco. The series continued until July 1958.

1953   February 1 marked the first television broadcast of *You Are There*, a series of dramatic re-enactments of historic events with CBS newscasters giving "on-the-spot" reports.

1954   The News and Public Affairs departments of CBS Radio and CBS Television were integrated as one department with Mr. Mickelson as Vice President of CBS and General Manager of CBS News.

On March 9, Senator Joseph McCarthy was the subject of a half-hour broadcast of *See It Now*. Senator McCarthy, offered the opportunity to reply, did so on *See It Now* on April 6. On April 22, the Army-McCarthy hearings began.

By November, CBS Television and Radio introduced *Face the Nation*, an interview broadcast with individuals close to recent news events. On the first broadcast on November 7, the guest was Senator Joseph McCarthy. The interview took place just two days before the Senate began ten days of debate ending in a vote to condemn Senator McCarthy.

CBS supplemented its regular schedule of Public Affairs programs with a number of special broadcasts that made it possible for families across America to witness many historic events that occurred during 1954—televised summaries of the Army-McCarthy hearings, the first cabinet meeting ever televised, and the President's State of the Union Message.

1957 Soviet Premier Nikita Khrushchev was interviewed on *Face the Nation,* the first time on television in any country.

On April 8, the *CBS Morning News* began on television with Richard C. Hottelet. The broadcast has since been anchored by such correspondents as Harry Reasoner (1961–63), Mike Wallace (1963–66), Joseph Benti (1966–70), John Hart (1970–73), Hughes Rudd (1973–75), and Hughes Rudd and Bruce Morton (1975–77), Lesley Stahl and Hughes Rudd (October 3, 1977–October 28, 1977), Lesley Stahl and Richard Threlkeld (October 31, 1977–Present).

The Twentieth Century, a highly acclaimed news broadcast profiling the people of our time, premièred on October 20 with a special hour-long program paying tribute to Sir Winston Churchill.

1959 In October, CBS News was made a full division of the corporation, with Sig Mickelson as President.

On October 27, CBS News presented the first broadcast of *CBS Reports.* Through the years, *CBS Reports* has offered to its audience such outstanding, in-depth reports as:

Harvest of Shame	*1960*
The Volga	*1966*
Hunger in America	*1968*
The Selling of the Pentagon	*1971*
Justice in America (Parts 1–3)	*1971*
Castro, Cuba and the U.S.A.	*1974*
The American Way of Cancer	*1975*
The Americans Assassins (Parts 1–4)	*1975/76*
The Fire Next Door	*1977*
The Battle of South Africa	*1978*

1960   By 1960, CBS News had established a regular news bureau in major foreign cities including London, Paris, Rome, Bonn, Tokyo, Moscow and Beirut.

1961   In February, RICHARD S. SALANT was appointed President of CBS News.

1962   CBS announced the formation of six domestic news bureaus: New York City for the Northeast, Chicago in the Midwest, Washington, D.C., in the Mid-Atlantic, Atlanta in the South, Dallas in the Southwest and Los Angeles covering the West Coast, Hawaii and Alaska.

With the launching of the "Early Bird" satellite, CBS was first in the regularly scheduled use of satellite television for news.

CBS News announced the formation of the CBS News Election Unit, the first year-round political reporting organization in network television.

In April, WALTER CRONKITE became the anchorman of the *CBS Evening News*.

1963   The *CBS Evening News with Walter Cronkite* was expanded to a half-hour broadcast on September 2.

1964   RICHARD SALANT left CBS News to become Special Assistant to the President of CBS and CBS Vice President, Corporate Affairs.

FRED FRIENDLY was named President of CBS News.

1965   On March 1, CBS News presented *T-Minus 4 Years, 9 Months and 30 Days*, a one-hour news special from five key space centers in the U.S., the first in a series of videotaped broadcasts introducing a new approach to broadcast journalism.

1966   In February, RICHARD SALANT returned to CBS News as Acting President; and in April, he was formally appointed President of CBS News.

1967   The *Twenty-First Century* began on CBS as a series of broadcasts devoted to scientific and environmental subjects.

1968   *60 Minutes* began September 24. Its magazine format enabled CBS News to treat subjects in greater depth than

377

do daily news broadcasts. It has won virtually every major award in television news reporting and has received critical acclaim for its hard-hitting investigative reports and exclusive interviews.

1969   WALTER CRONKITE anchored CBS's extensive coverage of man's first landing on the moon, narrating the historic event continuously for eighteen hours and then, after a six-hour nap, returned for another nine hours.

On March 31, the *CBS Morning News* was expanded to become network television's first one-hour news broadcast.

1971   In September, CBS News began to broadcast *In the News,* two-and-one-half-minute segments every half hour on Saturday mornings, designed to explain current events to school-age viewers.

1974   On May 2, CBS News began *Magazine,* the daytime series for women. Because of its success, in 1977, this series was given a regular time slot, the first Thursday of each month.

By August, CBS News was involved in all aspects of electronic news gathering, adopting the use of Ikegami portable, hand-held color television cameras and Sony battery-operated ¾-inch videotape recorders. This news-gathering unit enabled coverage of events at any location on short notice.

1976   CBS News honored the nation's bicentennial with a sixteen-hour broadcast, *In Celebration of Us,* anchored by WALTER CRONKITE and described as the most extensive coverage of any single day since man landed on the moon in 1969.

1977   On March 5, President Carter took part in a two-hour nationwide call-in radio broadcast, which was suggested to him by CBS News.

In June, CBS News went all electronic in its domestic bureaus.

On August 31, CBS News broadcast *Energy: The Facts . . . The Fears . . . The Future;* it was the first in-depth look at this vital subject on network television.

On November 14, WALTER CRONKITE conducted interviews by satellite with President Anwar Sadat of Egypt and Prime Minister Menachim Begin of Israel, which led to the historic visit of the President of Egypt to Israel and the subsequent Middle East peace talks.

1978 WILLIAM A. LEONARD, veteran newscaster, was named to succeed RICHARD S. SALANT as President of CBS News in 1979.

Your Turn: Letters to CBS News—CBS News series that is television's answer to newspapers' letters to the editor —first went on the air, February 5.

On August 22, 23, and 24, *Is Anyone Out There Learning?: A* Report Card on American Public Education, was broadcast as a three-hour special, one hour each night.

On September 16, CBS News inaugurated its unique children's broadcast, *30 Minutes.*

1931   WILLIAM SCHUDT, JR., Director of Television Programs Experimental station in New York City, W2XAB, was opened. Inaugural broadcast, July 21, 10:15–11:00 P.M. with Mayor James J. Walker, Kate Smith, the Boswell Sisters, George Gershwin, etc. CBS was the first broadcaster in New York to have a schedule of regular television programs for more than a year.

1933–38   GILBERT SELDES, Experimental Television Director, September 1937.
CBS worked on the technical aspects of television before resuming television broadcasting.

1939   Studio equipment for television broadcasting in New York was installed in the Grand Central Terminal Building and transmitters in the Chrysler Tower.

1940   Color television was first broadcast in August from the CBS transmitter at the top of the Chrysler Building and received in the CBS building at 485 Madison Avenue.

1941   On July 1, a black-and white television program service of fifteen hours a week began over the New York station WCBW. News was a regular feature of the schedule.

1942–43   War research took priority in television laboratories. The loss of personnel to World War II and the inability to replace equipment forced CBS Television to decrease its broadcast schedule to four hours a week.

1944   Starting May 5, CBS broadcast twice weekly "live" television programs over its New York station WCBW. CBS made use of technological improvements realized during the war so that bigger and better television pictures would result.

1945   By the end of the year, WCBW was broadcasting four hours of television per week.
Our television research engineers worked on the development of color television in the ultra-high frequencies. This culminated in actual broadcast transmission and reception of high-definition, full-color television pictures.

In July, CBS offered its television facilities and personnel to its clients to develop commercial programs and to test typical viewer preferences before and after the broadcasts.

1946 The first television advertising rate card was issued by WCBS-TV (formerly WCBW), New York.

Sports broadcasts came to the fore in 1946; college football games, ice hockey games, the National Horse Show and basketball tourneys from Madison Square Garden were televised.

CBS filed a petition with the FCC in September requesting the establishment of engineering standards and commercial status for color television.

At a hearing before the FCC in December, CBS requested that color television in the ultra-high frequencies be established commercially on an equal basis with black-and-white television.

1947 The FCC denied CBS's petition to authorize the operation of commercial color-television stations in the ultra-high frequencies.

Studio One, an outstanding dramatic series, had its première, April 29.

Sports events included the World Series baseball games between the New York Yankees and the Brooklyn Dodgers.

1948 The CBS Television Network was formed, with WCAU-TV, Philadelphia as the first television affiliate. Within the year there were thirty affiliate stations.

On March 20, the CBS Television Network broadcast the Philadelphia Symphony Orchestra with Eugene Ormandy, the first symphony orchestra to be televised.

Plans were announced for the construction of the largest and most modern television studios in the world in the Grand Central Terminal Building, New York City.

Tonight on Broadway premièred April 6, with excerpts from *Mister Roberts.* Other productions on this series were *High Button Shoes* and *The Heiress.*

381

We the People (6/1/48) began on CBS Television as the first regularly scheduled network program series simulcast.

ED SULLIVAN's *Toast of the Town,* a series which ran for twenty-three years, premièred June 20.

1949

DAVIDSON TAYLOR, Vice President and Director of Public Affairs (Radio and Television) 12/24/45–12/30/49.

HUBBELL ROBINSON, JR., Vice President in Charge of Network Programs (Radio and Television) 12/30/49–7/30/51.

The Goldbergs started January 17 on CBS Television.

Studio One presented its full-hour version of *Julius Caesar* in modern dress.

Mama, a series based on the play *I Remember Mama* had its première July 1.

The CBS color television system was used to show operations and clinical demonstrations to delegates attending the American Medical Association Convention in Atlantic City.

CBS presented its color television system before the FCC during open hearings on color television and TV frequency allocation.

CBS demonstrated its system of color television before the FCC in October and November in an attempt to gain authorization of its system.

The sessions of the United Nations General Assembly were seen daily (11 A.M.–1 P.M.; 3–4 P.M.) from early November into early December.

1950

The Garry Moore Show started on television June 26 and ran for seventeen years. Carol Burnett was discovered on this show.

George Burns and Gracie Allen began their first regular television series, October 12.

Jack Benny starred in his first CBS Television broadcast, October 28.

FCC adopted the CBS color television system for commercial broadcasts.

The FCC's decision for the adoption of the CBS color television standards was upheld by a federal district court in Chicago.

1951
J. L. VAN VOLKENBURG, President, CBS Television Division, 7/16/51–12/31/56.

HUBBELL ROBINSON, JR., Vice President and Director of Network Programs (TV only), 7/30/51–3/19/56.

HARRY S. ACKERMAN, Vice President in Charge of Network Programs, Hollywood, 6/13/51–6/1/55.

The United States Supreme Court upheld the FCC's decision in favor of CBS's color television system.

CBS Television Division was established on July 16 as part of the administrative reorganization of the company.

CBS Television began exclusive daily coverage of the United Nations General Assembly sessions in Paris.

I Love Lucy with Lucille Ball and Desi Arnaz had its première broadcast October 15.

1952
CBS Television completed construction of Television City, Hollywood, the first fully self-contained production unit.

Omnibus produced weekly by the TV-Radio Workshop of the Ford Foundation made its debut November 9.

Arthur Godfrey and His Friends, I Love Lucy, Our Miss Brooks, Toast of the Town, What's My Line? continued in popularity.

1953
Person to Person, with Edward R. Murrow as interviewer, premièred October 2 with Roy Campanella and Leopold Stokowski as the guests.

The CBS Production Center (now Broadcast Center) in New York City was put into full operation after much renovation.

CBS Television maintained its program popularity with shows such as Herb Shriner's *Two for the Money, Life with Father, My Favorite Husband, My Friend Irma,* and *The Red Skelton Hour.*

Television City in Hollywood marks its first full year of operation.

The FCC reversed its previous decision and adopted the National Television System Committee standards for color broadcasting. CBS Television was on the air within an hour after the announcement with a color program using the new standards.

1954   *CBS Editorial* by DR. FRANK STANTON, CBS President, sought support from viewers for radio and television to have the same opportunity as other branches of the press to cover congressional hearings. This was the first editorial to be delivered by a national network.

Twenty-three new entertainment series were introduced, including *Climax!, December Bride, Father Knows Best, Lassie, General Electric Theater.*

The *Jack Benny Program* premièred as a regular series October 3.

The Kentucky Derby, The Preakness, The Belmont Stakes were among the exclusive sports broadcasts.

1955   HARRY G. OMMERLE, Vice President in Charge of Network Programs, New York (reporting to H. Robinson, Jr.), 5/31/55–3/26/58.

ALFRED J. SCALPONE, Vice President in Charge of Network Programs, Hollywood (reporting to H. Robinson, Jr.), 7/1/55–4/3/58.

The *64,000 Question* attracted the largest audience for a regularly scheduled program.

Ford Star Jubilee television broadcasts in color were: *The Judy Garland Show, The Caine Mutiny Court Martial, I Hear America Singing,* and *Together with Music* (Noel Coward and Mary Martin).

Gunsmoke premièred September 10 and continued for twenty years.

Captain Kangaroo had its first broadcast on October 3, and is still continuing.

Other programs making their debuts were: *Alfred Hitchcock Presents,* the *Bob Cummings Show, The Honeymooners,* the *Phil Silvers Show,* and *United States Steel Hour.*

Sports broadcasts included exclusive coverage of the Orange and Gator Bowl Games, intercollegiate football games; major league baseball games; The Kentucky Derby, The Preakness and The Belmont Stakes.

1956 HUBBELL ROBINSON, JR., Executive Vice President overseeing all program area, 3/18/56–5/26/59.

CBS Television averaged one color broadcast per day this year.

CBS was the first network to acquire and use the Ampex videotape recorder system to record television pictures and sound on a single magnetic tape, enabling a faster rebroadcast of television programs with better quality.

Playhouse 90 was the first hour-and-a-half dramatic series to be broadcast on a regular weekly basis. Outstanding dramas of its first season included: *Requiem for a Heavyweight, Forbidden Area, Sizeman and Son, Rendezvous in Black, Heritage of Anger, Eloise* and *The Family Nobody Wanted.*

1957 MERLE S. JONES, President, CBS Television Division, 1/1/57–3/11/58.

New series included: the *Danny Thomas Show, Have Gun—Will Travel, The Lucille Ball–Desi Arnaz Show, Richard Diamond, Private Detective, Cinderella,* and the *Edsel Show.*

More on-the-spot coverage of sports was broadcast by the CBS Television Network than during any previous year.

1958 LOUIS G. COWAN, President, CBS Television Network Division, 3/12/58–12/8/59.

HARRY G. OMMERLE, Vice President in Charge of Network Programs (reporting to H. Robinson, Jr.), 3/25/58–8/10/59.

MICHAEL DANN, Vice President in Charge of Network Programs, New York (reporting to H. Ommerle), 3/25/58–3/11/63.

The *Du Pont Show of the Month* dramas were *The Bridge of San Luis Rey, A Tale of Two Cities, Wuthering Heights, Harvey, The Member of the Wedding, The Count of Monte Cristo,* and *The Hasty Heart. New York Philharmonic Young People's Concerts* with Leonard Bernstein premièred January 18.

1959   JAMES T. AUBREY, JR., President, CBS Television Network, 12/8/59–3/1/65.

Outstanding dramatic television broadcasts included *Playhouse 90* presenting *For Whom the Bell Tolls, The Wings of the Dove, Misalliance, A Child of Our Time,* and *Made in Japan. Du Pont Show of the Month* offered *What Every Woman Knows, The Human Comedy, Billy Budd, The Fallen Idol, Oliver Twist* and *The Browning Version.*

More people saw The Old Vic Company perform *Hamlet* on CBS than had ever seen it on the stage.

Rod Serling's *Twilight Zone* premièred October 2.

The CBS Television Workshop was established to develop professional writers, actors and directors for television through seminars and a weekly hour of network time for experimental programs.

1960   HUNT STROMBERG, JR., Vice President, Program Development, Hollywood, 11/60–3/64.

The Fabulous Fifties, an entertainment special, featured Julie Andrews, Shelley Berman, Betty Comden and Adolph Green, Jackie Gleason, Rex Harrison, Mike Nichols and Elaine May, Eric Sevareid, and Dick Van Dyke.

Danny Kaye appeared in his first entertainment special, October 30.

Fifty-seven entertainment specials were broadcast this year.

1961   JOHN T. REYNOLDS, Vice President and General Manager, Network Programs, Hollywood (reporting to Guy della Cioppa) 9/5/61–3/7/62.

The CBS Sports Department became a part of the CBS Television Network.

Thirty-seven entertainment specials were broadcast, including the *Gershwin Years, Victor Borge's Twentieth Anniversary Show, Carnegie Hall Salutes Jack Benny,* and Danny Kaye in a comedy special. *The Power and the Glory,* a dramatic special, was hailed by one critic as "the year's most searching and significant television drama.

Daytime audiences grew to a new record high. *Password* was one of the new popular daytime shows.

1962   HUBBELL ROBINSON, JR., returned 3/12/62–3/11/63 as Senior Vice President, Programs.

JOHN T. REYNOLDS, Senior Vice President, Hollywood, 3/7/62–2/9/66.

The *Beverly Hillbillies* premièred September 29.

Julie and Carol at Carnegie Hall was broadcast June 11.

The opening of Lincoln Center for the Performing Arts in New York, September 23, was televised nationally.

Captain Kangaroo, The Adventures of Rin Tin Tin, Dennis the Menace, G. E. College Bowl, and *Mister Ed* were some of the children's shows.

In sports, CBS Television Network obtained the broadcast rights to both NFL professional and NCAA college football games. This was a first.

1963   MICHAEL H. DANN, Vice President, Programs, 3/11/63–7/11/66.

Eastside/Westside with George C. Scott had its première September 23.

Petticoat Junction and *My Favorite Martian* were two new comedy series.

Henrik Ibsen's *Hedda Gabler* with Ingrid Bergman, Sir Michael Redgrave, Sir Ralph Richardson, and Trevor Howard was one of the year's outstanding specials.

In the daytime schedule *As the World Turns* and *The Edge of Night* each reached its 2,000th broadcast, having been on the air eight years.

1964   BRUCE LANSBURY, Vice President, Programs, New York, 9/23/64–6/28/65.

HUNT STROMBERG, JR., Vice President, Programs, Hollywood, 3/64–3/4/65.

New comedies such as *Gomer Pyle USMC, Gilligan's Island,* and *The Munsters* were added to the schedule.

The *Jackie Gleason Show* started its third season from Florida, its point of origination from then on.

Once Upon a Mattress with Carol Burnett premièred June 3.

CBS Television Network broadcast more sports events than any other network.

1965 JOHN A. SCHNEIDER, President, CBS Television Network, 3/1/65–2/9/66.

PERRY LAFFERTY, Vice President, Programs, Hollywood, 4/12/65–4/29/76.

IRWIN SEGELSTEIN, Vice President, Programs, New York, 6/28/65–9/8/70.

Fifty per cent of the CBS network regular nighttime schedule was broadcast in color.

The *CBS Thursday Night Movies* was added to the regular network schedule.

New broadcasts added to the network television schedule were *Hogan's Heroes, Green Acres, The Wild, Wild West* and *Lost in Space*.

Gian Carlo Menotti's opera, *Martin's Lie* made its American première on the CBS Television Network.

The National Geographic Specials began September 10 and continued to April 12, 1973.

A Charlie Brown Christmas, December 9, was the first Charles Schulz animated cartoon special.

1966 JOHN A. SCHNEIDER, President of newly created CBS Broadcast Group, 2/9/66–2/17/69.

JOHN T. REYNOLDS, President, CBS Television Network, 2/9/66–12/15/66.

THOMAS H. DAWSON, President, CBS Television Network, 12/15/66–2/14/69.

MICHAEL H. DANN, Senior Vice President, Programs, 7/11/66–6/22/70.

FRED SILVERMAN, Vice President, Daytime Programs, 7/18/66–6/23/70.

Entertainment specials continued to be a big item on the network schedule. Among these were Arthur Miller's *Death of a Salesman,* Tennessee Williams' *The Glass Menagerie, Carol + 2* with Carol Burnett, Lucille Ball and Zero Mostel, and *An Evening with Carol Channing*.

Mission Impossible premièred September 17.

Dr. Seuss: How the Grinch Stole Christmas, December 18, was the first of these children's specials.

1967 ALAN WAGNER, Vice President, Program Development, Hollywood, 10/4/67–9/8/70.

ROBERT B. HOAG, Vice President, Program Administration, 10/4/67–9/8/70.

Two new series, *Carol Burnett Show* and *Gentle Ben* were added to the network schedule.

CBS Playhouse was established to find new writing talent. The dramas shown were *The Final War of Ollie Winter* by Ronald Ribman, *Do Not Go Gentle into That Good Night* by Loring Mandel, and *Dear Friends* by Reginald Rose.

Specials broadcast were: Hal Holbrook's *Mark Twain Tonight, The Crucible, The Don Knotts Show.*

1968 *Vladimir Horowitz: A Television Concert at Carnegie Hall,* September 22 was his first television recital.

From Chekhov, with Love, starring John Gielgud, Dame Peggy Ashcroft, Wendy Hiller, and Dorothy Tutin, was broadcast on September 11.

CBS Playhouse produced four original plays: *The People Next Door* by J. P. Miller, *My Father and My Mother* by Robert Crean, *Secrets* by Tad Mosel, and *Saturday Adoption* by Ron Cowen.

Hawaii Five-O premièred September 26.

1969 RICHARD W. JENCKS, President, CBS Broadcast Group, 2/17/69–7/20/71.

ROBERT D. WOOD, President, CBS Television Network, 2/17/69–4/4/76.

FRED SILVERMAN, added responsibilities of long-range nighttime program planning, 4/18/69–2/4/70.

CBS Playhouse: Appalachian Autumn by Earl Hamner, *Sadbird* by George Bellak, *Shadow Game* by Loring Mandel, and *The Experiment* by Ellen M. Violett.

A special marking the 100th anniversary of the Museum of Natural History, *The Natural History of Our World: The Time of Man,* was broadcast September 18.

Juilliard Comes to Lincoln Center, A Dedication Concert was broadcast October 26.

CBS Children's Hour, a Saturday daytime broadcast, premièred with *J.T.,* December 13 and was repeated in prime evening time on December 22.

1970   FRED SILVERMAN, Vice President, Program Planning and Development, New York, 2/4/70–6/23/70 (continued to supervise daytime program schedule); Vice President, Programs, 6/23/70–5/23/75.

IRWIN SEGELSTEIN, Vice President, Program Administration, 9/8/70–5/29/75.

ALAN WAGNER, Vice President, Program Development for the Network, 9/8/70–11/22/72.

PAUL RAUCH, Vice President, Programs, New York, 9/8/70–8/2/71.

Jackie Gleason Christmas Special, Sol Hurok Presents—Part IV (David Oistrak and Sviatoslav Richter), *The CBS Thanksgiving Parade Jubilee, A Connecticut Yankee in King Arthur's Court* were one-time specials.

The Mary Tyler Moore Show premièred September 19.

The *Children's Hour* continued with *Summer Is Forever* and *Toby.*

1971   JOHN A. SCHNEIDER, President, CBS Broadcast Group, 7/20/71–10/17/77.

A drastic overhaul in the network schedule was necessitated by the prime time access rule. (Restricted stations in top fifty markets from using more than three hours in prime time of network programming a night.)

Appointment with Destiny, a series of seven one-hour drama specials, premièred November 19.

All in the Family had its first broadcast January 12.

A special, *The Homecoming* (12/19/71), starring Patricia Neal was said to have inspired the series, *The Waltons.*

Beethoven's Birthday: A Celebration in Vienna with Leonard Bernstein was televised December 24.

Three musical specials were: *The Doris Maryanne Kapplehoff (Doris Day) Special, Julie and Carol at Lincoln Center* and *The Burt Bacharach Special.*

1972   B. DONALD (BUD) GRANT, Vice President, Daytime Programs, 1/10/72–4/19/76.

New series added this year to the network schedule were: *Maude, The Waltons, M*A*S*H*, and the *Bob Newhart Show.*

Bill Cosby's *Fat Albert and the Cosby Kids* was added to the children's Saturday morning schedule.

Salute to a Cockeyed Optimist: Oscar Hammerstein II was broadcast July 3.

A five-part series about Leonardo Da Vinci was televised (8/13/72–9/10/72).

1973   *Barnaby Jones* and *Kojak* were new series on the network schedule.

Among the specials were: *Much Ado About Nothing* and *Sticks and Bones,* both produced by Joseph Papp.

Famous Classic Tales' broadcast *The Count of Monte Cristo* (9/23/73) started a series of animated specials for children which continued to September 30, 1978.

The *General Electric Theater* premièred December 18 with *I Heard the Owl Call My Name.*

CBS Festival of the Lively Arts for Young People presented two specials of note on its Saturday morning broadcasts: Dylan Thomas' *A Child's Christmas in Wales,* performed by the National Theatre for the Deaf, and Gilbert and Sullivan's *H.M.S. Pinafore.*

CBS Sports continued to schedule the Triple Crown, NFL football, and added the NBA Basketball.

1974   *Rhoda* was the new comedy series in the fall schedule. (Valerie Harper, the lead, had been in the *Mary Tyler Moore Show.*)

The Autobiography of Miss Jane Pittman with Cicely Tyson became the outstanding television drama of the year.

The *General Electric Theater* televised *It's Good to Be Alive* and *Tell Me Where It Hurts.*

Entertainment specials were: *6 Rooms Riv Vu, The Incredible Flight of the Snow Geese,* and *Applause.*

A Smithsonian Special: Monsters, Mysteries and Myths? was televised November 25.

The first of the *Benjamin Franklin* series, *The Ambassador,* premièred November 21, and the second episode, *The Whirlwind,* on December 17.

Bicentennial Minutes, descriptions of incidents in American history, started on July 4, 1974, and continued until July 4, 1976.

1975   LEE CURRLIN, Vice President, Programs, 5/23/75–4/19/76.

The *Price Is Right,* a game series, and the daytime serial, *As the World Turns,* were expanded to one hour.

Queen of the Stardust Ballroom with Maureen Stapleton, *Babe,* a program portraying the life of Babe Didrikson Zaharias, *Fear on Trial,* a drama about Henry Faulk's account of blacklisting, and *In This House of Brede* with Diana Rigg were outstanding dramas.

Another *Smithsonian Special: The Legendary Curse of the Hope Diamond* was broadcast March 27.

1976   ROBERT J. WUSSLER, President, CBS Television Network, 4/11/76–10/17/77.

B. DONALD (BUD) GRANT, Vice President, Programs, 4/19/76–10/17/77.

WILLIAM SELF, Vice President, Programs, Hollywood, 4/29/76–10/3/77.

Alice, a new situation comedy with Linda Lavin had its initial broadcast September 29.

Some of the specials presented were: *America Salutes Richard Rodgers: The Sound of Music, Sills and Burnett at the Met, The Bolshoi Ballet: Romeo and Juliet* with Mary Tyler Moore as hostess, and *CBS Salutes Lucy, the First 25 Years.*

1977   GENE JANKOWSKI, President, CBS Broadcasting Group, 10/17/77–

ROBERT A. DALY, President, CBS Entertainment Division, 10/17/77–

JAMES H. ROSENFIELD, President, CBS Television Network Division, 10/17/77–

ROBERT J. WUSSLER, President, CBS Sports Division, 10/17/77–4/15/78 (newly established).

B. DONALD (BUD) GRANT, Vice President, Programs, CBS Entertainment Division, 10/17/77–

Among the specials presented this year were: *Carol Burnett Show—10th Anniversary*, *All in the Family—Edith's 50th Birthday*, *The Lucille Ball Special* and the *George Burns One-Man Show*.

Dramatic specials on the network were: *A Circle of Children*, *Something for Joey*, *The Amazing Howard Hughes* and *Minstrel Man*.

The Body Human: The Miracle Months by Vivian Moss was a unique broadcast tracing human development from conception to birth.

The *Winners*, a monthly half-hour dramatic series for young viewers, featuring real-life experiences and the accomplishments of young men and women who have overcome their problems.

Lou Grant with Ed Asner premièred September 20 as a one-hour series.

1978

The specials were: *The Kraft 75th Anniversary*, *Julie Andrews: One Step into Spring*, *Gene Kelly: An American in Pasadena* and *A Special Evening with Carol Burnett* (the last show of her series).

The Paper Chase and *Dallas* were two new series.

The CBS Television Network ranged from 268 to 277 affiliated stations.

PHOTO CREDITS

Paul Whiteman. CBS

Franklin D. Roosevelt. CBS

Anschluss, the Nazis on the march. WIDE WORLD

The World News Roundup, with Robert Trout. CBS

Orson Welles at a news conference after *The War of the Worlds.* CBS

Goodbye, Mr. Chips brought James Hilton, Laurence Olivier, and Cecil B. DeMille to *Lux Radio Theater.* CBS

With Paul Kesten. CBS

With souvenirs of early CBS affiliates. CBS

Elmer Davis. CBS

At a wartime dinner for Ed Murrow, with Archibald MacLeish (l.). CBS

In World War II, I served as Deputy Chief of the Psychological Warfare Division of SHAEF under General Eisenhower. PERSONAL PHOTOGRAPH

At SHAEF with General Eisenhower (front right), RAF Marshal Tedder (front left), and a few others. U. S. SIGNAL CORPS

Correspondents Murrow, Daly, and Trout (l. to r.), with Paul Manning next to Murrow. CBS

Winston Churchill. WIDE WORLD

Charles Collingwood in working clothes. CBS

Presenting an eighteenth-century Chinese bowl to Lowell Thomas on his twentieth anniversary on the air. CBS

Frank Sinatra starting out on CBS. CBS

PICTURE SECTION III

Babe and I starting our honeymoon trip to Europe. WIDE WORLD

It was always funny with Burns and Allen and the Jack Bennys. CBS

With Amos 'n' Andy (Freeman Gosden, left, and Charles Correll, right). CBS

Edgar Bergen and Charlie McCarthy. CBS

Hubbell Robinson headed TV programming. CBS

Lucy and Desi. CBS

Frank White and Ed Wallerstein found long-playing records stacked up well against the same music on old-fashioned discs. CBS

The Materials Policy Commission submits its report to President Truman. WHITE HOUSE PHOTOGRAPH

Secretary of War Robert Patterson giving me the Medal for Merit. U. S. DEPARTMENT OF DEFENSE

Stokowski conducts. CBS

Election Night 1956 with Walter Cronkite. CBS

Alistair Cooke when *Omnibus* was on the air. CBS

Ed Murrow and *See It Now* showing both coasts at the same time. CBS

With an early color camera. CBS

Faye Emerson and Arthur Godfrey. CBS

When Television City opened, Frank Stanton and I surveyed the scene. CBS

PICTURE SECTION IV

In my office at the new CBS Headquarters Building. MUSEUM OF MODERN ART

At the University of Pennsylvania, May 1968, for an honorary doctor of laws degree and a commencement address. UNIVERSITY OF PENNSYLVANIA

Columbia University's Board of Trustees with University President Dwight D. Eisenhower. COLUMBIA UNIVERSITY

I enjoyed Arthur Godfrey. CBS

The Honeymooners, Art Carney, Jackie Gleason, and Audrey Meadows. CBS

Shooting with Ed Murrow. PERSONAL PHOTOGRAPH

Recording *My Fair Lady* with Robert Coote, Julie Andrews and Rex Harrison. CBS

Studio One: George Orwell's *1984*. CBS

Larry Kert and Carol Lawrence record *West Side Story*. CBS

(l to r.) Danny Thomas, Merle Jones, and Phil Silvers. CBS

With Frank Stanton in a television studio during the 1960 presidential election campaign. CBS

Ed Murrow's *Person to Person* visits Salvador Dali. CBS

With Red Skelton. CBS

Danny Kaye's television debut, touring for UNICEF. CBS

Mildred Dunnock and Lee J. Cobb in *Death of a Salesman*. CBS

Cliff Robertson and Piper Laurie in *Days of Wine and Roses*. CBS

Keenan Wynn, Jack Palance, and Ed Wynn in *Requiem for a Heavyweight*. CBS

With Eric Sevareid. CBS

Captain Kangaroo (Bob Keeshan). CBS

Carol Burnett. CBS

PICTURE SECTION V

Off the shore of Normandy for *D-Day Plus 20 Years* with Fred Friendly, President Eisenhower, and Walter Cronkite. CBS

The first Kennedy-Nixon debate, at WBBM-TV, our Chicago station. CBS

With Senator Kennedy. CBS

The senator with Bob Sarnoff, Frank Stanton, and me. CBS

Vice-President Nixon with Frank Stanton and me. CBS

Lyndon Johnson at the last party in the Johnson White House. WHITE HOUSE PHOTOGRAPH

In the Congo with Robert Murphy (left, standing) as Patrice Lumumba sits with clasped hands. STATE DEPARTMENT

With Winston Burdett in Africa. STATE DEPARTMENT

Leonard Bernstein. CBS

John Hammond. CBS

Goddard Lieberson. CBS

Bob Dylan. CBS

Simon and Garfunkel. CBS

Barbra Streisand. CBS

Eero Saarinen, original architect of CBS's new headquarters building. RICHARD KNIGHT

Feeling the unique texture of the granite on the building. CBS

The Headquarters Building—a matter of great pride. CBS

As the building began. CBS

Work in progress. CBS

Picasso's "Boy Leading A Horse," in my city apartment. CBS

PICTURE SECTION VI

With my sister Blanche and my mother. PERSONAL PHOTOGRAPH

Babe with Amanda and Tony. RINALDI

In Venice. PERSONAL PHOTOGRAPH

With my sister-in-law Minnie, Noel Coward, and Babe. PERSONAL PHOTOGRAPH

Babe and I posed separately with four of our children in the same setting. PERSONAL PHOTOGRAPHS

Christmas 1952 with some of the children. PERSONAL PHOTOGRAPH

Babe sketching. PERSONAL PHOTOGRAPH

Family portrait at Kiluna. PERSONAL PHOTOGRAPH

Jeff. PERSONAL PHOTOGRAPH

Amanda. PERSONAL PHOTOGRAPH

Kate. PERSONAL PHOTOGRAPH

Hilary. PERSONAL PHOTOGRAPH

Tony. PERSONAL PHOTOGRAPH

Bill. PERSONAL PHOTOGRAPH

Amanda's coming-out party. PERSONAL PHOTOGRAPH

Hilary's coming-out party. PERSONAL PHOTOGRAPH

A favorite picture of Babe. PERSONAL PHOTOGRAPH

With Babe and Amanda. PERSONAL PHOTOGRAPH

Relaxing. PERSONAL PHOTOGRAPH

Sightseeing in Rome with Babe. PERSONAL PHOTOGRAPH

A favorite photo I took after the wedding of Tony and Siri, with the newlyweds (upper center) surrounded by family well-wishers at Kiluna in February 1971. PERSONAL PHOTOGRAPH

The living room of our Nassau home in the Bahamas. PERSONAL PHOTOGRAPH

Posing for portrait painters. PERSONAL PHOTOGRAPH

The three Cushing sisters, Minnie (l.), Babe, and Betsey. PERSONAL PHOTOGRAPH

With my friend and brother-in-law, Jock Whitney (l.), and my friend, Walter N. Thayer. PERSONAL PHOTOGRAPH

PICTURE SECTION VII

Babe and I met Chou En-lai in China. CHINESE NEWS SERVICE

A visit with Chinese youngsters. PERSONAL PHOTOGRAPH

At the Whitney plantation in Thomasville, Georgia, with Babe, the Whitneys, and Roy Atwood. PERSONAL PHOTOGRAPH

Mr. and Mrs. Robert Sherwood. PERSONAL PHOTOGRAPH

Babe with Picasso at his home in southern France. PERSONAL PHOTOGRAPH

Jack Baragwanath with Dominguin, the matador. PERSONAL PHOTOGRAPH

With Picasso. PERSONAL PHOTOGRAPH

The Loel Guinnesses. PERSONAL PHOTOGRAPH

The Guinness yacht, the *Sarina*. PERSONAL PHOTOGRAPH

The Earl and Countess of Avon (the Anthony Edens). PERSONAL PHOTOGRAPH

Michael and Lady Anne Tree. PERSONAL PHOTOGRAPH

Lord Beaverbrook (l.) with Babe and John Minary. PERSONAL PHOTOGRAPH

Lord Victor Rothschild. © ARNOLD NEWMAN

Starting a walk after lunch with Queen Elizabeth, Prince Philip, and party. PERSONAL PHOTOGRAPH

Lord Mountbatten. PERSONAL PHOTOGRAPH

The David Somersets. PERSONAL PHOTOGRAPH

A family gathering on the terrace at Kiluna. PERSONAL PHOTOGRAPH
Babe with Randolph Churchill at Kiluna. PERSONAL PHOTOGRAPH
Jeremy Tree. PERSONAL PHOTOGRAPH
Babe and our son Bill with guide in Leningrad. PERSONAL PHOTOGRAPH
Babe in Venice. PERSONAL PHOTOGRAPH
I try for salmon in Canada. PERSONAL PHOTOGRAPH

PICTURE SECTION VIII

The waterfall at Paley Park, New York City. CBS
With Carter Burden and Jeff, Brooke and Hilary Byers at the opening of Paley Park. CBS
Ed Sullivan with Ella Fitzgerald. CBS
With Joe Iglehart (l.) and Arthur B. Tourtellot at the Paley Park opening. CBS
Election Night 1972, with Frank Stanton and Dick Salant. CBS
With Walter Cronkite while working on our fiftieth-anniversary program. CBS
Visiting President Nixon at the White House with (l. to r.) Bob Wood, Dick Jencks, Frank Stanton, and Jack Schneider. WHITE HOUSE PHOTOGRAPH
Speaking at the Museum of Modern Art. COURTESY OF THE MUSEUM OF MODERN ART
Cutting the 60 Minutes tenth-birthday cake. CBS
Mary Tyler Moore. CBS
Alan Alda and Mike Farrell of M*A*S*H. CBS
Carroll O'Connor and Jean Stapleton of All in the Family. CBS
Consul General Trexler making me a Commander of Italy's Order of Merit. CBS
With the Television Academy's Governors Award Emmy in 1978. CBS
Looking at model of the Paley Art Center in Jerusalem in honor of my mother. CBS
At the opening of the Museum of Broadcasting. CBS
Using the camera—one of my delights. PERSONAL PHOTOGRAPH
With Bob Saudek at a Museum of Broadcasting carrel. CBS
At the 1977 Annual Meeting, with John D. Backe. CBS

Index

414

Copy 1   B
                                       Paley

Paley, William S.
  As it Happened.

                                        $14.95